queer

art

Quarto

First published in 2024 by Frances Lincoln,
an imprint of The Quarto Group.
One Triptych Place, London, SE1 9SH,
United Kingdom
T (0)20 7700 9000
www.Quarto.com

A catalogue record for this book is available from the British Library.

ISBN 978-0-7112-8267-4
Ebook ISBN 978-0-7112-8268-1

10 9 8 7 6 5 4 3 2 1

Publisher: Philip Cooper
Commissioning Editor: John Parton
Senior Editor: Laura Bulbeck
Project Editor: Clare Churly
Picture Research: Laura Bulbeck, Stephen Behan, Katerina Menhennet
Art Director: Paileen Currie
Design by Leonardo Collina
Production Controller: Eliza Walsh

Printed in Bosnia and Herzegovina

queer art

Gemma Rolls-Bentley

Foreword by Sir Isaac Julien

From canvas to club, and the spaces between

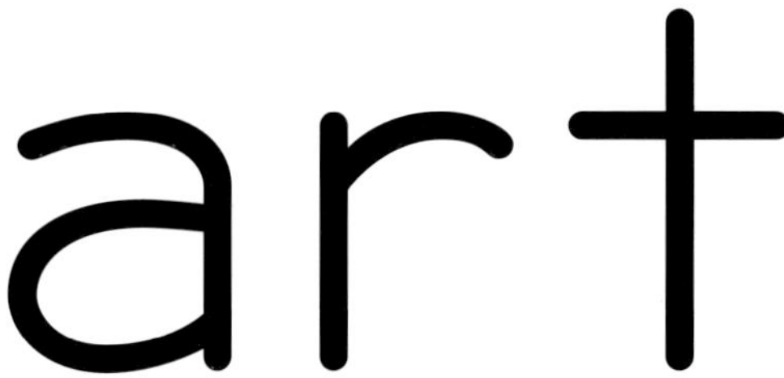

Contents

Foreword

Throughout the history of the visual arts, artists have produced work that reflects the vibrancy, resilience and unapologetic self-expression of queer life, from the 1920s Harlem Renaissance to the 1990s New Queer Cinema. *Queer Art: From Canvas to Club, and the Spaces Between* emerges as a long-awaited beacon, illuminating the dynamic intersections of creativity and activism which spearheaded the movements connected to the LGBTQIA+ experience.

The groups that emerged during the AIDS crisis of the 1980s and 1990s, such as Act UP and Queer Nation, influenced the contemporary art world. A new generation of artists joins the clarion call within these pages astutely assembled by Gemma Rolls-Bentley, who invites us on a journey through the vibrant landscapes of queer art now. In three beautifully curated acts: Queer Spaces, Queer Bodies and Queer Power, artists from across the globe converge to share their unique perspectives, aspirations and truths.

As a pioneer of New Queer Cinema, I have witnessed firsthand the transformative potential of art to challenge norms, provoke thought, and spark change. Queer Cinema made a vital intervention, calling into question the boundaries that the normative assumptions imposed onto its aesthetics. *Queer Art* critically celebrates the richness and diversity of queer creativity and amplifies voices that have long been placed on the margins or silenced. But no longer. Through Gemma Rolls-Bentley's meticulous curation and insightful commentary, she establishes herself as the leading voice in contemporary queer art, tirelessly working to provide artists with the visibility and recognition they deserve. For a number of decades, the contemporary art world turned its back on these voices. Now, urgency surrounding these concerns beckons us to pay closer attention to the signifying practices of queer artists today.

From painting and photography, to protest art and nightclub performances, this book transverses and transcends traditional boundaries, embracing the myriad forms and articulations of queer art.

Each artist featured here contributes to a contemporaneous moment of urgency, enabling a new reading of a collective visibility and resistance in reshaping our understanding of identity and belonging today. Their work is not only inspiring but also essential, offering a poignant reflection of our shared humanity and the kaleidoscopic spectrum of queer experiences.

Queer Art is a testament to the profound impact of art and culture and the resilience of the human spirit, and will undoubtedly resonate with readers of all backgrounds and identities. This book is not just for the LGBTQIA+ community; it is for anyone who believes in the power of art to transcend boundaries, foster empathy, and ignite change. As you embark on this journey through *Queer Art*, may you be inspired, challenged, and moved. May you discover new perspectives, forge connections, and celebrate the beauty of diversity in all its forms. And may you join us in honouring the voices and visions of queer artists around the world, as we continue to strive for more inclusive and equitable futures for all.

Sir Isaac Julien, RA

Introduction

In 1992 artist and filmmaker Derek Jarman staged an exhibition at Manchester Art Gallery in the north of England called 'Queer'. He very deliberately chose the provocative title, knowing that it would cause public debate, which it did. As with many artists before and after him, Jarman used his artistic practice to amplify, memorialize and impact the future of the community that he was a part of. When I was discussing this book with Jarman's close friend the painter Maggi Hambling, she told me that before his death he had made her promise to always use the word queer rather than gay. He believed gay sounded too polite, and perhaps even apologetic, whereas queer 'really means something'. Originally meaning 'odd' or 'strange', the word queer was used as a pejorative term to describe LGBTQIA+ (lesbian, gay, bisexual, transgender, queer, intersex or asexual) people for a long time. Since the late 1980s the word has been reclaimed as a term that rejects narrow definitions of sexuality or gender identity, creates space for intersectional identities and takes an expansive and creative approach to navigating the world, described beautifully by bell hooks:

> queer as not being about who you're having sex with – that can be a dimension of it – but 'queer' as being about the self that is at odds with everything around it and has to invent and create and find a place to speak and to thrive and to live.

I'm often asked what makes art queer, does queer art have distinguishing features, does all art made by queer artists qualify as queer art? These are not easy questions to answer. What I do know is that art can tell a story, share an experience, pose a question or start a conversation. Art has the power to encourage its audiences to consider different perspectives and develop empathy. For this book, I have selected artwork that relates to the queer experience, implicitly or explicitly; art that offers some insight into queer life, past, present or future. I've taken the late 1960s as a loose starting point because, even though there is a long history of queer art, we had to start somewhere. With the pivotal 1969 Stonewall Uprising in New York, led by heroes like Marsha P. Johnson, and the launch of

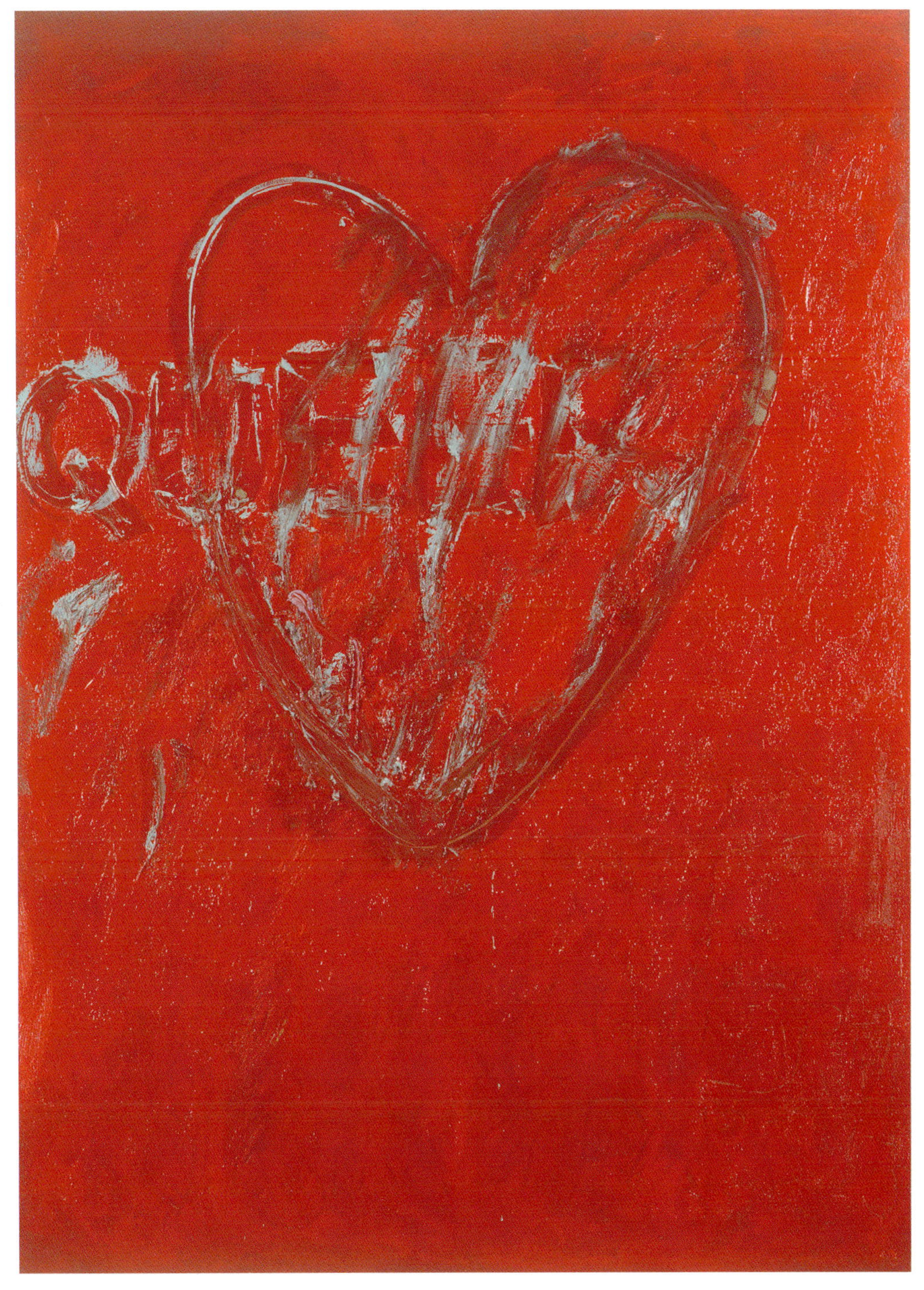

Queer, **Derek Jarman**, 1992

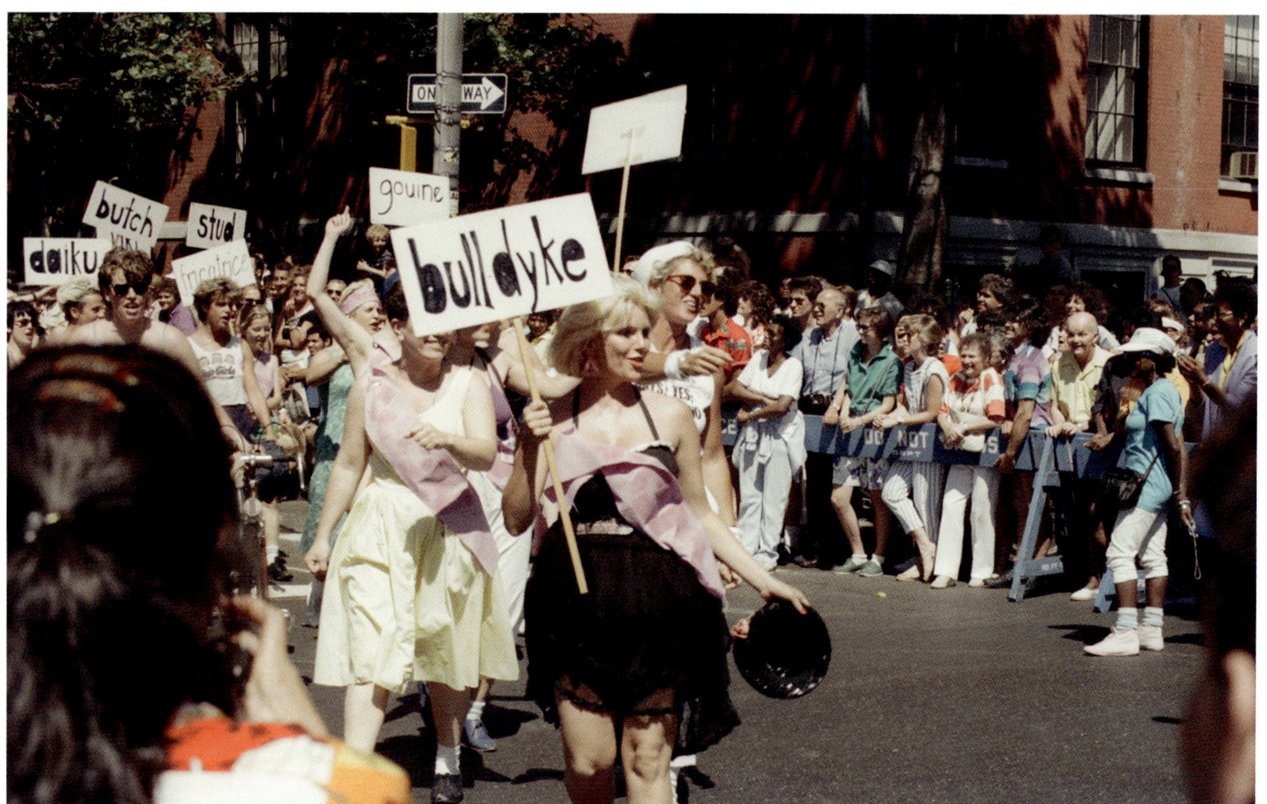

Lois Weaver and others from the infamous WOW Cafe Theater march down Fifth Avenue with The Lesbian Herstory Archives in the 1985 New York Gay Pride March, photo by Janice Wilde, 1985

gay rights movements around the world, we saw the idea of queerness gain wider visibility and political acceptance, and queer art truly begin to thrive.

Many brilliant artists make work that could be described as queer but for the purposes of this book I've primarily selected artists that identify as LGBTQIA+ because we had only so much space to work with and these artists have increased odds of facing challenges due to their identity, as their art often demonstrates. It is my hope that this can be the starting point for many more books, social media accounts and collections of queer art. When compiling the book, we contacted all artists and their estates to ensure that they were happy to be included under the title of *Queer Art*. Because the pathways to existing openly have not been straightforward for queer people, some of the greatest queer art isn't found in a gallery or museum but in nightclubs, theatres, the street, a protest or a parade. Queer art is being made all around the world and I've tried my best to present a global view of queer art, but in the places where it's not safe to

Introduction

live freely that art is harder to find. This book celebrates a diverse range of artistic mediums and artists, some you may have seen in a museum, some perhaps on social media, and others will be new to you. I've brought this work together here to present a vibrant and powerful picture of queerness, and to honour the contributions of the queer artists and ancestors that have paved the way for the freedoms that we experience in most of the world today.

A decade after Jarman's 'Queer' exhibition, I embarked on an art history course at university. In the five years of studying that followed, I began to figure out my own identity, entered my first queer relationship and struggled to find peace within myself. During two art history degrees there wasn't a single mention of queer art. I feel confident that if I'd seen a book like this one, I'd have had an easier time understanding who I was. I did of course study some of the artists in this book, but their work was not contextualized as queer and I missed the opportunity to see myself reflected. Viewing art through a queer lens helps add a layer of understanding: it's just one of many lenses and rather than being reductive it should be an enriching process. I've dedicated my career to art because I believe passionately that art has the power to change things. To all of the artists included in this book, thank you for sharing your work with the world and for helping to make it a better place.

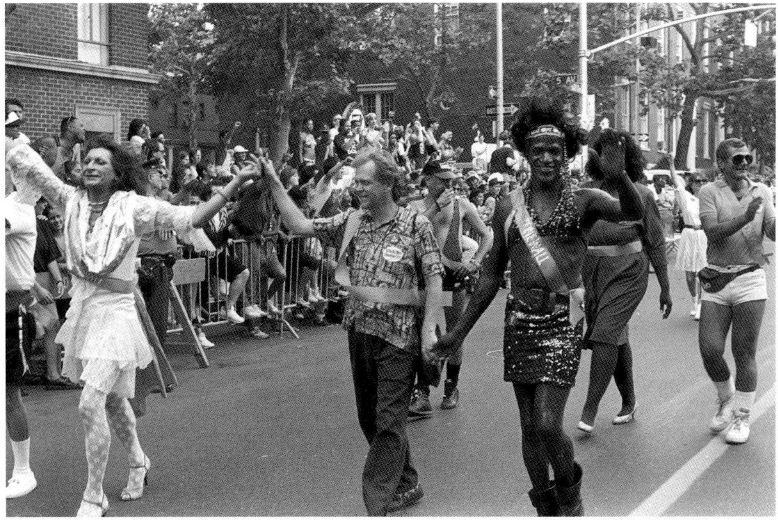

Gay liberation and transgender rights activists Sylvia Rivera, Jim Fouratt and Marsha P. Johnson marching together wearing 'Stonewall' sashes at Pride, New York, 1991

spaces

queer

Act I

The rejection and exclusion of queerness from mainstream life throughout history means that LGBTQIA+ people have been forced to find and create their own spaces in which to exist openly, congregate safely and form community. Home can shift from somewhere oppressive, unstable or transient to a site of radical self-discovery, a refuge for free expression and where connections with chosen family can be built. Beyond the domestic realm, queer people find home in the spaces that provide safety, validation and a sense of belonging: queering a space by inhabiting it. Where queer life is forced to exist on the peripheries, queer people are often found outside. Outside in the streets fighting for their rights, outside in public spaces secretly established as gay cruising grounds, or outside of urban centres forming alternative communities or connecting with the land. In places where there is a risk of being harmed, outed or arrested, queer spaces have needed to be clandestine and would often be found operating after dark, under the cover of night. From bars and pubs that became known as meet-up spots for like-minded people to queer-led clubs and parties fostering joy among queers and their allies, these spaces offered individuals the opportunity to be their authentic selves, to explore their desires and to creatively express their identity, as captured in the 1980s and 1990s photography of Ingrid Pollard.

Ever since the violation and retaliation that occurred when the Stonewall Inn was raided by police in 1969, giving birth to the global pride movement, queer spaces have been fought for and defended as front lines, refuges and frontier lands. David McDermott and Peter McGough's *The Oscar Wilde Temple* (see pages 16–17) is an immersive installation paying homage to the ancestors who paved the way for contemporary queer life, often at huge personal cost. Envisioned as a secular space for private reflection and ceremonial gatherings of the LGBTQIA+ community, the temple demonstrates the power of having a space to call your own. As laws change and attitudes shift, queer spaces become less secretive and underground in many parts of the world; however, their role continues to be sacred and valued by the community they serve.

Performance Outside The Fridge,
Brixton, **Ingrid Pollard**, c. 1990

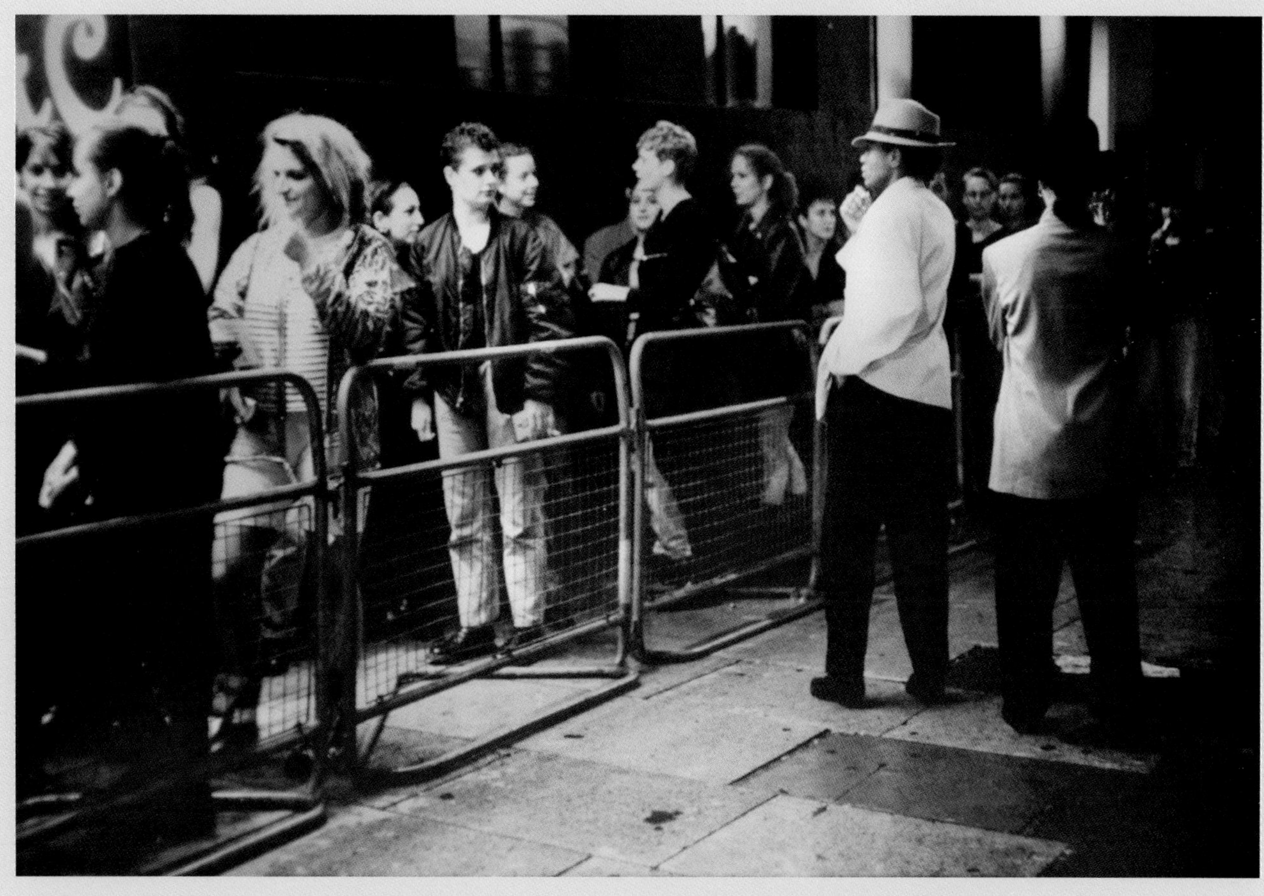

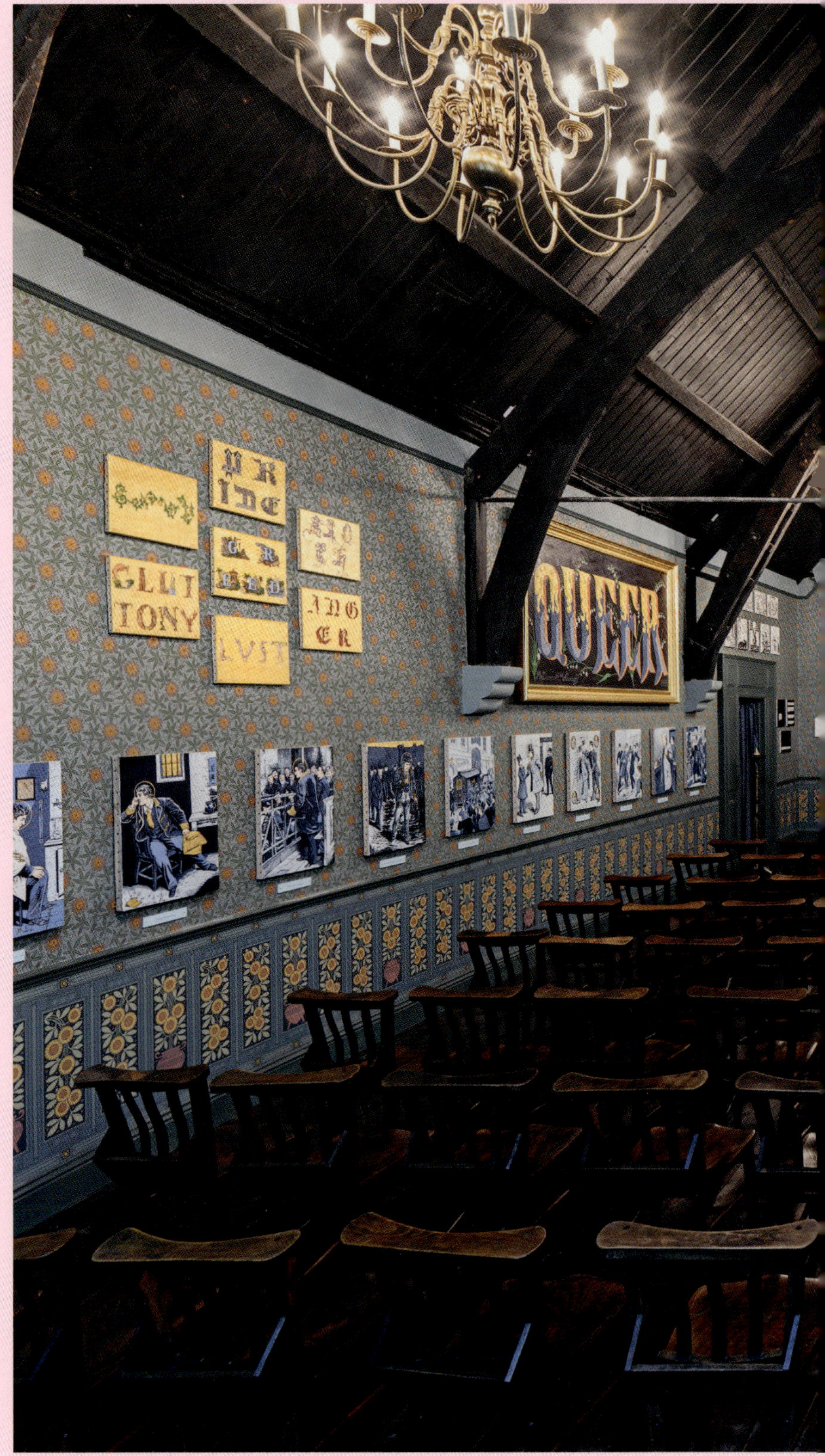

The Oscar Wilde Temple,
David McDermott and Peter McGough, 2018, installation view at Studio Voltaire Gallery, London

Act I. Queer Spaces

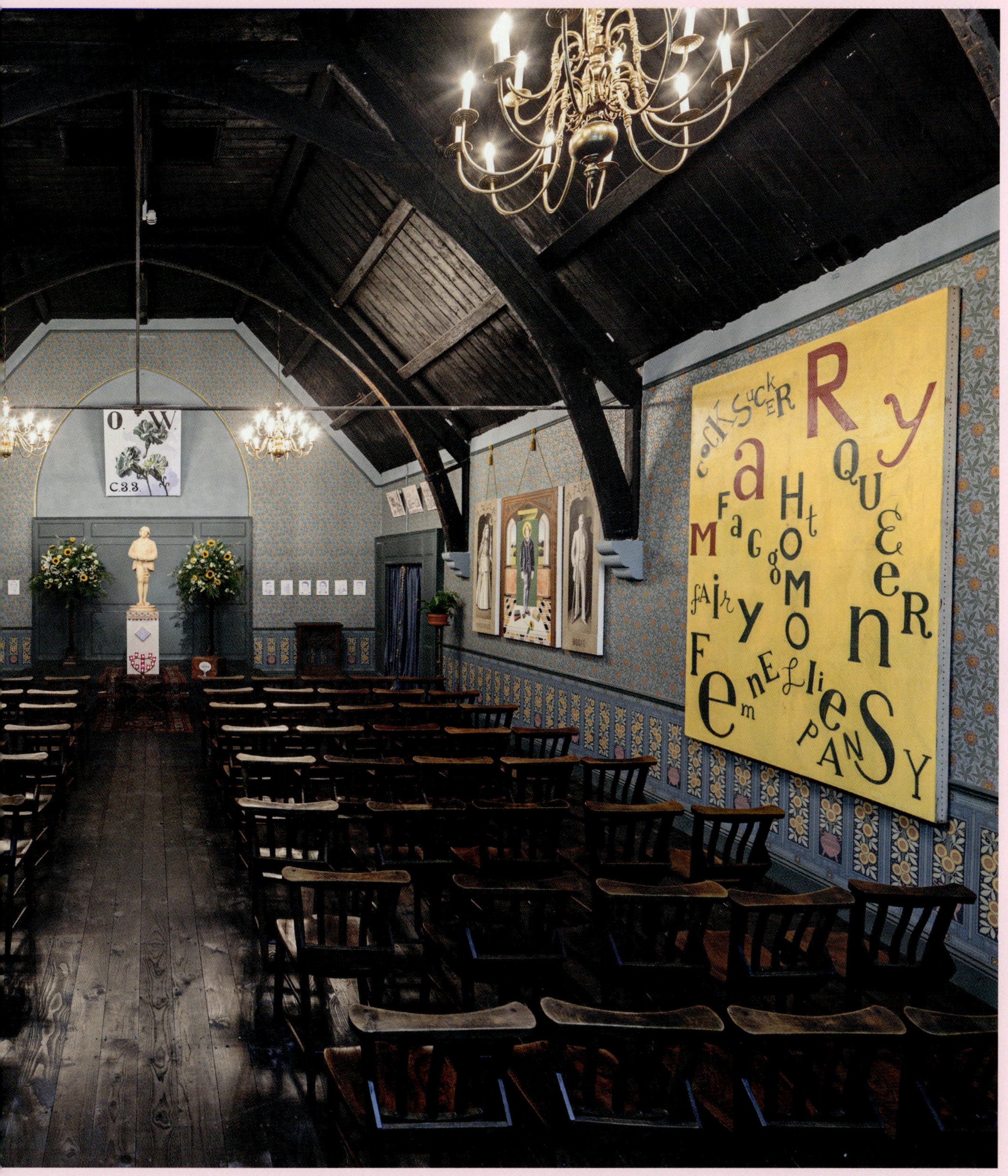

Home

Home is something we all dream of, whatever form that dream takes. For queer people, whose home life may have started out as unsafe and unwelcoming, the dream of home is a place to live securely and freely. For some people, survival and authentic existence is dependent on migration, leaving one home in search of another. In the face of censorship and oppression, the safety of home becomes all the more important. Establishing a home of one's own or creating shared space with fellow queers opens a world of possibility; home becomes a site of joy and self-discovery, a place to thrive. Rather than revolving around heteronormative definitions of domesticity, queer people reimagine what home looks like, pushing boundaries and challenging traditional means of housing and shared living.

Queer people don't have a blueprint to follow for what home looks like because queer life has been forced to exist behind closed doors and has gone undocumented, in official records and in art and culture. Charleston, the twentieth-century home and studio of Bloomsbury Group artists Vanessa Bell and Duncan Grant on the south coast of England, is a rare example of a historic home that's been preserved to commemorate the queer lives of its inhabitants. Within a historical narrative that deems domesticity to be at odds with queer life, there is a power in

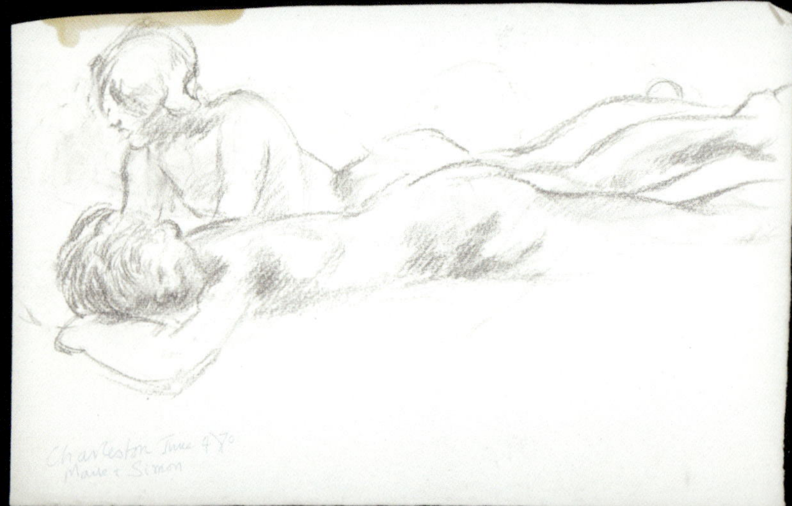

Charleston June 4 '70/ Mark and Simon,
Duncan Grant, 1970

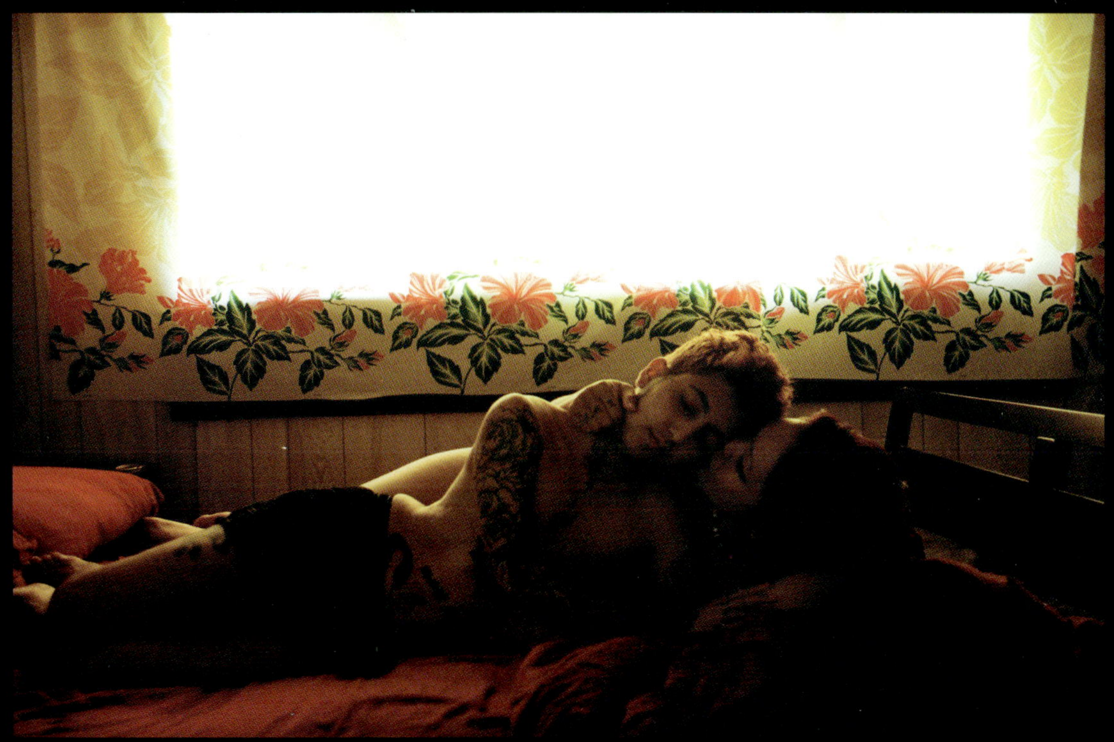

seeing evidence of LGBTQIA+ home life, which is why creatives take great inspiration from houses like Charleston and why we increasingly see home reflected in art.

As artists capture home in their work, we see them explore the myriad ways in which home manifests, from the unpacking of childhood experiences of home or reflecting on complex journeys of migration, to the imagining of past and future homes and documenting the sometimes hard-won reality of home. The instability and transient nature of the physical home for many queer people means that 'home' as a concept often exists within the community, with other people or within themselves. For 2spirit artist Coyote Park, home is not connected to a place but found in the embrace of another. The queerness of a physical home may not be explicit; in the absence of bodies we are left to read queer signifiers in coded imagery and titles, and the knowledge that queer people occupied the space imbues it with meaning. We see queer life revealed in art; spirituality, transformation, friendship and love, explored through the lens of home.

Home is in every bed space with you,
Coyote Park

Relationship #24 (The Shadow Self)
from the series 'Relationship',
Zackary Drucker and Rhys Ernst, 2011,
C-print face-mounted on UV acrylic,
50.8 x 76.2 cm (20 x 30 in)

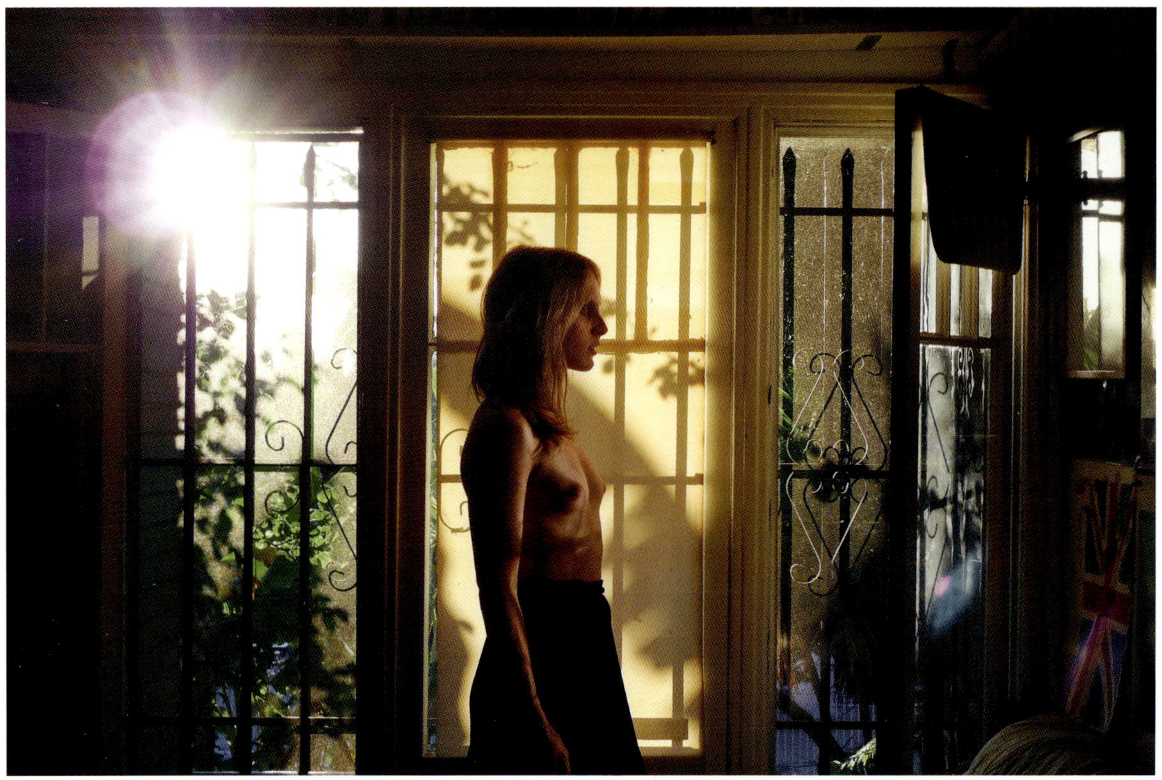

'Relationship' is an extensive photo project by Zackary Drucker and Rhys Ernst documenting their romantic relationship between 2008 and 2014, during which time Drucker transitioned from male to female and Ernst transitioned from female to male. Reminiscent of the domestic documentary photography of Nan Goldin, the images let the viewer into private moments shared by the couple in the safety of their home as they embarked on mirrored journeys of hormone-led gender transition. During the same period the couple produced the film *She Gone Rogue* (2012) together, which merges autobiography with a performed creative reality in a similar way to their photography. Drucker has shared her belief that the work of documenting and sharing trans life is both an artistic opportunity and a political responsibility. At its core, the series chronicles two people in love morphing and transforming together as they move through their shared life.

Bloom is a beautiful example of Jarvis Boyland's vivid hues, which bestow a softness and a sensitivity to his subjects. In this 2020 painting, we are transported to a particular moment in 1970s America when yellow interiors became a popular representation of a newfound optimism and our eye is drawn to the black panther on the window sill, a symbol of protection found in the living rooms of Black American families since the 1930s.

Inspired by the couple portraits of David Hockney and Emma Amos and their representations of love, Boyland reconfigures the scene, placing queer men of colour among the plush fabrics and soft furnishings of a living room, which he refers to as a site of 'queer interior fantasies'. Amid the golden hour lighting and curated detail of the scene, we feel the precious nature of this momentary bliss.

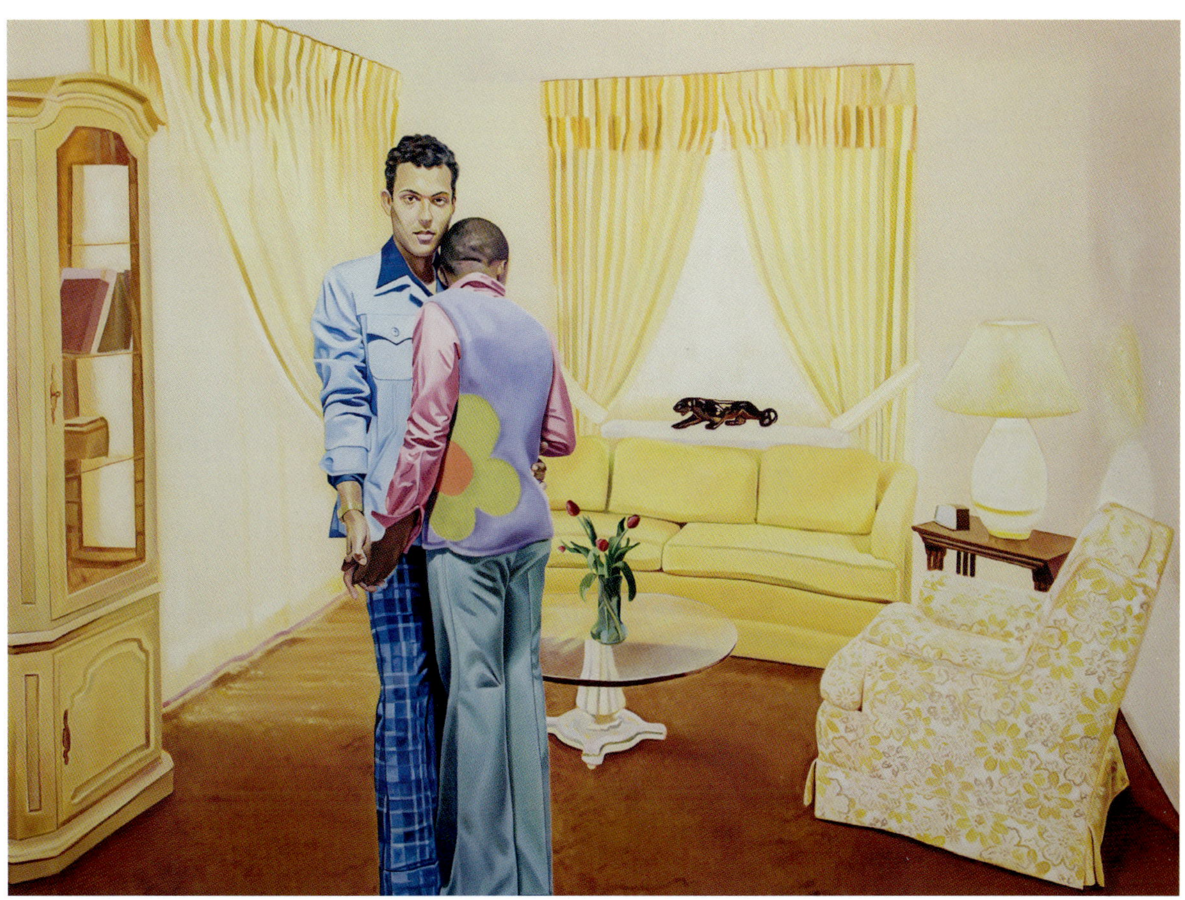

Bloom, **Jarvis Boyland**, 2020, oil on canvas, 182.8 x 243.8 cm (72 x 96 in)

Le Chemin des fous (The Path of Fools) is an ongoing multifaceted project initiated by Marseille-based artists Liam Warren and Arthur Eskenazi, after meeting Moussa Fofana, co-founder of Refuge Migrantes LGBTQIA+ de Marseille (RML). In a series of regular workshops, a space is established for RML members to express themselves safely in various artistic disciplines. Recording the encounters indirectly reveals the discrimination the RML members have faced due to their status as refugees and their sexual and gender identity. The stories are presented through performances and installations involving dance, song, text, film and art objects. Acknowledging the potential for problematic power dynamics between marginalized communities and their relatively privileged allies, in this instance the two artists who reside in France with citizen status, the project questions the ethical frameworks of such a collaboration and is structured to avoid any imbalance between participants. Guided by the values of solidarity, inclusion and emancipation, the stories of queer migration examine systemic failings and emphasize the power of collective action.

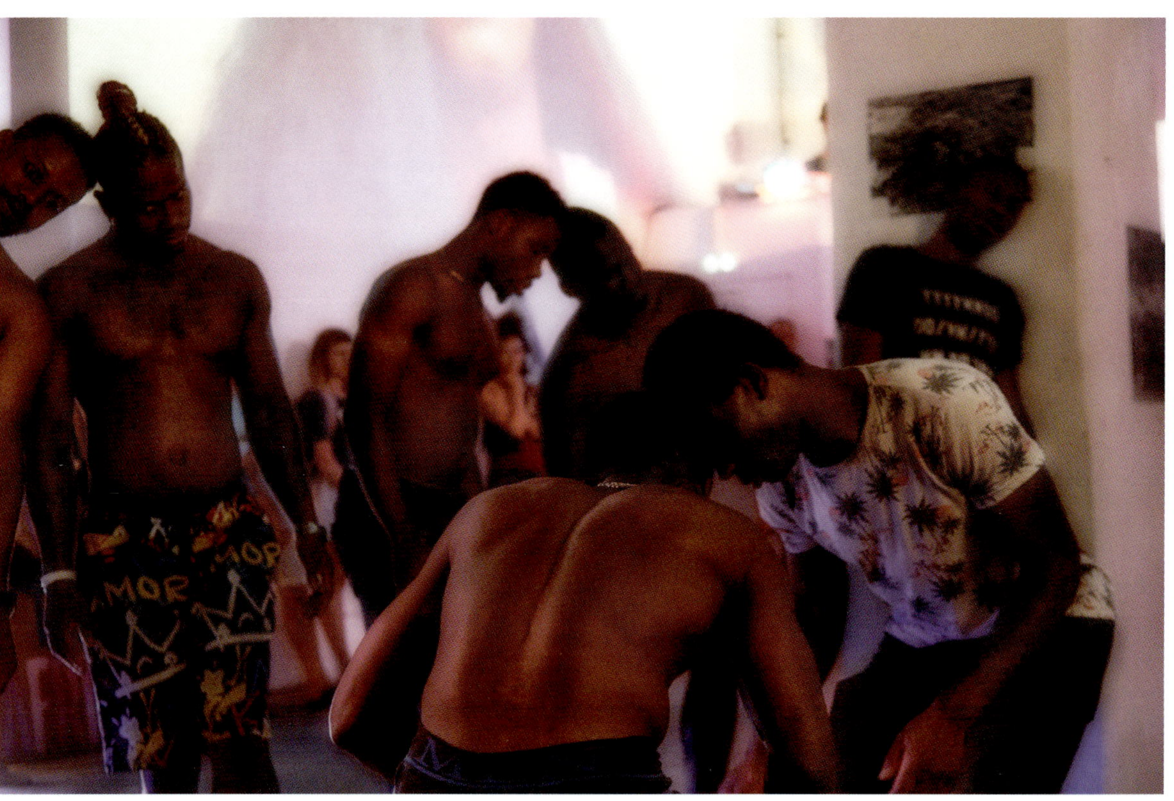

Le Chemin des fous, **Liam Warren,
Arthur Eskenazi and members of RML,**
2020–ongoing, performance
in Marseille, France, 2022

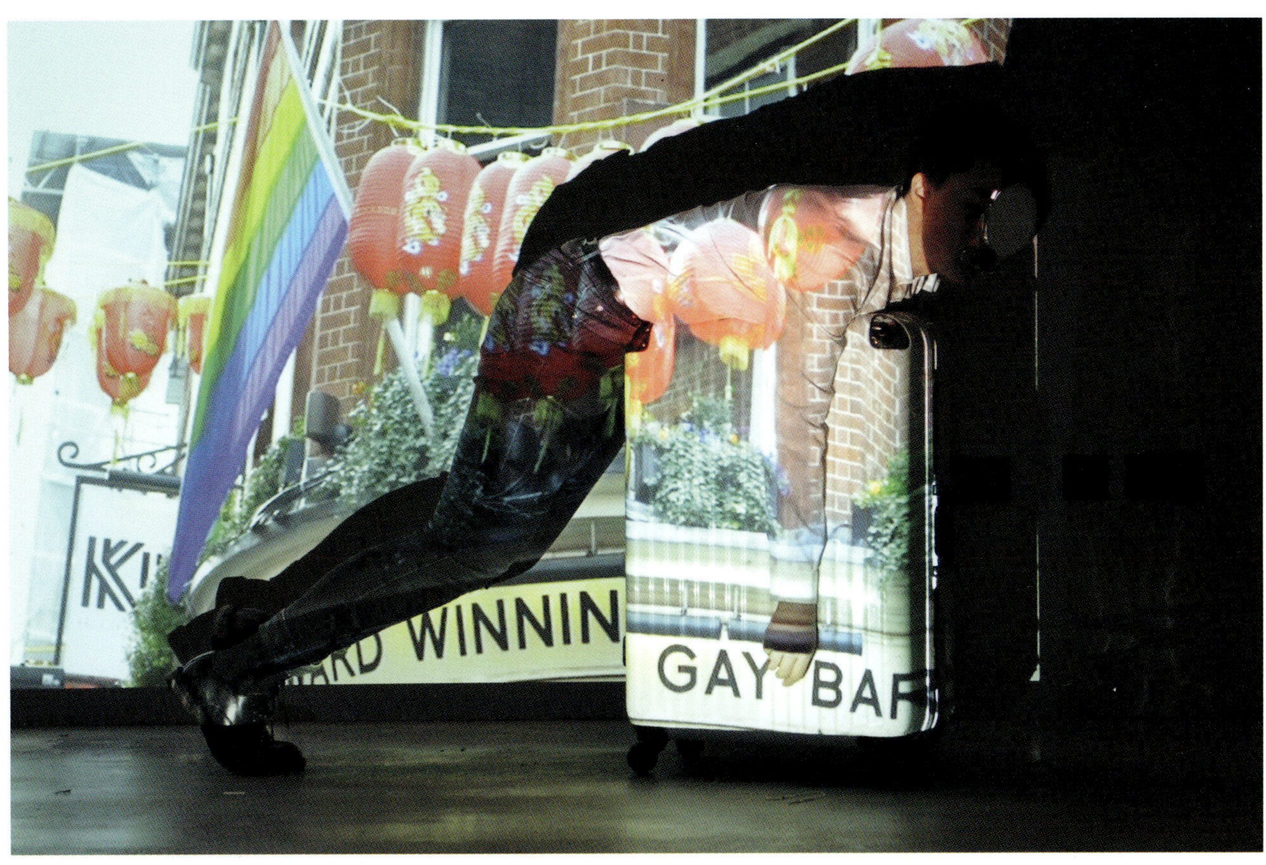

Whiskey Chow is a London-based Chinese artist, activist and drag king. Her interdisciplinary practice queers masculinity and interrogates stereotypical projections of Chinese and Asian identity. *Unhomeliness* is a three-channel video installation with live performance that explores identity and belonging from the perspective of a queer Chinese migrant recently arrived in London. Originally presented at Tate Modern in London, the films are projected onto Chow's crisp white shirt and the surface of the large white suitcase that contained her belongings when she arrived in the UK. Chow is silenced by steel wool blocking her mouth and her face is covered by a makeup mirror that reverses the audience's gaze. As she heads to adjoining neighbourhoods Chinatown and Soho in search of a home she is met with red lanterns and rainbow flags that represent commodified versions of Chineseness and queerness, leading her to ask, 'Who is generating a sense of belonging for whom?'.

Whiskey Chow

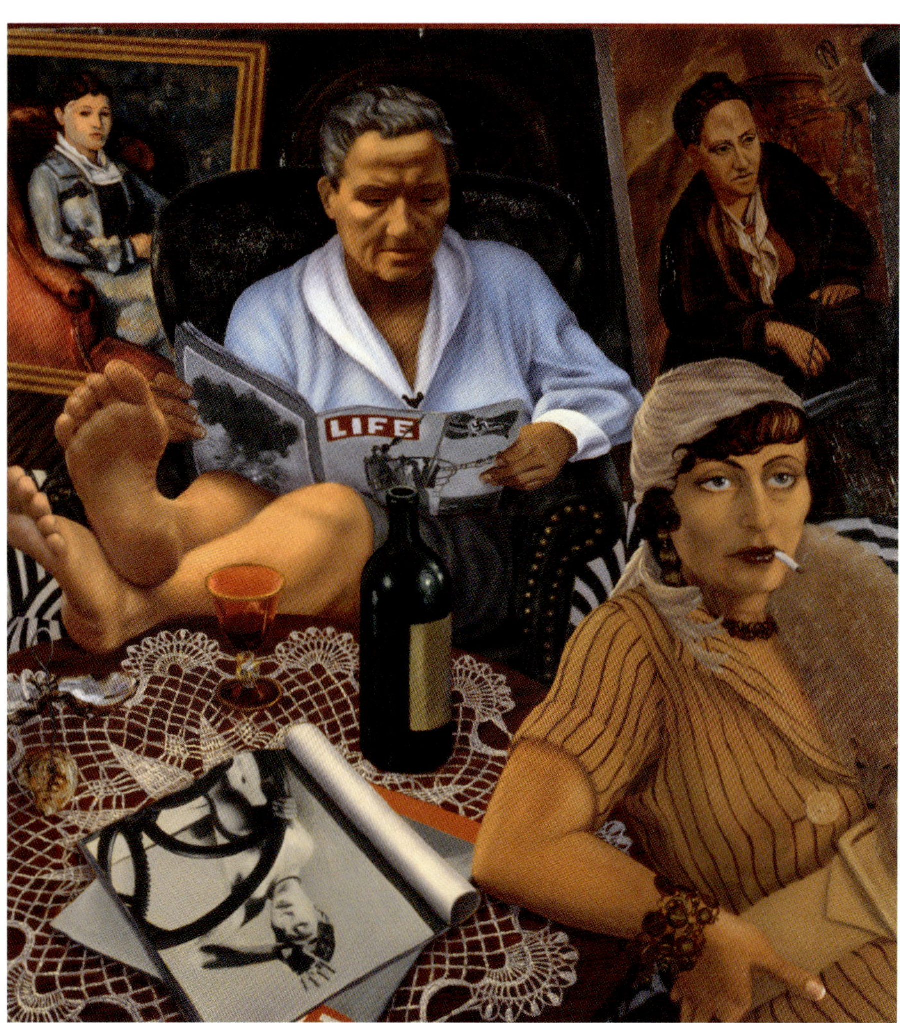

Gertrude Stein & Alice B. Toklas, Paris, October, 1939, **Hilary Harkness**, 2007–2008, oil on copper, 30.5 x 27.9 cm (12 x 11 in)

Hilary Harkness

Hilary Harkness's small oil painting on copper, *Gertrude Stein & Alice B. Toklas, Paris, October, 1939,* is part of a six-part series depicting imagined scenes from the shared life of the historical lesbian couple. Famed for hosting salons in their Parisian home where they welcomed the greatest writers and artists of the period, the pair are shown surrounded by the vast art collection Stein amassed through the success of her writing while feasting on oysters and wine.

Modelled for by the artist's mother, the tender-hearted butch Stein dominates the scene while the elegant, taciturn Toklas takes her place on the sidelines, reflecting historical accounts of their lavish life. A departure from the countless tiny figures in Harkness's surrealist paintings, the two-figure scene mirrors a personal shift in the artist's life from a decade of single life to a monogamous relationship rooted in the domestic.

Skuja Braden is the collaborative practice of artists Ingūna Skuja and Melissa D. Braden, which they describe as a symbiotic being formed over a period of more than 20 years of living and working together. 'Selling Water by the River' is their exhibition for the Latvian Pavilion at the 59th Venice Biennale, and it recreates the interior spaces of their shared home, every detail masterfully crafted from porcelain. The installation is titled after the Zen Buddhist concept that the path to enlightenment is within us, something that is central to their life and work. Walking through the rooms, we are privy to the couple's daily rituals and the intimate details of their life together. By opening up their domestic space they ask us to consider the social issues that home represents, like public and private territories, spaces of care and safety, and queer and feminist empowerment.

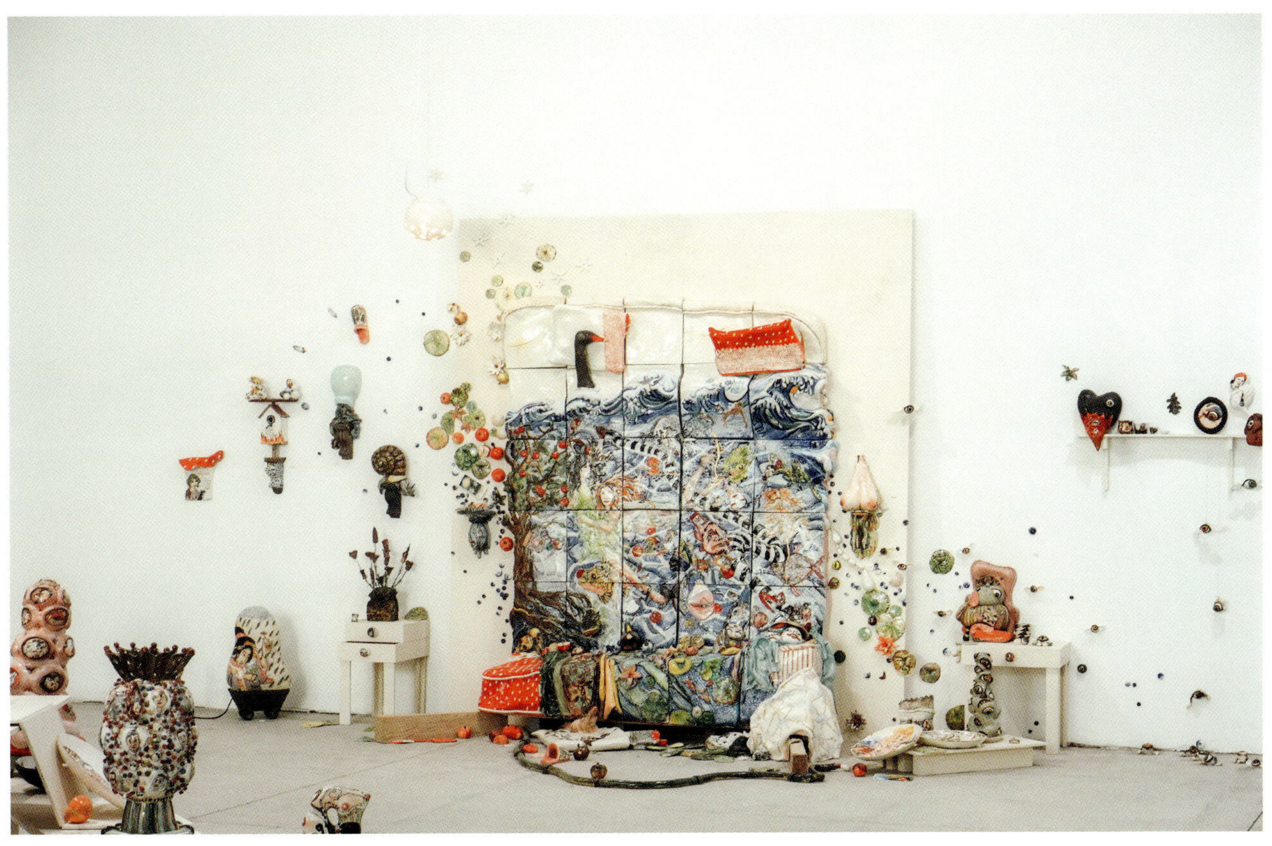

We Made Our Bed, **Skuja Braden**, 2022, porcelain, dimensions variable, installation view, 'Selling Water by the River', 59th Venice Biennale

Portrait of an Artist (Pool with Two Figures) is one of David Hockney's most well-known paintings. The two figures, an underwater swimmer and a clothed onlooker, combine two of Hockney's central motifs – double portraits and swimming pools. The large-scale painting, which is the subject of Jack Hazan's film *A Bigger Splash* (1973), is composed from many carefully staged preparatory photographs of the artist's friends and his former lover Peter Schlesinger. The Los Angeles pools, which provided the setting for much of his early painting, symbolize the freedom that Hockney found as a gay man in sexy, sunny California compared to rural Yorkshire where he'd been raised. In 2018 *Portrait of an Artist (Pool with Two Figures)* broke records as it became the highest-priced painting by a living artist to sell at auction, demonstrating Hockney's enduring impact in both the art world and wider discussions around LGBTQIA+ representation.

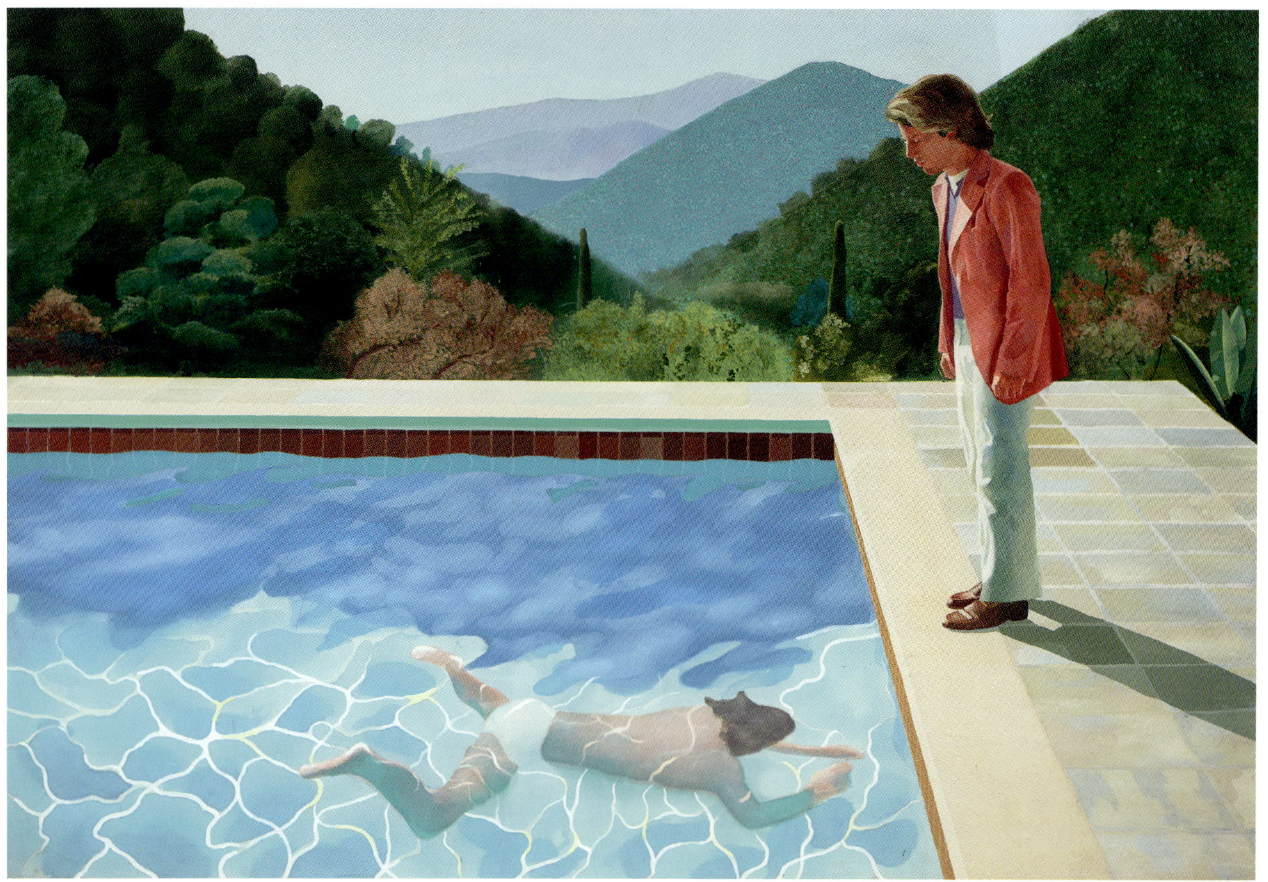

Portrait of an Artist (Pool with Two Figures),
David Hockney, 1972, acrylic on canvas,
213.4 x 304.8 cm (84 x 120 in)

ngochani mumhuri, **Kudzanai-Violet Hwami**, 2022, oil and acrylic on canvas, 100 x 100 cm (39⅜ x 39⅜ in)

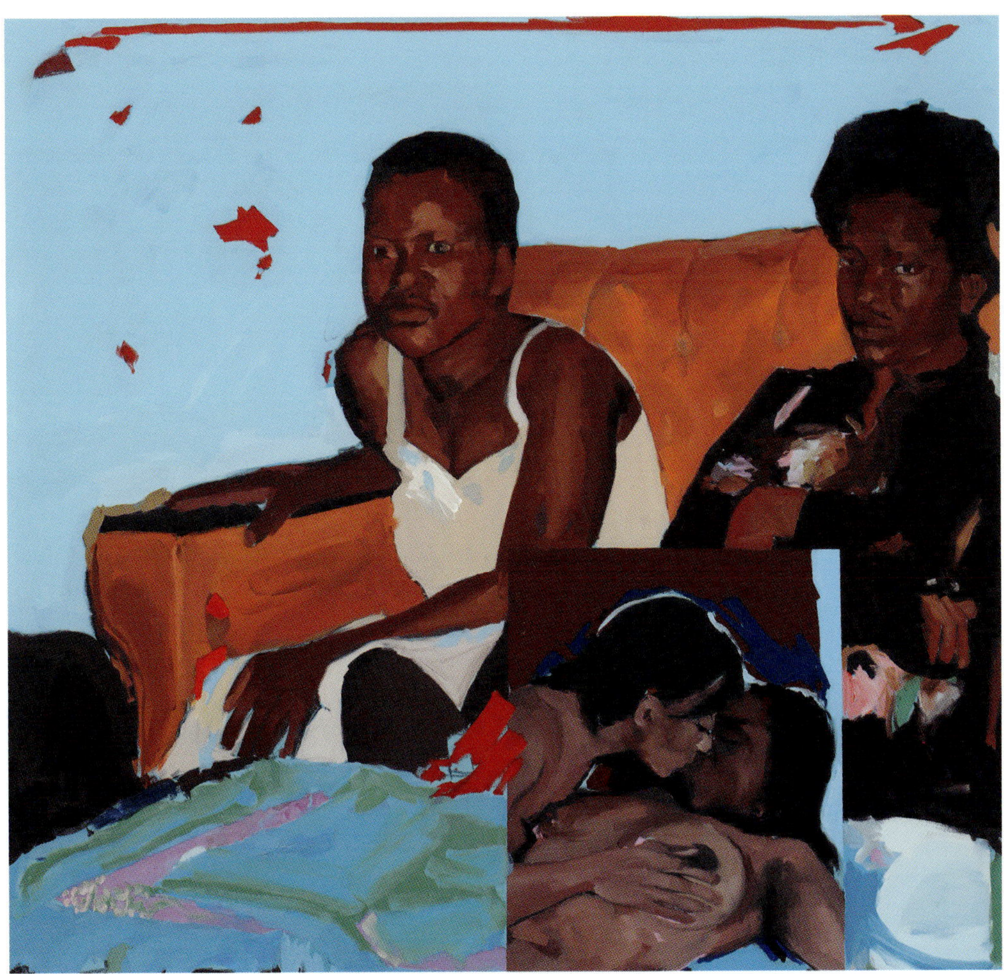

UK-based artist Kudzanai-Violet Hwami's work considers the complex intersection of spirituality, community, identity and home. She masterfully collages photographs taken in her native country, Zimbabwe, with images found online, seeking to reconstruct a fictional family in response to her own displacement. In Shona, the language Hwami grew up speaking, *ngochani mumhuri* translates to 'homosexual in the family'. The word *ngochani* has negative connotations in Zimbabwe and has recently been widely adopted by the nation's media and public when addressing LGBTQIA+ topics. The painting juxtaposes an archival family photograph with an image from a porn site, two sources often brought together by the artist as she navigates alternative sides to her own identity. The two figurative images represent two versions of intimacy occurring in the privacy of home united in a single painting in the spirit of openness.

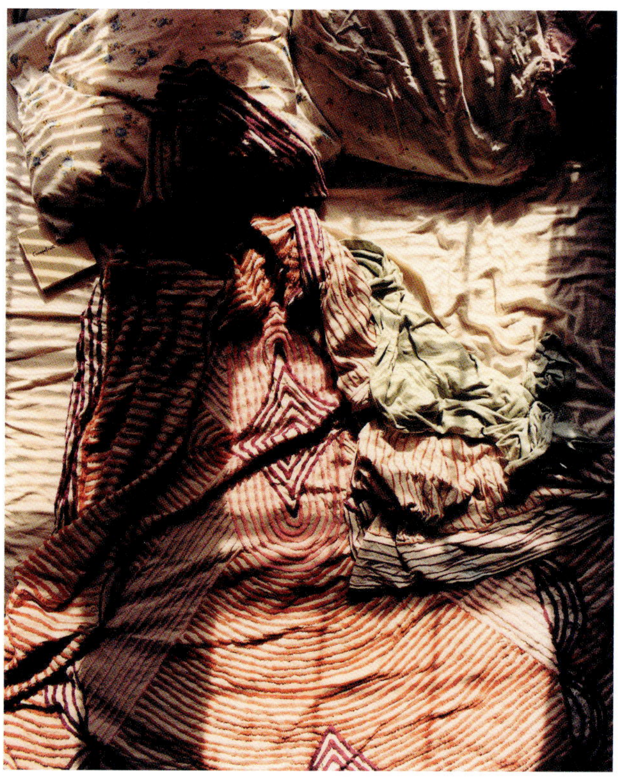

'Lesbian Beds' by Tammy Rae Carland is a series of large-format photographs of unmade beds shot from above, which invites us in to the most private of spaces. Crumpled sheets and indented pillows suggest the beds were occupied moments before the photographs were taken. The textured space left behind elicits a physical response from the viewer who can almost feel the warmth of the bodies once there. At first glance, the brightly coloured, beautifully lit beds could belong to anyone. Looking deeper, subtle visual clues hint at the identity of each bed's occupants – a cat, a baseball cap, a book – the lesbian context only made explicit by the artwork titles. In presenting this perfectly ordinary and inviting series of beds, the photographer encourages us to consider domesticity, love, family, relationships and home through a queer lens.

'Lesbian Beds', **Tammy Rae Carland**, 2002,
from left to right: *Untitled #1* (2002),
Untitled #3 (2002), *Untitled #5* (2002); all
images C-print, 101.6 x 76.2 cm (40 x 30 in)

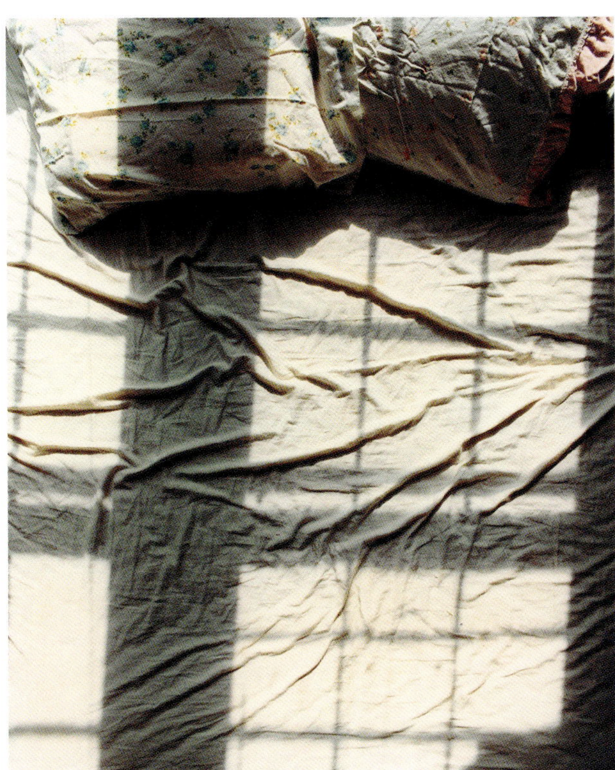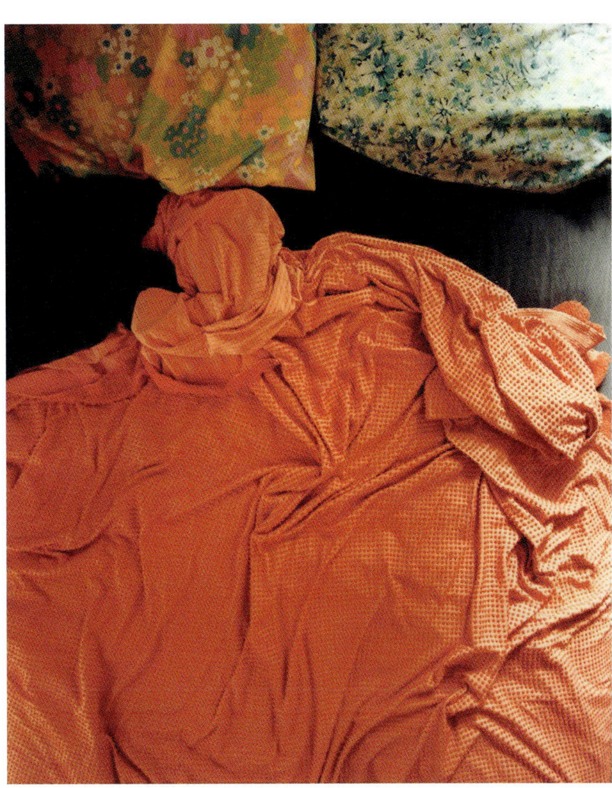

B & P v3 is one of a series of black-and-white ink drawings of couples that Amy Sillman made in her friends' homes. The drawings comprise the first stage in a three-step process of transmuting depiction into abstraction, in which bodies and soft furnishings are reduced to simple lines and shapes, ending with the large process-based paintings that Sillman is best known for. Gay men B and P are one of many queer couples included in the series. Titled with initials rather than names, the drawings exist as something other than portraits. With distinguishing features abstracted, the figures coexist on an equal plane, regardless of gender or identity. The intimate interactions experienced in the comfort of home are familiar, leaving room for the viewer to imagine themselves in the role of either figure, to step into someone else's shoes and gain a different perspective.

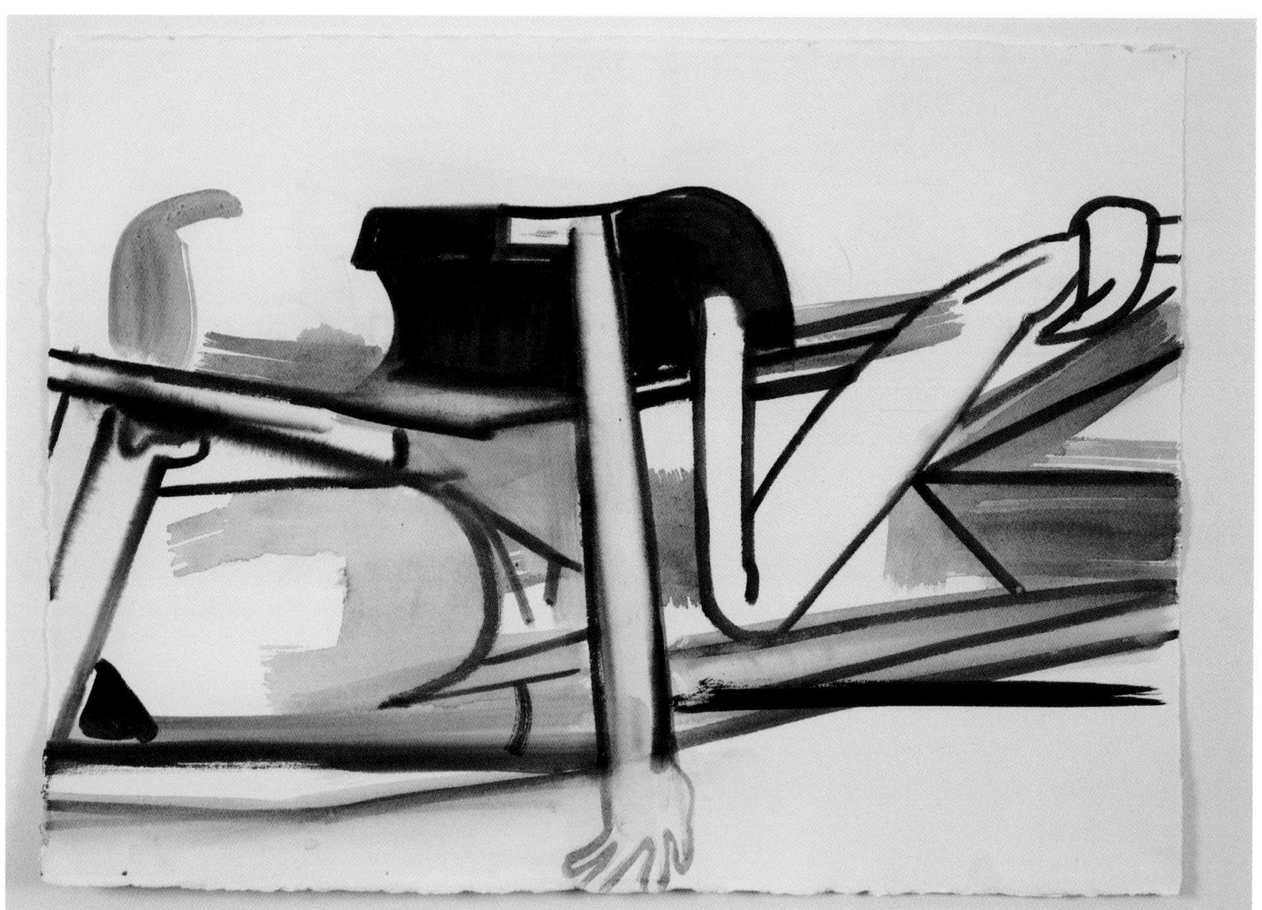

B & P v3, **Amy Sillman**, 2007,
ink on paper, 57.8 x 76.2 cm
(22¾ x 30 in)

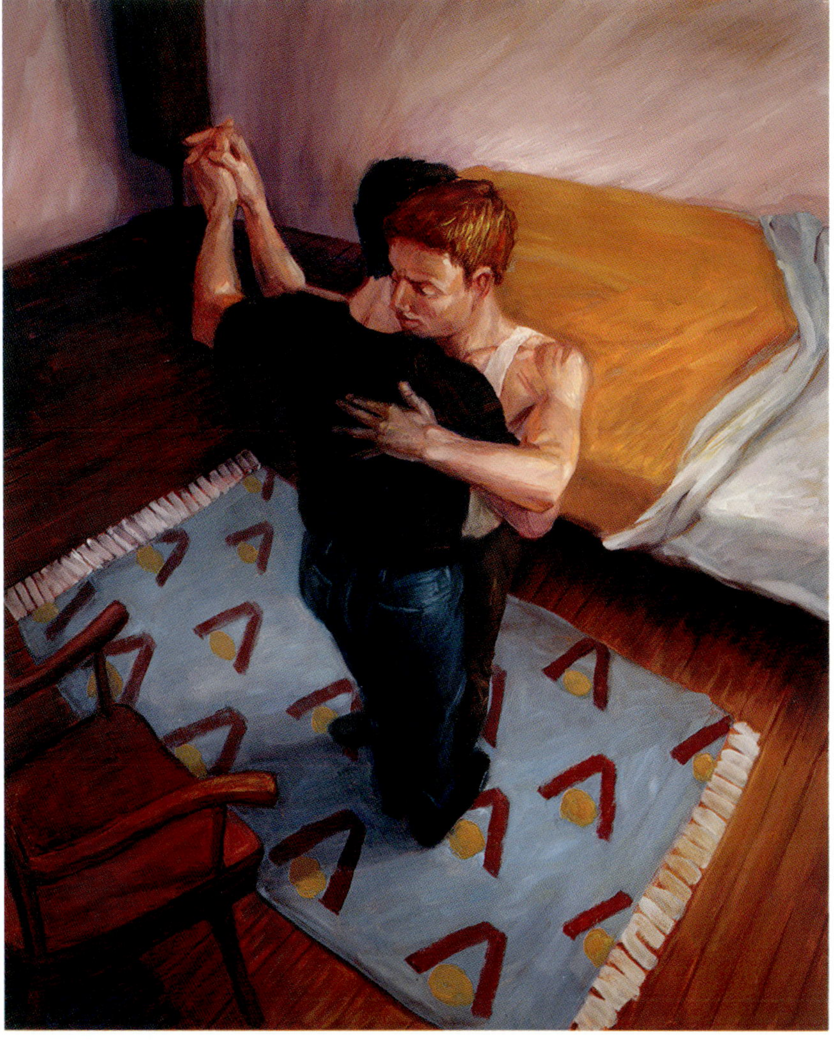

Blue Rug, **Hugh Steers**, 1994, oil on canvas, 115.6 x 91.4 cm (45½ x 36 in)

Hugh Steers

Painted at the end of Hugh Steers' life and later reproduced as a lithograph, *Blue Rug* reflects on the solace found through human connection as death loomed over his community during the AIDS epidemic, to which he fell victim at the young age of 32. Steers often painted from an unusual perspective, his scenes capturing intimate views of everyday moments within the domestic space in a style that he described as 'gorgeous bleakness'. In *Blue Rug*, we see the fragile nature of the dancing figures' bodies as they share a tender moment, finding strength in their embrace and challenging the isolation of the illness. His paintings of male couples caring for and loving each other at home are a powerful reminder of the need for safe spaces and to value the potentially limited time we have together.

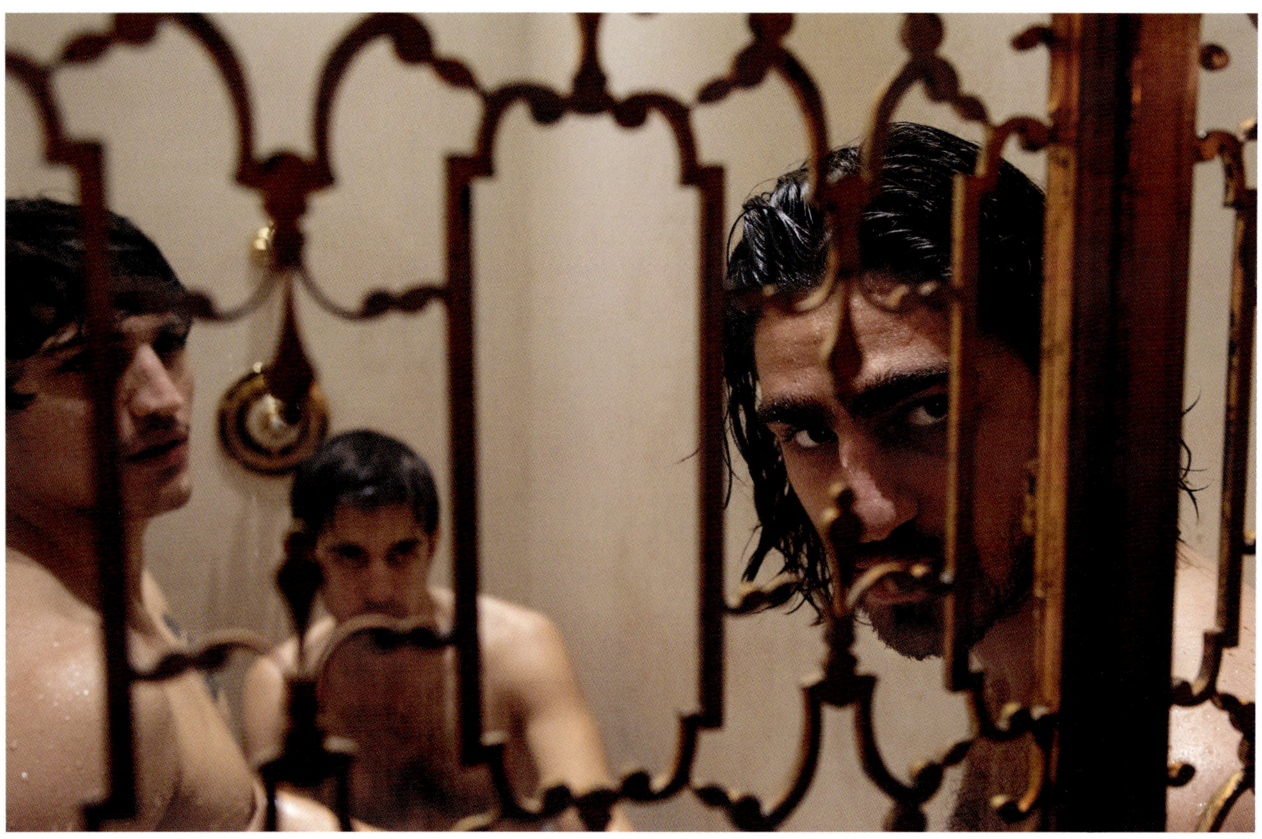

Sarp Kerem Yavuz

Sarp Kerem Yavuz's *Selamlık* is named after the spaces in the Ottoman court where only men were allowed, the counterpart of *haremlik*, where the Sultan's concubines lived. The three male figures in the photograph are visible through the ornate protective screen of a Turkish bath, their gazes fixed on something beyond the picture plane in anticipation of a disturbance to the safe space in which they interact with each other with ease. Yavuz's practice explores the homoerotic implications of patriarchal structures within an Islamic context, a result of his upbringing in Istanbul, which meant navigating 'contradictory narratives around male camaraderie, homosocial behaviours and homophobia'. Yavuz often borrows from the language of cinema, and this particular image, shot in a private home designed to evoke the golden age of the Ottoman Empire, is a love letter to Turkish-Italian director Ferzan Özpetek's scandalous 1997 queer film, *Hamam*.

Clifford Prince King's photography presents an intimate look at Black queer masculinity. Appearing in the tender image *Safe Space* himself, King's hair is being braided by a companion who has a spliff held to his mouth by the third figure. Together, they form a trio of mutual respect and caregiving. King reads a copy of James Baldwin's novel *Giovanni's Room* (1956), a story of two gay male lovers who poignantly find solace in the bedroom in question amid the unacceptance and eventual tragedy of the outside world. The richness of King's work is inspired by influences alongside Baldwin such as filmmaker Isaac Julien and poet Langston Hughes. As the three shirtless men smoke and read together, they take pleasure in each other's company, relaxing and existing authentically in the 'safe space' of someone's home.

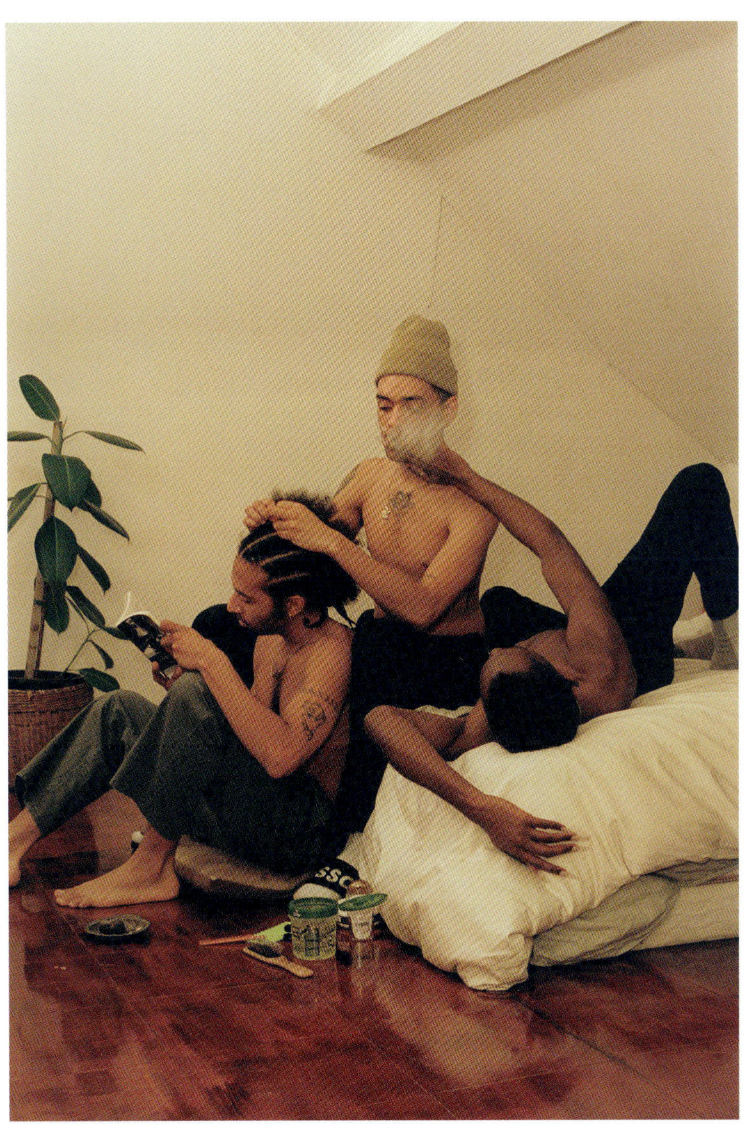

Safe Space, **Clifford Prince King**, 2020, 35mm photograph, 121.9 x 81.3 cm (48 x 32 in)

Laurence Philomene constructs tranquil images of space and place that are full of magic. The autobiographical photographic series 'Puberty' 'looks at the intimate and vital process of caring for oneself as a non-binary transgender person undergoing hormonal replacement therapy (HRT)'. The saturated scenes, photographed within the artist's home, evoke comfort, safety and security – qualities of life that are regularly denied to queer people. Through these dreamlike photographs, Philomene offers a glimpse into their daily life and the habitual practices of bedtime routine, conjuring new forms of spirituality and ritual found through queerness. The colourful spaces created and documented by Philomene celebrate the freedom of expression and exploration found in transition and embrace notions of home for those seldom represented.

Bedroom Candles from the series 'Puberty', **Laurence Philomene**, 2020, digital photograph, dimensions variable

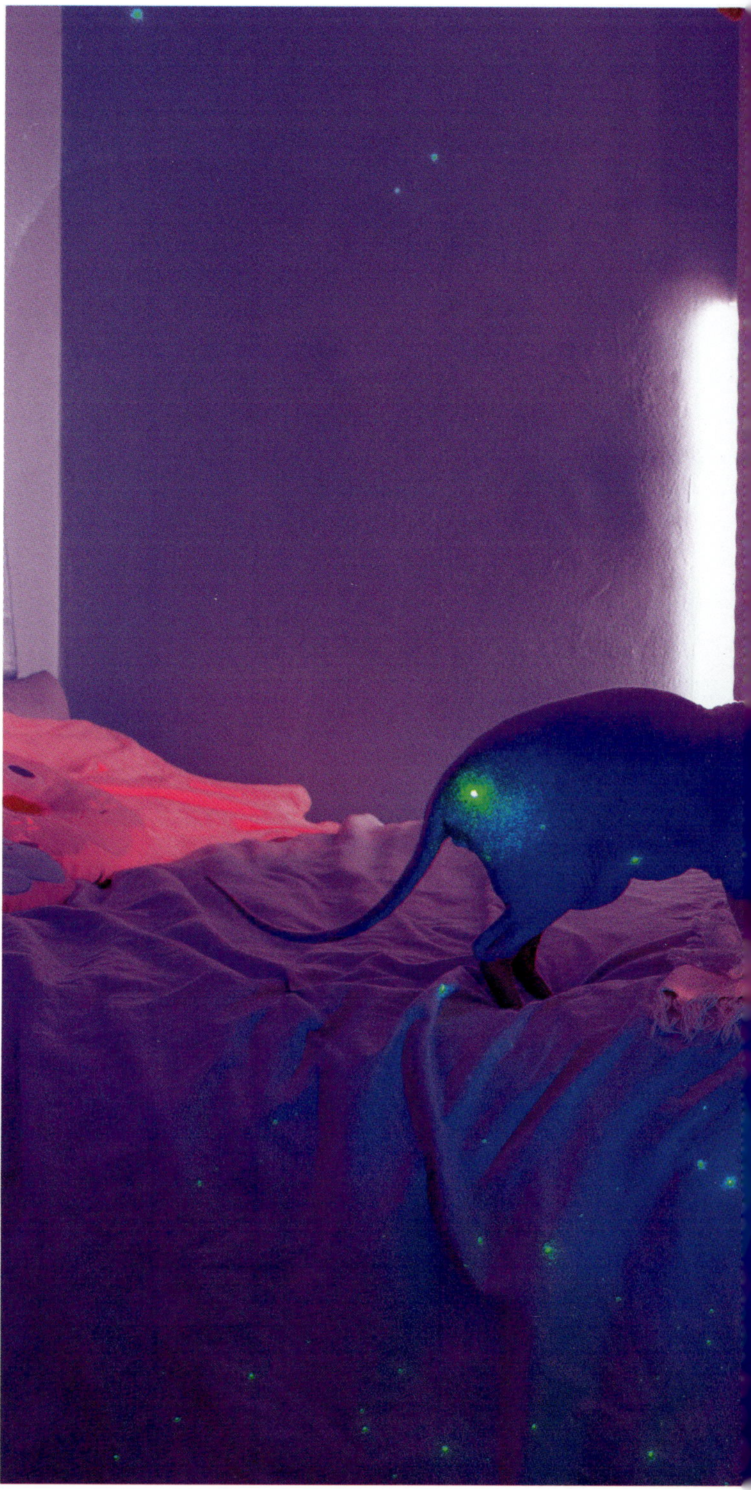

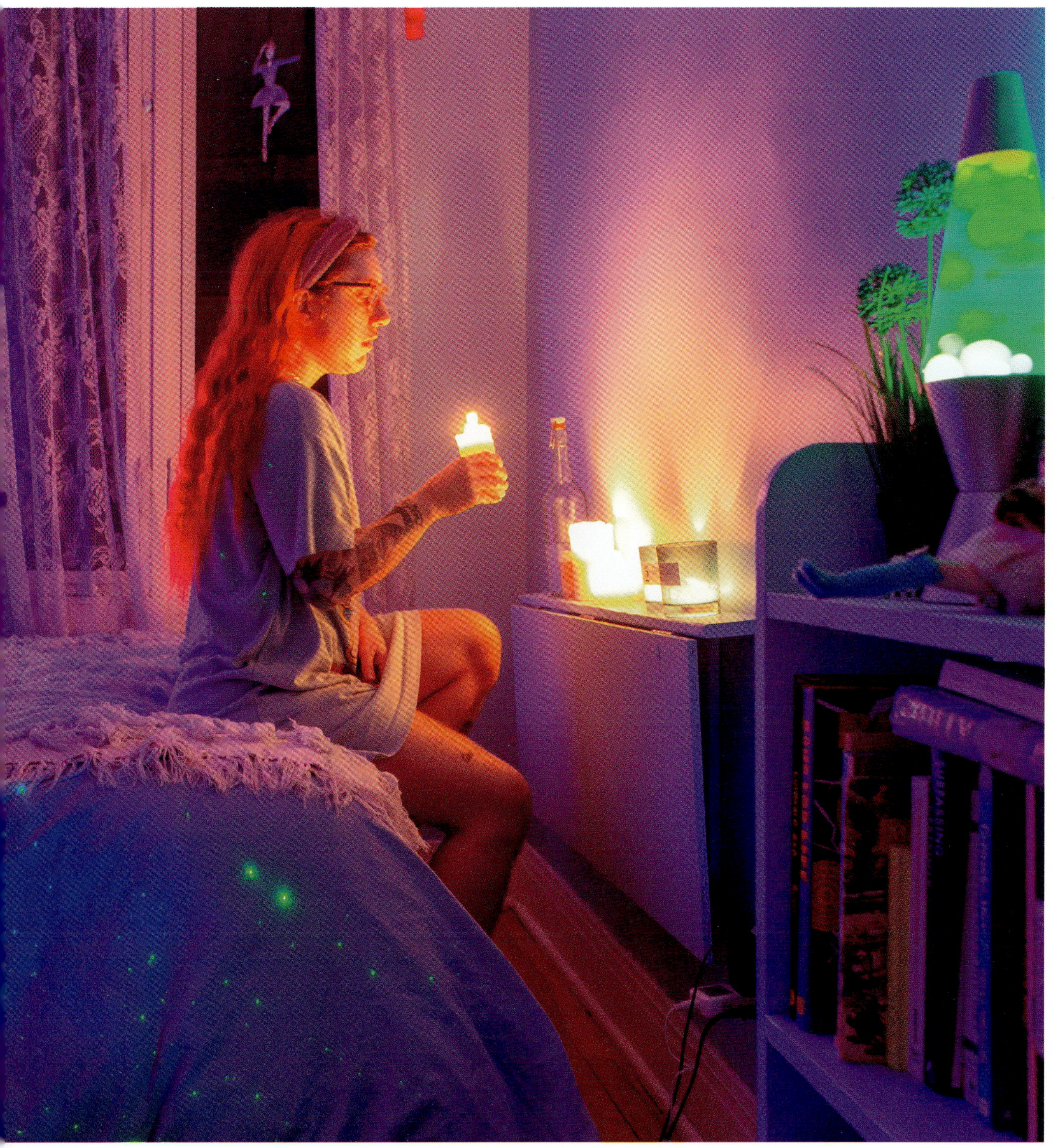

Club

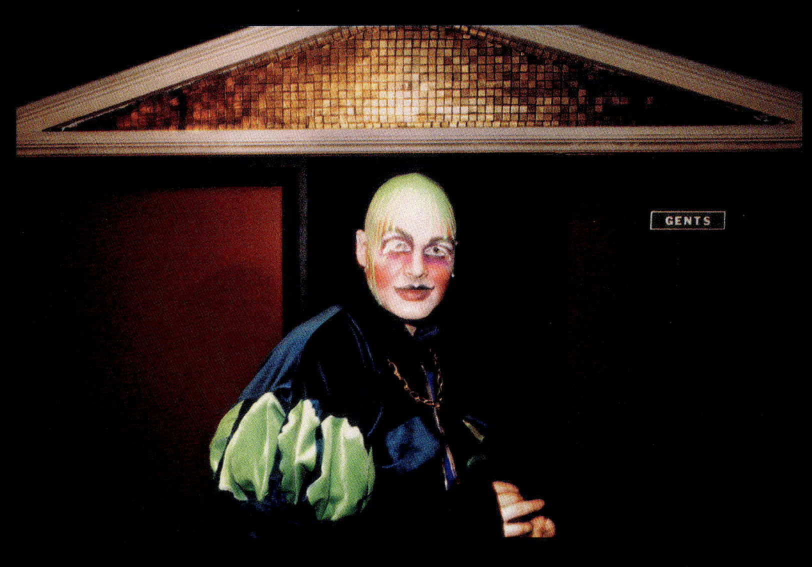

Gay spaces began opening as early as the late nineteenth century in places like Berlin, which according to historical records had as many as six gay bars by 1900. Since then clubs and bars have nurtured the LGBTQIA+ community all over the world. Whether underground and operating in secret, or well known as queer destinations and proudly identifiable by rainbow flags above the door, clubs have offered sanctuary to queers who find each other and themselves on the sweaty and steamy dancefloors. Queer creatives have become legendary for shaping the direction of their community's nightlife, such as Andrew Logan and Leigh Bowery, who took London's club scene of the 1970s and 80s to a new frontier through radical performance, makeup and costume that brought the queer community together in creative spectacle. In turn, LGBTQIA+ people have pioneered ways of partying, and queer nightlife has influenced and shaped mainstream club culture, from disco, house and pop music, to ballroom, pageants and drag performance.

Artists have played a critical role in the archiving of queer nightlife by documenting contemporary spaces that play home to their own communities. Reynaldo Rivera's large body of photographic work captures the parties and clubs that were

Leigh Bowery at his club night Taboo,
photo by Dave Swindells, 1986

home to Los Angeles' queer Latinx community in the 1980s and 90s, offering insight into a scene that died along with many of its participants and may otherwise be forgotten.

As queer people celebrate new rights and freedoms in the majority of the world, their spaces come under a very different kind of threat to the raids, attacks and forced closures that they have historically faced. Significant progress in LGBTQIA+ rights, illustrated by landmark wins across the Western world, can lead to a perception of equality that overlooks the nuanced challenges still facing the wider community. The result is a lack of prioritization and protection of the spaces that have come to be called home against a hungry wave of gentrification that sweeps across gay villages turning the once iconic clubs and bars into offices and residential blocks. The mass closure of queer spaces is a worldwide threat. Queer bars and clubs in London and New York began closing at a rapid rate in the decades following 2000 and it is now estimated that both of these cities have fewer than half of the queer venues they had in the 1990s. Artists have responded to these closures by memorializing the spaces that nurtured their histories and played a key role in their own self-realization.

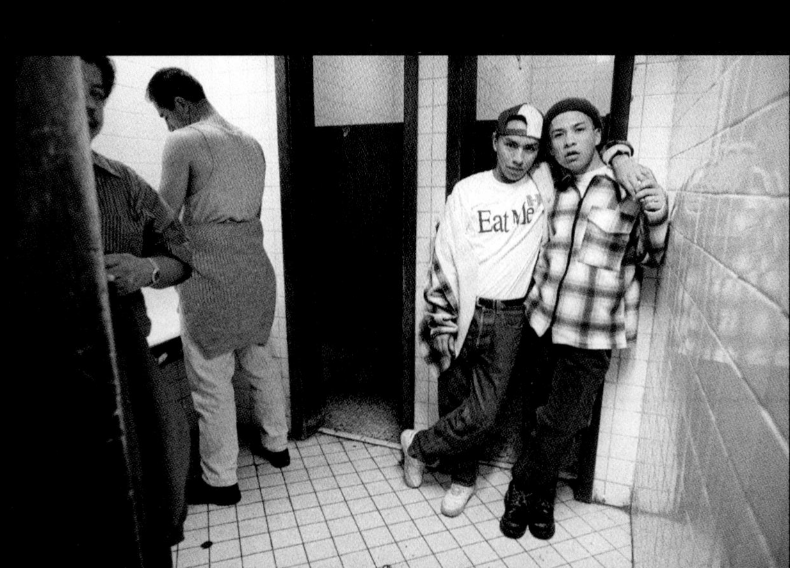

Hannah Quinlan & Rosie Hastings

UK Gay Bar Directory (*UKGBD*) is a moving image archive of over one hundred gay bars filmed by artist duo Hannah Quinlan and Rosie Hastings in 2016. With a running time of over four and three-quarter hours, the film memorializes the UK's gay bars as they face the threat of closure in response to increasing costs, gentrification and safety threats. According to a 2017 report from London's City Hall, 58 per cent of the capital city's LGBTQIA+ bars and clubs had closed in the decade prior to *UKGBD* being made. The artists believe that documenting these disappearing spaces is an 'important historical gesture and a strategy for resisting assimilation'. Filming these hallowed spaces while they are empty, with the lights flashing and the music pumping, the artists reflect on the ways in which gay bars serve the queer community, and the joy, liberation and solidarity that can be found on the dance floor.

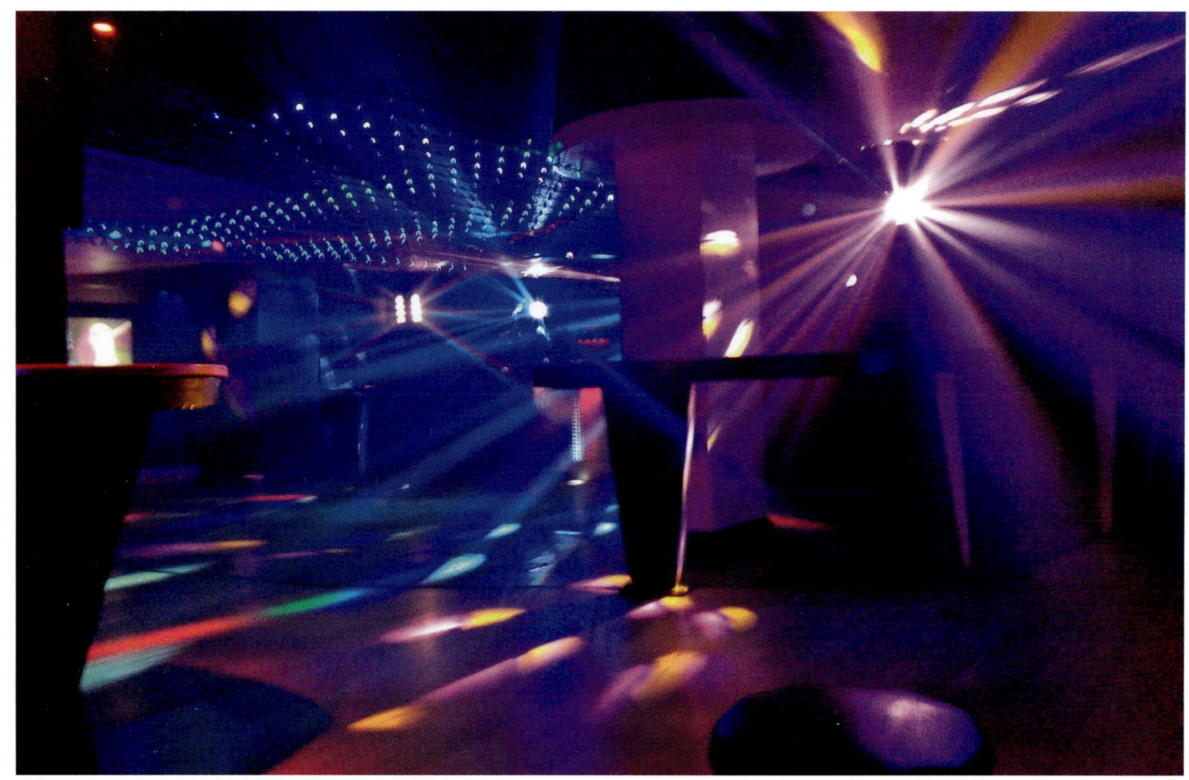

UK Gay Bar Directory, **Hannah Quinlan & Rosie Hastings**, 2016, HD video with sound on hard drive, 4 hrs 47 mins

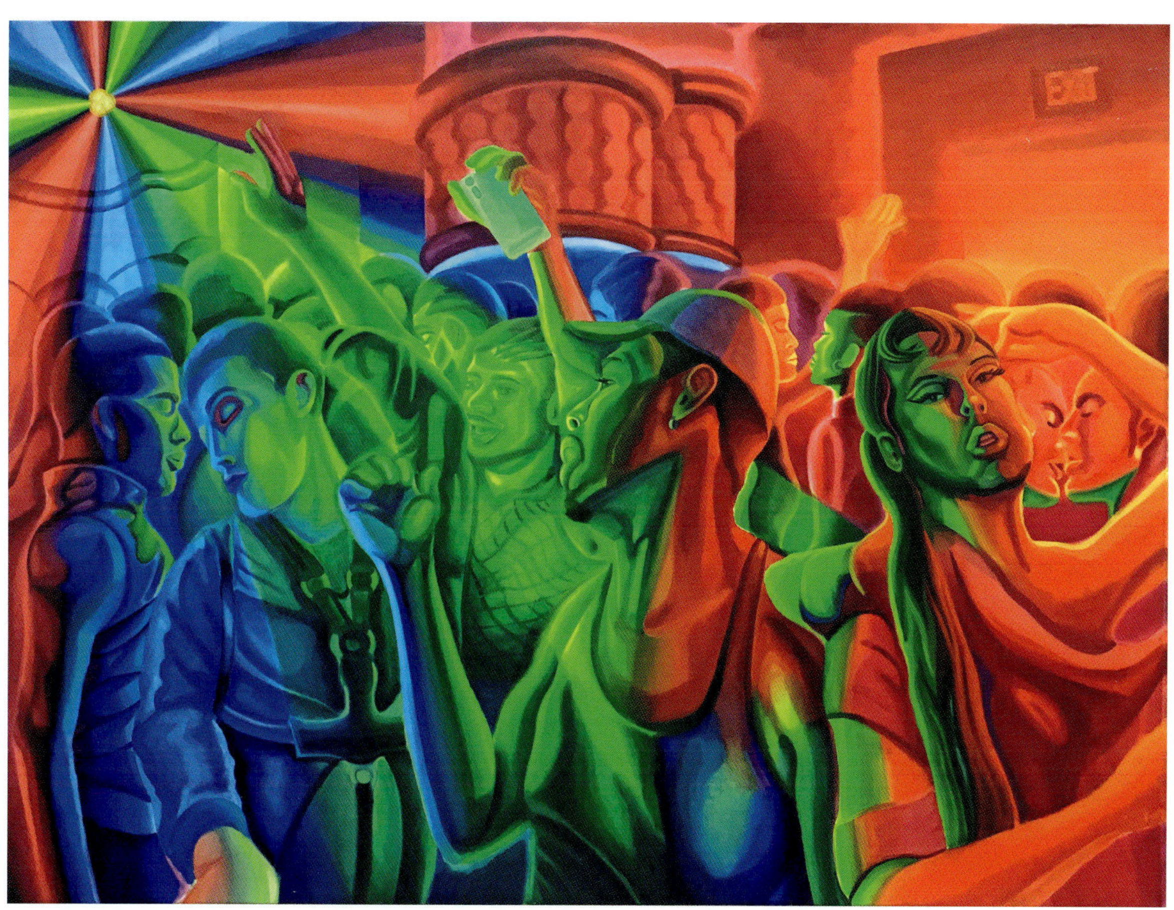

Painted during the Covid pandemic, James Bartolacci's neon painting *Spectrum Closing Party* mourns the loss of the bodily contact once shared on the sweaty dance floors of New York's queer clubs. Prior to the pandemic, the young artist had been nostalgically painting gay clubs and bars impacted by the consistent and systematic closure of LGBTQIA+ party spaces across the United States. The pandemic-induced ban on social gatherings, which heightened the permanent closure of the already disproportionately affected queer spaces, prompted Bartolacci to dig deeper into the power of physical human connection and the life-giving force of queer spaces. Bartolacci situates his audience in the midst of the crowded Brooklyn club, inviting us to share in the ecstasy of the glistening bodies rhythmically moving together under the fluorescent lights of the Spectrum dancefloor.

Salman Toor's paintings present intoxicating
scenes of contemporary queer life often
rendered in his signature palette of lustrous
and acidic green hues. His figures are languid
and fluid, dressed in richly textured fabrics
that hang seductively from their frames. *Bar
Boy* features a solitary central figure amid a
crowded bar, his pensive face lit by the phone
in his hand. In the foreground a couple tenderly
embrace and the blond locks of a sleeping
figure tumble onto the bar. There is an aching
romanticism and nostalgia to the painting,
unsettled by a hauntingly ominous edge. The
scene brings to mind the loss of LGBTQIA+
night-time spaces in the artist's home city of
New York and the rise of online dating apps
serving the pursuit of human connection,
underlining the critical need for queer spaces
in which marginalized individuals can find their
communities and thrive.

Bar Boy, **Salman Toor**, 2019, oil on
plywood, 121.9 x 152.4 cm (48 x 60 in)

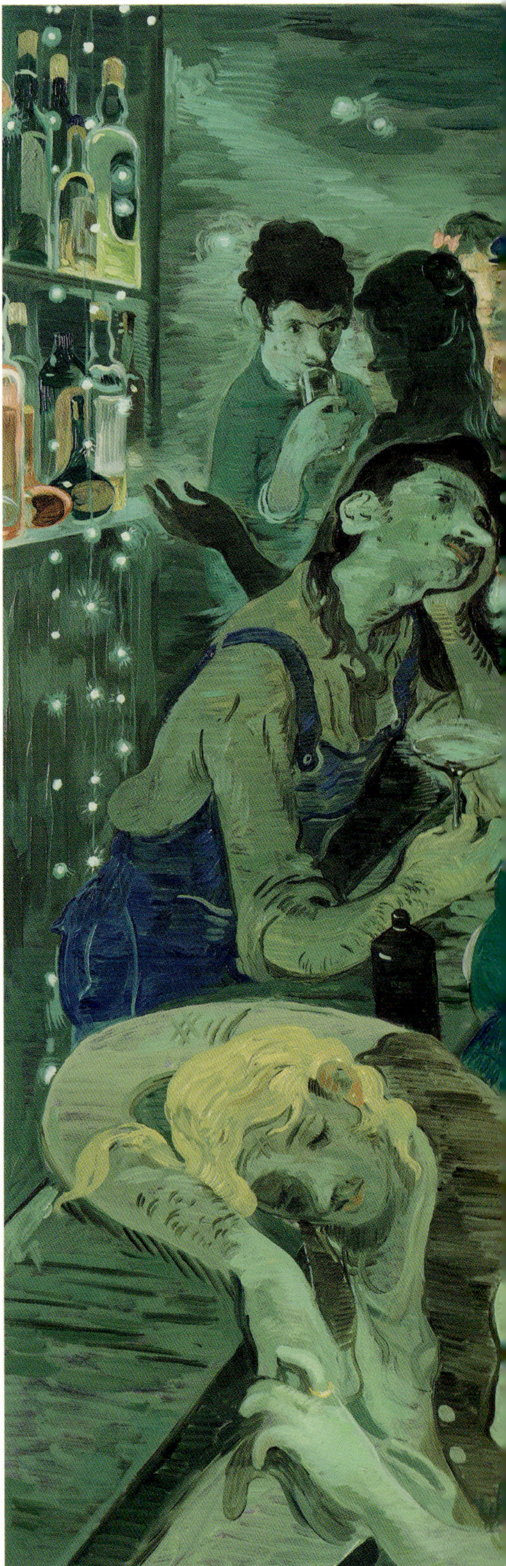

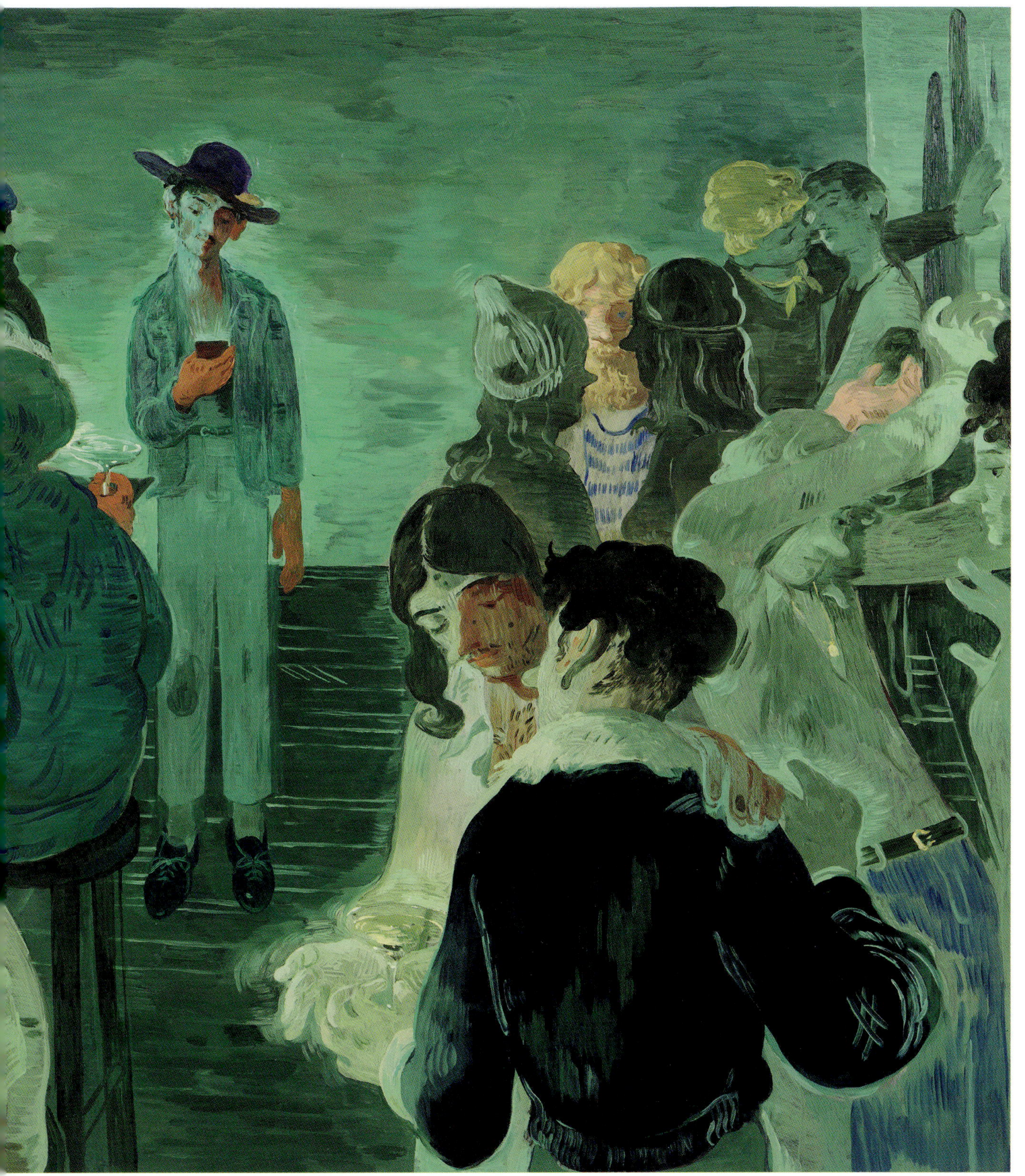

homocrap #1 is a multimedia installation by the collective assume vivid astro focus, which immerses viewers in a vibrant, sensory-rich environment. In celebration of LGBTQIA+ culture, the installation simulates a gay club, complete with pulsing music, smoke machine, mirrored floor and disco lights. A giant tan-lined sex doll with both male and female-presenting faces does a backbend across the space, which is decorated with densely patterned wallpaper and an animated geometric ceiling referencing the maximalist aesthetic of Op art-influenced discos. The artists' desire to bring the communal energy of the club to their work is amplified by hosting dance parties in the installation, shifting the focus from the work itself to the self-expression and identity of the community being celebrated.

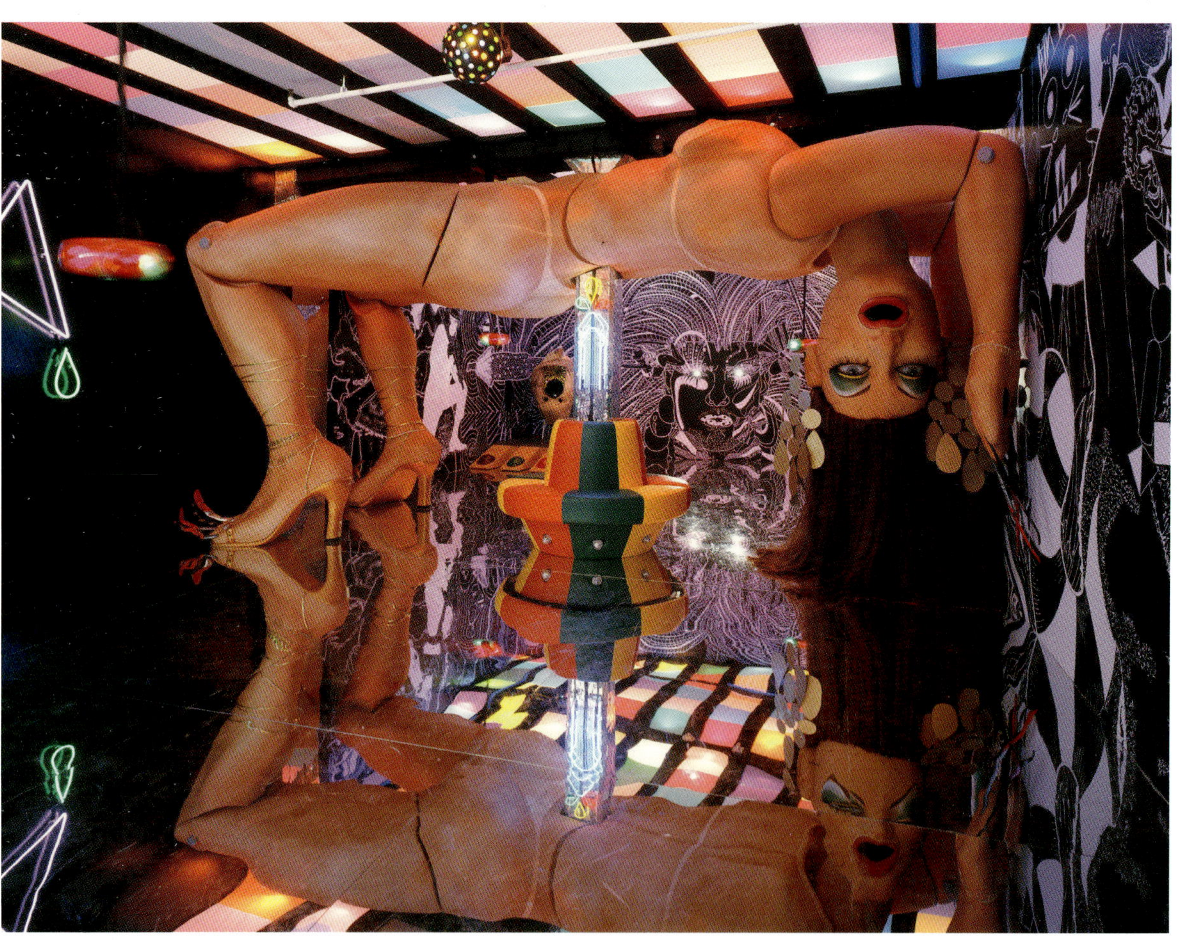

homocrap #1, **assume vivid astro focus**,
2005, mixed-media installation

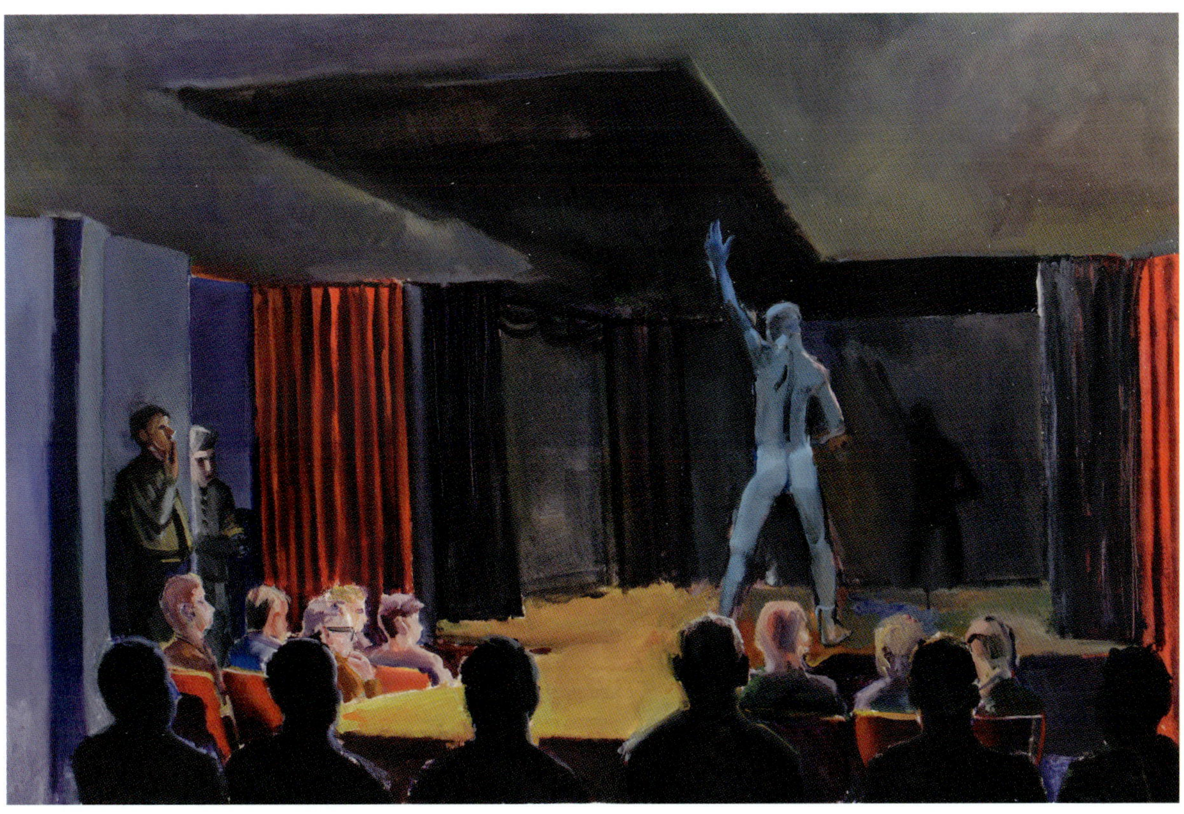

Patrick Angus's paintings depict the private spaces of New York City's gay world in the 1980s. He painted the bedrooms, bathhouses, cinemas, theatres, bars and clubs occupied by a community that had been pushed underground during the AIDS epidemic. Rather than addressing the disease directly in his work, even as he began to suffer from its symptoms himself, Angus tackled the looming spectre by applying empathy and sensitivity to the figures that congregated in these spaces. Like many of his night-time paintings, *Slave to the Rhythm* evokes an atmosphere of loneliness and longing even within a crowded room. His work serves to document the hallowed queer spaces that provided solace to a social scene in mortal crisis and the transient interactions that would otherwise go unrecorded.

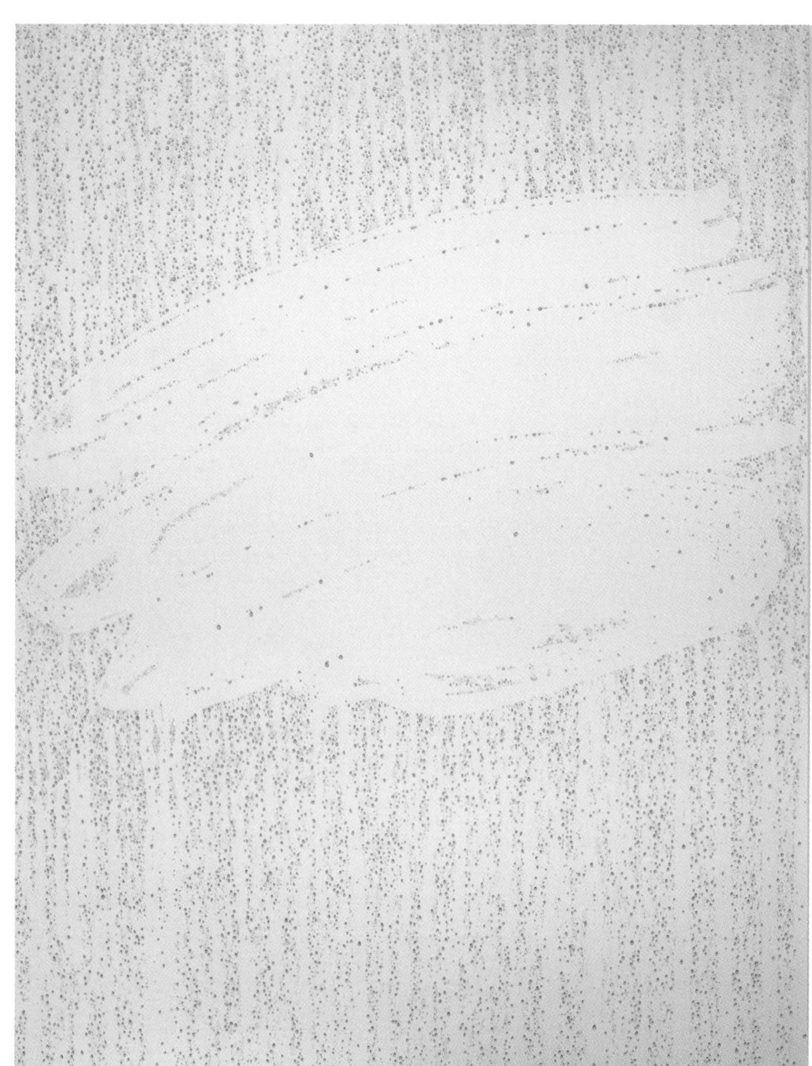

Work That Body IX, **Prem Sahib**, 2013, aluminium and resin, 74 x 54 cm (29 x 21¼ in)

Prem Sahib

Multidisciplinary artist Prem Sahib's *Work That Body IX* is part of a series that he informally calls 'sweat panels'. The anodized aluminium panel 'sweats' with droplets of resin that appear to drip vertically down the panel, interrupted by a large smear mark that could have been created by a single motion. In actuality, each resin drop is painstakingly painted by hand and quite rigid. The artwork's surface resembles a steamy window or mirror, or the interior wall of a sweaty club or sauna, the smear evidence of the body referred to by the title. Sahib's seemingly minimalist works are inspired by a long history of queer spaces and the interconnected bodies that occupy them. The work is bursting with sexy energy, heightened by the tension between the droplets of resin, evoking bodily fluids, and the smooth aluminium, which dares us to run our own hand across the surface.

Wu Tsang's 2012 film tells the story of the wildness found at Silver Platter, a bar that has nurtured the Latin queer community in Los Angeles since 1963. Narrated by an older drag queen, the film is told from the perspective of the bar herself, as she contemplates her legacy and reflects on the thousands of queers who have found safety, support and freedom on her dancefloors. A story of survival, solidarity and intergenerational love and respect is woven around documentary footage of the trans women and gay men who call the club home, alongside footage of Tsang and friends as they fight to defend Silver Platter and throw their own wild party. *Wildness* is a story based on truth and full of magic.

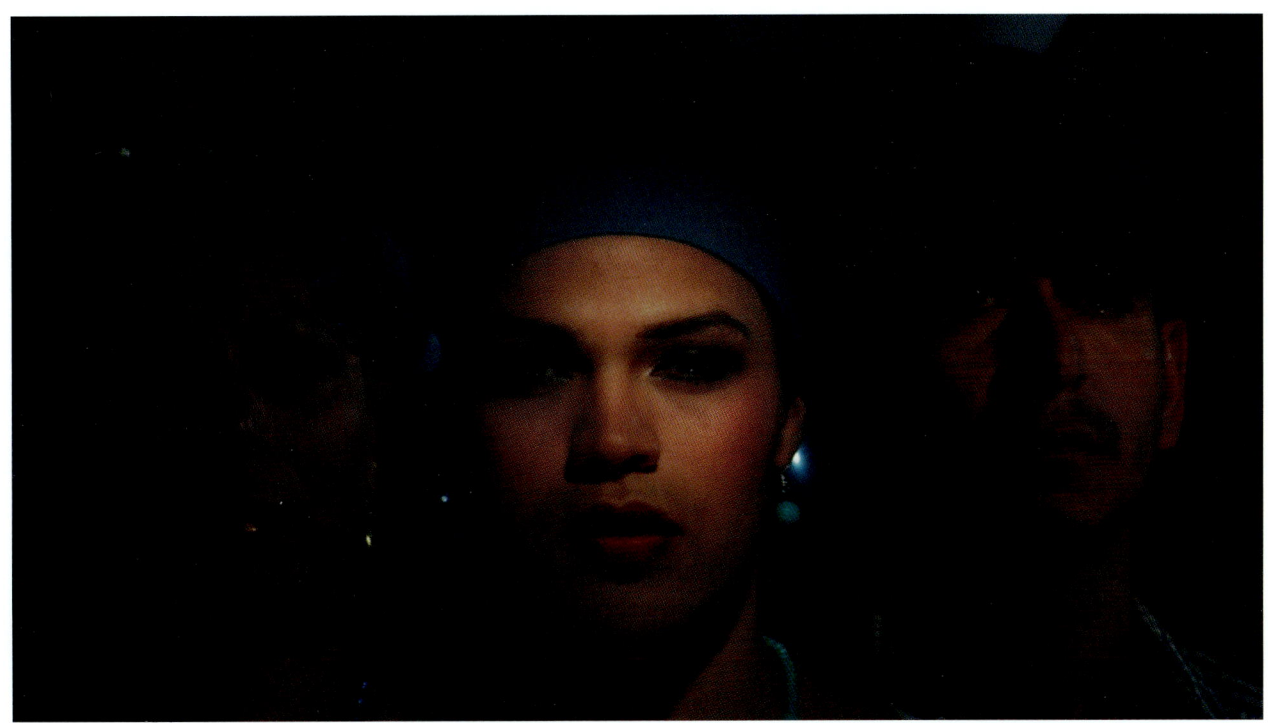

Wildness, **Wu Tsang**, 2012, single-channel
HD video, stereo sound, 74 mins

Andrew Logan describes Alternative Miss World as 'a surreal art event for all-round family entertainment'. Blending cabaret, drag show and pageant, the first event was staged in London in 1972 in the format of Crufts Dog Show, with three categories: daywear, swimwear and eveningwear, and with Logan playing both host and hostess, each half of his body immaculately dressed as one or the other. What began as a party in Logan's studio has become an institution for London's queer creative scene, with leading figures from the arts, music and fashion, such as David Hockney, Grayson Perry, Brian Eno and Leigh Bowery, appearing as contestants and judges. Most recently the event was presented at Shakespeare's Globe on the River Thames.

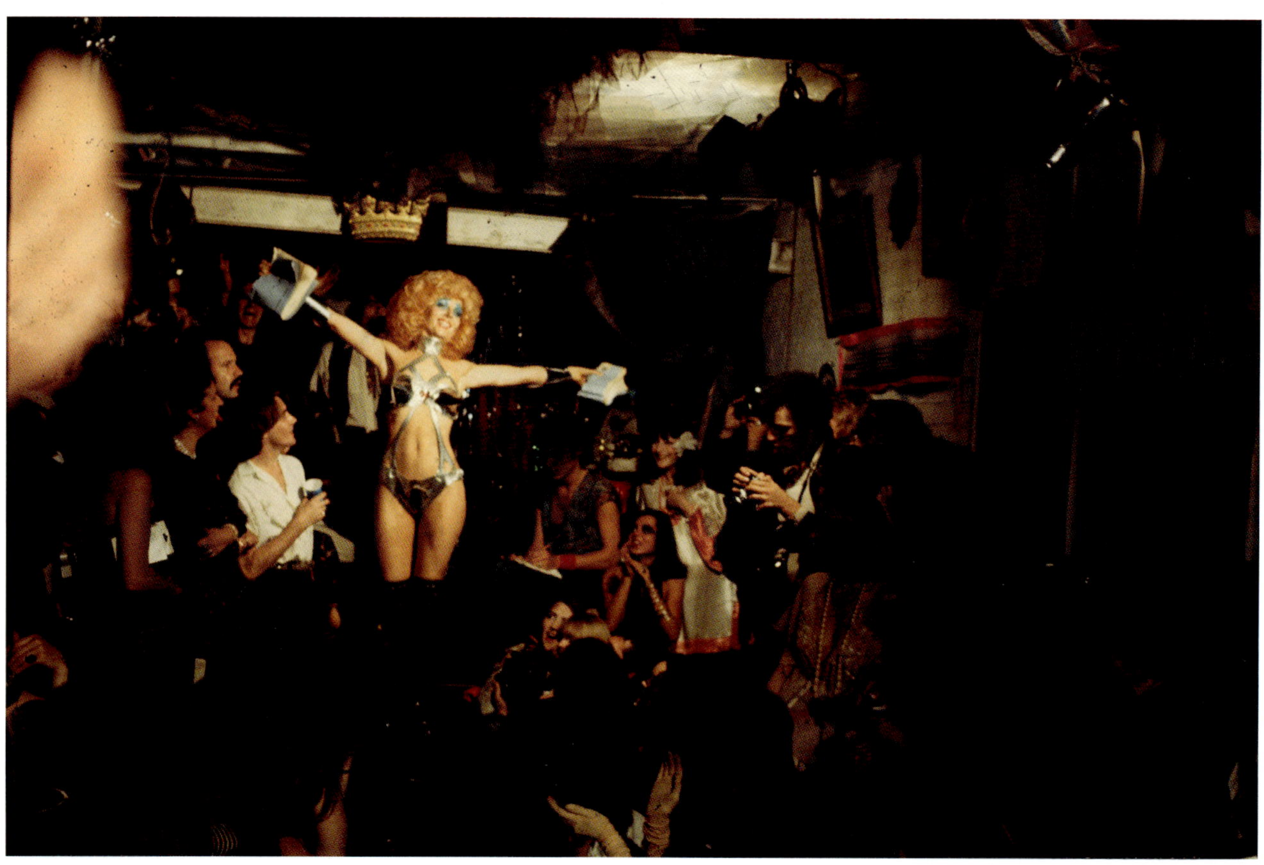

Miss Hackney in the swimwear category, Alternative Miss World, **Andrew Logan**, 1972

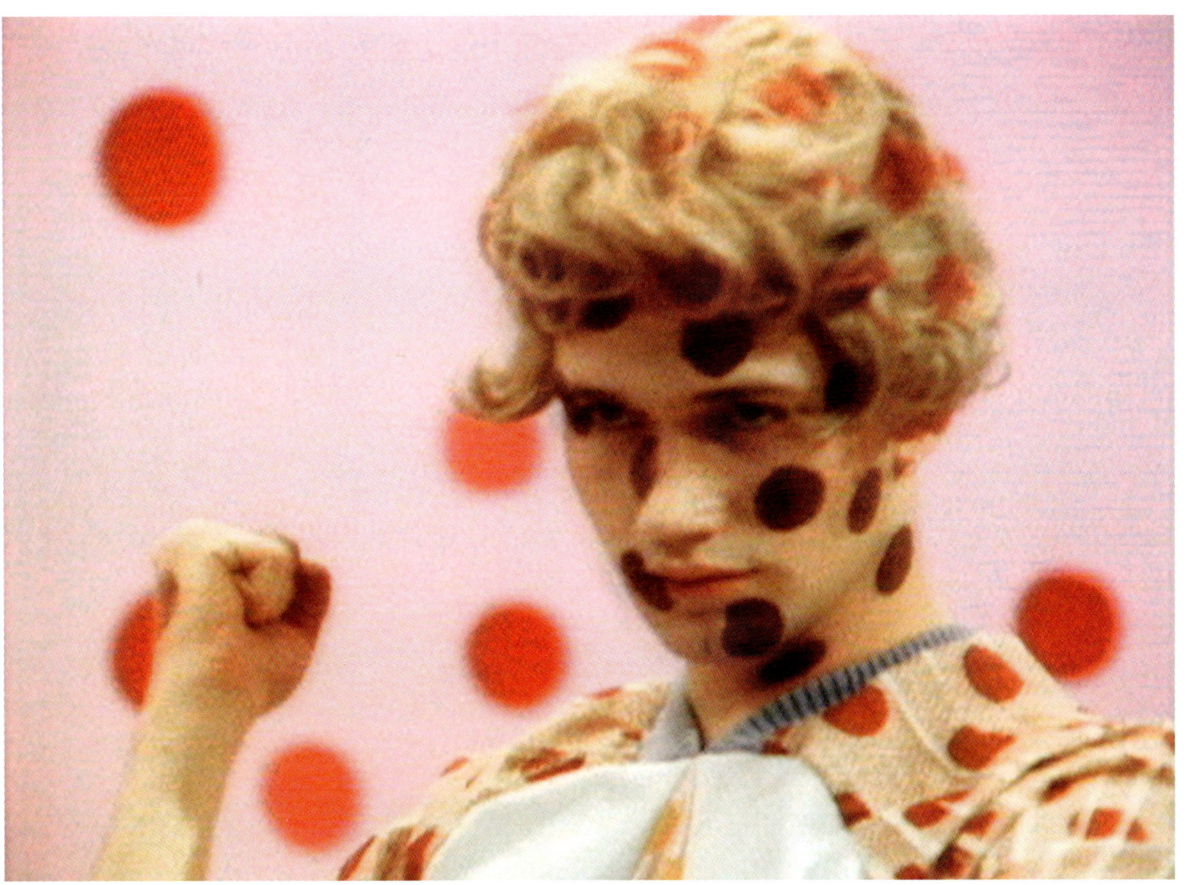

Charles Atlas is a pioneering figure in film
and video. *Hail the New Puritan* depicts a
fictionalized day in the life of the Scottish
dancer and choreographer Michael Clark,
as he and his company prepare for a
performance of his 1984 work *New Puritans*.
Celebrated as a defining cultural figure,
Clark is known for provocative dance that
challenges society's perceptions of sexuality
and gender. Dance performances occur
within a set designed by Leigh Bowery

and Trojan, accompanied by a soundtrack
with contributions from English post-punk
band The Fall and American avant-garde
musician Glenn Branca. Both Atlas and Clark
collaborated with key figures across music,
fashion, performance and film throughout
their careers. The film is indicative of their
approach to cross-disciplinary practice
and the fruitful relationships and vibrant
creativity that emerged from London's queer
clubs and art spaces in the 1980s.

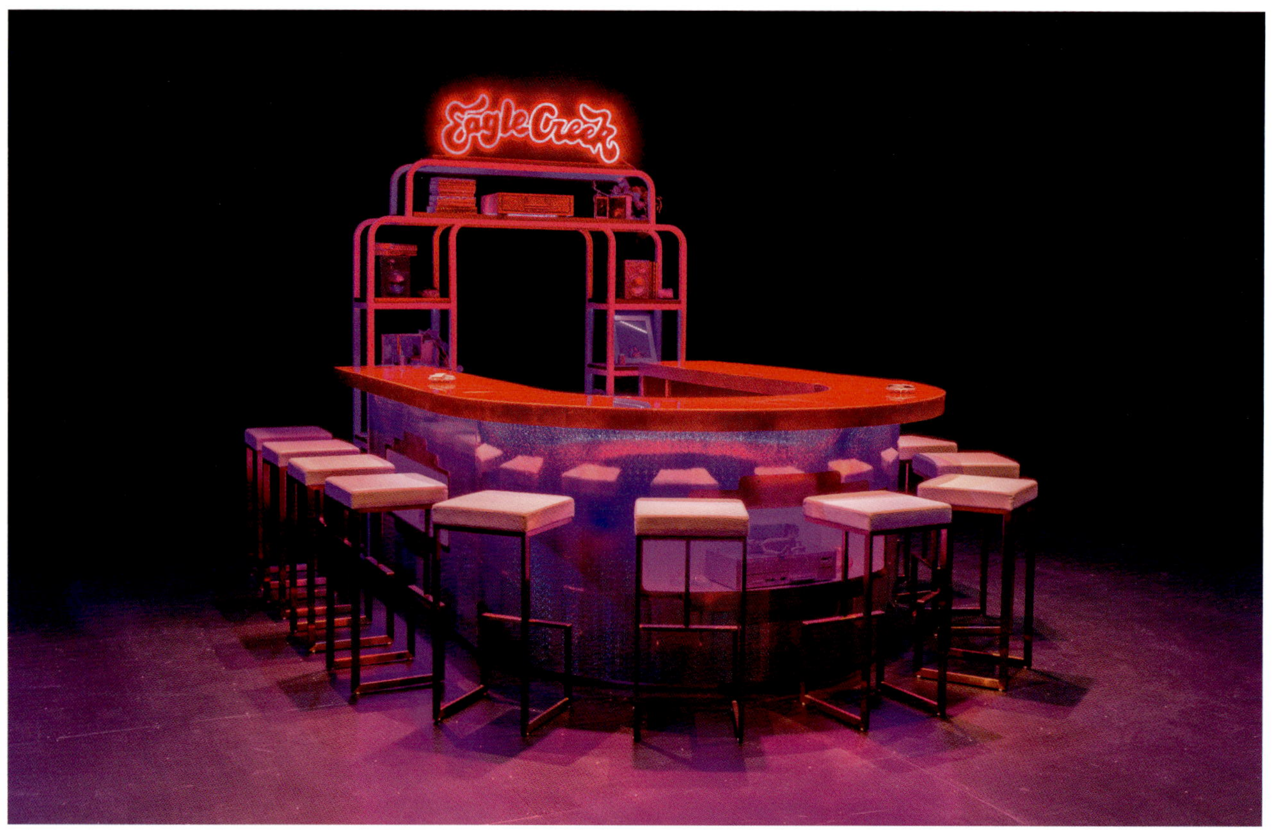

Sadie Barnette

The New Eagle Creek Saloon is an installation and performance series by the artist Sadie Barnette. It reimagines San Francisco's first Black-owned gay bar, which was opened by the artist's father, Rodney Barnette, in 1990 and closed only three years later. Operating with the tagline 'a friendly place, with a funky bass, for every race', the bar served as a safe meeting place for the city's multiracial queer community. Activations taking place within the installation connect to the history of loss, activism and solidarity that inhabited the bar as the LGBTQIA+ community endured the AIDS epidemic, rising violence and marginalization in the early 1990s. In Barnette's own words: 'I built the glittering bar structure – glowing somewhere between a monument and an altar – as an invitation, a place to be, and an invocation … It is permission to dance and dream, to call the names of those lost, and to see one another as we are in the glow of our own small moments of freedom.'

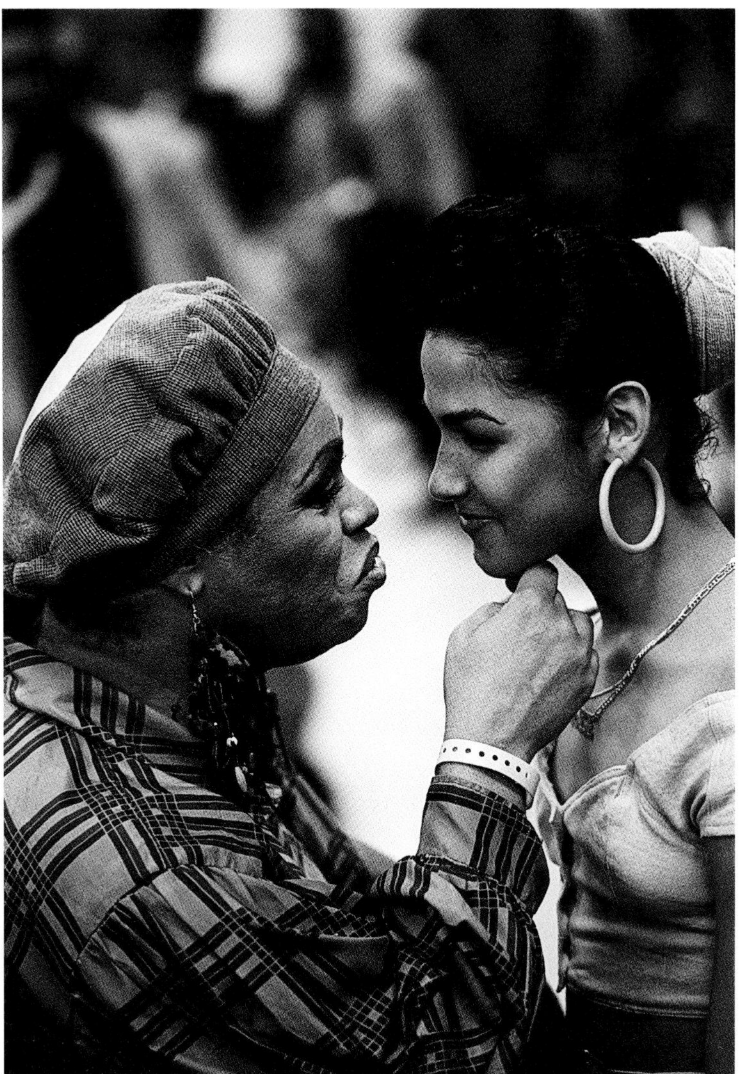

Iconic Mother Avis Pendavis and Daughter Evie, House of Chanel Ball, Marc Ballroom New York, 1990, **Chantal Regnault**, 1990

Chantal Regnault photographed the most legendary queens of the Harlem House Ballroom scene between 1989 and 1992. During this period, queer clubs in New York City were facing extinction because of the threat of violence, particularly impacting femme-presenting queer and trans people of colour, and the vast AIDS-related loss of life within the community. Regnault, a cisgender heterosexual French woman, gained permission to photograph the balls and the individuals and Houses who competed, describing her role as an appreciator rather than an observer and her photography as a way to understand others. The traditional drag shows that inspired ballroom culture were unappreciative and unaccepting of Black and Hispanic queens, so they created their own houses and club nights. Regnault's studio portraits and action shots from the dance floor document the exquisite elegance and love found in these spaces, including a tender moment between house mother Avis Pendavis and her daughter Evie.

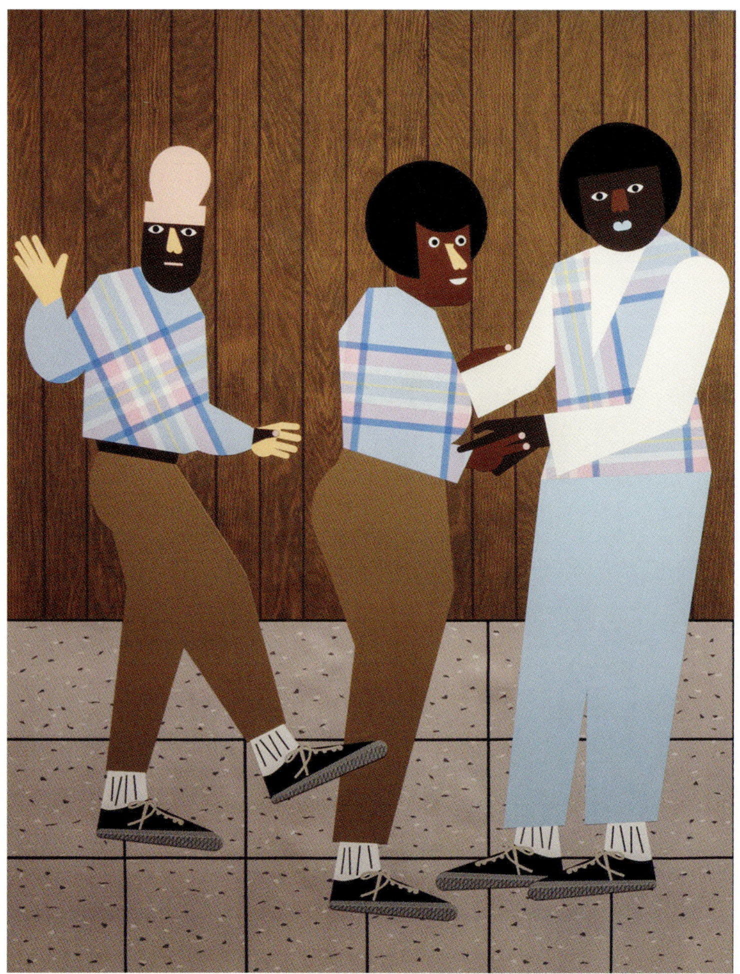

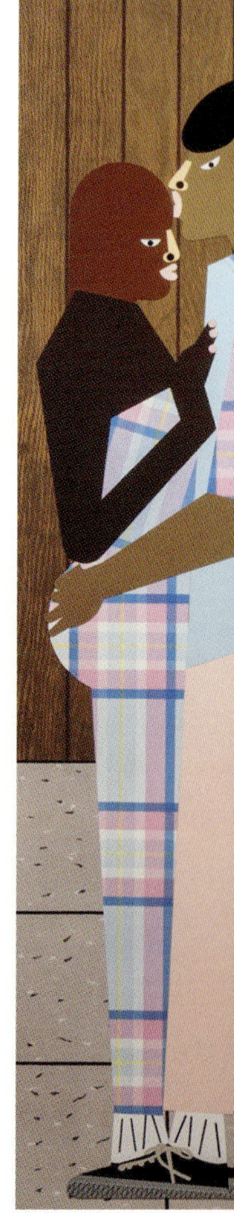

Nina Chanel Abney's collaged triptych *Day Party, Gay Party* belongs to a body of work titled 'Big Butch Synergy', which, together with the earlier series 'Big Butch Energy', explores the intersection of Black and queer identity in America. These series springboard from coming-of-age movies set on American high school and university campuses, like *National Lampoon's Animal House* (1978), *Porky's* (1981) and *American Pie* (1999), which were popular in mainstream culture during the artist's youth; films that asserted gender binaries and queer erasure. Reimagining scenes from such movies, the artist centralizes the experience of masculine-of-centre women. The Black and Brown dancing figures wear harmoniously colour-coordinated clothing that incorporates the light blue, light pink and white of the transgender flag. In her recognizably graphic style, Abney presents alternative realities built on female solidarity, freedom of sexuality and butch empowerment.

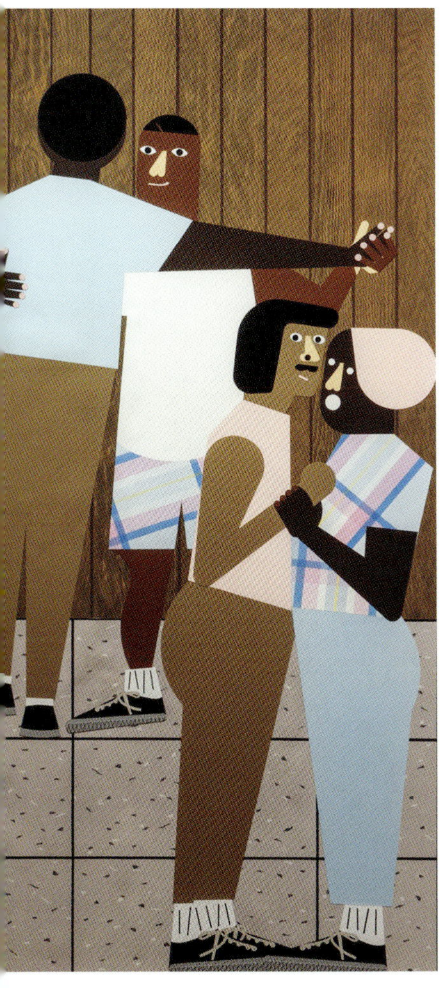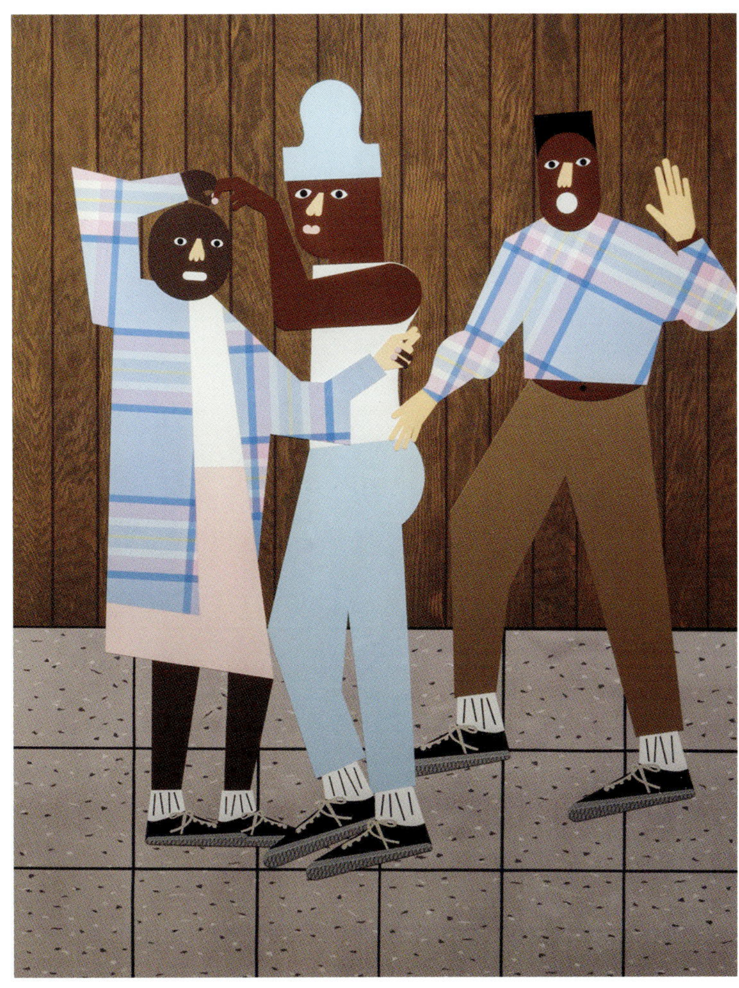

Day Party, Gay Party from the series
'Big Butch Synergy', **Nina Chanel Abney**, 2022,
paper collage on panel, triptych, each panel
243.8 x 182.9 cm (96 x 72 in)

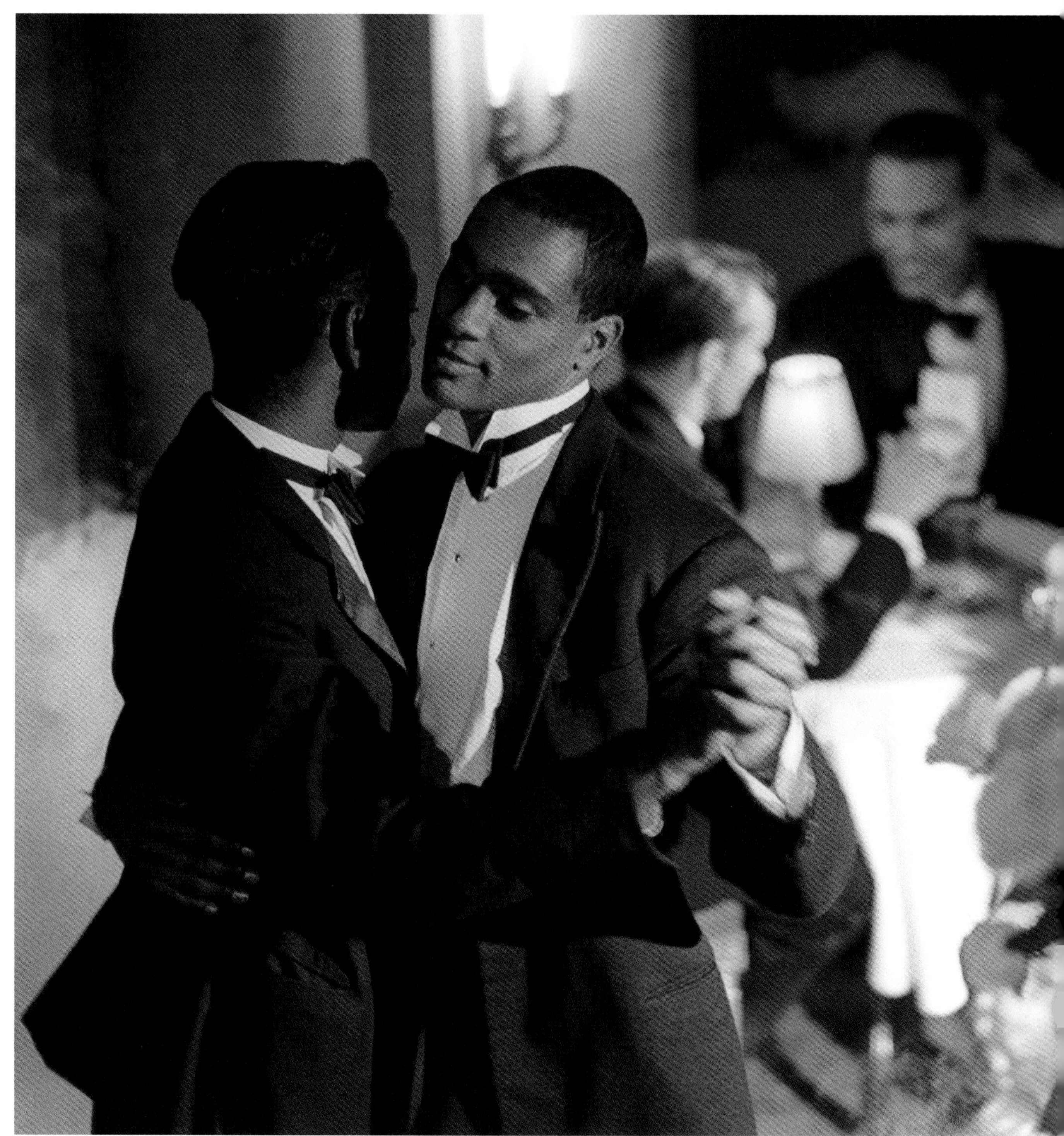

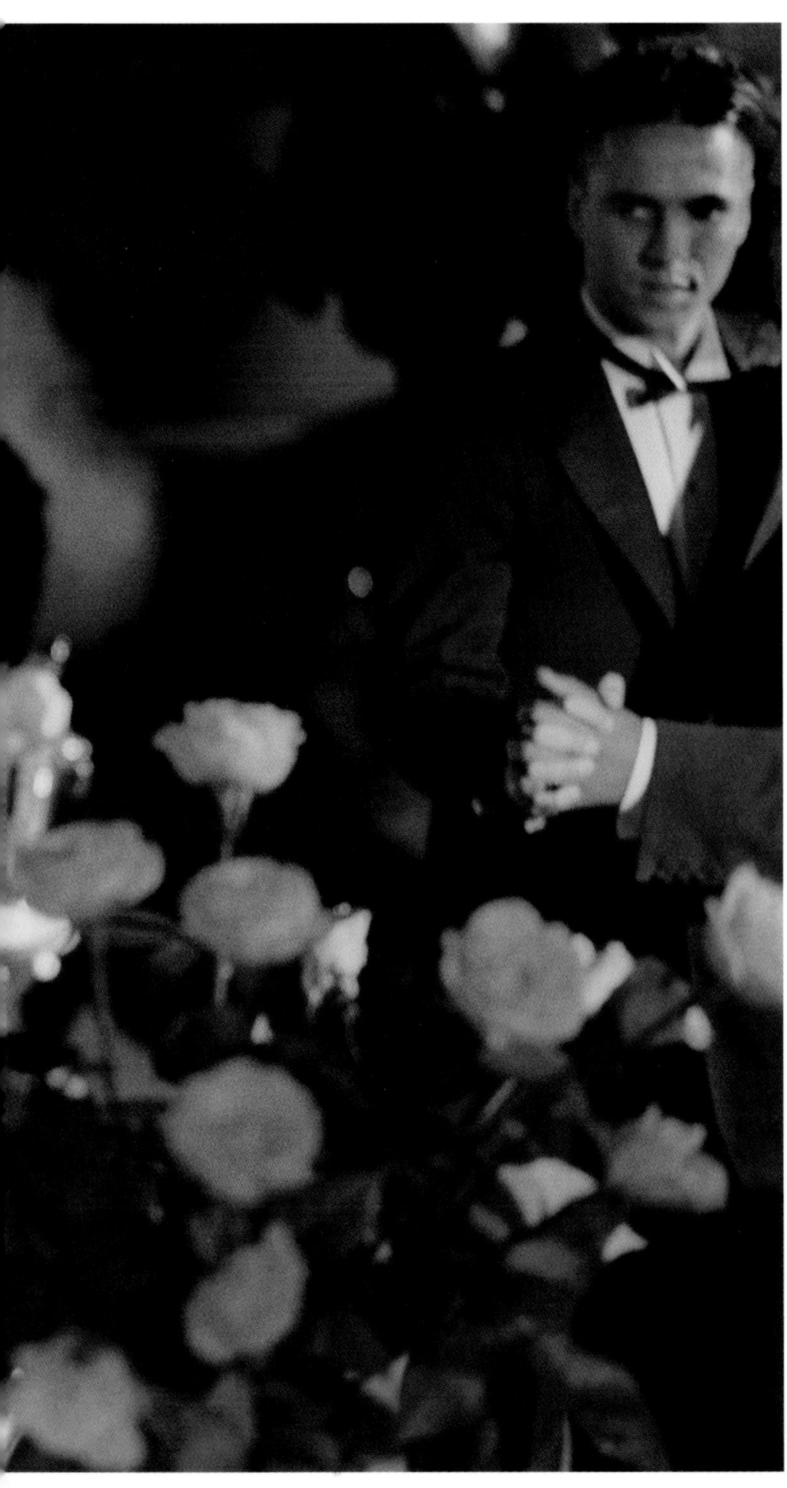

Sir Isaac Julien's work, which gives a voice to disregarded narratives, has played a significant role in the development of contemporary art, inspiring generations of artists. Made at the height of the AIDS crisis, his 1989 film *Looking for Langston* recreates the private world of Langston Hughes, the African American poet, writer and social activist. Acknowledged as a landmark moment in New Queer Cinema, the 42-minute black-and-white film is a stunning exploration of desire and the Black queer gaze. A memoriam to the Harlem Renaissance, the film takes place in a speakeasy inspired by the Cotton Club, New York's prohibition and segregation era nightclub, which appears through found footage. Scenes of Black men dancing together are spliced with Robert Mapplethorpe's photography, accompanied by the poetry of Hughes, Richard Bruce Nugent, James Baldwin and Essex Hemphill. Having earned a cult status, the seminal work feels timeless and just as relevant now as it did then.

Pas de Deux with Roses from the 'Looking for Langston Vintage Series', **Sir Isaac Julien**, 1989/2016, Ilford classic silver gelatin fine art paper, 39.4 x 57.2 cm (15½ x 22½ in)

Outside

historically excluded from mainstream culture, LGBTQIA+ people occupy outside spaces in a way that is shaped by their particular experiences, needs and desires. Whether outside of the home, outside of cities or outside in nature, queer identity resonates with the notion of 'outside'. Within towns and cities, queers have occupied streets as sites of activism, situating themselves in the public realm to assert their existence and demand their rights. Within urban centres, queer cruising grounds are established as locations for men to meet other men and for sex workers to operate: from public bathrooms and parks, to New York's famous piers in the 1980s, documented by Alvin Baltrop (see below).

Historically at odds with the dominant heteronormative structures of urban spaces, many queer bodies reject the marginalization of city life in favour of rural locations where they form non-traditional communities with likeminded people and find new ways to create home and shared space. Congregating within open spaces that are free from oppression presents the opportunity to connect more freely with each other and with the land. For many, particularly young LGBTQIA+ people, finding themselves outside may

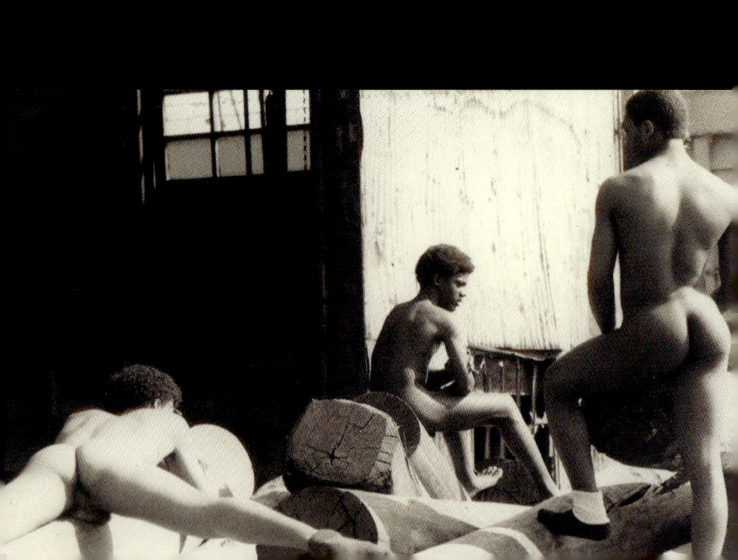

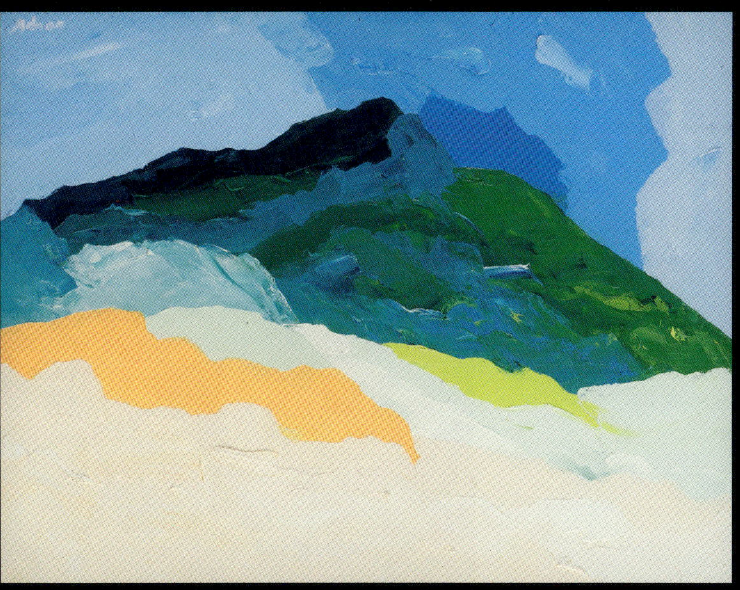

not be a choice. Forced out of a home, family or community, outside spaces may in fact be the safest locations to exist openly and meet others.

For queer people, who know that their identity and desires couldn't be more natural, there is solace and safety to be found in the natural world. The non-judgemental and nurturing qualities of nature are reinforced by the many examples of same-sex behaviour, non-binary organisms and imagery that has symbolic meaning for LGBTQIA+ identity. Whether depicting the restorative solitude offered by natural landscapes, or intimacy with each other and the land, artists present a nuanced perspective on how queer bodies individually and collectively thrive through a meaningful and immersive connection with nature. As in the painting of Etel Adnan (see above), queer resonance with landscapes may not be explicit; instead it is discernible in the undertones of the transformational power of nature. As queer artists explore the daily lives, memories and fantasies of themselves and their communities we see a range of outside experiences reflected in their art.

Untitled, **Etel Adnan**, c. 1980s

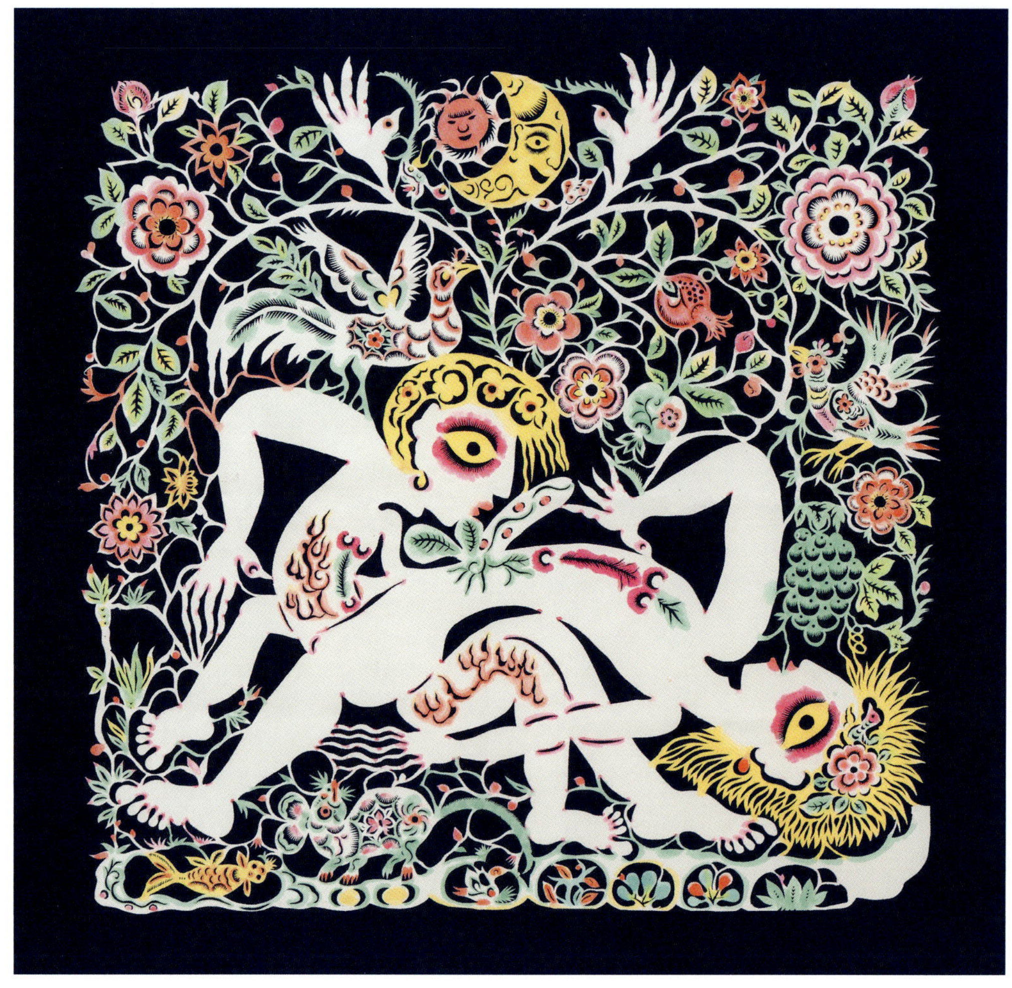

The artist Xiyadie works under a pseudonym because of the risks of being out and making explicitly homoerotic art in China. Despite acknowledging his sexuality at a young age he married a woman and had children, before moving from rural China to Beijing in 2005, where he connected with the underground queer community. It was at this point in his life that he adopted his chosen name, which means Siberian Butterfly, a symbol of survival in the harshest conditions, and began exhibiting his art. His intricate scenes are made using the ancient Chinese tradition of papercutting, usually considered a feminine craft, which he learned from his mother. Recalling clandestine outdoor moments from his own life engulfed by luminous elements from the natural world, Xiyadie's work represents queer joy, abandon and bliss amid a life of oppression.

Joy 乐, **Xiyadie**, 1999, papercut with water-based dye and Chinese pigments on Xuan paper, 176 x 176 x 4 cm (69¼ x 69¼ x 1½ in)

Nash Glynn is known for nude self-portraits that centralize her own transfeminine form. *Self Portrait with One Foot Forward and One Hand Reaching Out* presents the artist's naked body stepping into a dreamy landscape as she turns and offers a beckoning hand, her knowing gaze and raised eyebrow daring us to follow her. In a play with scale and perspective, her tall figure towers over the forest, imbuing her with a mythical presence and power: she holds the keys to this ethereal paradise. Glynn's signature palette runs through the painting, baby pink and cerulean blue meet in the undulating texture of the fleshy clouds and her luminous skin. There is coolness where there should be warmth, revealing a subtle tension under the surface. Stepping into the future towards a distant rainbow beyond the horizon, the artist leads us into a world full of hope and promise.

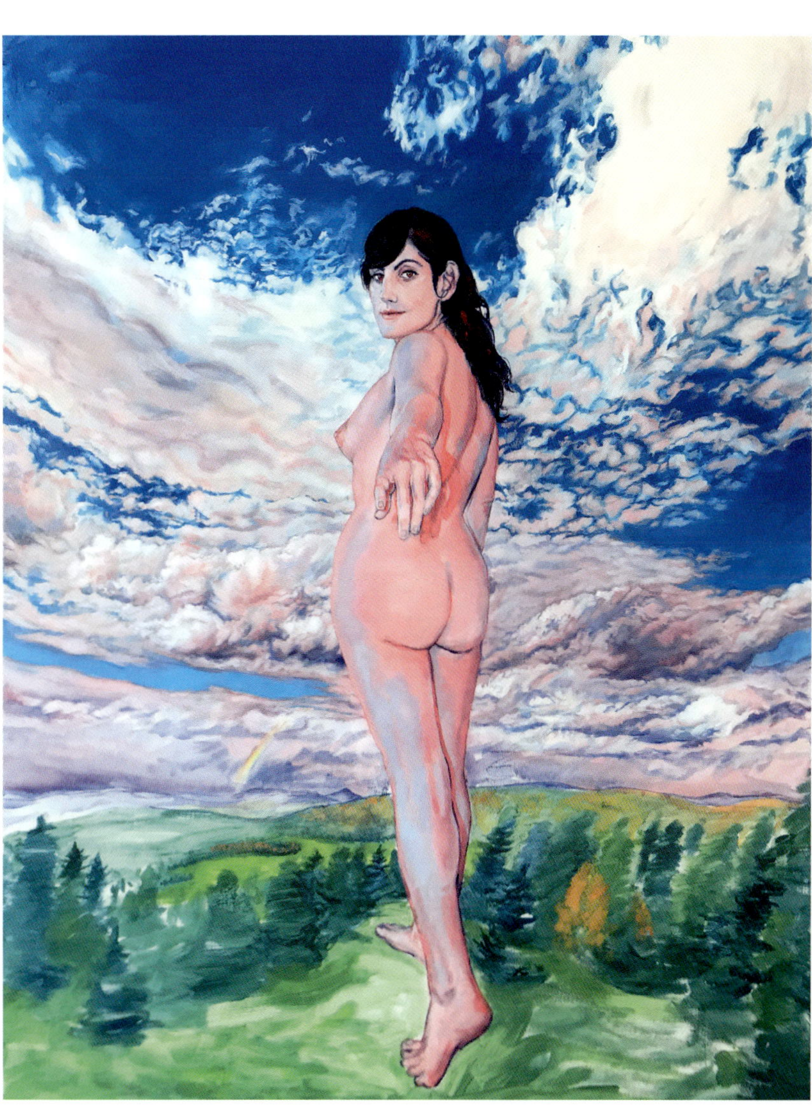

Self Portrait with One Foot Forward and One Hand Reaching Out, **Nash Glynn**, 2020, acrylic on canvas, 121.9 x 90 cm (48 x 36 in)

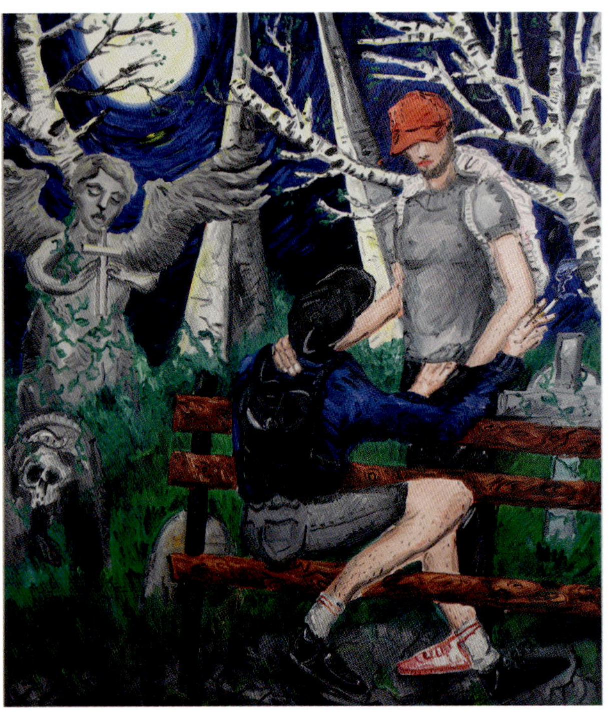 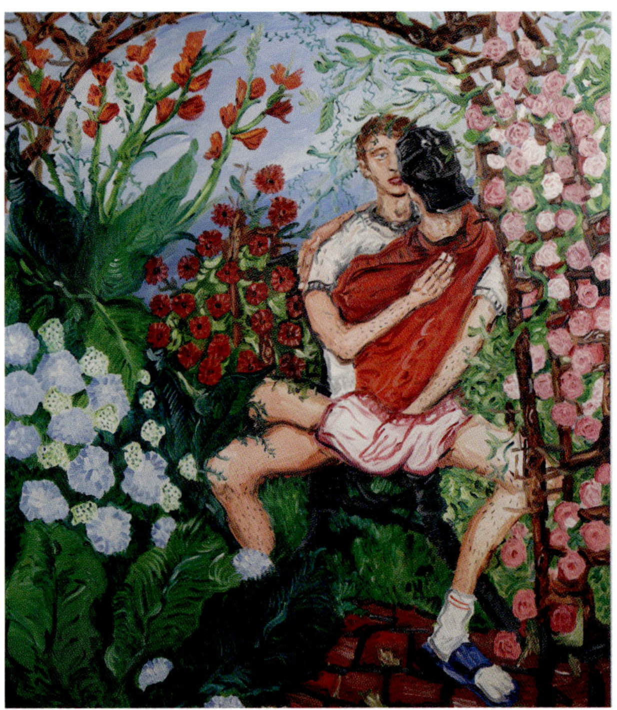

'Seasons Meatings', **Dale Lewis**, 2021,
from left to right: *Caretakers* (2021),
Constant Gardener (2021), *Migration* (2021),
The Herd (2021); all images oil and acrylic on
canvas, 200 x 170 cm (78¾ x 66⅞ in)

In 'Seasons Meatings', Dale Lewis's series of four large-scale paintings, life-size male figures engage in outdoor sexual acts through each of the seasons. The changing seasons are communicated through the subjects' attire and nature's cues: the colour of the sky, bare trees, plants in bloom and the appearance of (comically voyeuristic) animals. Lavish and gestural use of paint adds a fullness and frenetic energy to each scene. Rich with art historical references, the series is inspired by Pieter Bruegel the Elder's seasonal paintings and uses the traditional format of four seasons paintings, while the three-figure groups are modelled on poses of the Three Graces. Refreshingly explicit in representing cruising, the artist wants viewers to feel as though they've stumbled across each scene while out walking the dog, being left with no ambiguity about what's happening.

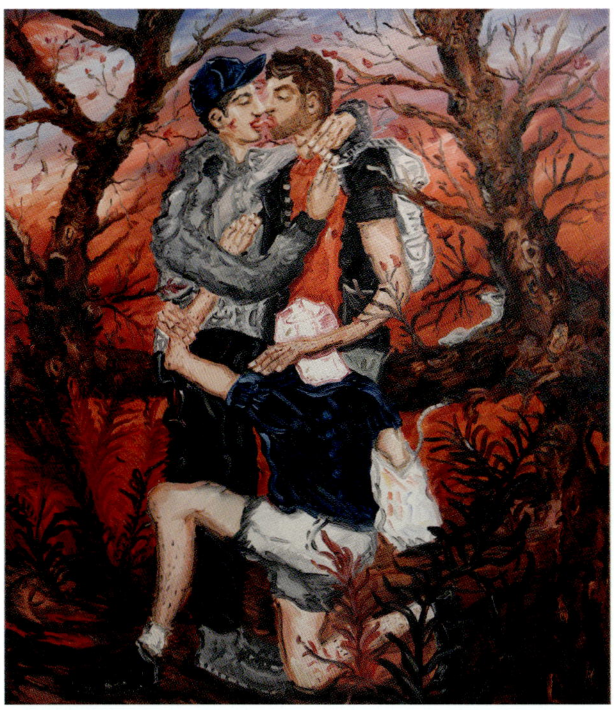

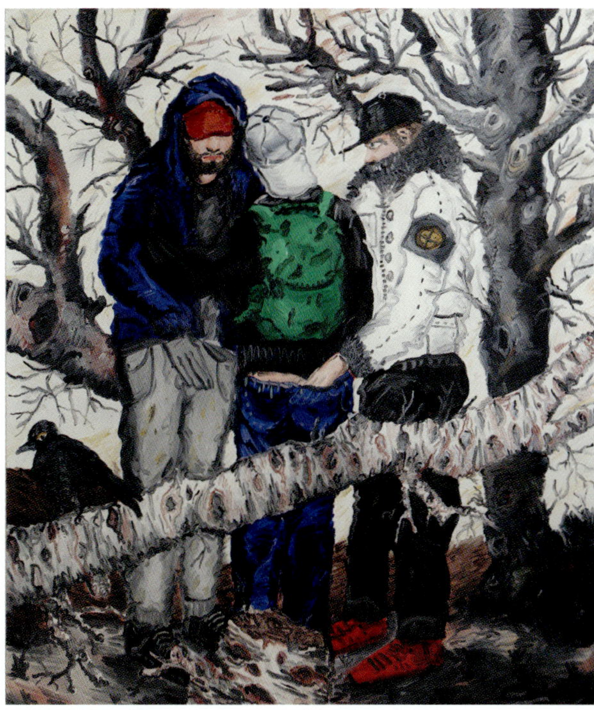

Public Toilet was part of Jaanus Samma's exhibition 'Not Suitable for Work. A Chairman's Tale' at the Estonian Pavilion for the 56th Venice Biennale in 2015. The exhibition, which explores Estonian gay history during the Soviet period, takes the form of a fragmented opera presented as a multimedia installation. The 'chairman' who appears in this photograph was based on a real historical character who was expelled from the Communist Party for being implicated in a court case about homosexual acts. The opera follows the chairman's incarceration, the loss of his family, home and employment, and his murder in 1990, two years before Estonia decriminalized homosexuality.

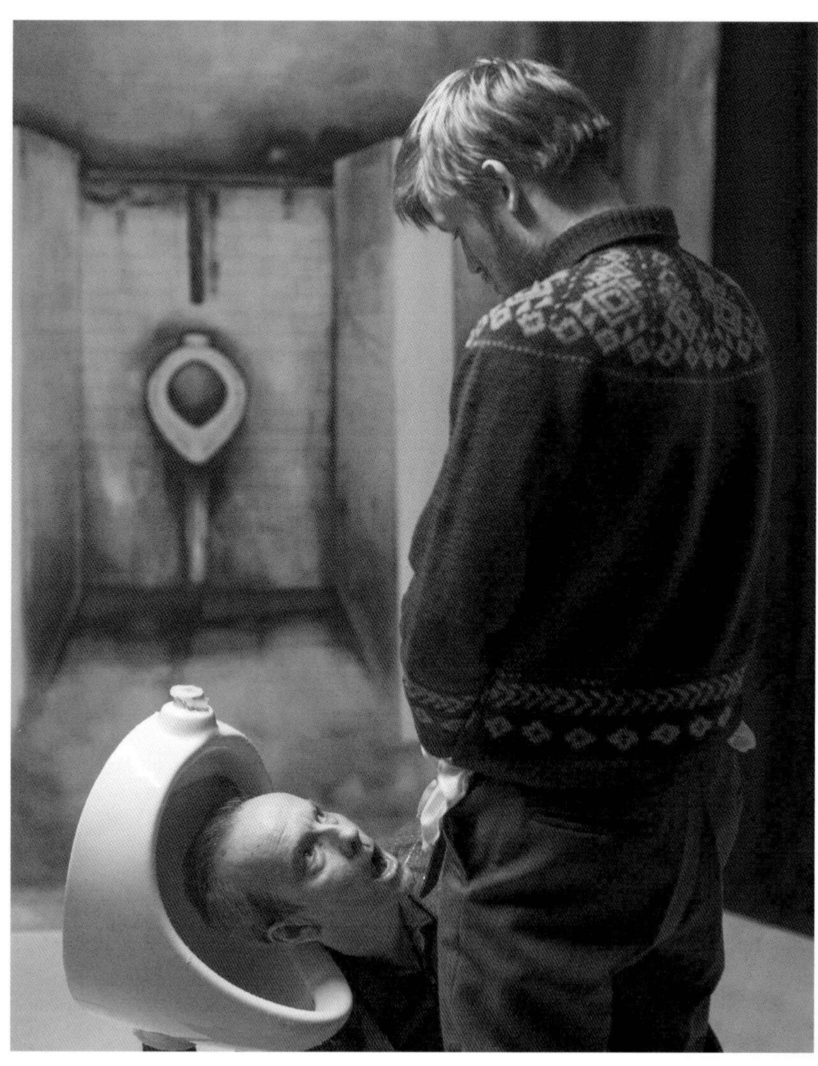

Public Toilet, **Jaanus Samma**, 2015, pigment print, 120 x 92cm (47¼ x 36¼ in)

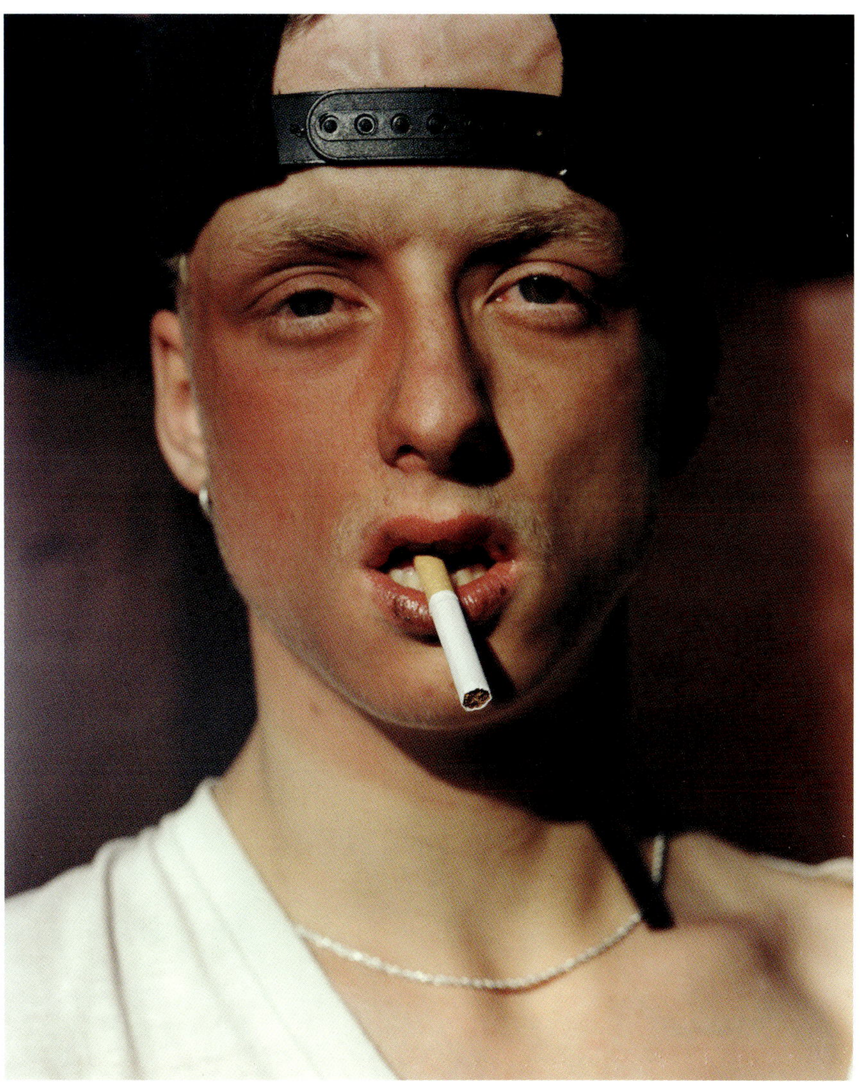

Untitled from the series 'Hustlers',
Eve Fowler, 1996, C-print, 35.6 x
27.9 cm (14 x 11 in)

Eve Fowler came to prominence with
'Hustlers', her 1990s photo series of the male
sex workers of New York's West Village and
Los Angeles' Santa Monica Boulevard. Her
dramatically lit portraits of the young men
present an intense study of masculine allure
and vulnerability. In 2014 the photographs
were turned into a book; each image was
printed without a caption and left open to
viewer interpretation and imagination. The
only textual accompaniment to the series
is a short tale by queer writer Kevin Killian,
which poetically traces the bleak realities
of a fictional young sex worker called Jesse.
Fowler's more recent work explores the
format of billboards, posters and installation,
featuring the words of Gertrude Stein.
Running through these various bodies of
work is an interest in outside space and how
the process of being othered can sometimes
make the street the only place to form and
confront our queer identities.

Eve Fowler

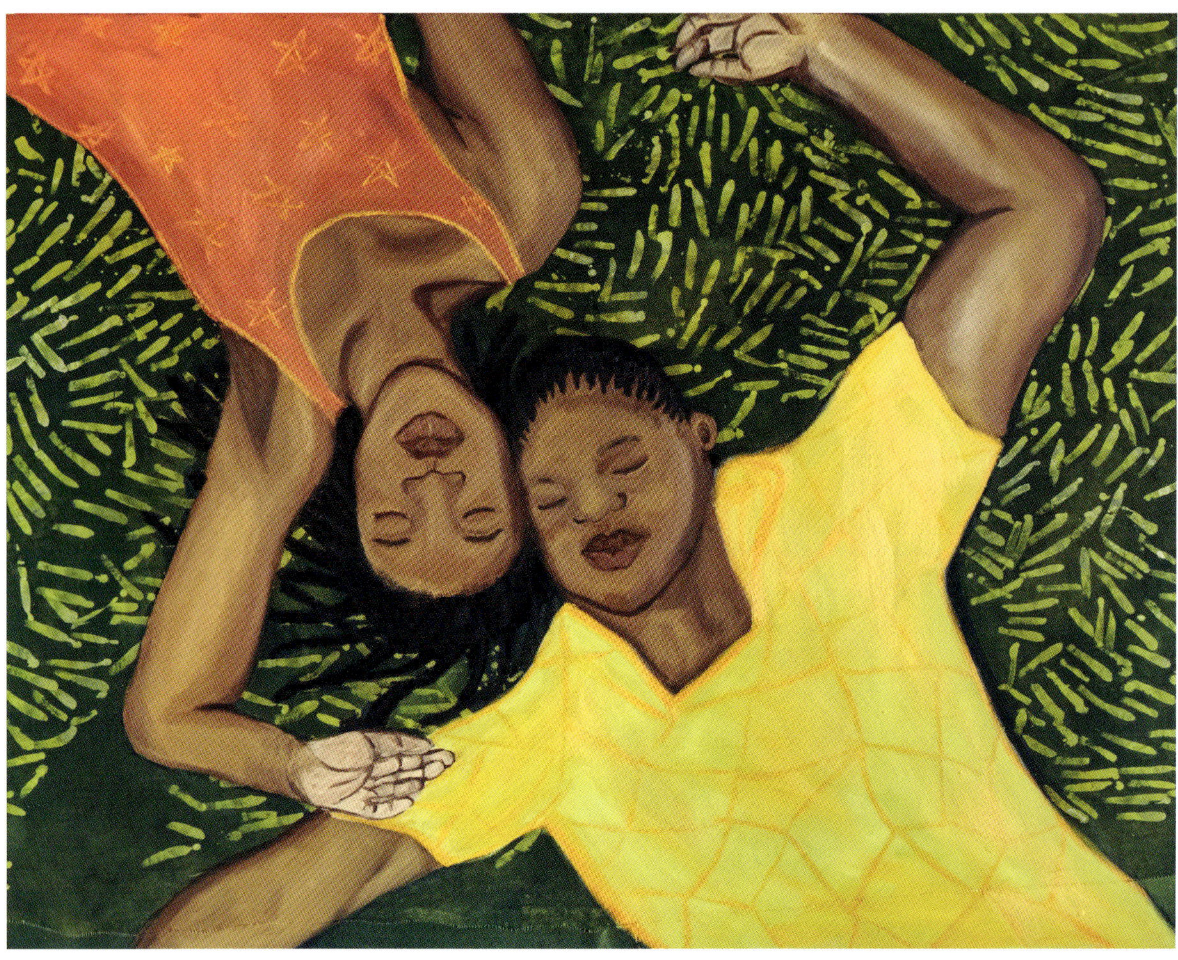

Sola Olulode paints dream-like vignettes as a refuge for Black queer love. Her work emerges from the vibrant tapestry of South London, where she finds inspiration in pole dancing, city romance and the joy of intimate encounters. Made with her own version of Nigerian *adire* textiles – hand-dyed fabrics using the wax-resist method of batik, Olulode's painting embraces the complexity of seemingly simple figures. Usually painted in couples, her figures appear in environments of safety and nurture – in bed, at dance parties or in outdoor spaces. Elements such as the moon, sun, sea and grass recur as anchors of the natural world, bringing a sense of serenity to Olulode's scenes. *Laying in the Grass I* is one of many paintings of the same title, where couples relax in the comfort of each other's company and find peace amid the vivid green and yellow hues of the grass.

Hernan Bas's painting *Secret Hideout of the Flamingo Gang* depicts three young people, characteristically androgynous and ambiguous in their relationship to each other, among the flamingo paddle boats and luscious foliage of a lakeside setting. Bas's painterly style merges figuration and abstraction, emphasizing the ambiguity and fragility of the dream-like scene, and the birds and figures that inhabit it. Inspired by the flamboyance of nineteenth-century writers such as Oscar Wilde and Arthur Rimbaud, Bas's characters channel the energy of the historical figure of the youthful dandy and are described by the artist as being in 'fag limbo', somewhere between adolescence and adulthood, between knowing and coming out, as they appear from the shadows.

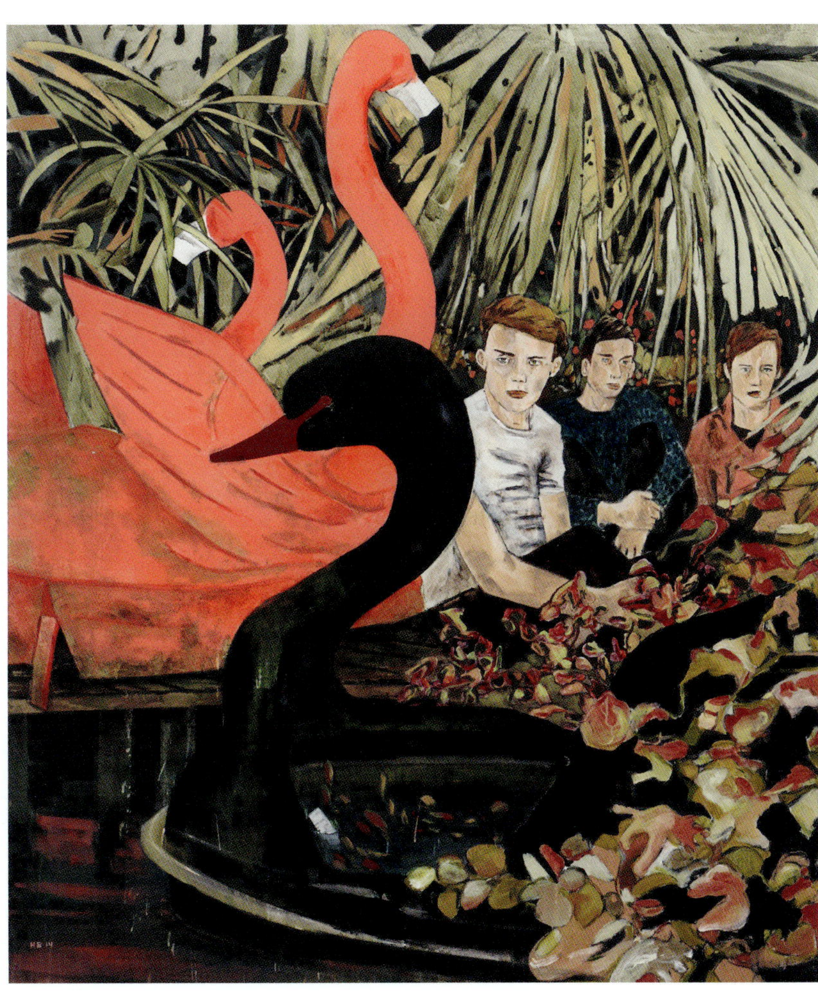

Secret Hideout of the Flamingo Gang (Abandoned Paddle Boats), **Hernan Bas**, 2014, acrylic on linen, 182.9 x 152.4 cm (72 x 60 in)

Chinese-American artist Martin Wong was raised in San Francisco's Chinatown, at the epicentre of the city's counterculture movement. In 1978 he moved to New York and spent the 1980s painting the urban landscapes of the Lower East Side where he was introduced to the underground art scene by the poet Miguel Piñero, who became his boyfriend. Typical of the fantasy and desire often infused into his urban scenes, *Big Heat* depicts two kissing firemen in front of an imposing, dilapidated tower block engulfed in flames. As the child of immigrants and as a gay man who would eventually die prematurely due to AIDS-related illnesses, Wong represents that feeling of being an outsider through the oppressive brick facades that run through his work. His eroticized firemen, about whom he once wrote 'I really like the way firemen smell when they get off work. It's like hickory smoked rubber and B.O.', offer a moment of freedom.

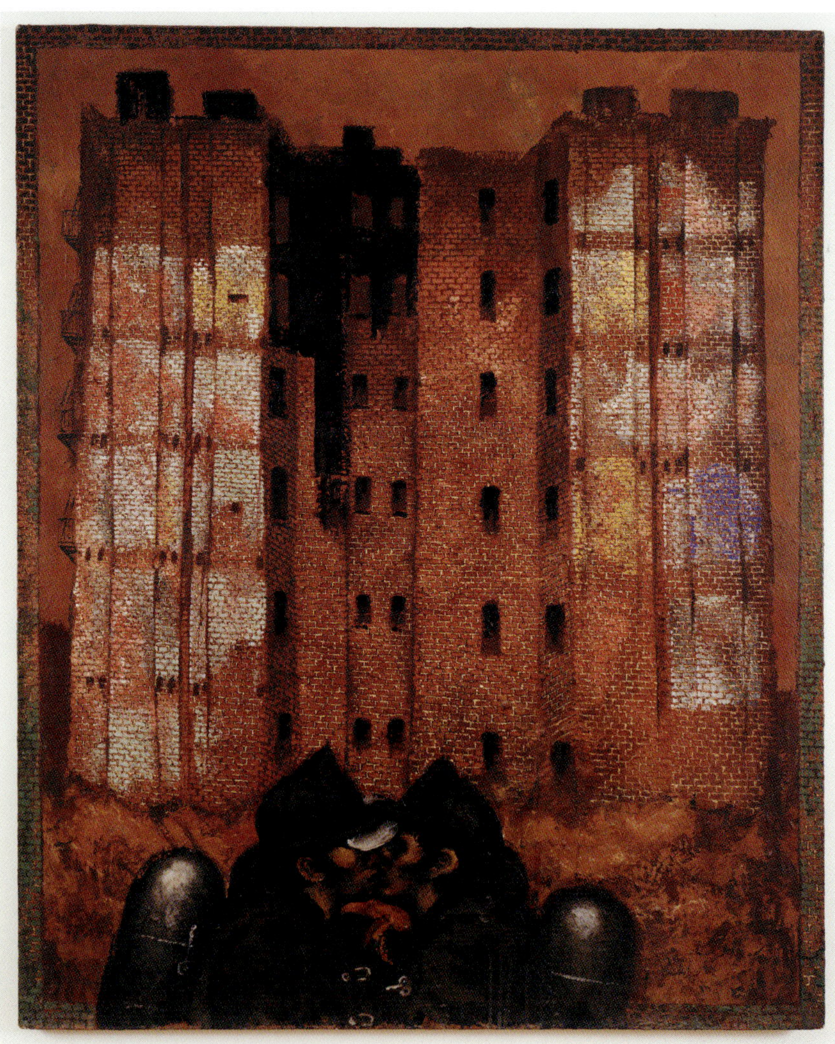

Big Heat, **Martin Wong**, 1986–1988, acrylic on canvas, 152.7 x 122.2 cm (60⅛ x 48⅛ in)

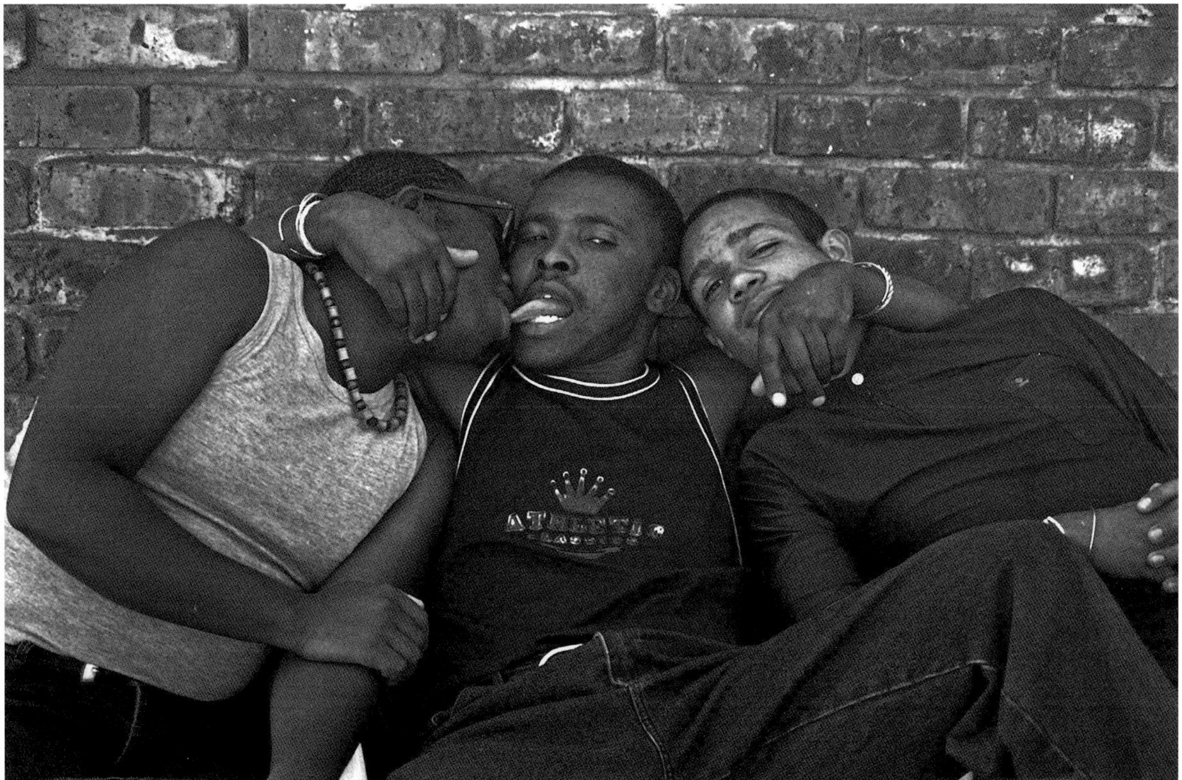

Sabelo Mlangeni

Sabelo Mlangeni extensively documents contemporary queer African life through black-and-white photography. *uMakhosi Gadisa* is from the series 'Country Girls', completed over a six-year period from 2003 to 2009, in which Mlangeni captures the beauty, glamour and resilience of queer and trans people living in the South African countryside. Many of those making home for themselves outside of the city work as Zulu healers called *sangomas*; the title *uMakhosi Gadisa* refers to the ancestral wives of *sangomas*, who are often the same gender as the healers. By connecting a Zulu concept with the three men who share a moment of playful intimacy, the photographer gives visibility to queer experiences that are often erased and deemed 'unAfrican', shining a light on the love and community found in the otherwise bleak and sparse rural landscapes.

Chicago-based artist Leasho Johnson was born and raised in Jamaica, where his 'Anansi' painting series originates. Anansi is a figure in the oral folktales that travelled from West Africa to the Caribbean along the transatlantic slave trade routes, ancient stories that the artist turns to for affirmation and explanation. Usually depicted as a trickster spider and known for defying and outsmarting the gods, Anansi is used by Johnson as a 'metaphor for finding psychological space for Black queer love'. The limbs of the black charcoal figures at the centre of the painting are intertwined in an anthropomorphic abstraction that moves fluidly through the vibrant plant life of the tropics. The artist conjures the pulsating energy of a secret outdoor party in the mountains, where queer people congregate among the bushes to a dancehall soundtrack.

Anansi and the river maiden (Anansi #16) from the series 'Anansi', **Leasho Johnson**, 2022, charcoal, watercolours, distemper, indigo dye, logwood dye, oil, collage and gesso on paper mounted on canvas, 171.5 x 264.2 x 5.1 cm (67½ x 104 x 2 in)

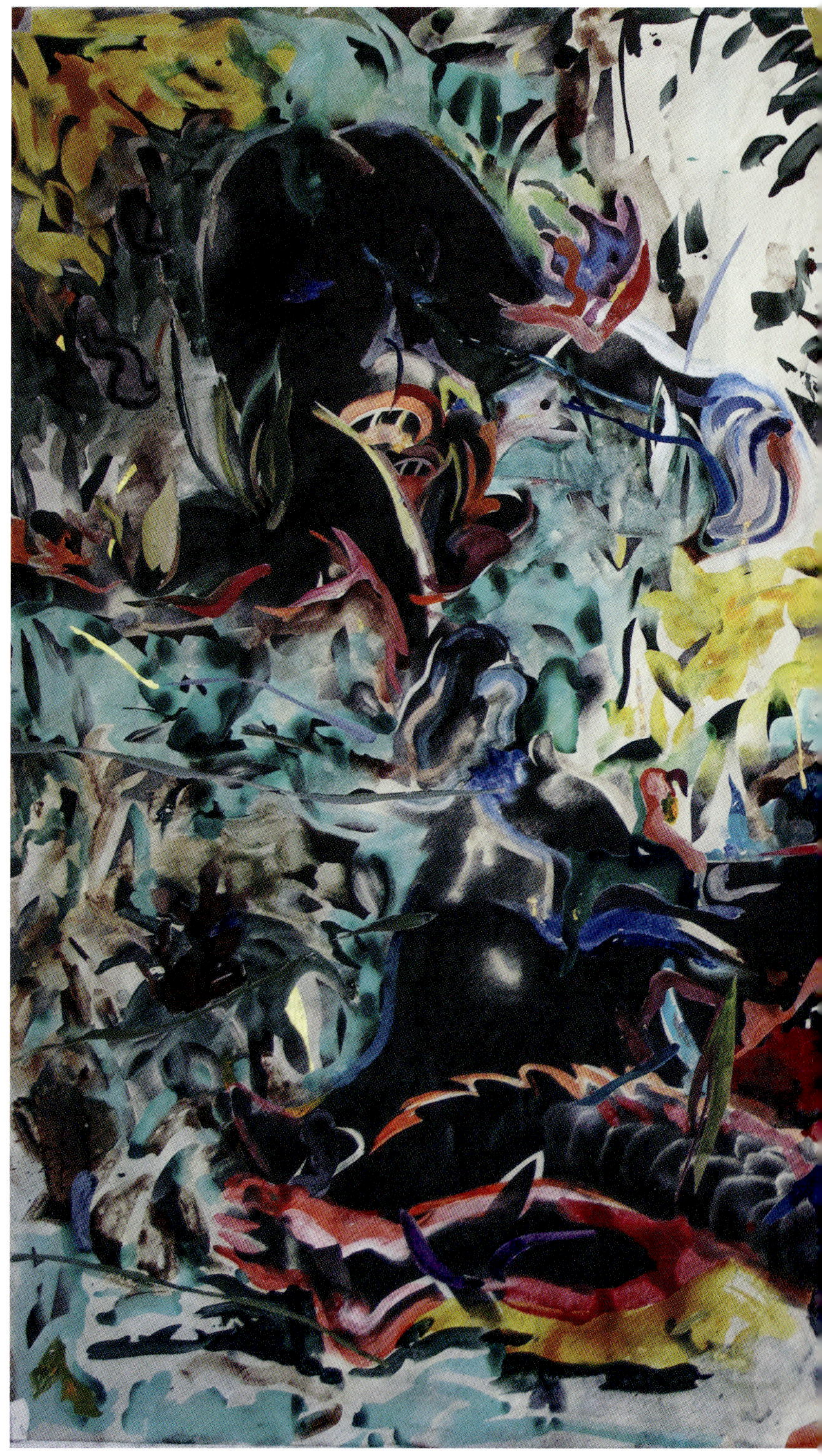

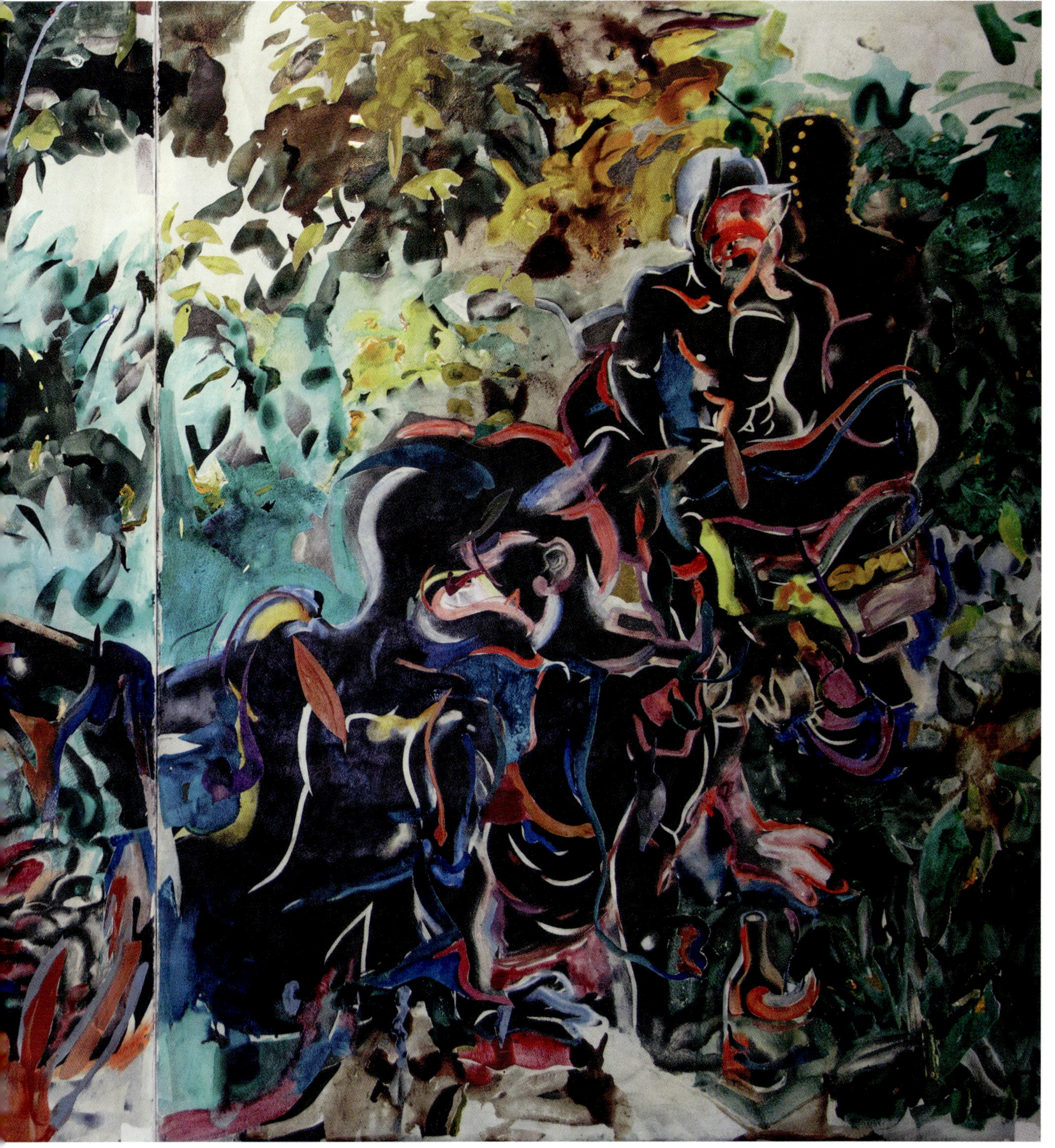

Jonathan Baldock

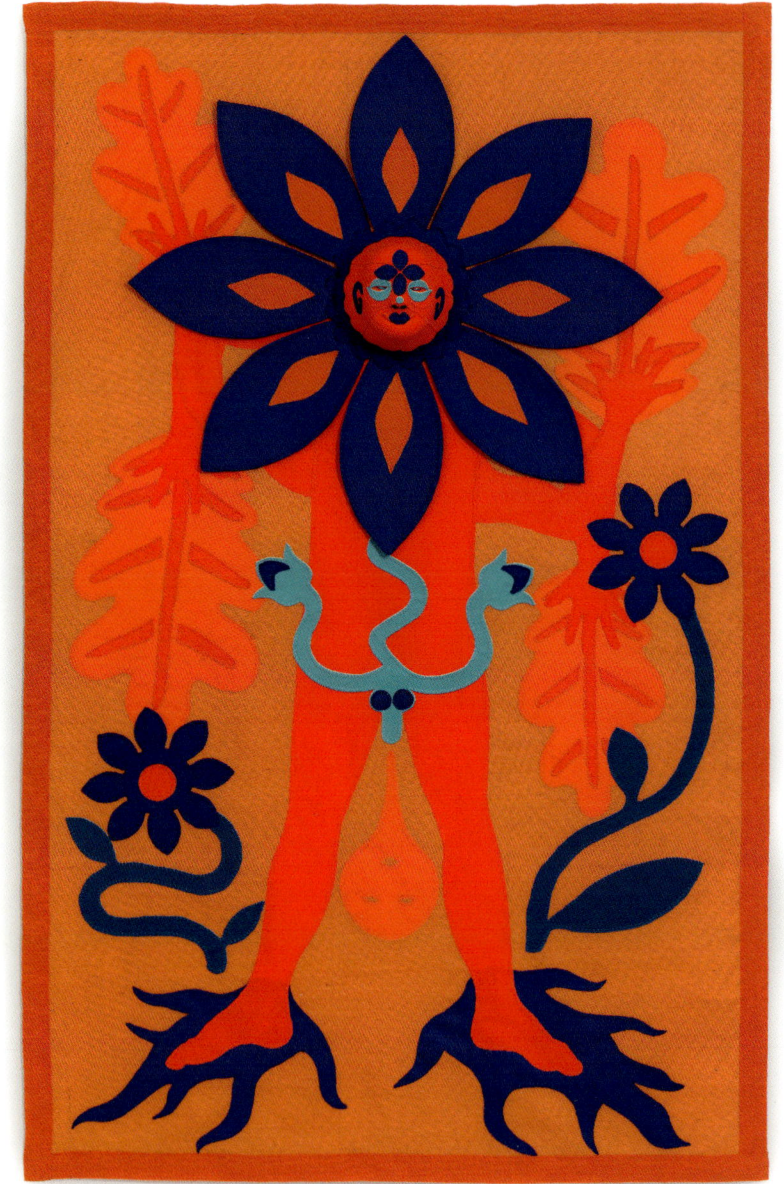

Moment in the Sun, **Jonathan Baldock**, 2023, felt, hessian, polymer, turquoise and quartz, 253 x 158 cm (99⅝ x 62¼ in)

Jonathan Baldock works across installation and performance, with ceramics and textiles being central to his practice. Viewing sewing as an extension of his own body, his textile works become second skins through a lengthy process of hand stitching. *Moment in the Sun* is from an informal series of fabric wall hangings that feature a silhouette of the artist's body, which Baldock describes as a kind of self-portrait. Each one depicts a figure drawn from the artist's body taking on different guises or characters. In accordance with his wider practice, this work explores human connection to the earth and the power of the natural world, particularly in relation to the nurturing qualities of the land for the queer body. Hybrid beings from myth and folklore appear throughout Baldock's work. Here he references the foliate being or Green Man as a symbol of rebirth, to explore the ancient idea that we are constantly in a state of transition and transformation.

Stone (Butch), **Ro Robertson**, 2021,
Cor-Ten steel, Jesmonite and paint,
220 x 130 x 156 cm (86⅝ x 51 x 61½ in)

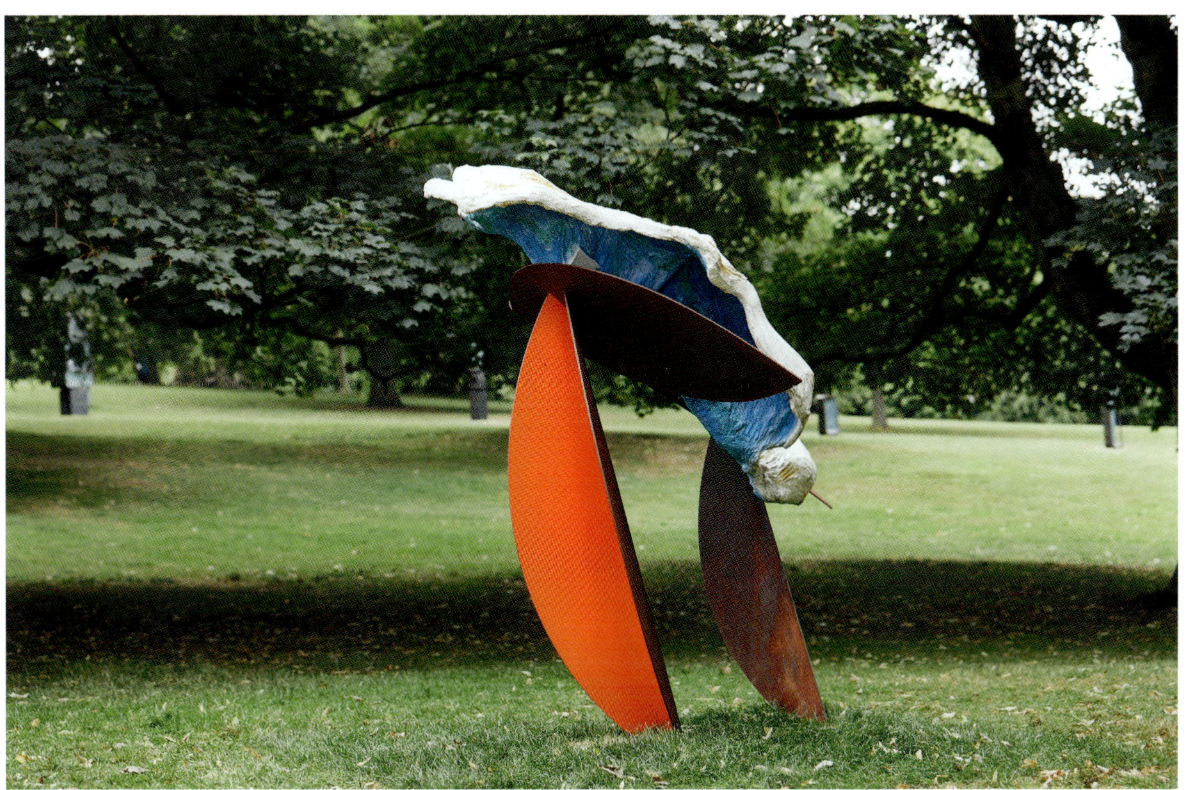

Ro Robertson's *Stone (Butch)* takes its title from the writing of Leslie Feinberg, whose novel *Stone Butch Blues* (1993) explores the 'complexities of being a transgendered person in a world demanding simple explanations'. The sculpture, formed by casting plaster directly into the crevices of natural rock formations, is an investigation of the queer body in relation to the natural landscape.

Challenging the notion that people existing outside of a binary understanding of gender go 'against nature', the work demonstrates a deep kinship between queer bodies and the natural world. Conceived as a public sculpture, the Jesmonite and Cor-Ten steel sculpture prompts us to question who is depicted and commemorated in art and who has permission to take up space and exist freely outside.

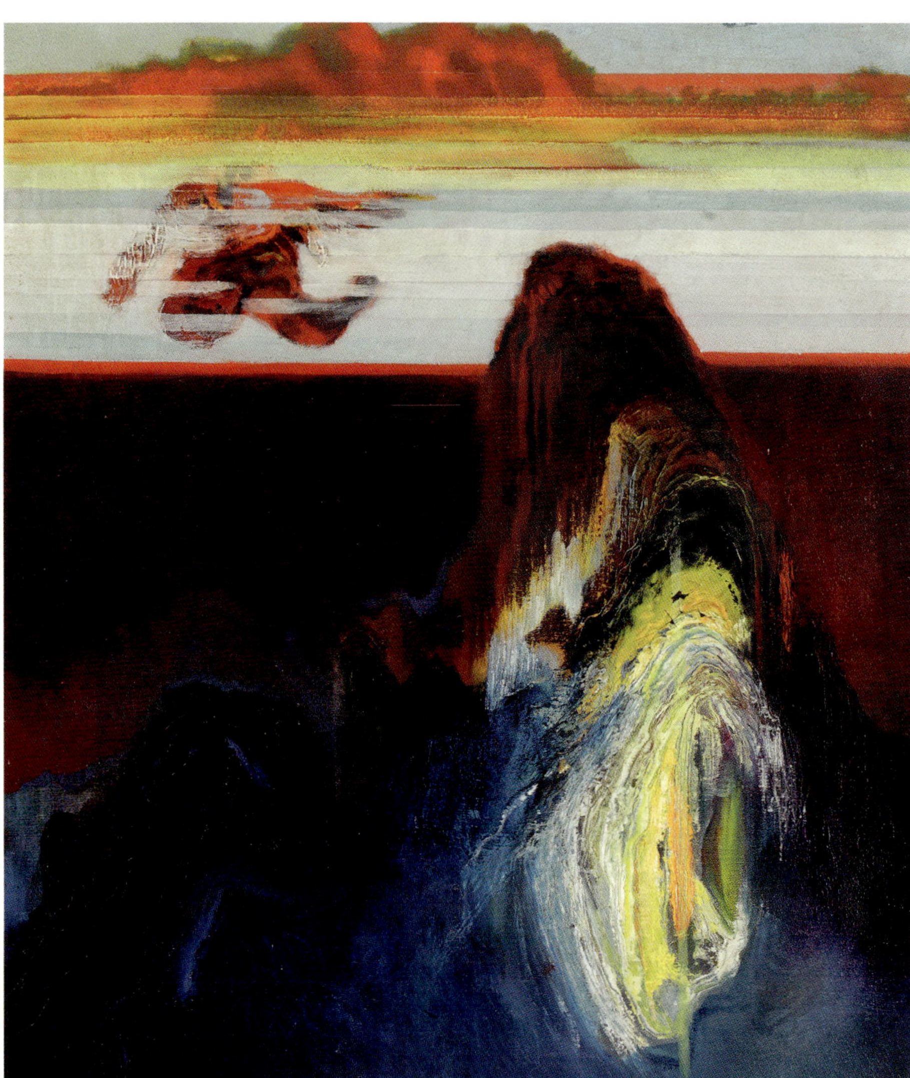

Bernice Bing

Despite being a core part of San Francisco's cultural scene in the second half of the twentieth century, Bernice Bing has largely been forgotten by art history. More than two decades after her death in 1998 the artist's work began receiving due attention from museums and critics. Orphaned at an early age and raised mostly in foster care, Bing was a third-generation Chinese-American out lesbian and community activist. Her paintings, which synthesize Abstract Expressionism with Chinese calligraphy, reflect a lifelong search for autonomy, spirituality, belonging and a clear sense of identity. This quest often led to an immersion in nature where she experienced a sense of 'overpowering spirituality' as seen in her depiction of *Big Sur*, which was made during a residency at a Jungian mystical retreat in the Californian mountain range that changed the course of her work.

Historian and visual artist Leah DeVun's photographic series takes its title from *Lesbian Land*, a collection of writings by lesbians who lived in women's intentional communities in the 1970s and 1980s, published in 1985. These revolutionary communities, formed and occupied by women who opted out of mainstream society in response to their marginalization, were established in rural areas all around the world as separatist sites of freedom, liberation and creativity. DeVun combines documentary photography of communities that are still in existence with staged photography that recreates images from lesbian zines of the same era. Her ongoing exhibitions of the work are often accompanied by performances connecting the history of Lesbian Lands to contemporary non-traditional living spaces that encourage the viewer to reimagine what future living could look like.

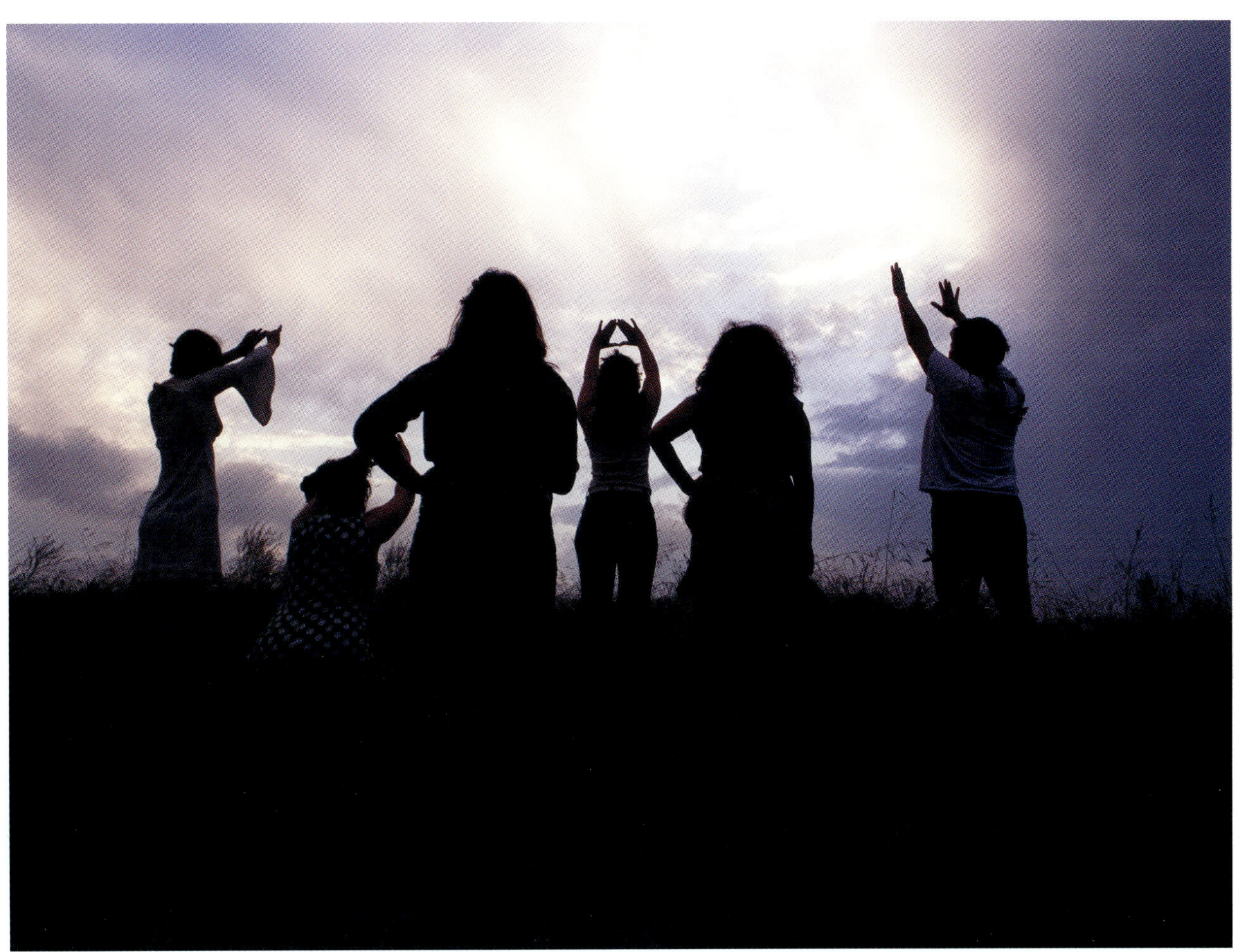

Early Morning Goodbye from the series
'Lesbian Land', **Leah DeVun**, 2010, archival
inkjet print, 75 x 101.6 cm (30 x 40 in)

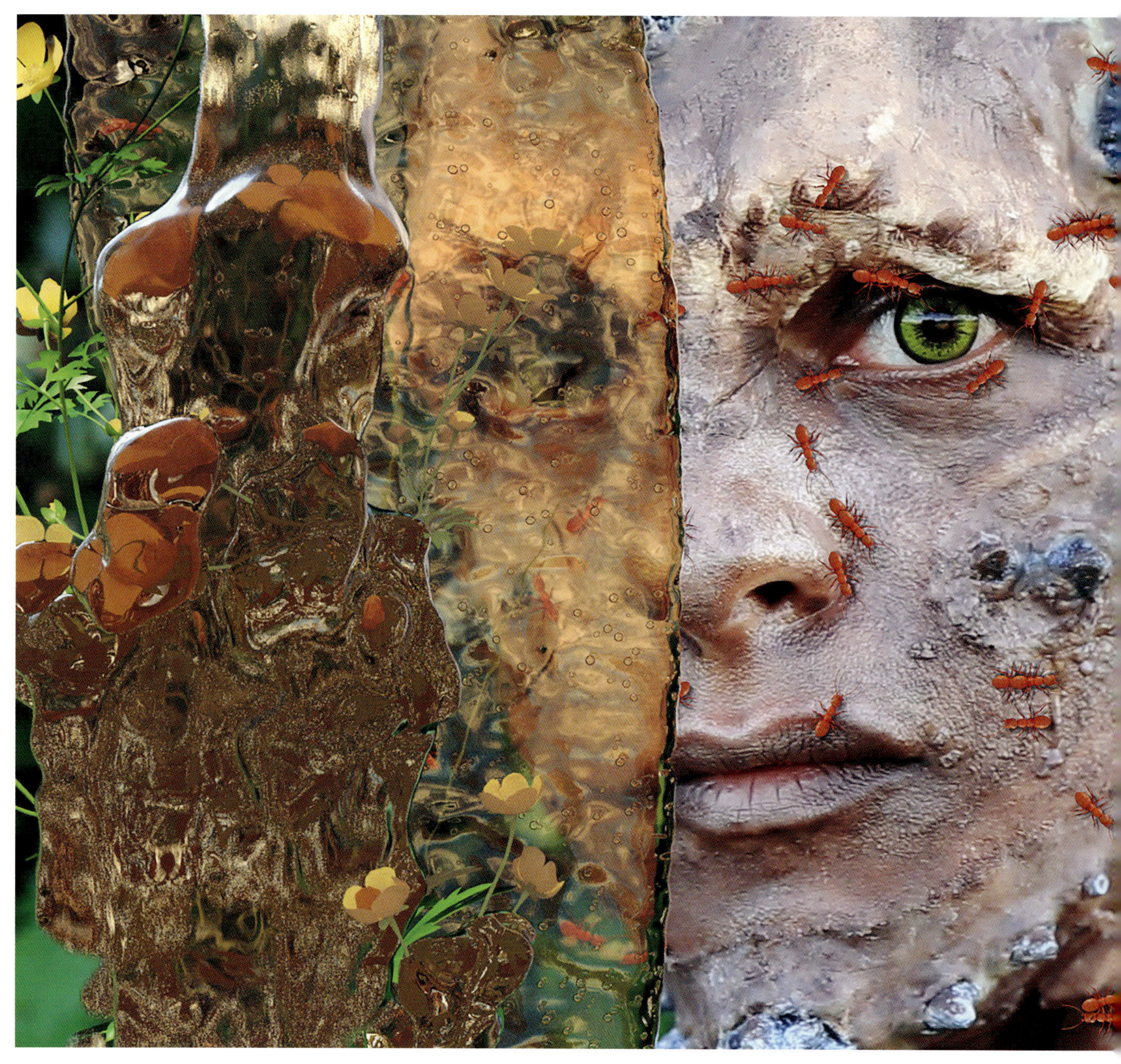

The heart wants what the heart wants,
Adham Faramawy, 2021, video, 21 mins

        Outside

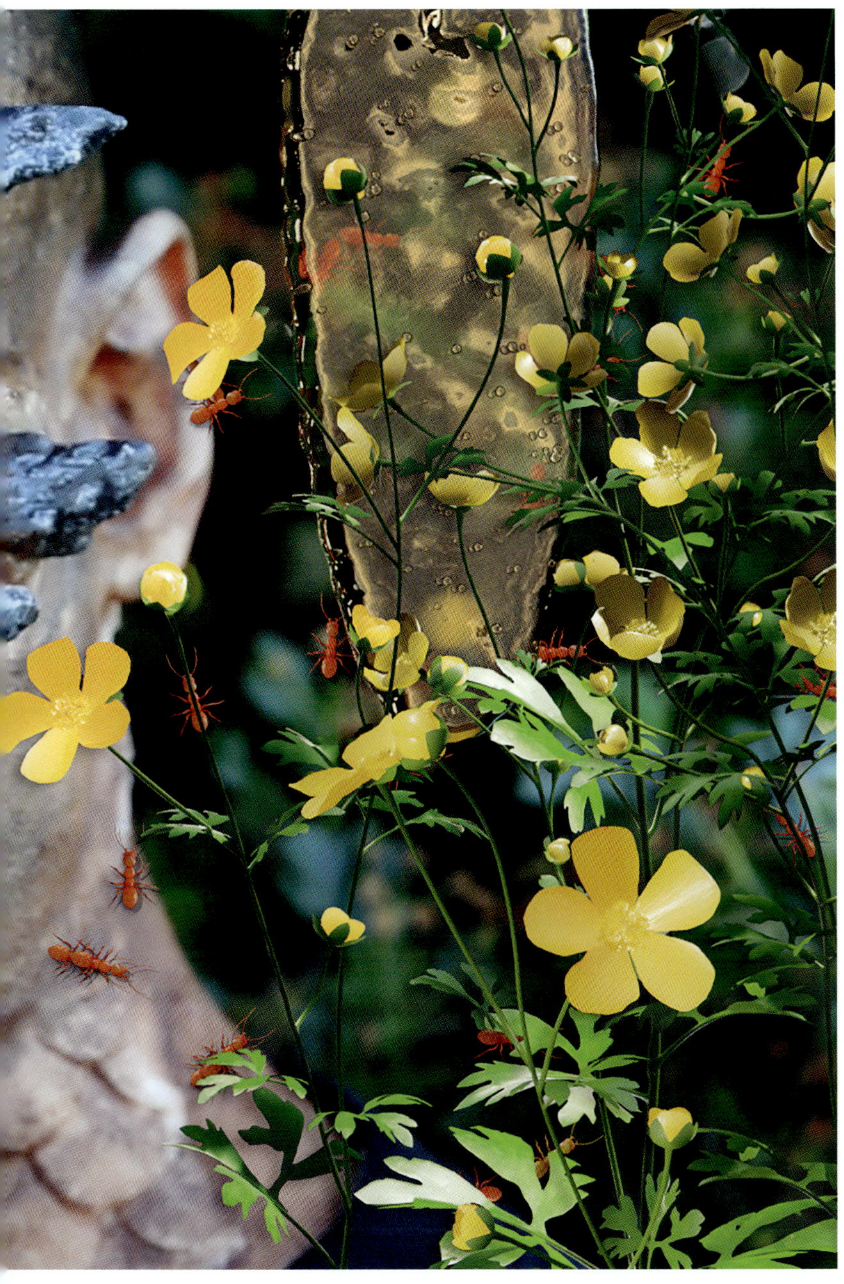

Adham Faramawy's practice stems from a body of research into identity, bodies, desire and queering ideas of the natural. *The heart wants what the heart wants* is a film centred on entanglements of multi-species ecologies; three dancers weave in and out of an English garden as trees lactate, nectar oozes and insects crawl across the screen to a musical score interspersed with birdsong and rustling leaves. Appearing in the film in the form of an otherworldly being with prosthetic spikes and shimmering skin, Faramawy shares stories of young people as they navigate migration, desire, gender and belonging. Tracing examples of queer existence in Arabic language and Middle Eastern traditions and drawing parallels with symbolic plant forms, Faramawy concludes 'what comfort there is in knowing there's a precedent'.

bodies

queer

Throughout history LGBTQIA+ people have had their bodies
judged, criminalized, threatened and restricted. Art is a
powerful platform for processing and communicating the
experience of queer bodies, for asserting their presence,
mourning their loss and manifesting hopeful futures.
Queer bodies appear throughout art history and increasingly
in contemporary art, via self-portraiture and via the shared
experiences and intimate connections between artists and
their subjects. In such works queer bodies can be distorted
and fragmented, made up, reimagined and made visible
in ways that are simultaneously vulnerable and powerful.

Robert Mapplethorpe shocked audiences when he first
exhibited his now iconic black-and-white photographs of
explicit gay male sexuality. His images of New York City's BDSM
scene of the 1970s and 80s shone a light on a subculture that
the American public was not used to seeing, sparking debate
about the censorship of art and essentially confirming art as a
powerful arena within which to explore the experiences of queer
bodies. As a white photographer, Mapplethorpe's seemingly
overt sexualization of Black men causes many contemporary
artists to carefully consider who is being portrayed by whom
and how power dynamics within portraiture are structured.

Art about queer bodies is not necessarily figurative or
representational; abstract or text-based work is sometimes
a more effective and intense way of communicating about
the queer experience. The body can become a canvas,
altered with makeup and clothes, body modification and digital
enhancements. Or it can be used for expression through
performance or dance, as in the work of Paul Maheke
(see pages 84–85). By centralizing the body in their work,
artists viscerally communicate the wide-ranging experiences
of LGBTQIA+ people, carving space for queer people to exist
openly and freely.

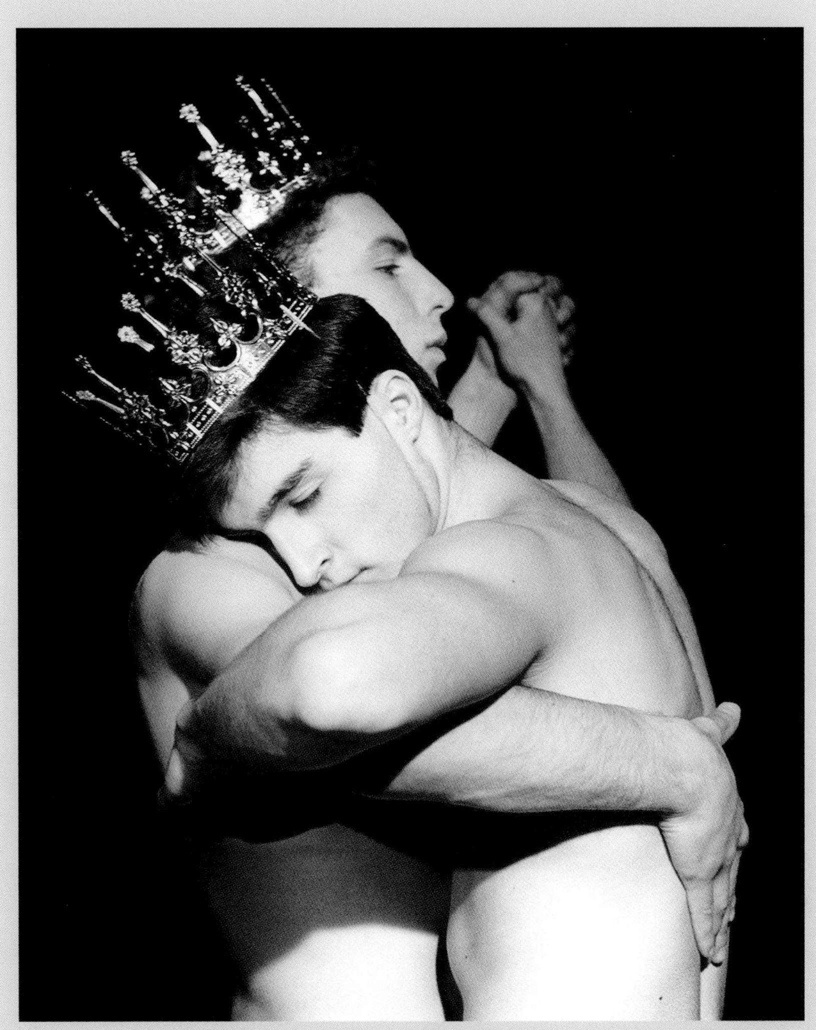

Two Men Dancing,
Robert Mapplethorpe, 1984

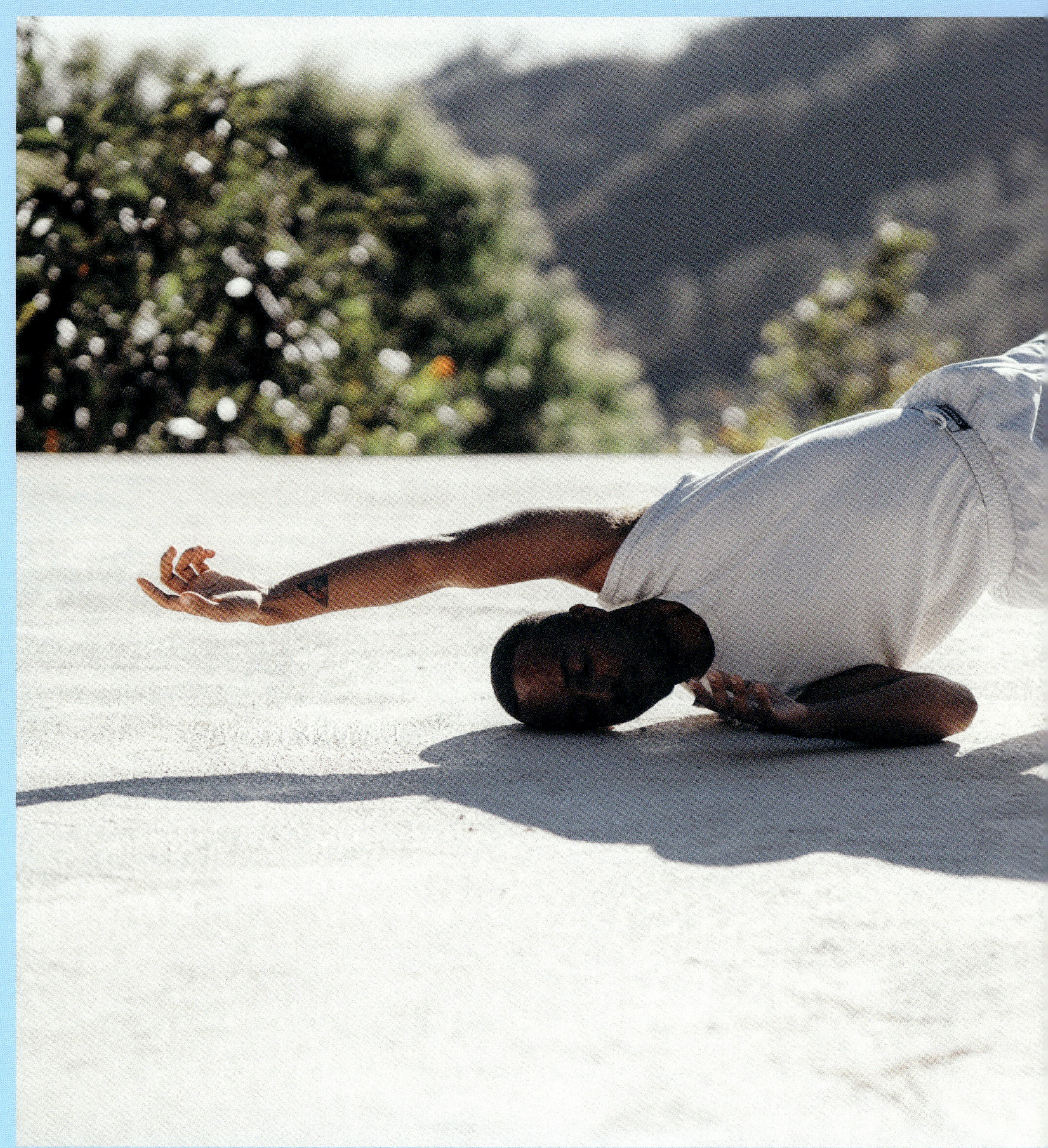

     Act II. Queer Bodies

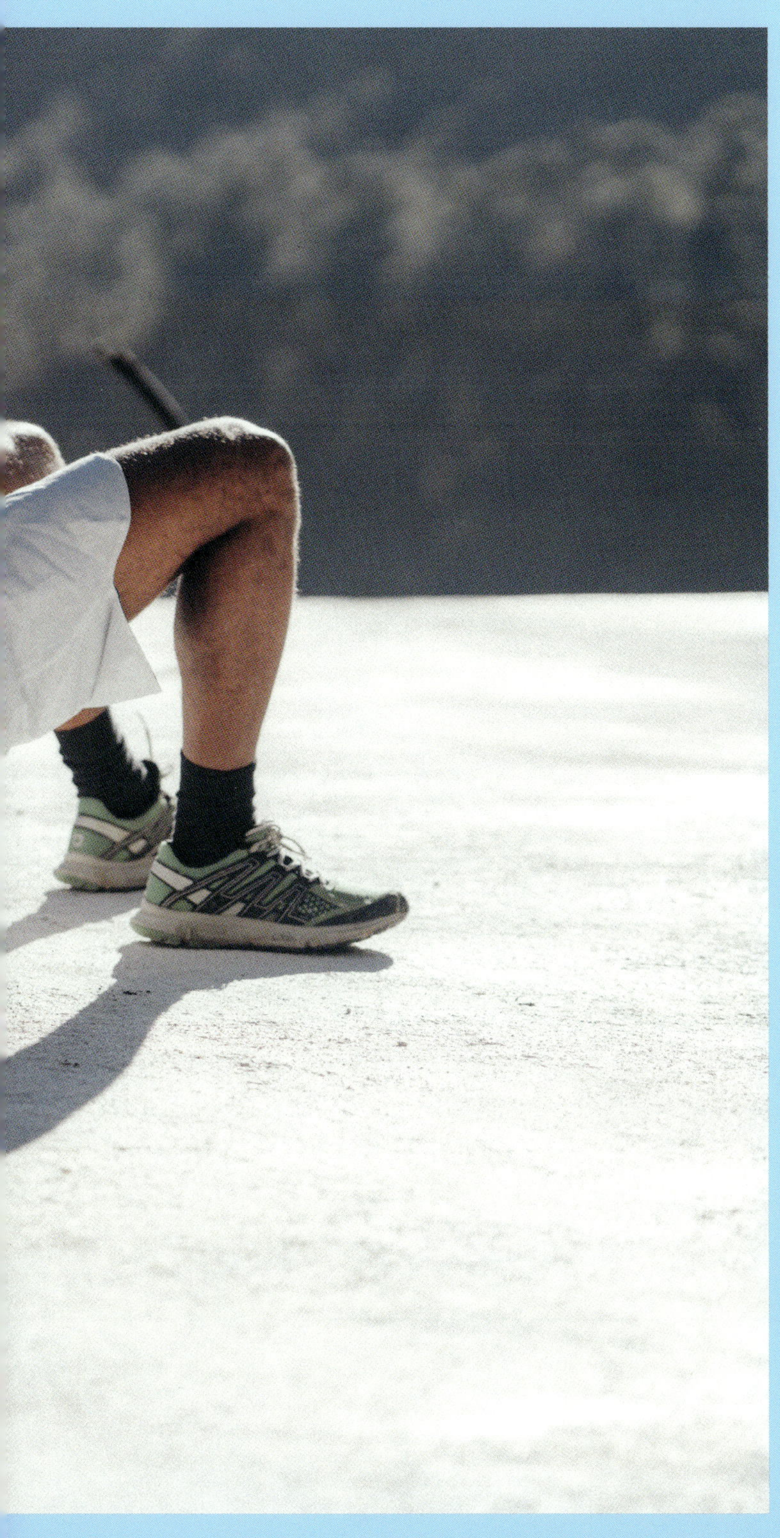

Seeking After the Fully Grown Dancer
'deep within', **Paul Maheke**, 2016–2018,
performance part of 'Meetings on Art',
58th Venice Biennale, 2019

Self

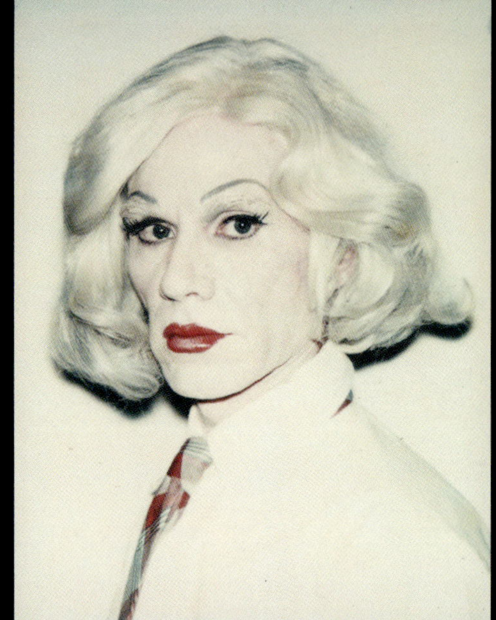

Self Portrait in Drag (blond wig),
Andy Warhol, 1982

Since the beginning of time people have been expressing themselves through art. As every person embarks on a lifelong journey of self-discovery, creativity can be a powerful tool for understanding and developing our identity and navigating who we are. For LGBTQIA+ people growing up in a world where they don't see themselves reflected – dominant heteronormative narratives in culture and media leaving a void of identification – the process of self-realization can be more challenging. In the quest to discover and articulate the self, queer artists bring together references that reflect their cultural context. Symbols and motifs are recontextualized, lifted from pop culture, literature, sports and religion, and pieced together to form new identities that sit outside of the mainstream. Part of the multifaceted reality of selfhood, queerness often intersects with other marginalized identities – race, class, gender, ability – making the formation of self all the more complex. Creative frameworks built through a process of deconstruction and reconstruction offer new possibilities for queer freedom, hope, spirituality and joy. Many artists centralize their own body. Self-portraiture is used as a means to assert oneself and to communicate the internal tensions borne from the experience of feeling at odds with society's expectations. Building on a long history of queer expression through makeup and clothes, we see artists getting creative with their appearance in order to challenge society's perception of LGBTQIA+ people. Art creates space for experimentation and pushing boundaries, to reflect on how we feel versus how we are seen and to project the version of ourselves that feels authentic.

Andy Warhol's iconic self-portrait of the artist wearing a wig and makeup (see opposite) is at once vulnerable and bold. It has been revisited by many artists in the decades since it was made, its reappearance in contemporary art a testament to its success as an exploration of self that challenges the narrow frameworks for gender expression society continues to offer us. Chiffon Thomas's sculpture *Ruse* (see below) is a similarly impactful self-portrait, approached from the perspective of a Black trans artist coming to terms with his identity against the backdrop of a deeply religious upbringing. By taking ownership of their narratives and celebrating queer difference, the artists in this chapter demonstrate the power of self-expression through art.

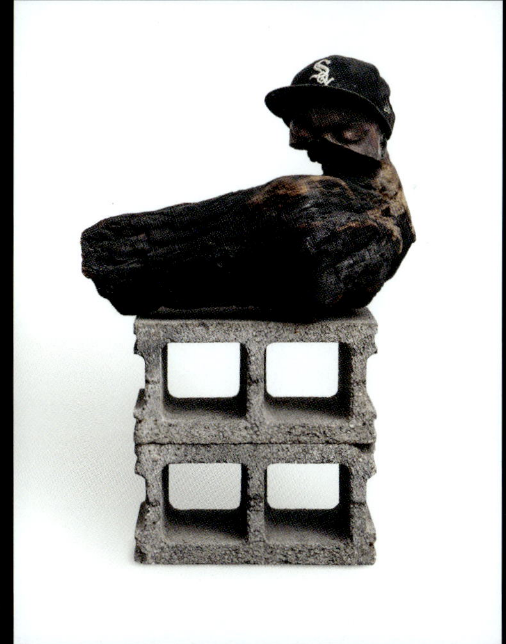

Ruse, **Chiffon Thomas,** 2023

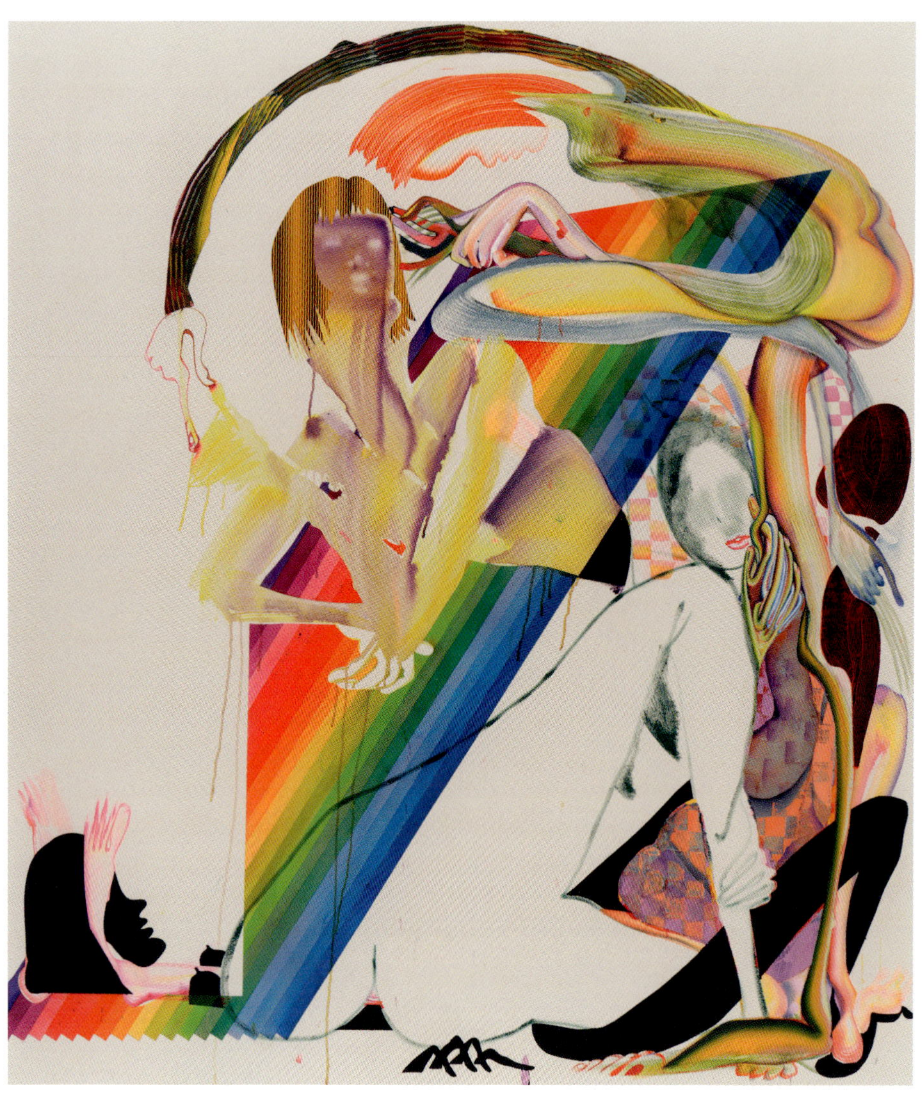

In *Try n' Pull tha Rains in on Me*, Christina Quarles draws inspiration from the intricate and multifaceted experience of existing within a body that embodies multiple identities as a mixed-race queer cis-gendered woman, embracing what she describes as an 'excess of identity'. Quarles's painterly techniques create a range of textures that dance across the canvas, imbuing it with the vibrancy and intensity of the queer experience. Five figures interweave intimacy and unknowing, some faceless, silhouetted or dissolving into each other and the surface of the canvas. The scene is set amid an ethereal landscape, the sharp stripes of a rainbow slice through the picture plane and the rainbow's arc overhead. Quarles invites viewers to explore the profound meaning of inhabiting one's own body and the power of connection with other queer bodies and the world around us.

Try n' Pull tha Rains in on Me,
Christina Quarles, 2022, acrylic on canvas, 213.4 x 182.9 x 5.1 cm
(84 x 72 x 2 in)

Multidisciplinary artist Carlos Motta's project *We Who Feel Differently* is an online 'database documentary' comprising interviews, conversations and journals addressing 'critical issues of contemporary queer culture'. The central tenet is that we'd arrive at a more socially just world by embracing difference and resisting assimilation, that sexual and gender difference is a position for alliance-building, solidarity and self-determination. The project manifests as publications, exhibitions, event series and symposiums in different cities, which continue to expand the dialogue and consider the nuances of local queer politics.

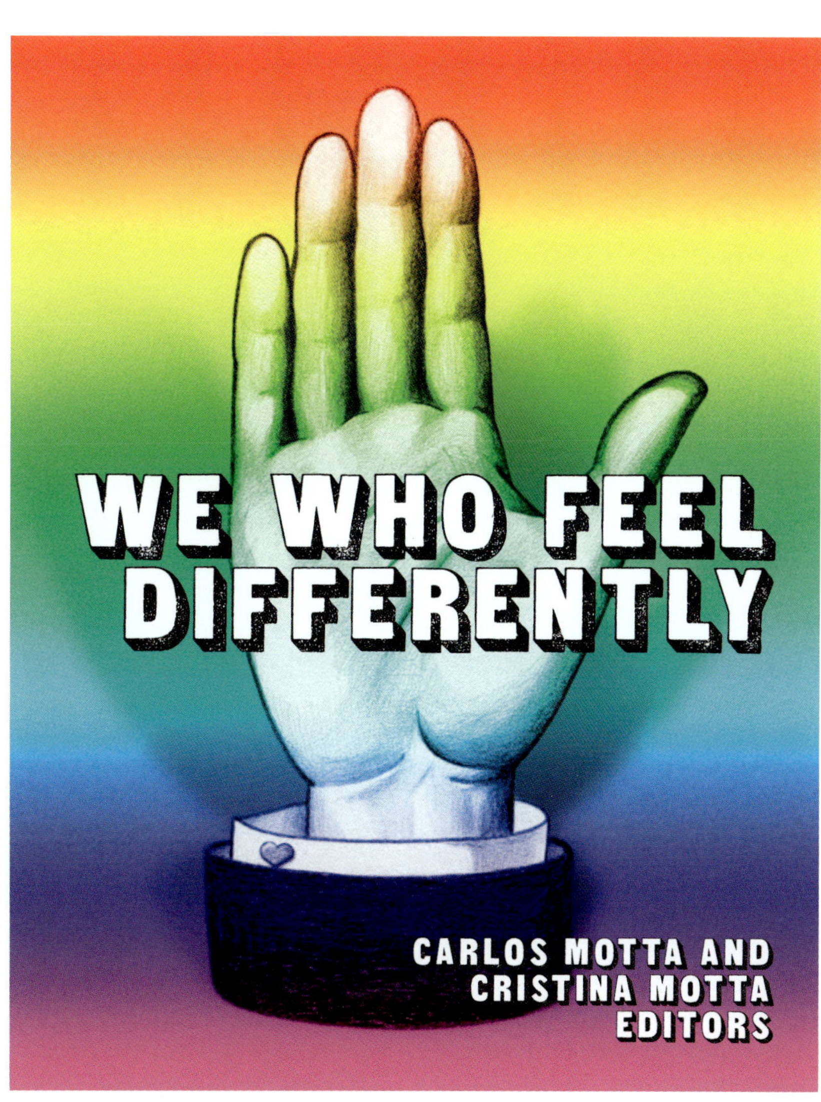

Front cover of *We Who Feel Differently*,
Carlos Motta, 2011

In *Doublonnage (Marcel)* Yasumasa Morimura takes the position of Marcel Duchamp's alter ego Rrose Sélavy as famously photographed by Man Ray in 1920. The image is part of an extensive body of work ongoing since the 1980s, in which Morimura recreates key moments from the cultural canon of the West, from the iconic poses of Hollywood actresses to European masterpieces from art history and landmark moments in contemporary art. The work unpicks the influence of Western values on Japanese culture, and challenges the lack of Asian representation in his own art historical training by literally inserting himself into the centre of the reference images. In *Doublonnage (Marcel)*, Morimura's version of Duchamp's exploration of the construction of self and the ambiguity of gender becomes all the more complex as Morimura introduces considerations of race and sexuality, doubling up on hands, hats and identities.

Yasumasa Morimura

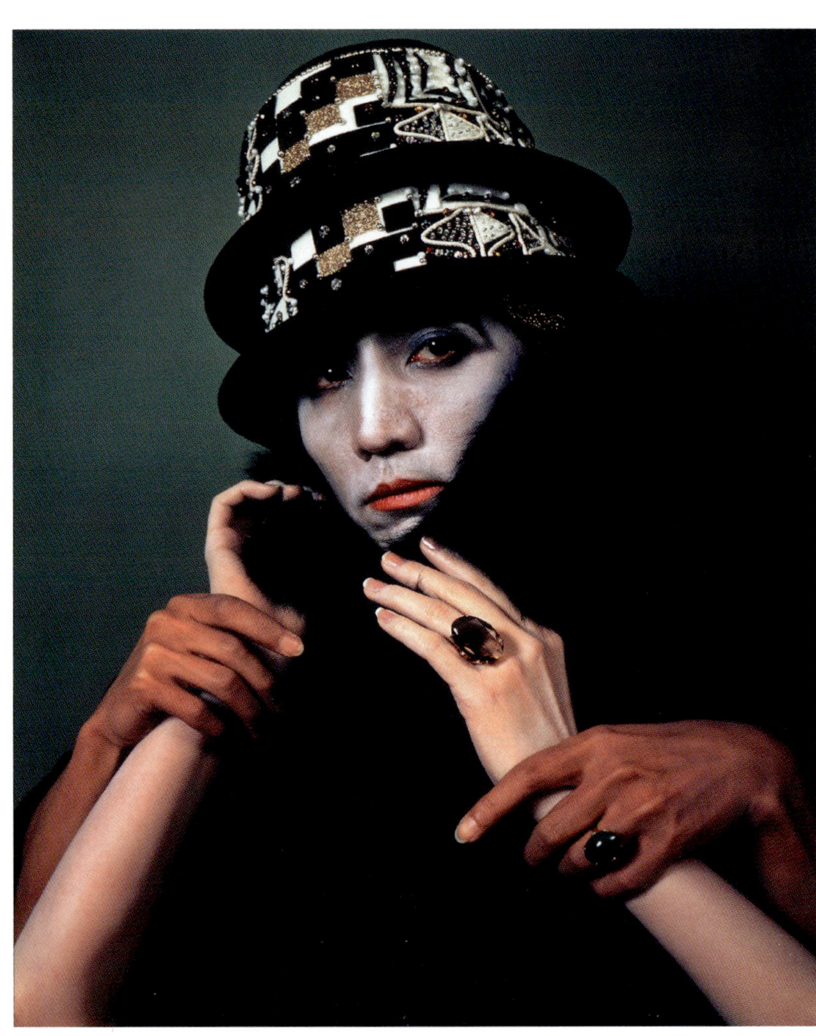

Doublonnage (Marcel),
Yasumasa Morimura, 1988, colour
photograph, 149.9 x 120 cm
(59 x 47¼ in)

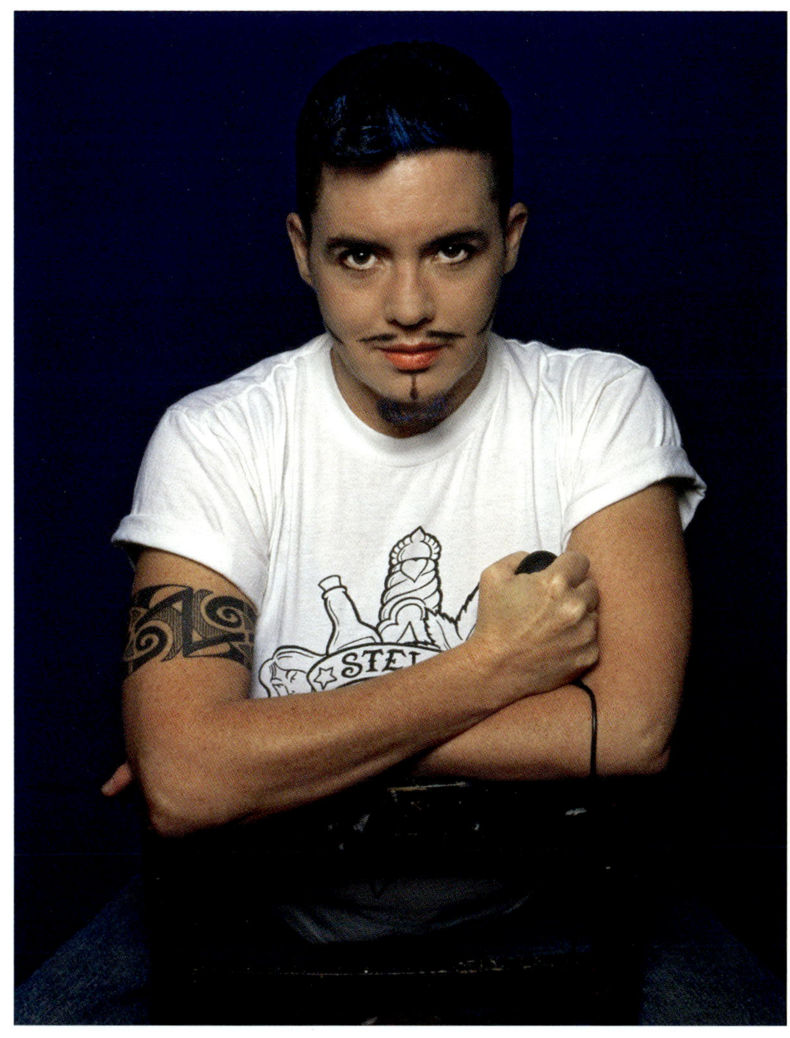

Self Portrait with Blue Beard,
Del LaGrace Volcano, 1995

Pioneer of queer photography, Del LaGrace Volcano's *Self Portrait with Blue Beard* was taken in their home studio in London in 1995. Known for making work inspired by their life and body, the photograph represents a moment in their gender journey, described by them as a move from being perceived as female to being perceived as male, exploring gender ambiguity and coming to terms with the fact that they were born intersex. The blue mascara worn in their hair and beard, which chimes with the bold blue background, and the makeup on their face speaks to a newfound confidence in experimenting with masculinity, influenced by their recent participation in a drag king competition. Volcano's self-portrait has become a symbol of non-binary gender identity, a celebration of the possibilities presented by what the artist refers to as the 'spaces in between'.

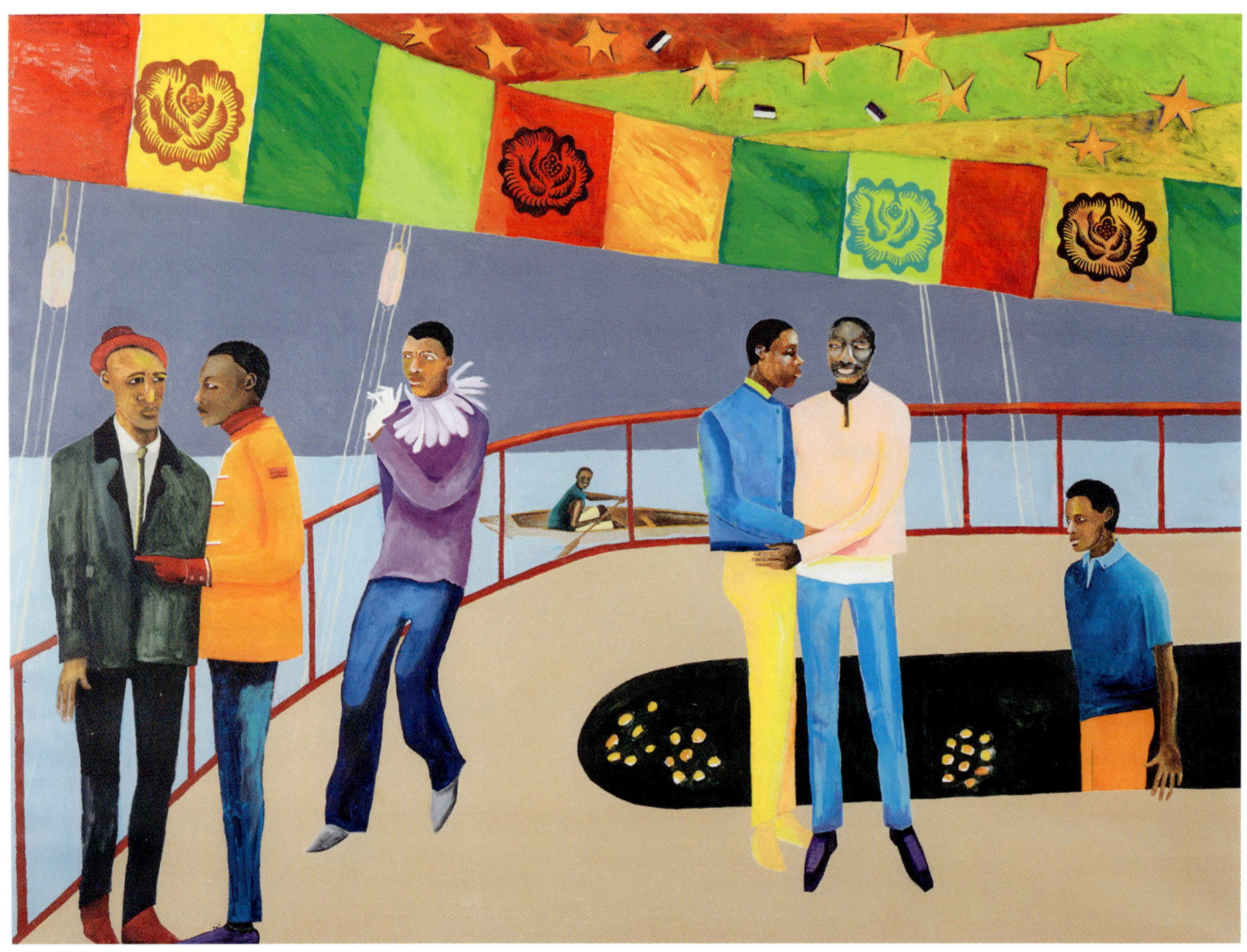

Lubaina Himid is an artist, curator, educator and cultural activist who has been making work since her early involvement with the British Black Arts Movement in the 1980s. Only really receiving cultural acclaim in later life, she became the first Black woman to win the Turner Prize in 2017. Born in Zanzibar and raised in the UK, her work tackles questions of race, class and gender, with a particular focus on uncovering marginalized and silenced histories. *Ball on Shipboard* features seven men, six on the deck of a ship and one looking on longingly from a rowing boat in the distance. Discussing this painting, Himid says her men 'fall in love with each other in front of you. They try to say what they mean to each other and attempt to begin to understand themselves by wearing whole outfits in combinations carefully chosen days before they put them on their bodies.' She describes them as 'pastry chefs' – working hard on something to be admired and consumed by someone else.

Ball on Shipboard, **Lubaina Himid**, 2018, acrylic on canvas, 72 x 96.1 x 1.6 cm (28⅓ x 37¾ x ⅔ in)

Jonathan Lyndon Chase's work explores Blackness, queerness and gender in America. Informed by personal experience growing up in a Christian Baptist community in Philadelphia and powered by a deeply physical and meditative creative process, Chase's paintings take on a spiritual power that rests on the cornerstones of 1990s hip hop culture and the opulence of rhinestones and sparkle. Titled after a Lil' Kim lyric, *butt naked dressed in nothing but pearls* presents painted figures and Styrofoam heads adorned with gold spray paint, red lipstick and strings of pearls surrounded by floating lemons. The figures challenge the limitations of a traditional understanding of gender expression, presenting an alternative to dominant masculinities, as they connect in a series of tender moments within the safe space of the painting.

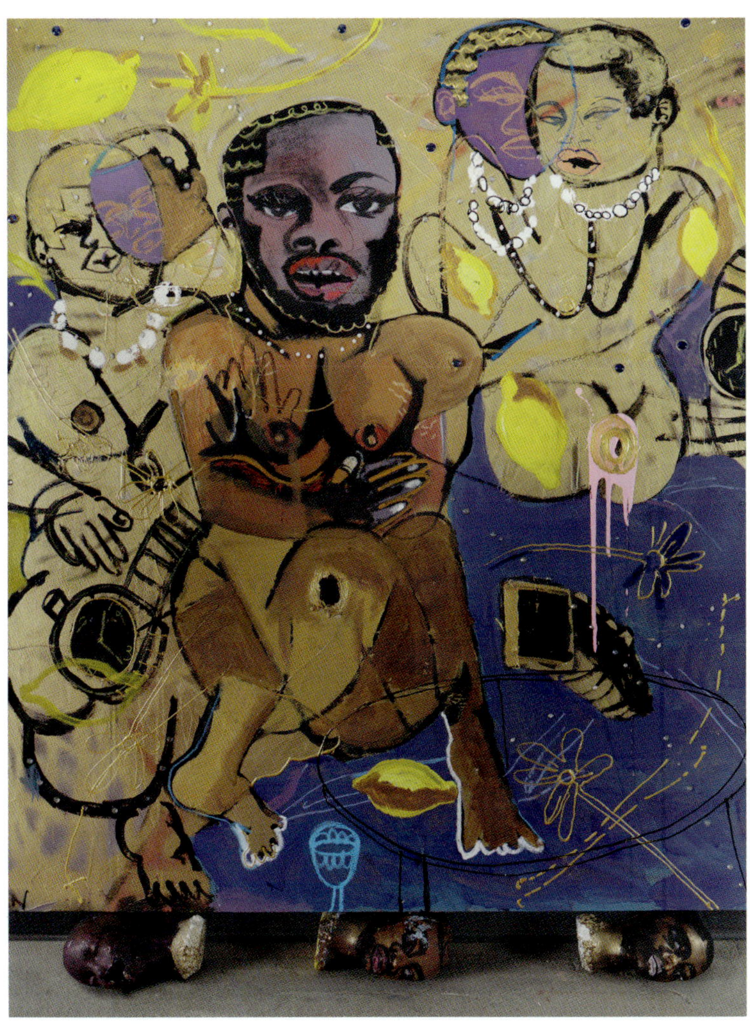

butt naked dressed in nothing but pearls,
Jonathan Lyndon Chase, 2018, marker, acrylic, oil, spray paint on canvas, Styrofoam heads; canvas: 182.9 x 152.4 cm (72 x 60 in), each head: 27.9 x 30.5 x 27.9 cm (11 x 12 x 11 in)

Jonathan Lyndon Chase

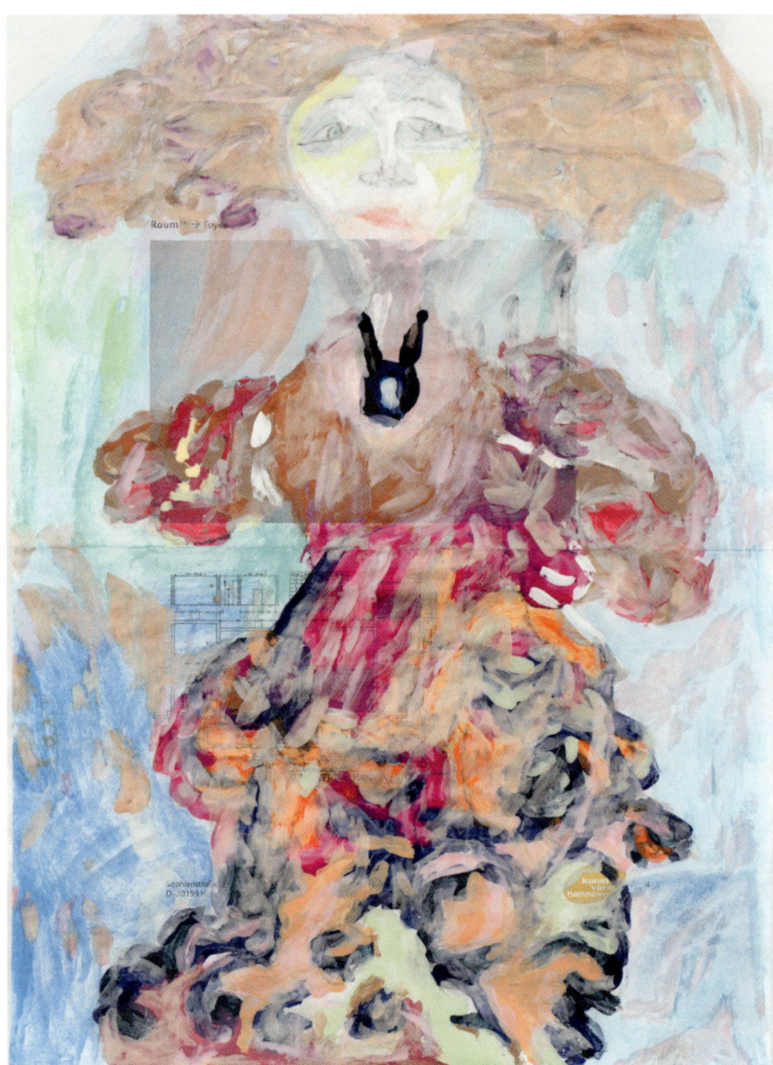

Julian Eltinge, The Countess Charming from the series 'Ladies on Paper', **Vaginal Davis**, 2018, hydrogen peroxide, glycerine, food colouring, watercolour pencil, coconut oil, nail enamel, varnish, lacquer, lipstick, mascara, eyebrow pencil, eye shadow, rouge, foundation, hamamelis water, mandrake, henbane, datura, hairspray and Iberogast, 41.5 x 29.4 cm (16⅓ x 11½ in)

Vaginal Davis

Vaginal Davis came to prominence in the queer and punk club performance scene in Los Angeles in the late 1970s for an aesthetic that's been described as 'Terrorist Drag'. Born intersex, assigned male at birth but addressed by female pronouns by her family as she was growing up, her educational performances interrogate her experience of being othered. She takes inspiration from strong pioneering women, including her mother, who was active in their local community where she created food gardens for the hungry, and the leading Black liberation and feminist activist Angela Davis, who the artist named herself after. *Julian Eltinge, The Countess Charming* is part of a series called 'Ladies on Paper', which remembers forgotten characters from history – here the women's fashion magazine editor and female impersonator Julian Eltinge. It is made from a pallet of sweetly scented, shiny, pastel beauty products.

     Self

Sin Wai Kin uses performance, and particularly drag, within their practice to deconstruct and challenge misogyny and racism in and outside of the queer community. Identifying as non-binary, their work prises apart femininity in order to expose gender as an elaborate social construct. The facial wipe works are made after performances or as part of the process of character development. Treating a fresh makeup wipe as a blank canvas, they carefully press their made up face onto the white surface, creating an archive of a meticulously painted look that would otherwise be wiped away and lost. Through the unique facial prints, each intimately capturing traces of Sin's own body, skin and sweat, we are asked to consider identity and the crafting of self through the lens of performance and spectatorship.

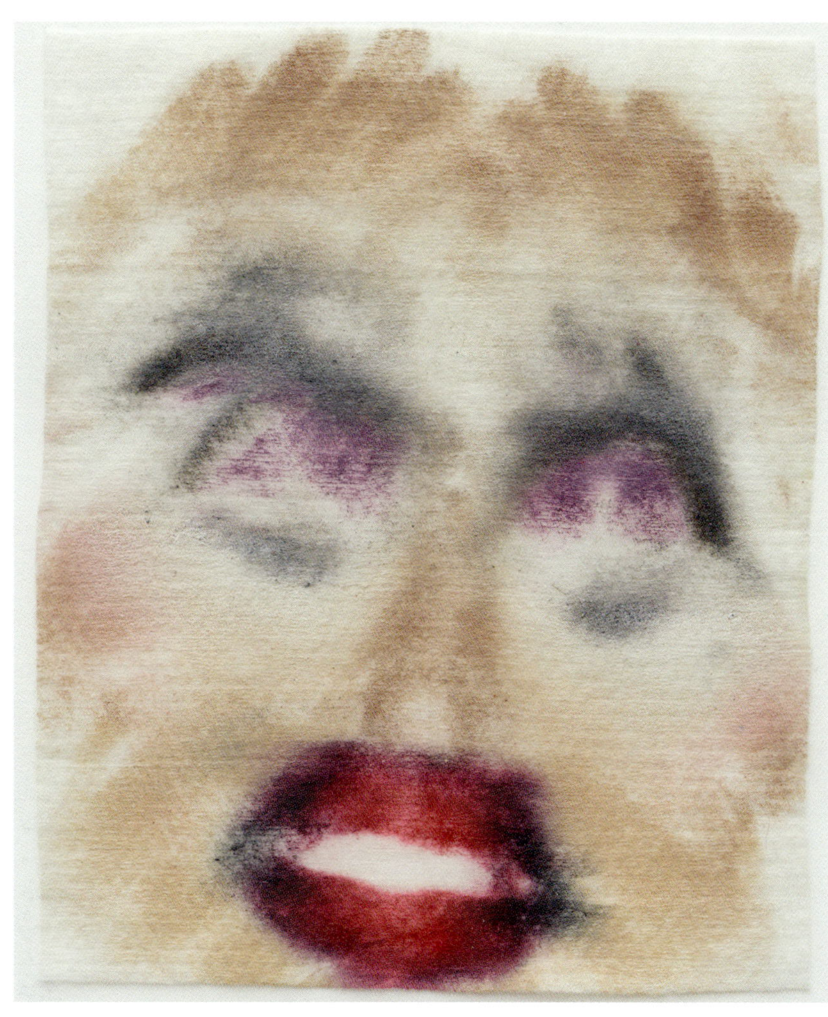

The expression wiped from her face,
Sin Wai Kin, 2016, makeup on facial wipe,
21 x 17 x 7 cm (8¼ x 6¾ x 2¾ in)

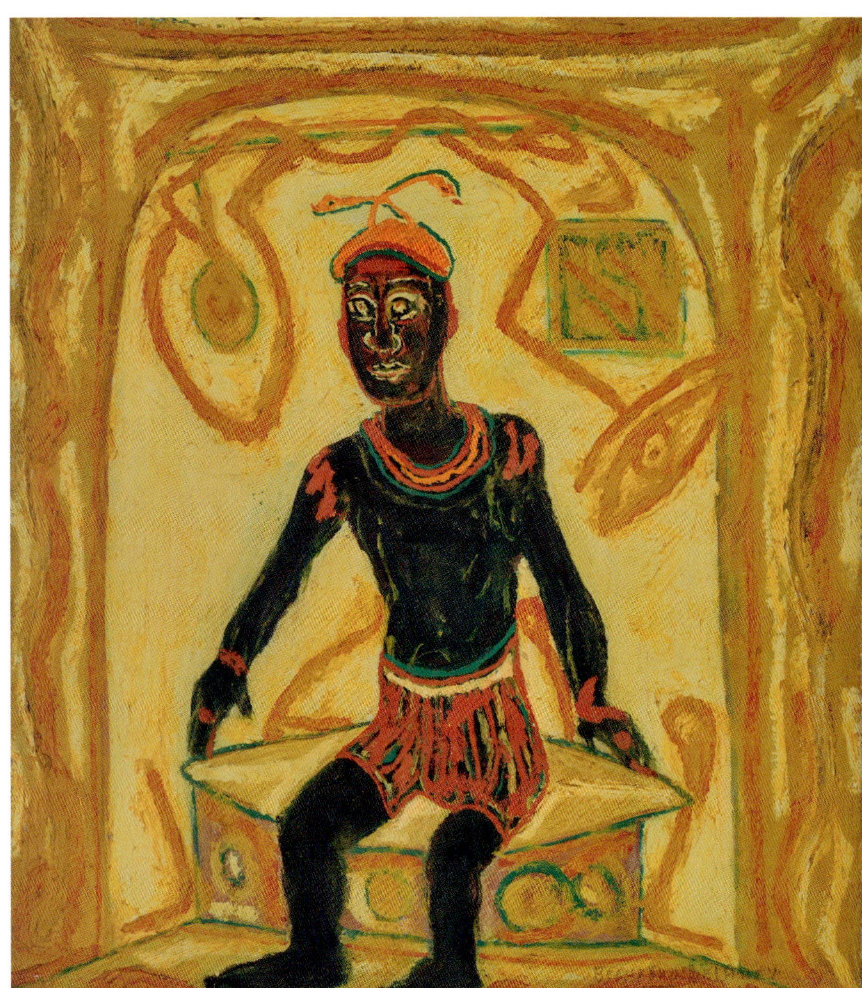

Self Portrait in a Paris Bath House,
Beauford Delaney, 1971, oil on canvas,
54.9 x 46 cm (21⅝ x 18⅛ in)

Beauford Delaney

Self Portrait in a Paris Bath House is the last-known self-portrait painted by Beauford Delaney. Born in 1901, he was raised with the strict Christian values of his deeply religious mother, who'd been born into slavery, and his Methodist Episcopal preacher father in Jefferson City, Missouri, where church dominated his and his nine siblings' lives. From a young age his artistic talent was nurtured by his family, who gave him the opportunity to spend time in local museums where he became inspired by the Impressionists and developed his own style of Colourist painting. Following in the footsteps of his close friend the writer James Baldwin, Delaney moved to Paris in 1953. The bath house self-portrait poignantly reflects the isolation and loneliness he experienced in later life as his mental health declined, after a lifetime of struggling with living openly as a gay Black man.

Greer Lankton appears in the 1980s and 90s photographs and films of her friends David Wojnarowicz, Peter Hujar and Nan Goldin. Her own work, which according to Goldin 'blurred the line between folk art and fine art', was modelled on other key figures of New York's creative scene, such as Candy Darling and Diana Vreeland, and queer and femme icons like Divine and Jackie Kennedy Onassis. From childhood she constructed elaborate dolls that reveal her lifelong fascination with the body, a fascination that intensified following gender affirming surgery when she was an art student. Her autobiographical character Sissy appears often, always with meticulously painted face and nails and intricately hand-stitched outfits. The life-size doll cuts a lonely and sometimes horrifying figure. Its exaggerated limbs and emaciated features reflect the gender dysphoria and body dysmorphia that Lankton experienced before her untimely death from drugs at age 38.

Greer Lankton

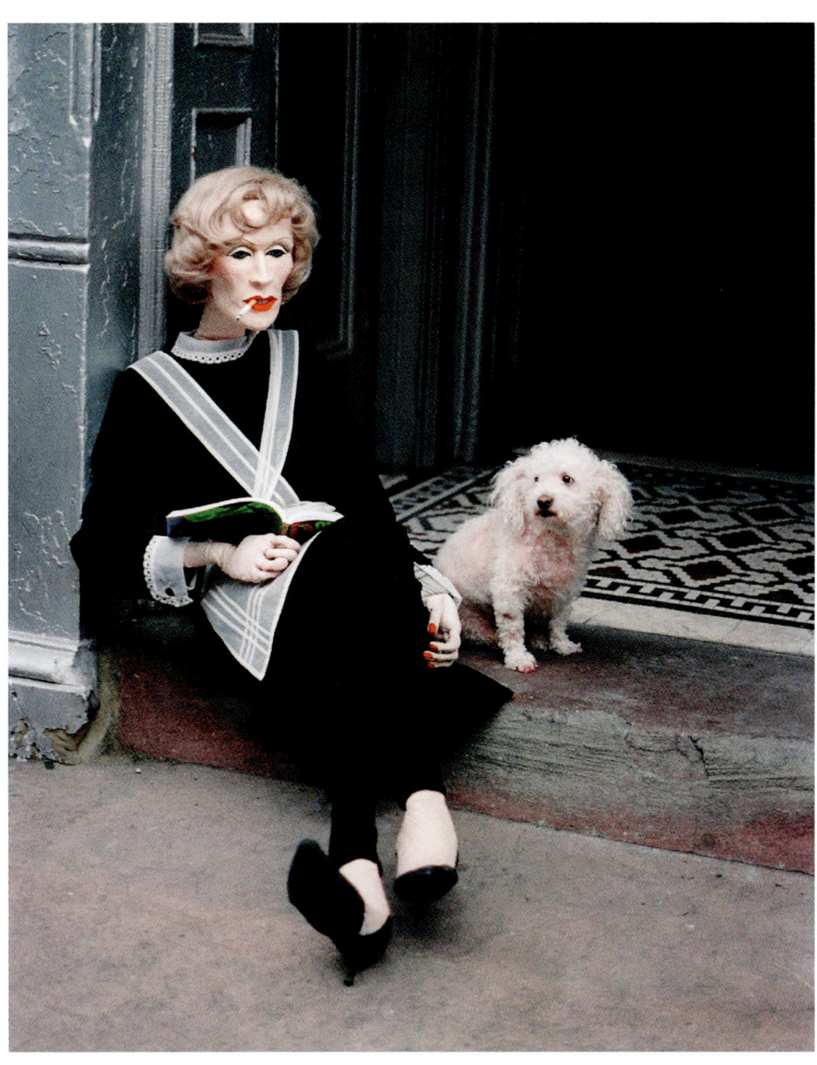

Sissy and Cherry on the Stoop of EINSTEINS, **Greer Lankton**, 1987, digital C-print, 45.7 x 30.5 cm (18 x 12 in)

Collier Schorr is best known for her fashion photography and portraits of adolescents. Her work upends traditional power structures relating to photographer and model, queerness and gender. *Daydreaming II* (page 131) is part of Schorr's book *Jens F.* (2005), which features collaged photographs of Jens F., a young boy who she met on a train. Jens recreates poses of the German model Helga, who was painted more than two hundred and fifty times in the 1970s and 1980s by Andrew Wyeth for his series 'The Helga Pictures'. We see the influence of Schorr's fashion background in her moodboard-esque collages that meddle with biography and fiction in an exploration of identification, performance and gender roles. The new relationship that the photographer develops with the boy can be seen as an allegory that frees Helga from being, in Schorr's words, 'trapped inside the female pose'.

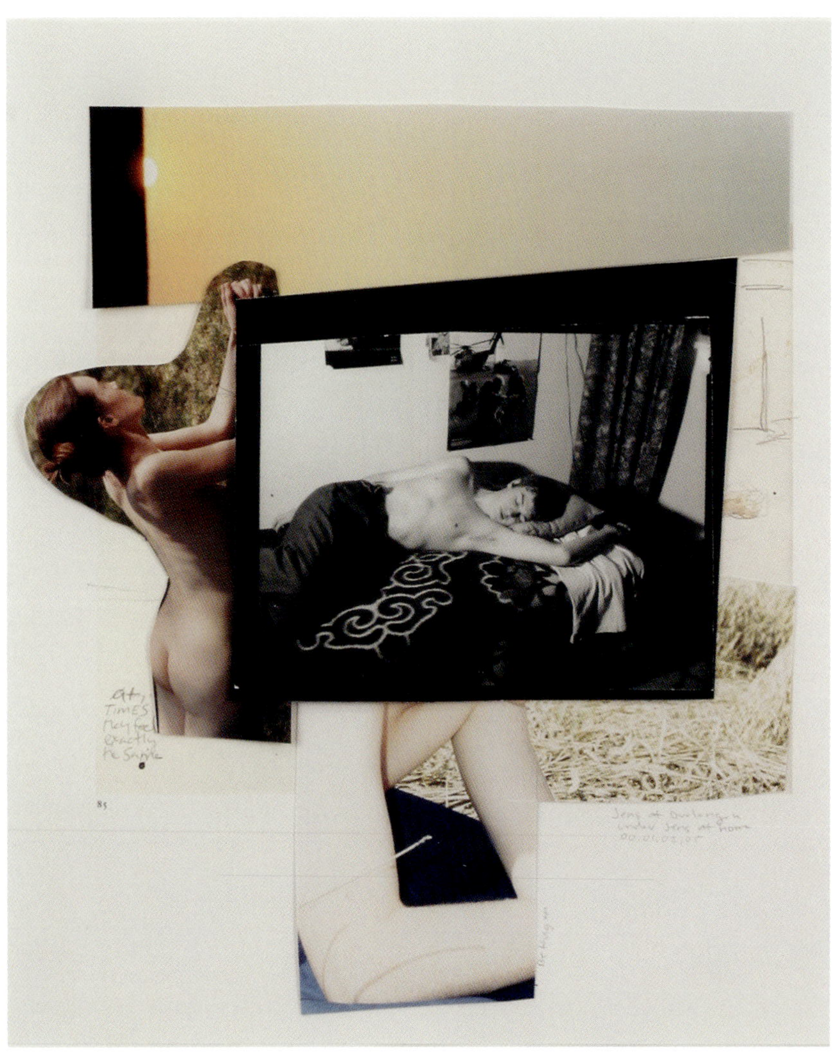

Daydreaming II (page 131), **Collier Schorr**, 2000–2002, colour photographs and pencil on paper, 27.9 x 24.1 cm (11 x 9½ in)

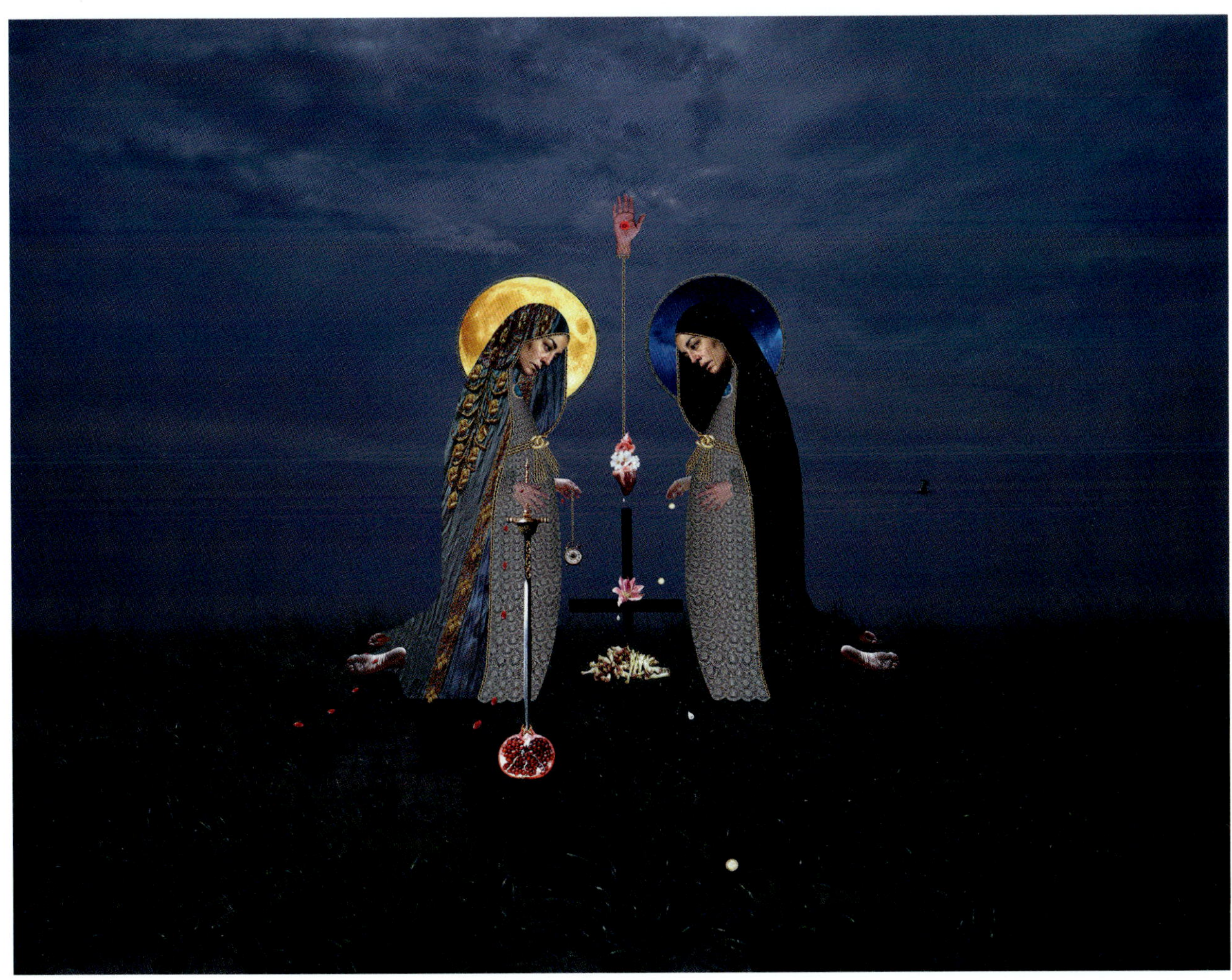

Ghada Khunji's photo montage *Maria, Myself and I* is a self-portrait in which two versions of herself participate in a ritual together. The artist uses symbols and religious iconography, such as stigmata, gold coins, a human heart, a ticking pocket watch and a sword puncturing a pomegranate, to question her life choices and communicate her fears. The image illustrates a void between her youth in a loving Bahrain that embraced diverse cultures and religions and the contemporary perceptions of Muslims and the scrutiny of Middle Eastern art she experiences in the West. Having lived in the United States for more than 25 years, she returned to live in her native Bahrain, where, despite it being difficult to live openly as her full self, she uses her art to explore all aspects of her identity, including her faith and her belief that 'God is in all of us'.

Maria, Myself and I from the series 'The Dark Ages', **Ghada Khunji**, 2016, photomontage

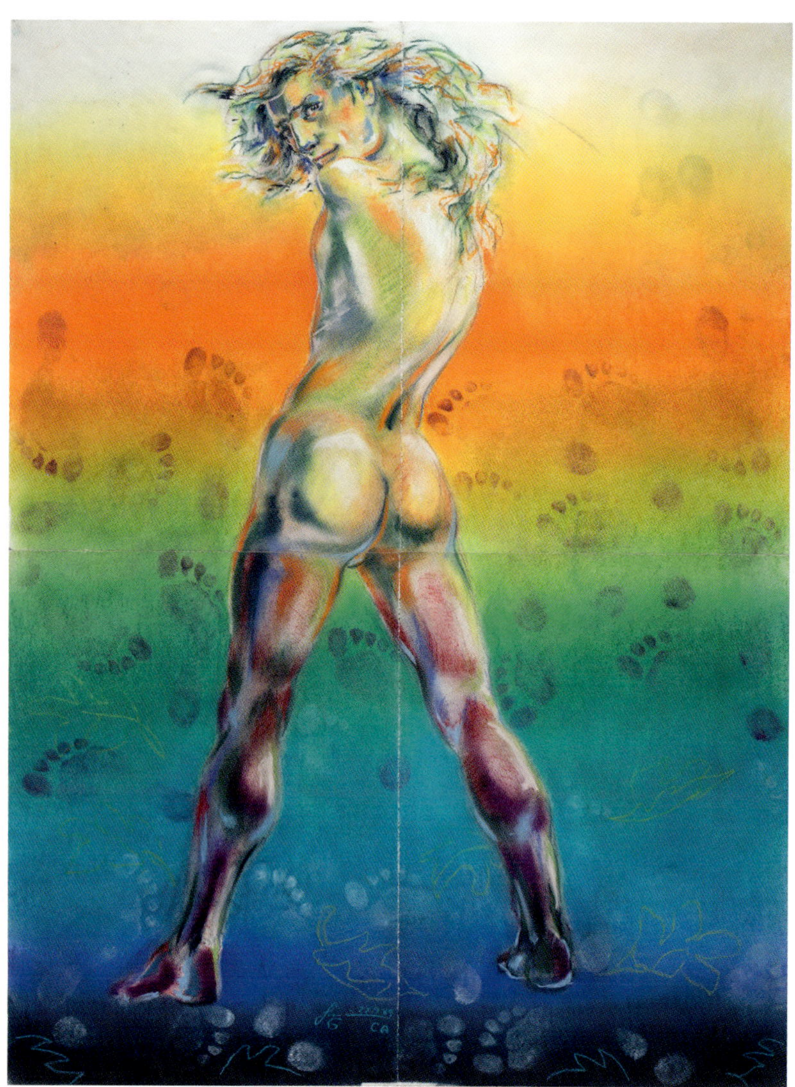

Untitled, **Lorenza Böttner**, 1989, pastel on paper, 152.4 x 114.3 cm (60 x 45 in)

Lorenza Böttner

Working with painting, drawing, photography, dance and performance, German-Chilean artist Lorenza Böttner's work centralizes her own transfeminine armless body. Before she died at the age of 34 from AIDS-related complications, her work was seen around the world via the Disabled Artists Network, of which she was an active member, and in her own public art performances in which she made live paintings with her toes. Drawing parallels with Venus de Milo, the armless classical sculpture widely revered as a beautiful object, Böttner questions the perception of disabled bodies, asking why her own body isn't accepted in the same way. Her photographic and painted self-portraits celebrate her physical form, transcending gender boundaries. The 1989 self-portrait pictured here is scattered with chalky footprints that trace her process and give joyful movement to her seductively posed naked body bathed in rainbow light.

     Self

Juliana Huxtable's *Untitled (Psychosocial Stuntin')* features the artist at the centre of the work, but delivers something beyond a typical self-portrait. To 'stunt' is to show off and flaunt, while 'psychosocial' points to the ways in which the self is always inscribed within a broader landscape. In this digitally created work, the artist abstracts representation by altering the colour of her hair and skin, adopting an Afrofuturist style. Set against a moonlit backdrop referencing what she calls 'household Black imagery', her defiant pose challenges the viewer's perception of her and her art. The image is part of the series 'Universal Crop Tops for All the Self Canonized Saints of Becoming', which uses politically charged visual motifs to explore race, gender, identity and queerness.

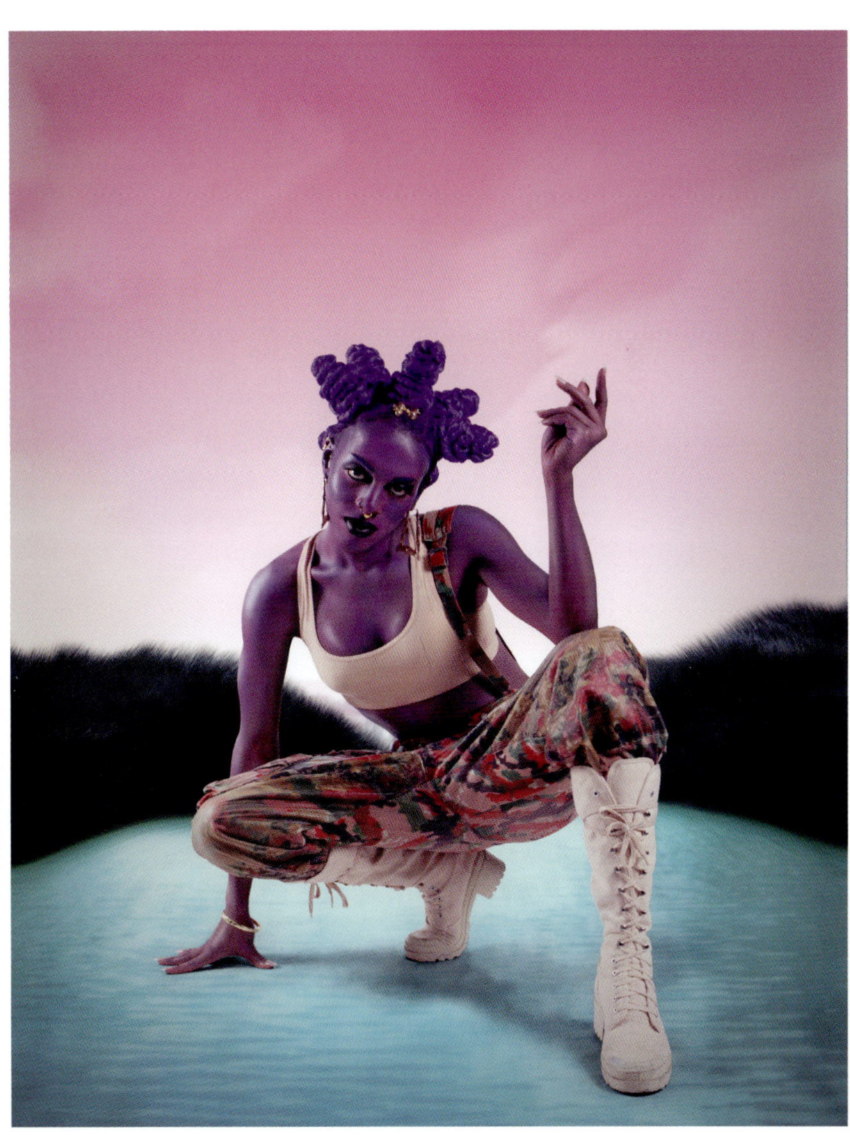

Juliana Huxtable

Untitled (Psychosocial Stuntin')
from the series 'Universal Crop Tops
 for All the Self Canonized Saints of
Becoming', **Juliana Huxtable**, 2015, colour
inkjet print, 101.6 x 76.2 cm (40 x 30 in)

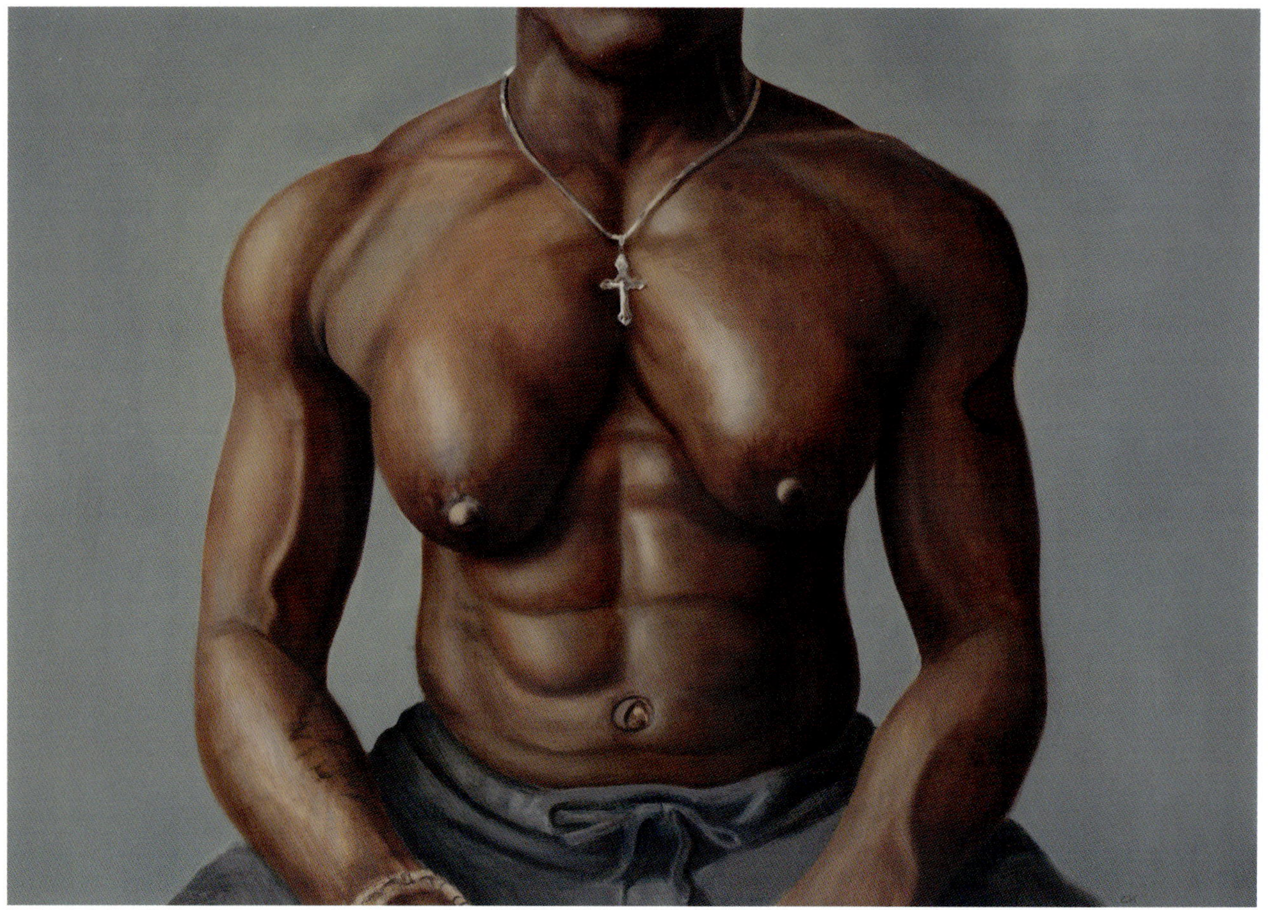

Clarity Haynes has been involved with groups operating at the intersection of art and activism throughout her career and the ethos of self-organized community extends to her practice itself. The Breast/Chest Portrait Project, ongoing for more than 25 years, is an exploration of the torso as a site for portraiture from the perspective of the lesbian gaze. Over the years, Haynes has painted and drawn torso portraits of several hundred people, documenting the process by photographing participants with their portraits and inviting them to write about their relationships with their bodies.

She thinks of the series as landscapes of the body, revealing far more of life's intimate secrets than a painting of the face. In Haynes's portrait of Roxanne, a professional bodybuilder, we see a study of outward female strength. The ripped torso adorned with a silver crucifix speaks to the faith and labour that goes into the relentless building and maintaining of queer resilience.

Roxanne, **Clarity Haynes**, 2012, oil on linen, 147.3 x 200.6 cm (58 x 79 in)

     Self

Gray Wielebinski's practice explores the intersections of mythology, identity, gender, nationhood and memory. He reconfigures and transforms iconography and visual codes in order to question society's frameworks and belief systems, proposing alternative imagined realities. His upbringing in Dallas, Texas, created a deep fascination with Americana, particularly the narratives that surround cowboys and sports. He uses these motifs of a particular version of masculinity as cultural reference points by which to navigate his own transmasculine identity. In *The Kelpie (Mulholland)*, a detailed ink-on-paper work, Wielebinski explores our relationship to animals and our tendency to view them through an anthropomorphized lens; the recurring symbols of spurs and horseshoes represent our desire to control nature. Referencing the parable of St Dunstan, who tricked Satan by horseshoeing his hooves, and interrogating the machismo often associated with horses, Wielebinski reinterprets historical visual signifiers to inform his own mythmaking.

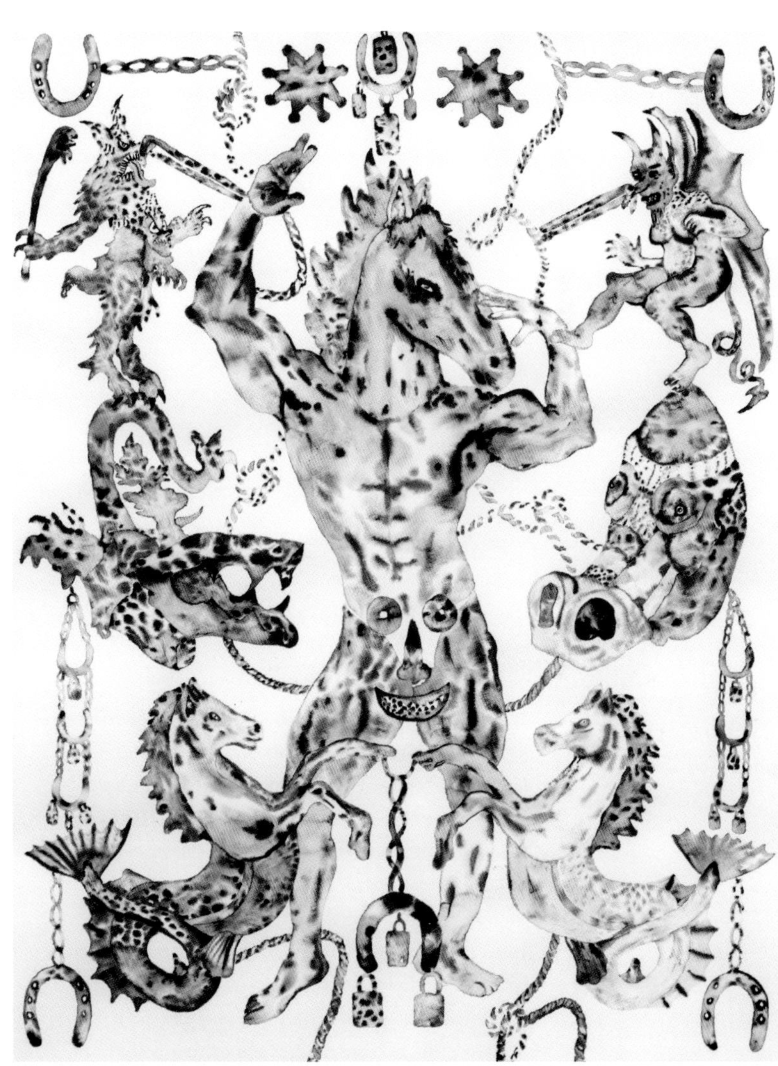

The Kelpie (Mulholland),
Gray Wielebinski, 2021, ink on paper,
68.9 x 50.7 cm (21⅛ x 20 in)

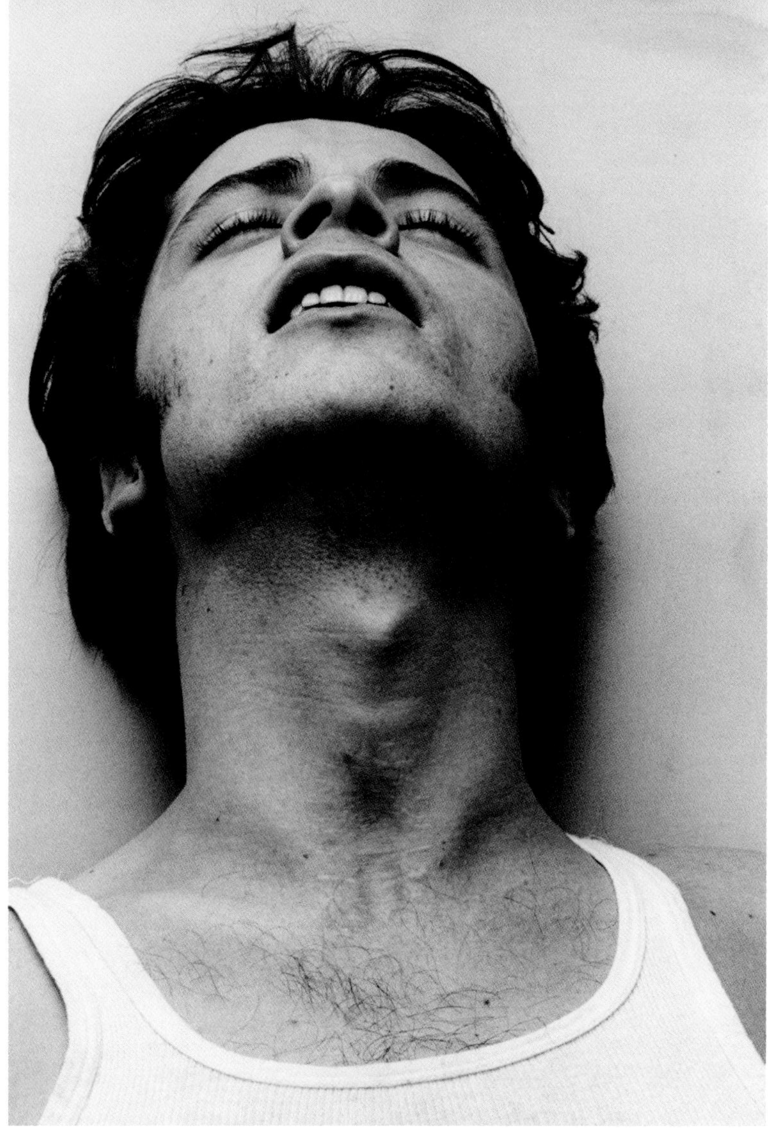

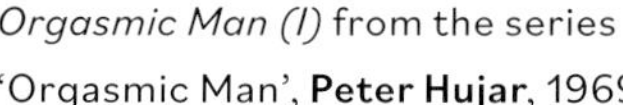
Orgasmic Man (I) from the series
'Orgasmic Man', **Peter Hujar**, 1969

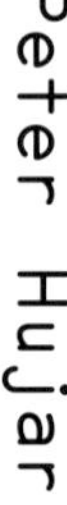

Peter Hujar

Studio and fashion photographer Peter Hujar shot portraits of members of Downtown New York's creative subculture, in which he was a prominent figure during the 1970s and 80s. His photography wasn't particularly celebrated during his lifetime, which meant he lived in relative poverty, and he doesn't tend to feature in traditional art histories. However, his images began appearing in contemporary culture in the twenty-first century – for example, on the covers of

Anohni and the Johnsons' album *I Am a Bird Now* (2005) and Hanya Yanagihara's novel *A Little Life* (2015) – and his work is now a regular feature of leading gallery and museum programmes. Hujar captures his subjects in moments of vulnerability, as in 'Orgasmic Man', an intimate series of photographs exploring the queer male gaze and desire. As the subject in the portraits throws his head back, we feel both the anguish and ecstasy of the orgasmic man's uninhibited sexuality.

　　Self

In Shikeith's sexually charged portrait, the model Prince Luxury experiences a moment of transcendence, his eyes closed as his tongue runs across his grills, sweat beading across his face and tattooed chest, clinging to the golden crucifix around his neck. According to the photographer, who is influenced by hauntology and spiritual traditions from the African diaspora, he seems to have caught his subject during 'an act of deviance', an act which transports him to some higher realm beyond the picture plane. As with many of his sitters, Shikeith has known Prince Luxury for many years, building the deep connection necessary to create such an intensely intimate photograph. Inspired by the work of James Baldwin and Marlon T. Riggs, Shikeith creates spaces where Black men can 'tap into the emotional tonalities of their being that have been restricted into one-dimensional spaces by way of patriarchal definitions of masculinity'.

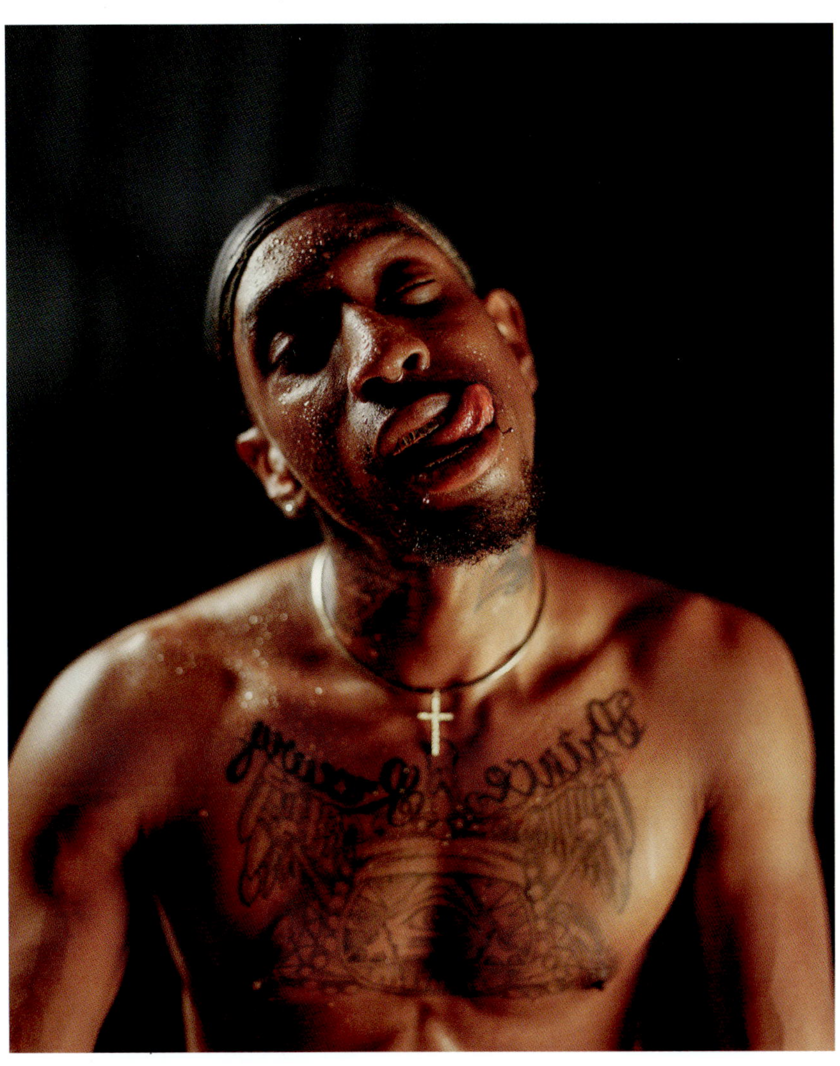

Prince, **Shikeith**, 2019, archival inkjet print on Canson Infinity Plantine, 96. x 76 cm (37⅞ x 30 in)

Lyle Ashton Harris's *Constructs #10–#13* is a series of four black-and-white prints in which the artist appears nude and semi-nude wearing wigs, a halterneck top and a skirt fashioned from a length of white net. Adopting poses that resemble classical statues and ballet positions, he meets the viewer either face on or with his back turned. Fist raised and hand on hip, he asserts his position within the frame, exuding a sexual and bodily freedom that feels particularly bold at the height of the AIDS epidemic, when the works were made. Inspired by peers Isaac Julien, Marlon T. Riggs and bell hooks, who were reflecting on the policing of Black bodies, Ashton Harris's photographs thoughtfully express the vulnerability of intersectional marginalized identities.

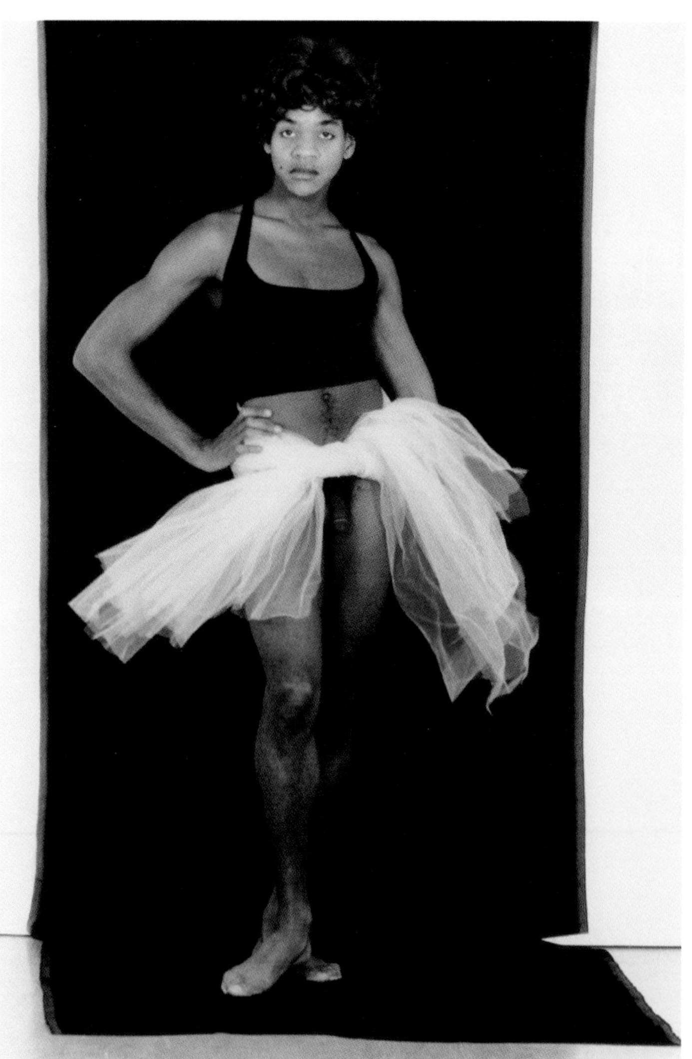

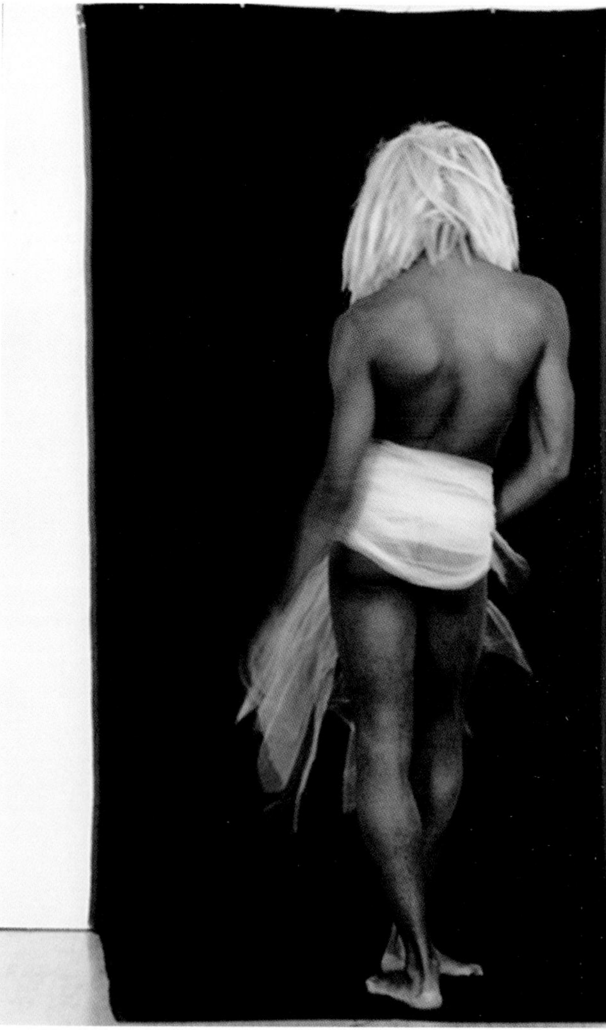

Constructs #10–#13, **Lyle Ashton Harris**,
1989, four black-and-white mural prints,
each print 208.3 x 109.2 cm (82 x 43 in)

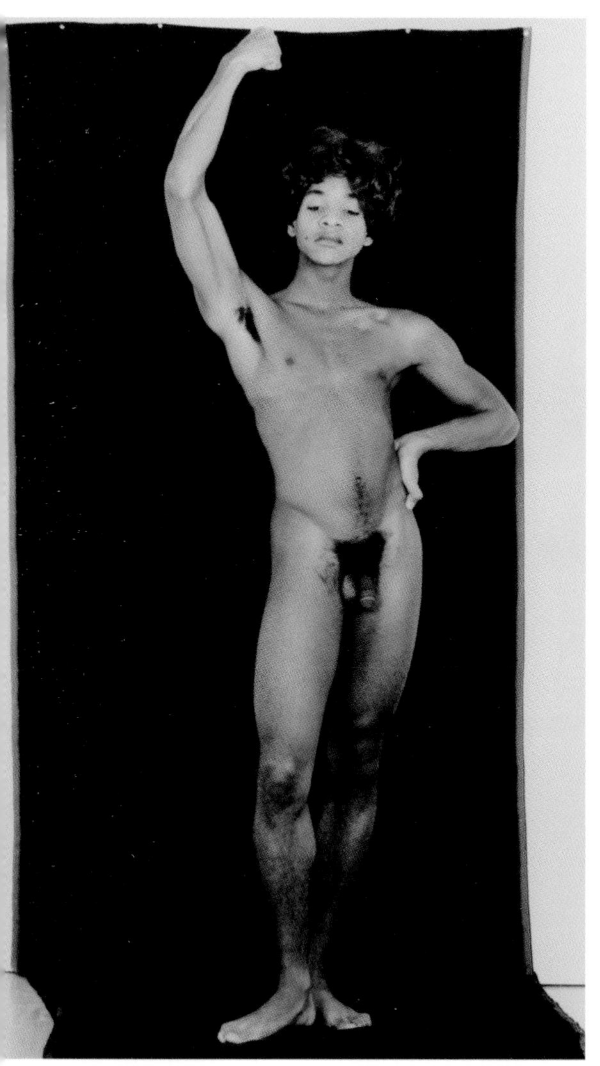

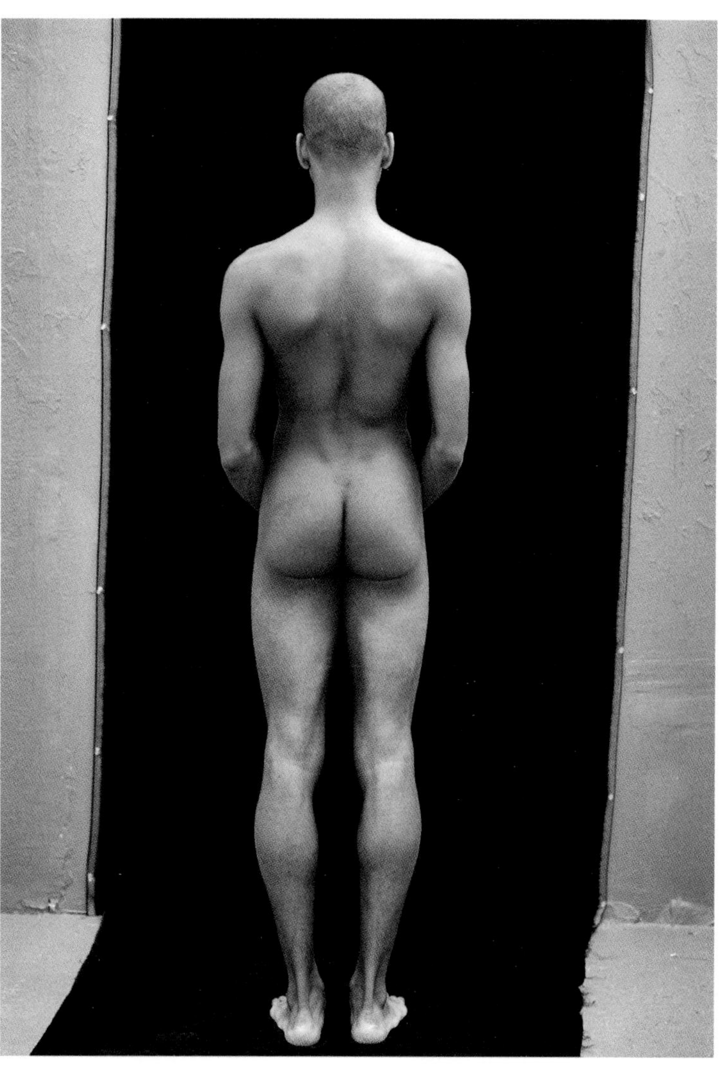

Intimacy

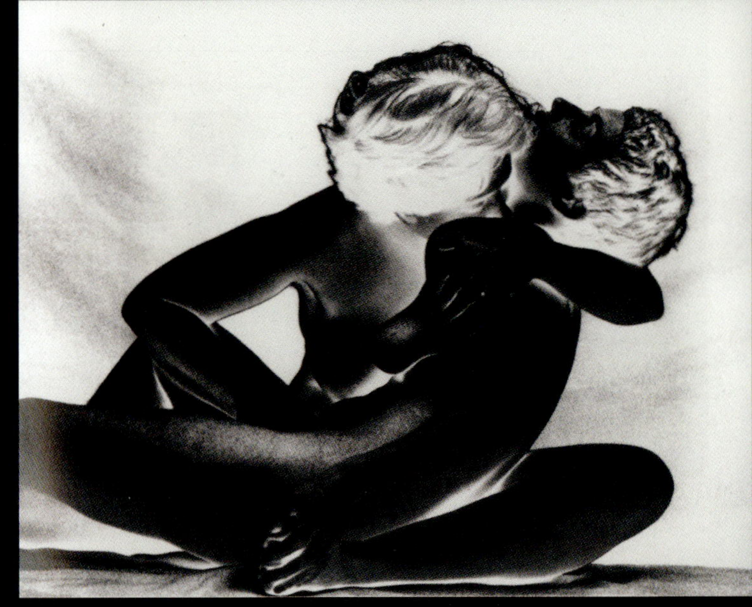

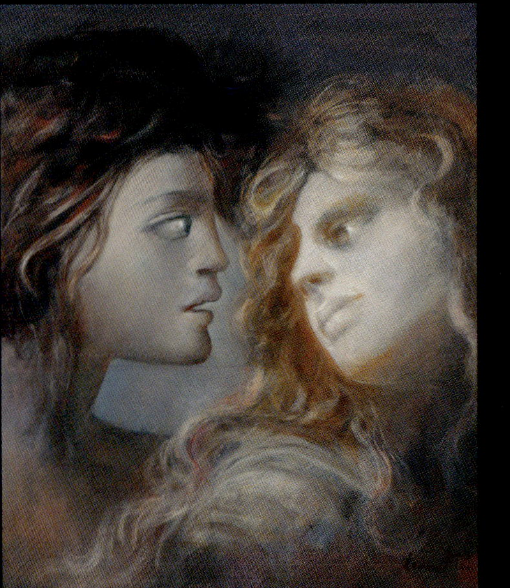

When thinking of queer art, intimacy is perhaps the way in which we expect to see queerness communicated. It's certainly true that seeing bodies entwined can make the queerness explicit, yet the intimacy we see reflected in art covers a spectrum of intimate connections, from romance and sex, to friendship and familial bonds. Artists navigate the hurdles – both internal and external – that must sometimes be overcome in pursuit of intimacy. Part of a process of experimentation and discovery, intimacy may be fleeting, a one-time thing, or it may be about relationships built over time. Queer intimacy in art is not necessarily figurative, in some cases it is represented through abstraction, using metaphor or reducing queerness to basic forms.

Challenging the mistreatment of queer bodies throughout art history, broader culture and society, many queer artists explore intimacy by calling into question the relationship between viewer, artist and subject. Approaching their queer subjects with tenderness and respect rather than voyeurism or objectification, we see single figures portrayed or the artist appearing in the work alongside others. From painting to photography, artists reveal elements of their technical process in order to shift traditional power structures. Within discourses on queer intimacy, it is typically gay cis men who are centralized, from the structures of discrimination, such as anti-gay laws that restrict sexual intimacy, to depictions in art, film and literature. There are, however, many poignant examples of queer female intimacy throughout art history and in contemporary art. Tee A. Corinne is celebrated for tackling lesbian sexuality in the 1970s when few others were so bold, applying her darkroom process of solarization that partially inverts light and dark tones to give her, often fat and disabled, figures an ethereal glow and an air of anonymity and abstraction to avoid male titillation. A decade later, Leonor Fini's silkscreen illustrations for her 1983 artist book *Carmilla*, inspired by the 1872 gothic novel by Sheridan Le Fanu, took the vampire at the heart of the story as an opportunity to explore female sexuality and lesbian desire.

Artists explore the intensity of being intimate with someone of the same gender and the liberation and deep sense of self that comes through intimate connections with other queer bodies and minds. The smoke passing between the three topless figures in LinZhipeng (aka No.223)'s *Smoking 3some* (see below) allegorically demonstrates something shared in this moment. Without knowing what happened before or after this scene was frozen in time by the camera, we see the ease with which their arms touch as they gaze intimately into each other's, and our, eyes. We witness a shared emotional and physical connection that goes beyond traditional heteronormative bonds.

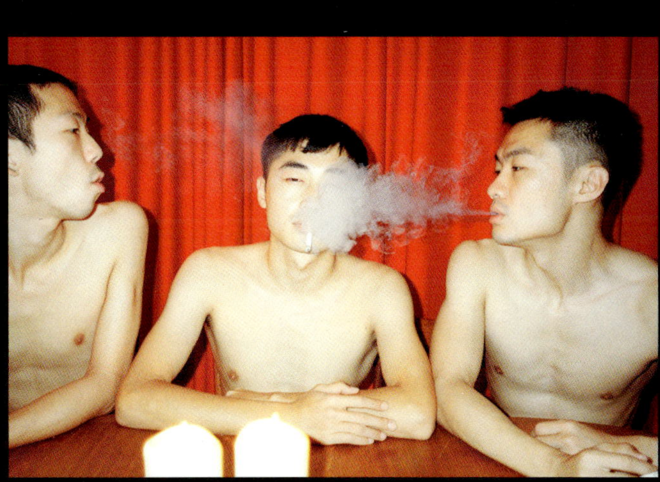

Smoking 3some,
LinZhipeng (aka No.223), 2018

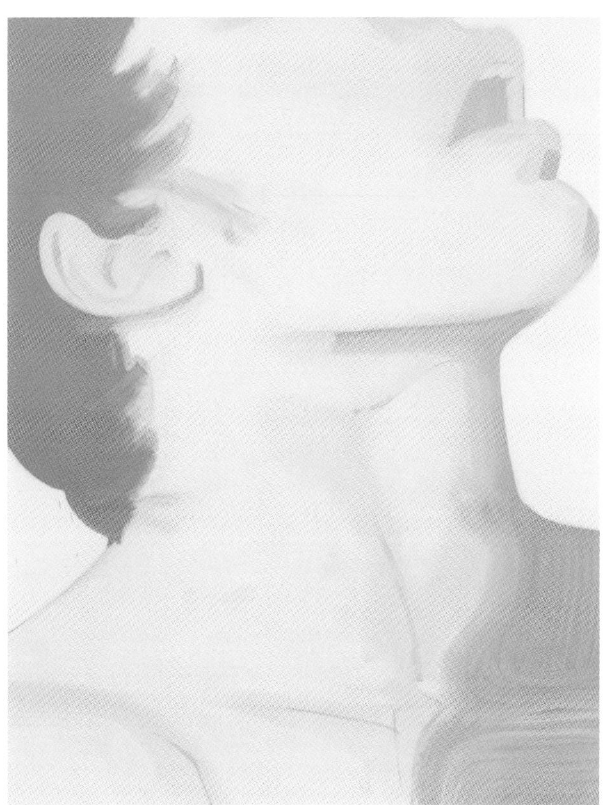 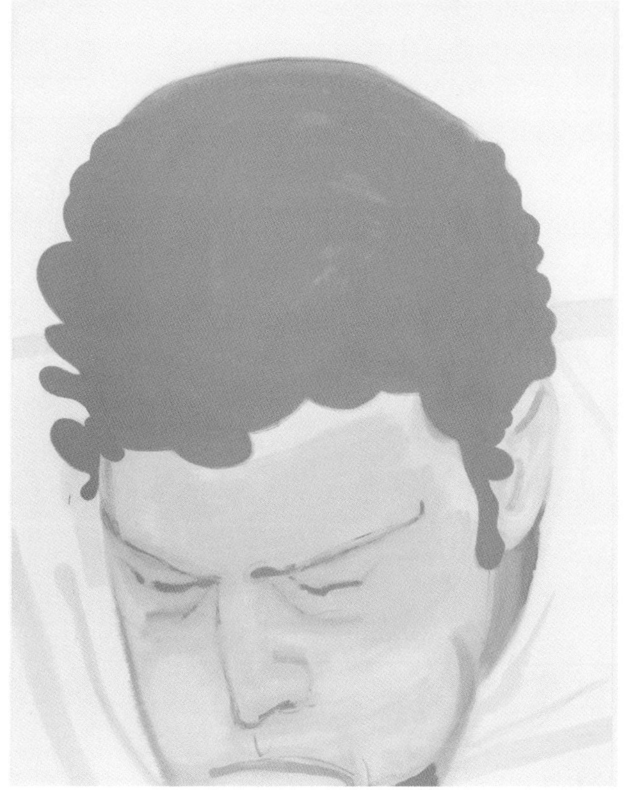

Jwan Yosef collectively refers to his series of greyscale portraits of young men as 'Floor Lickers'. Captured mid-action, each figure is removed from any context through a process of cropping and being placed in an empty white background. The picture frame ends abruptly before the mouth or eyes, deliberately omitting the features that might reveal the act that each subject is engaged in. What we are left with is a series of moments that suggest the same sexual tension, regardless of the source imagery – the artist reveals that one figure is actually vomiting onto a bar floor while the other is being ejaculated on. Yosef's long-standing fascination with the construction of images is further explored through an emphasis on the painting process, like visible underpainting and exaggerated brushstrokes. By playfully asking the viewer to reflect on where our mind takes us, Yosef questions the representation of young gay men and the over-saturation of sexualized images.

'Floor Lickers', **Jwan Yosef**, 2021, both images: *Head*, oil on linen, 254 x 190.5 cm (100 x 75 in)

arms and legs, **Wolfgang Tillmans**, 2014

Wolfgang Tillmans

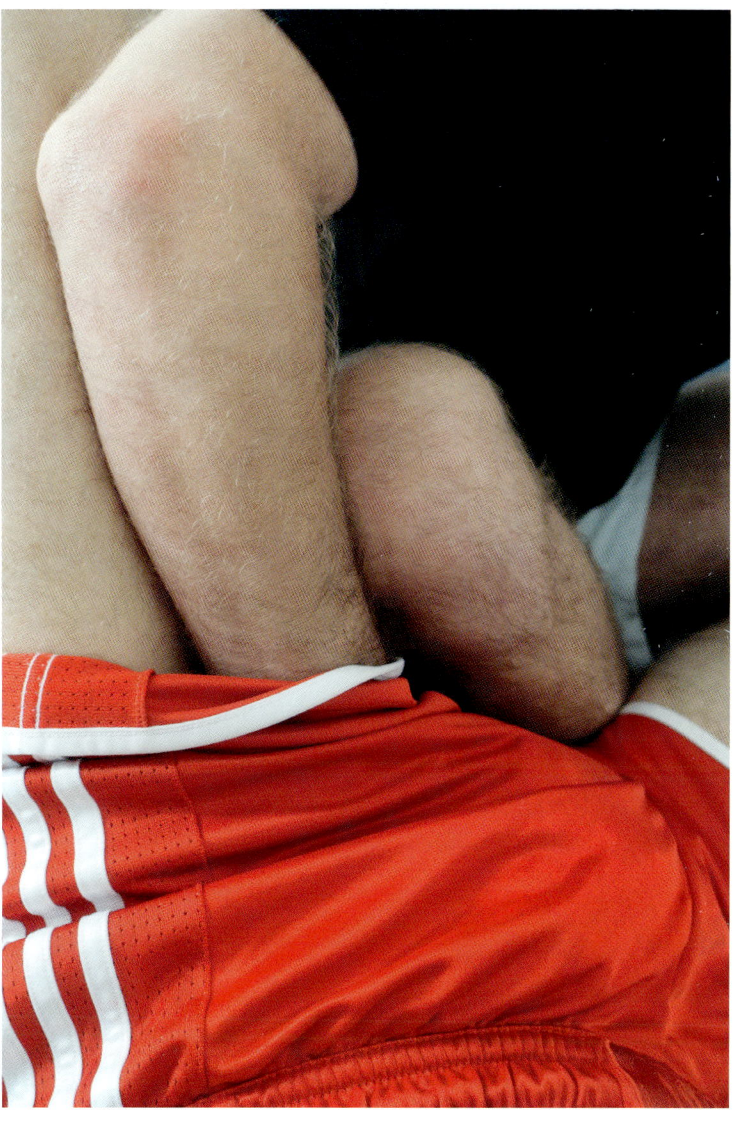

Wolfgang Tillmans' photography presents the world through his distinctive perspective. Whether capturing skyscapes, urban details, club scenes or human interactions, he assumes a role somewhere between participant, observer and chronicler. His portraits, often of queer creatives, friends and lovers, amplify their voices, memorialize their experiences and preserve their spaces.

As with all of his photography, *arms and legs* masterfully brings together the typically contradictory qualities of an effortless picture and a thoughtfully composed formal arrangement. The closely cropped confusion of limbs invites our eye to focus on the texture of skin, body hair and the creases of sports shorts at the centre of this moment of intimacy.

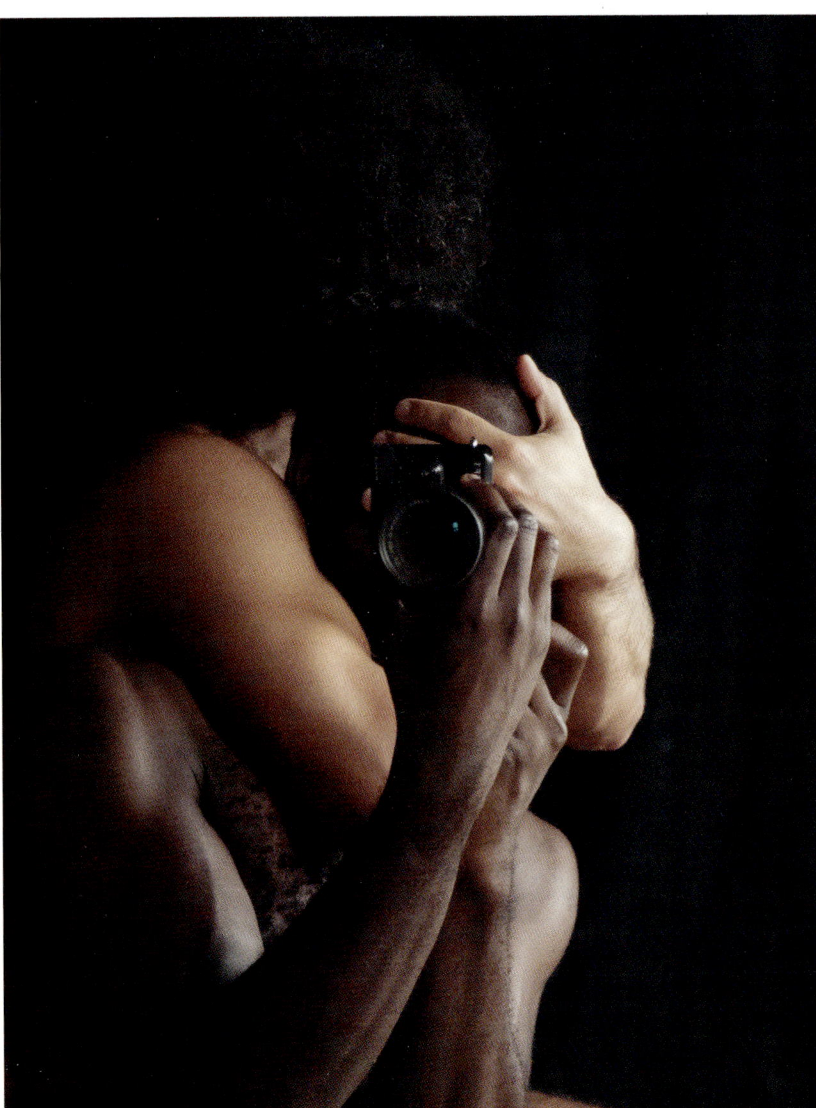

Darkroom Mirror (_2070386),
Paul Mpagi Sepuya, 2017, archival
pigment print, 81.3 x 61 cm (32 x 24 in)

As is typical for his photography, Paul Mpagi Sepuya places himself and his camera at the centre of *Darkroom Mirror (_2070386)*. In this self-portrait he is embraced by the arms of another man who turns away from the gaze of the camera. Sepuya's face is obscured by his camera, his eyes are covered by his companion's hand and the scene is reflected in a mirror that bears visible smudges. These very deliberate details reveal technical elements of the photographic and compositional process highlighting the different planes of existence within the image, calling into question the relationship between the viewer, the photograph, the subject, the photographed and the photographer. The entanglement of the two figures becomes a single mass that disappears into or emerges from the shadow of the darkroom, centralizing the experience potential of Blackness and queerness.

Jenna Gribbon's portraits of her most recognizable subject, her wife the musician Mackenzie Scott, are prolific, from candid domestic scenes and sexually tender moments to staged compositions that employ exaggerated lighting, such as *Examinationscape*. Her approach to painting dismantles the traditional relationship between artist, subject and viewer, shifting the power dynamics within the frame by revealing the tools of construction involved in the artistic process, from the thick texture of the brushstrokes to the harsh shadows cast by the visible clamp light. Through the monumentally romantic gesture of repeated looking and truly seeing, built on a foundation of consent and mutual respect, Gribbon crafts an allegorical figure, weaving together myth and reality in her representation of queer intimacy.

Jenna Gribbon

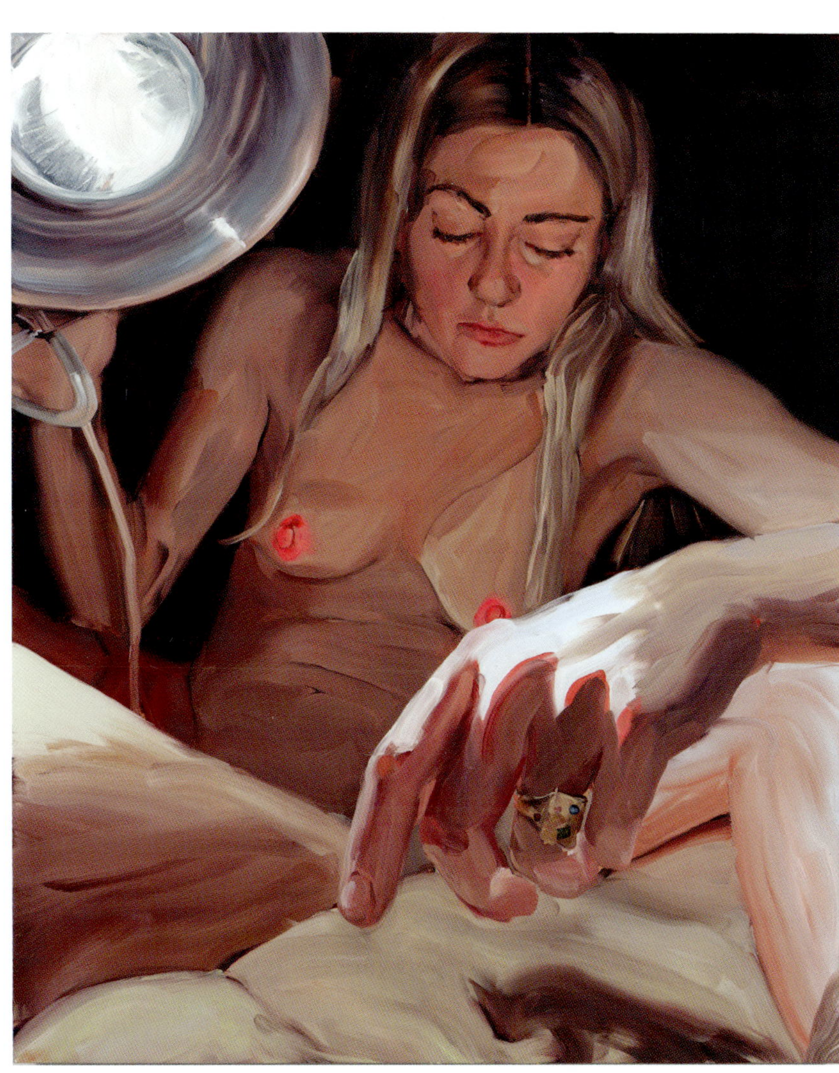

Examinationscape,
Jenna Gribbon, 2021, oil on canvas,
203.2 x 165.1 cm (80 x 65 in)

Born to first-generation Eastern European immigrants in New York City where she still works and lives, Roni Horn is a writer and visual artist whose diverse practice focuses on the 'protean nature of identity, meaning and perception', as well as the notion of doubling. In the 1980s she produced a series of sculptural installations called 'Pair Objects', in which two identical geometric volumes made of metal are displayed in distinct spaces. *Things That Happen Again: A Here and a There* is a pair of solid copper truncated cones, each hand-lathed to duplicate mechanical identity. Horn has referred to the Pair Objects possessing an implicit possibility of queerness. Made during a period of heightened awareness of sexuality caused by the AIDS crisis, the objects, which are the same in every way, reflect a deep connection that endures any distance.

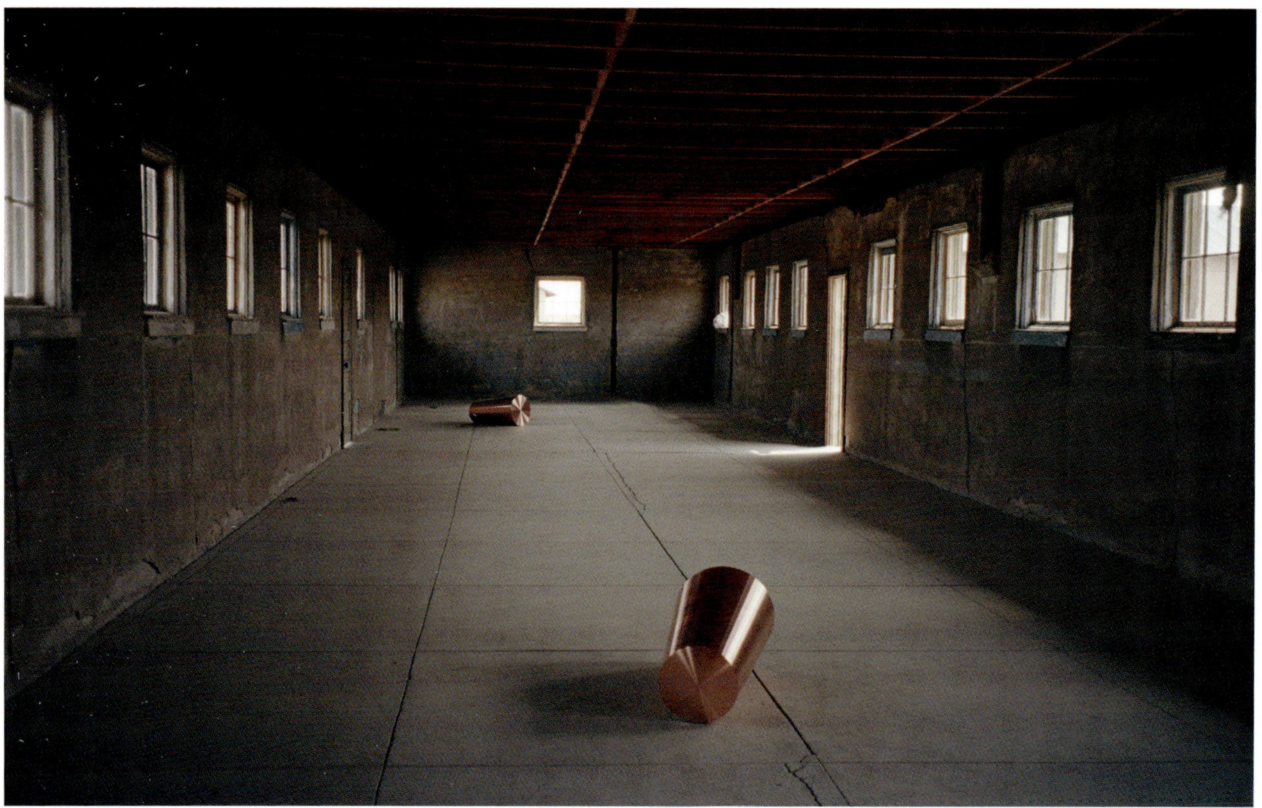

Things That Happen Again: A Here and a There from the series 'Pair Objects', **Roni Horn**, 1986, solid forged and machined copper, each of 2 units: diameter 29.2–43.2 (11½–17 in) and length 89 cm (35 in), installation view at Chianti Foundation, Marfa, Texas

     Intimacy

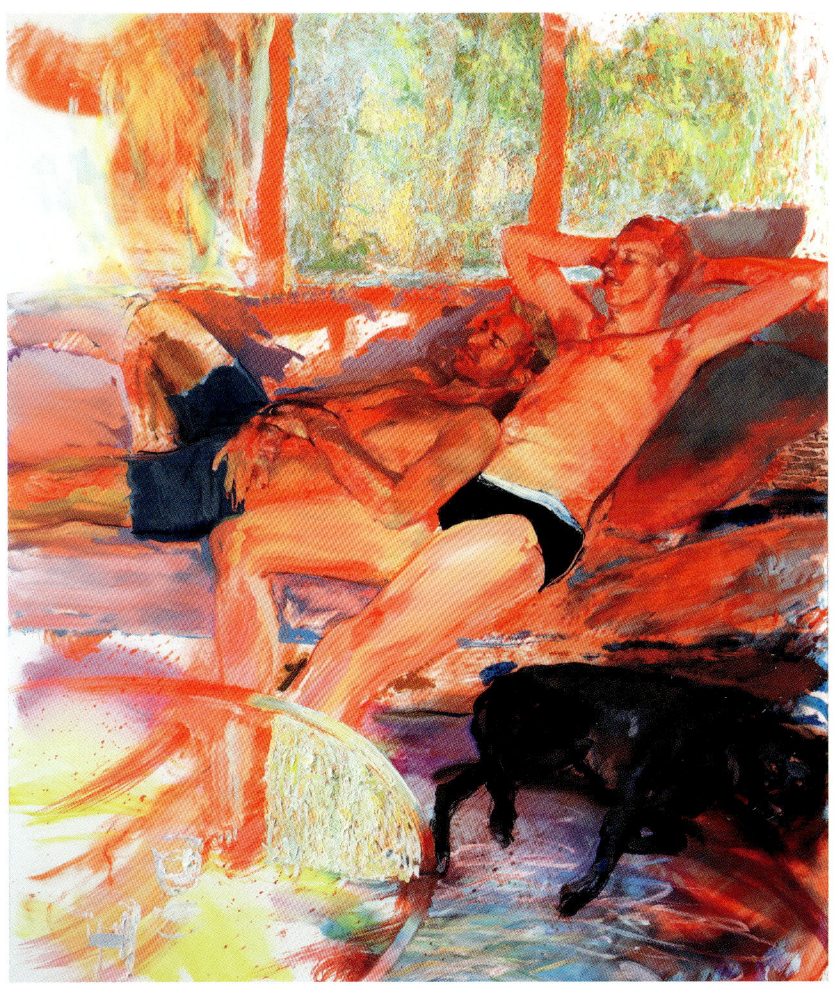

Joe and Edgar, **Doron Langberg**,
2020, oil on linen, 243.8 x 203.2 cm
(96 x 80 in)

Doron Langberg's paintings depict himself and his family, friends and lovers in a celebration of the physicality of touch and queer sensuality. Everyday scenes, rich in luminosity, are set in expressively painted interiors and landscapes. There is an intensity to the human interactions in his work, interactions between subjects and between subject and viewer that explore pleasure, friendship and intimacy. *Joe and Edgar* depicts an artist-couple known for their flag installations on New York's Fire Island and who form a key part of Langberg's close-knit community of emerging queer creatives. Painted from drawings made when the friends shared a summer house on the island, and later appearing as part of Public Art Fund's New York City-wide *Art on the Grid*, a public art exhibition appearing on bus shelters and wifi kiosks, the large-scale painting expresses the richness of queer familial bonds in saturated colour.

Doron Langberg

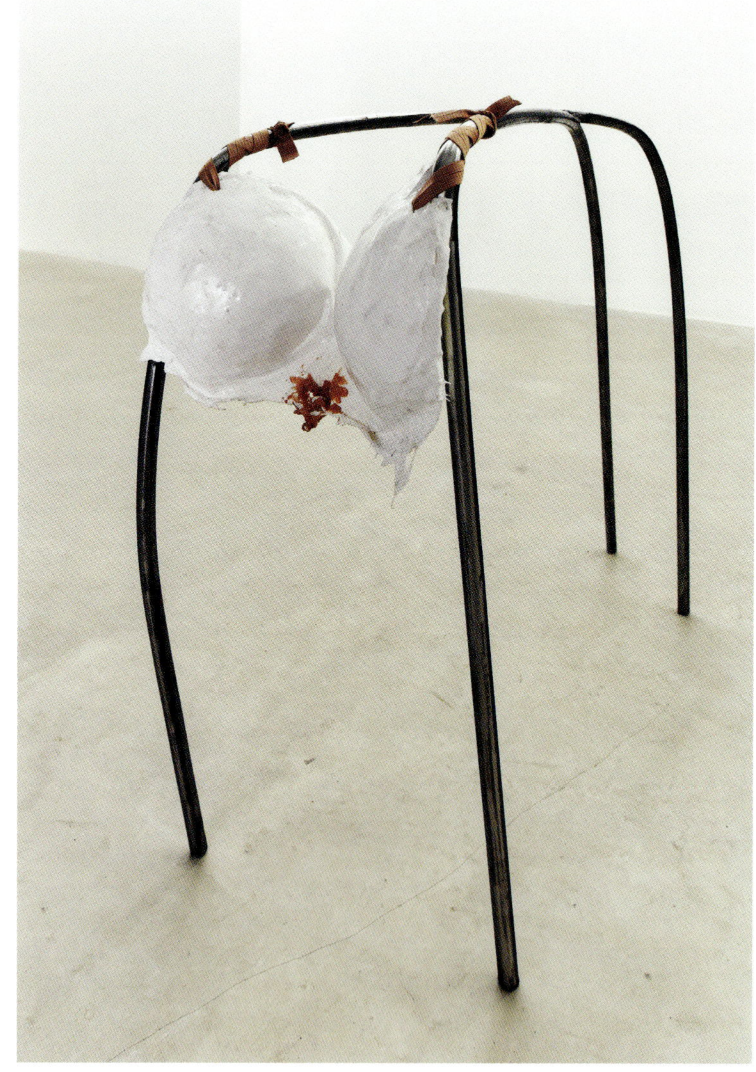

Uh Oh She's a Tourist, **Jesse Darling**, 2017, welded steel, cast silicone and silk ribbon, 87 x 85 x 40 cm (34⅜ x 33½ x 15⅞ in)

Jesse Darling's *Uh Oh She's a Tourist* is a cute animal-like form consisting of a cast silicone bum bound to welded steel legs with silk ballet ribbons. The sculpture assumes a coquettish pose, its white bum hovers in the air with its anus, denoted by a patch of darker silicone, skyward. The artist's intention for a queer reading of the work is apparent in the title, which alludes to sexual tourism. Who 'she' is is open to interpretation and would fit multiple queer tropes: a closeted she, a power bottom, a straight girl messing around. The affectionately satirical nature of the sculpture is typical of Darling's practice, often starting from a point of personal experience to comment or reflect on broader issues impacting society as a whole.

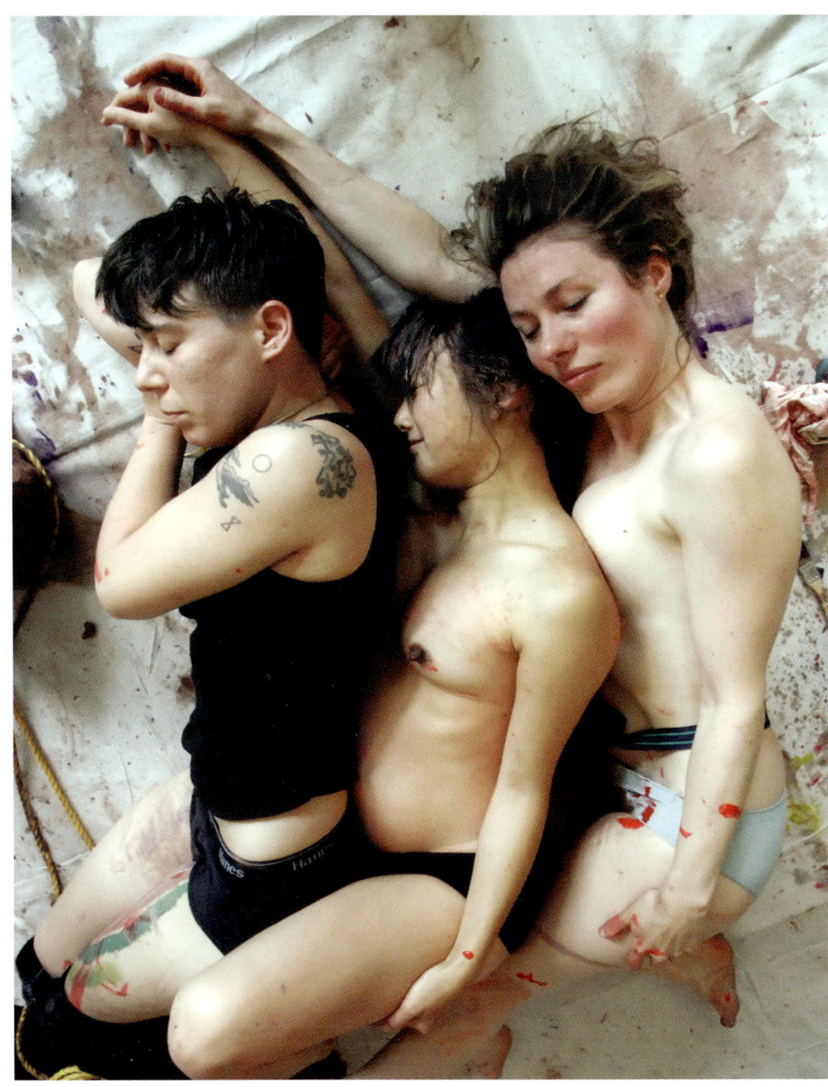

Community Action Center,
A.K. Burns and A.L. Steiner,
2010, SD single-channel video,
(colour, sound), 69 mins

A.K. Burns and A.L. Steiner describe *Community Action Center* as a 69-minute 'sociosexual video'. Centralizing an intergenerational 'womyn-centric community', the making involved more than 50 creative collaborators, such as the poet Eileen Myles and artists Nicole Eisenman and K8 Hardy. An original soundtrack includes new compositions by female musicians and a recitation of Jack Smith's poem 'Normal Love' by the performer Justin Vivian Bond. Inspired by 'porn-romance-liberation films', the artists take us on a journey that traverses the desire spectrum, from repulsion to attraction. Explicit in its sexiness, the film focuses on the body as a sexual organ and sexual creativity as an entire process, rather than simply focusing on sex or genitalia. The artists distributed the film themselves, touring Europe and America and presenting it at arts organizations via large-scale projections or screens that ensured the work took up space. Through a queer feminist lens underpinned by humour and joyful liberation, the project expands our view of how we define sex.

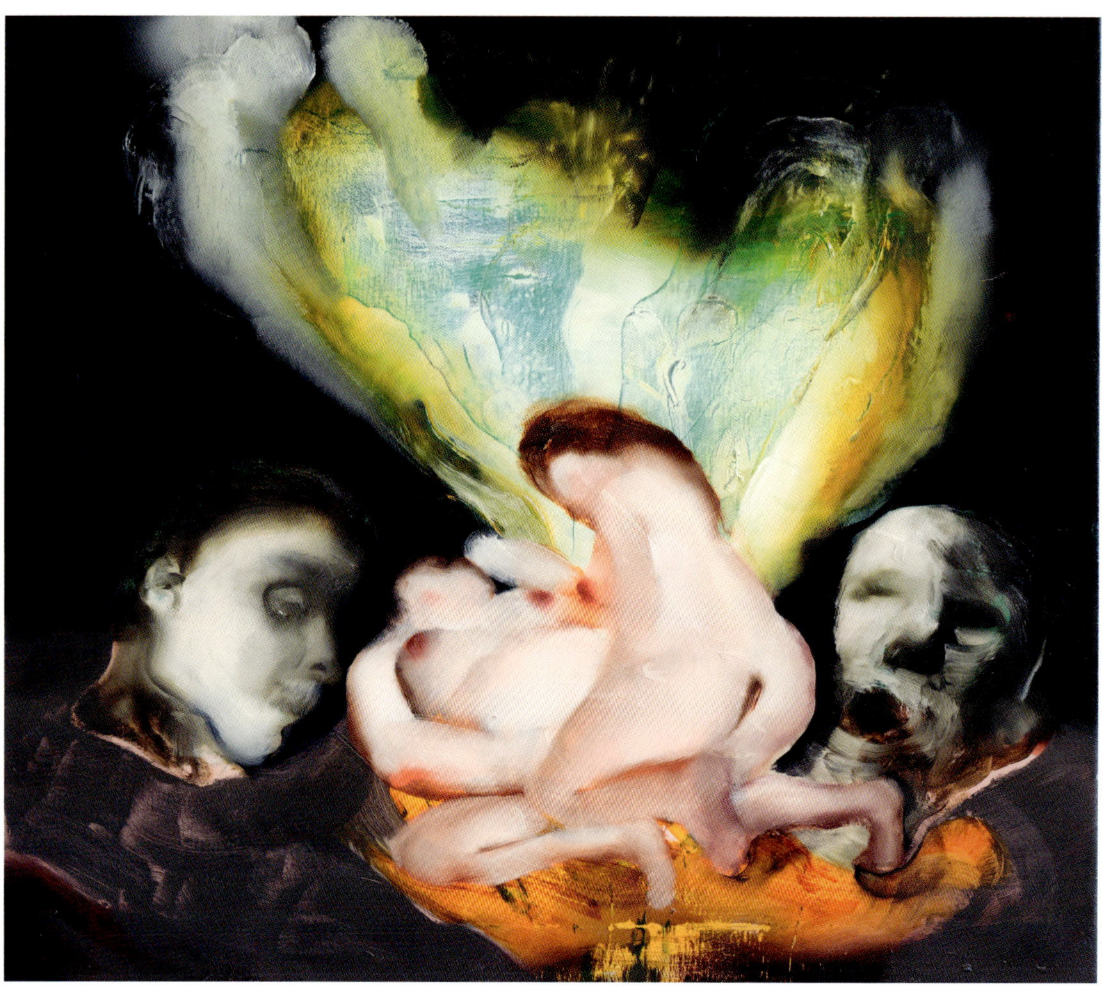

Ambera Wellmann paints complex dark scenes rich with historical references. *You Burn Me* takes its title from Canadian writer Anne Carson's translations of Sappho's poetry. Reflecting the intense and immediate yearning, desire and heartache of the ancient Greek lesbian love poems, the scene is centred around two amorphous figures lost in the throes of passion. As their bodies dissolve into one another, they are oblivious to the dark chaos surrounding them intensified by exposed layers of scraped paint. The two heads emerging from the shadows to ominously watch over the lovers are painted after Théodore Géricault's morgue study

The Severed Heads (1810) made during the French Revolution. The artist explains the painting is about 'situating the possibility of queerness in a context of violence'. Haunted by a deep history of aggression and conflict, the intimacy at the core of the painting provides a grounding force, a moment of meaning and radical resistance amid a burning world.

You Burn Me, **Ambera Wellmann**, 2022, oil on linen, 58.4 x 63.5 cm (23 x 25 in)

Cornel Brudaşcu is known internationally for his involvement with the American pop art movement, particularly for his 1970s portraits of fellow artists, Western pop icons and political figures. In his native Romania, he is celebrated as a leading painter who played a critical role in mentoring the Cluj School, an important group of painters whose loose figuration responded to post-Communist life. Born in 1937, Brudaşcu did not come out as gay until later life, which coincides with homoeroticness beginning to appear in his work. As in this untitled work, Brudaşcu's paintings of male nudes possess an ambiguity, darkness and melancholy suggestive of his own journey of coming to terms with his sexuality. With gestural movement he depicts a confusion of figures and bed sheets tumbling across the canvas in a moment of expressive intimacy.

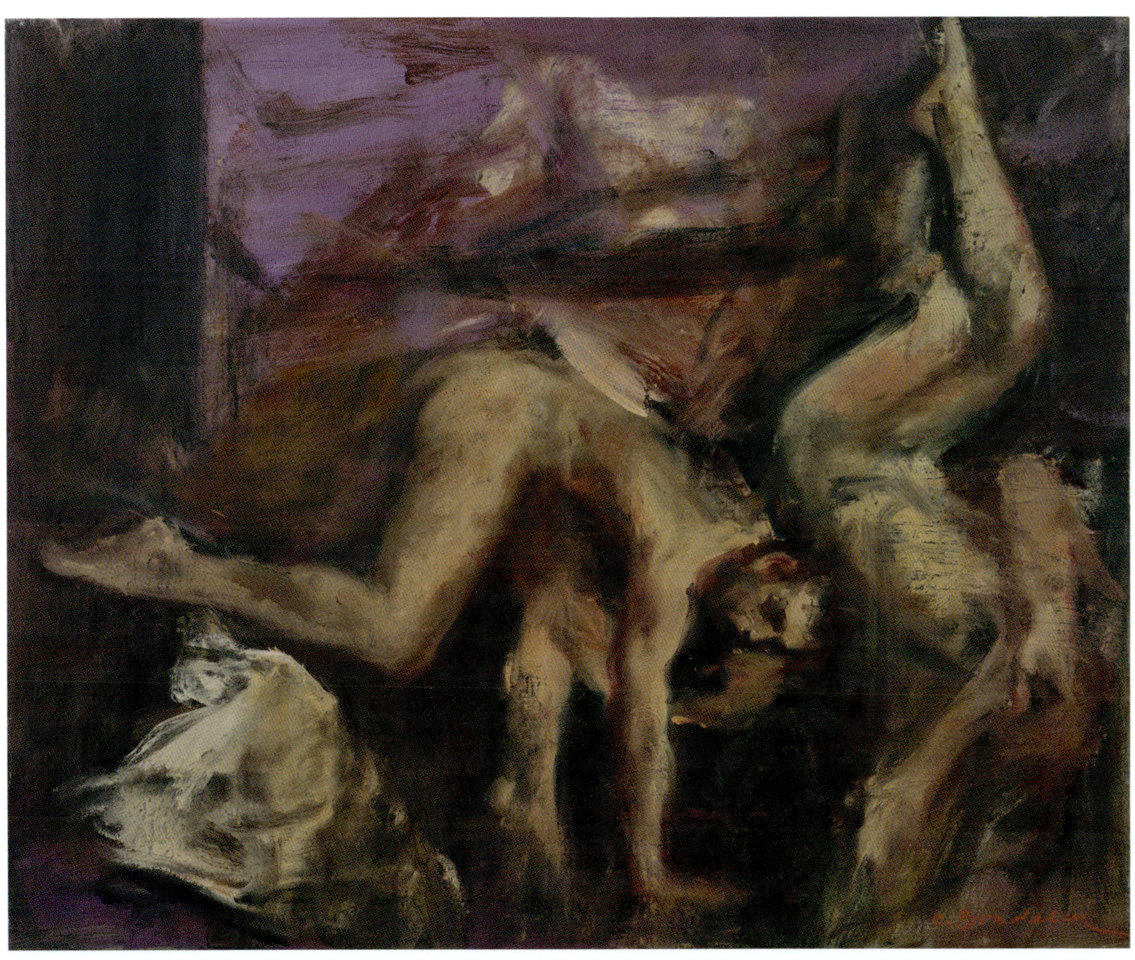

Untitled, **Cornel Brudaşcu**, 2016,
oil on canvas, 50 x 60 cm (20 x 24 in)

Cornel Brudaşcu

Widely considered one of the most significant artists of her time, Nicole Eisenman works in a distinctive style of painting and sculpture that takes inspiration from popular culture and art history. Painted seven years apart, *Night Studio* and *Morning Studio* each depict a pair of lovers, the skin tone of one a fleshy pink, the other a surreal mustard that blends with the makeshift studio bed they recline on. Set against a starry night sky, the figures in *Night Studio* are illuminated by a studio lamp, with books about the artists that inspire Eisenman piled next to the bed, alongside a beer, vitamin water and a pack of cigarettes. In *Morning Studio* the starry night sky appears in the desktop projected on the studio wall and the cigarettes have all been smoked, their butts in a tin on an upturned crate. In both paintings the intertwined couples appear to float through the cosmos, the power of the connection they share in these tender moments rendering everything outside of the studio inconsequential.

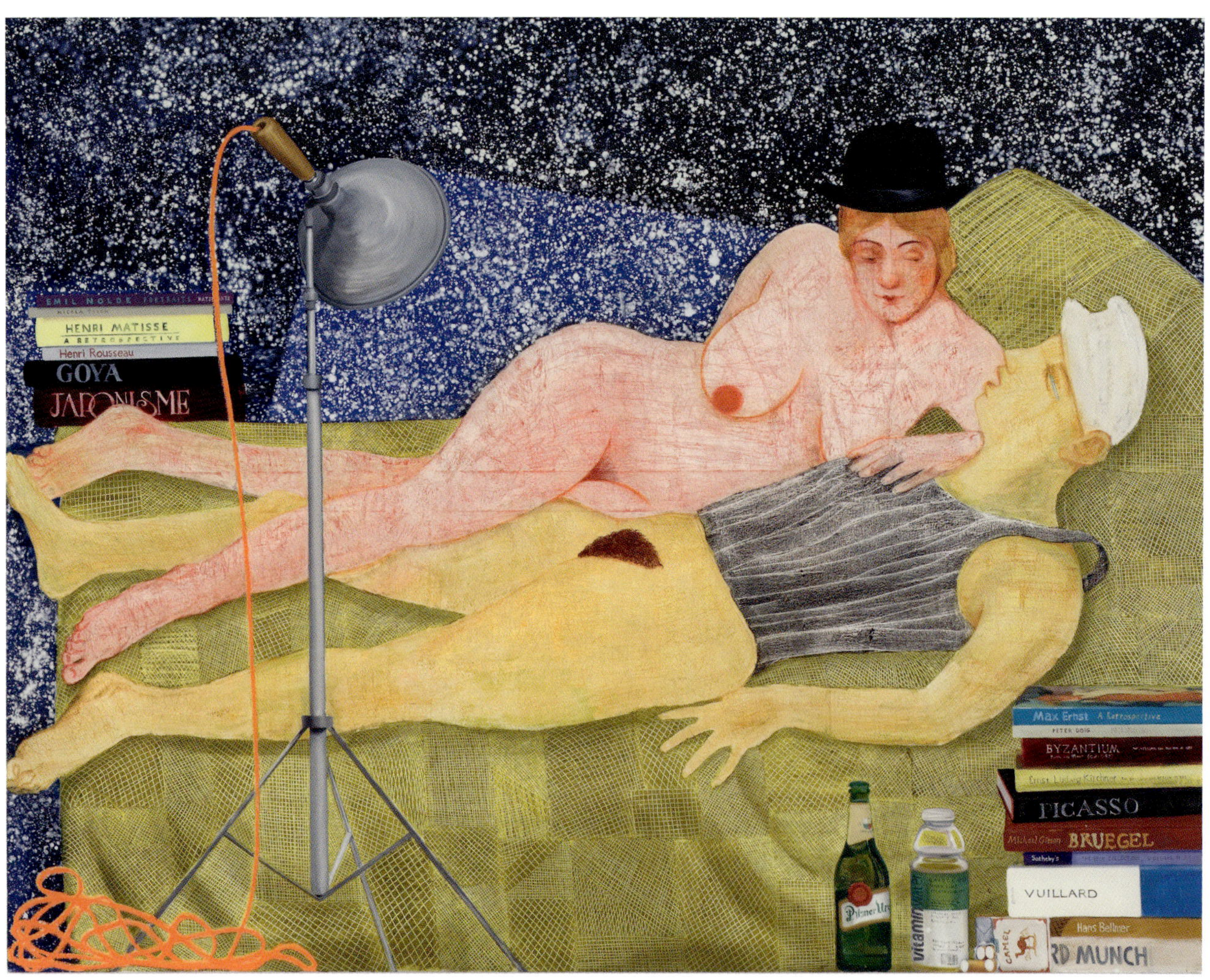

Opposite: *Night Studio*, **Nicole Eisenman**, 2009, oil on canvas, 165.1 x 208.3 cm (65 x 82 in); below: *Morning Studio*, **Nicole Eisenman**, 2016, oil on canvas, 167.6 x 210.8 cm (66 x 83 in)

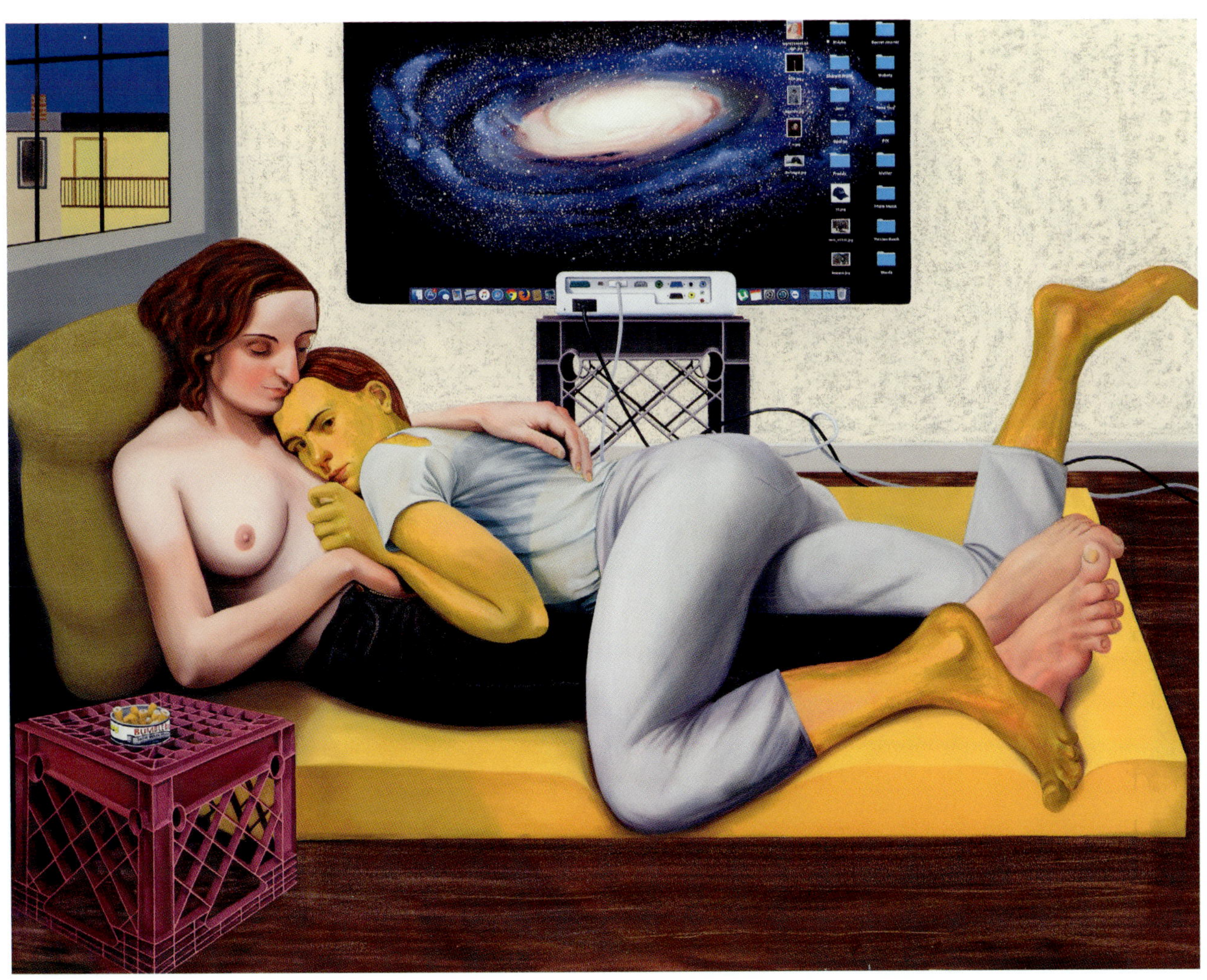

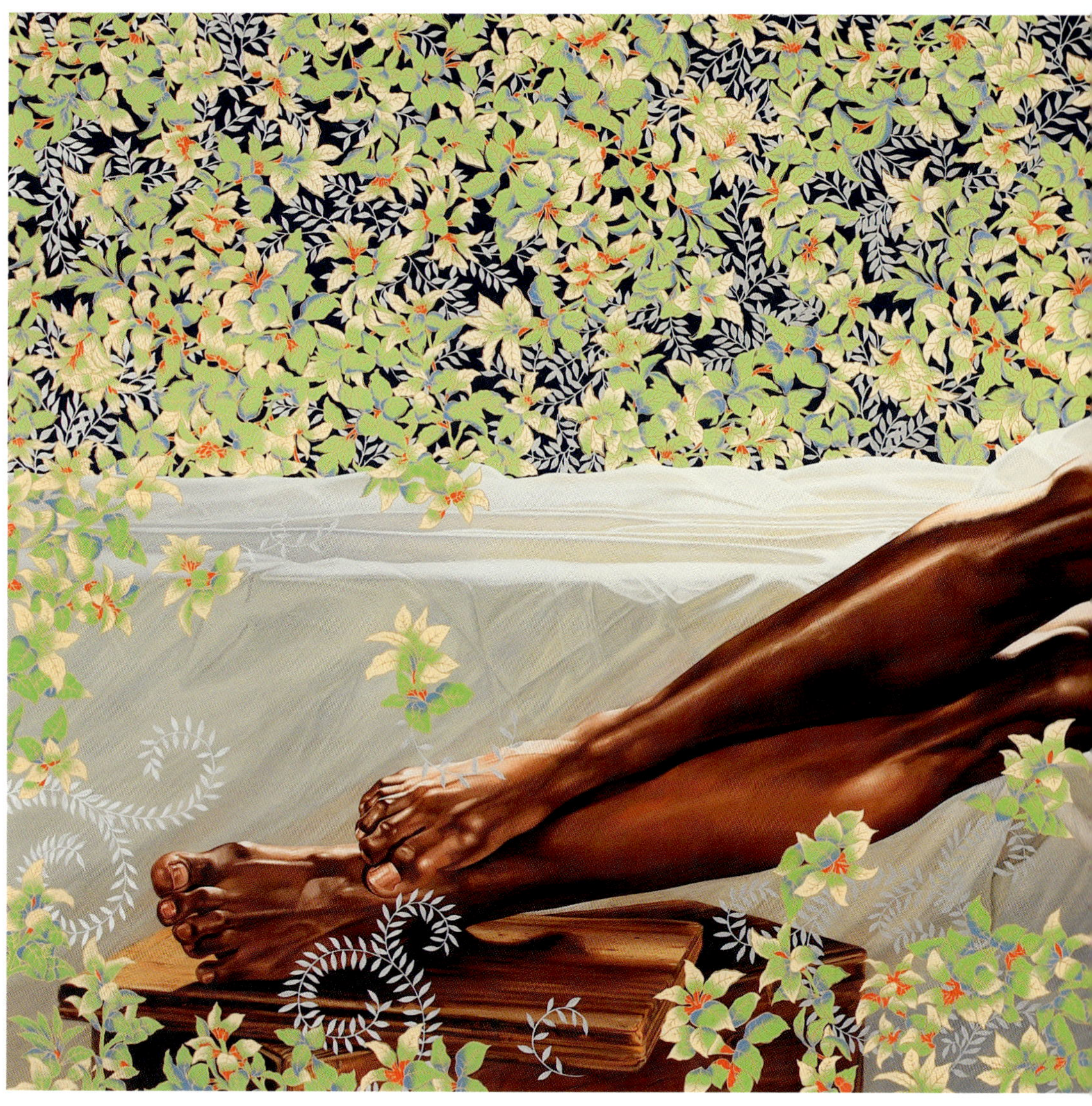

Kehinde Wiley's work is widely celebrated. He is best known for portraits of people of colour in the traditional settings of old master paintings. In 2018 he painted Barack Obama and became the first African American artist to be commissioned by the National Portrait Gallery to paint an official US presidential portrait. This monumental painting, *Sleep*, situates a contemporary Black figure in a classical pose, drawn directly from a *c.*1771 painting of the same name by Jean-Bernard Restout. It is part of a body of work featuring models in their late teens and early twenties, who were found in Downtown Brooklyn via the artist's infamous street casting method. The breathtaking scale of these paintings venerates subjects who have otherwise been invisible within the canon of painting. As a gay man Wiley approaches his subject with tenderness, every detail of the reclining nude is rendered with exquisite beauty, admiration and respect.

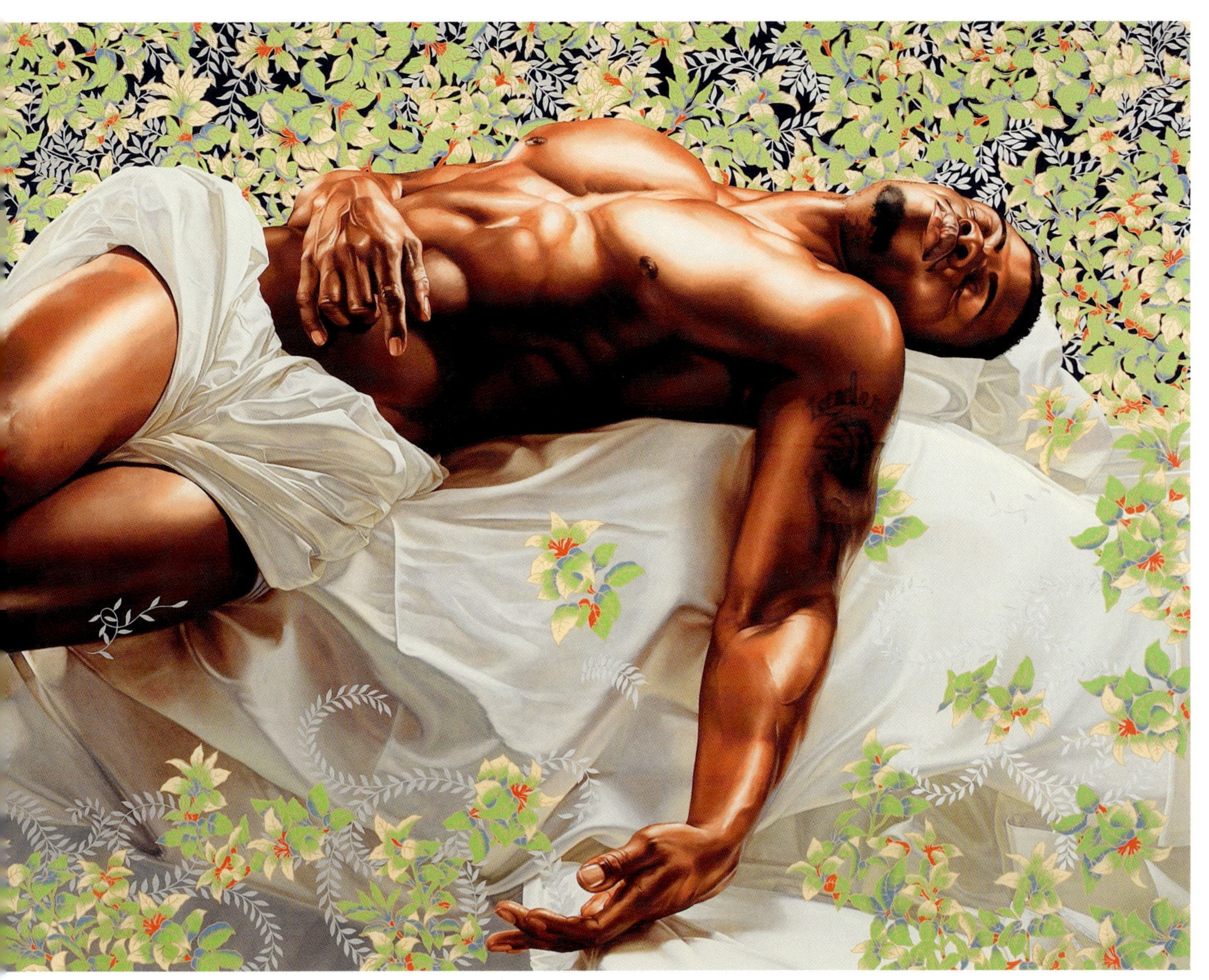

Sleep, **Kehinde Wiley**, 2008, oil on
canvas, 335.3 x 762 cm (132 x 300 in)

Survival

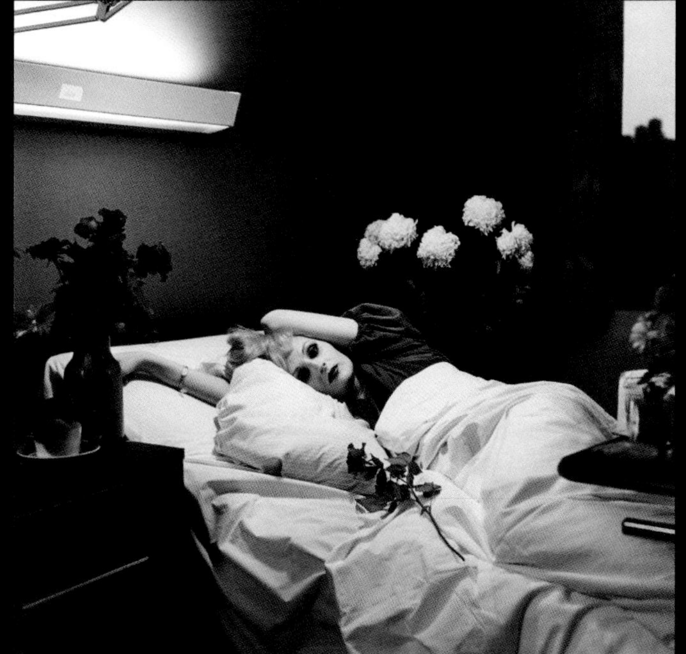

Candy Darling on Her Deathbed,
Peter Hujar, 1973

Living in a society that doesn't fully recognize or support you decreases your chances of survival. LGBTQIA+ people have been discriminated against throughout history. Today, in many areas of the world they are unrepresented and excluded from mainstream society, and even criminalized by laws targeting homosexual acts and gender nonconformity. Simply living openly and authentically becomes dangerous, putting queer people at risk of violence and murder. Existing within a world that considers your very nature unnatural or doesn't even acknowledge your existence can lead to trauma, mental health challenges and spiritual suffering, manifesting in high rates of addiction, self-harm and suicide among the queer community.

In the 1980s a new virus that became known as HIV/AIDS swept through the LGBTQIA+ community. As people became critically unwell and eventually died, their odds of survival were terrifyingly low as governments in the US and Europe failed to respond to the crisis. Many brilliant queer artists who died at very young ages from HIV/AIDS-related causes were prolific in their output before their artistic careers were cut short. Their art reflects on the feelings of abandonment, frustration and fear experienced by the community; the death of their friends and loved ones and their own illnesses and impending deaths.

The legacy of queer creatives lost to too soon endures in their work, in the retelling of their stories and in lives captured on film. The power of collaboration runs strong in the queer community; artists support and celebrate their peers and document shared histories, ensuring their work lives on and continues to inspire future generations. Candy Darling, the American actress and muse of Andy Warhol, was photographed on her death bed by Peter Hujar (see opposite), in a full face of makeup and surrounded by roses as the fearless trans superstar she's remembered as.

The new challenges that come with contemporary queer survival and the experiences of those fighting to stay alive are expressed through art. As different areas of the world are slower to make human rights progress, people are forced to flee their home countries in the name of survival, and in the West, new groups within the community are targeted, but often with the same old narratives and accusations. Culture wars have become gender wars, positioning trans and non-binary people as a danger to society, exacerbating their position as the most vulnerable in society, and queer and trans people of colour continue to face intersectional discrimination. As Deborah Kass's artwork (see left) suggests, the simple act of being alive is to defy the odds. Harnessing queer resilience and finding ways to survive and thrive, to find joy, love and connection is a powerful political act in itself.

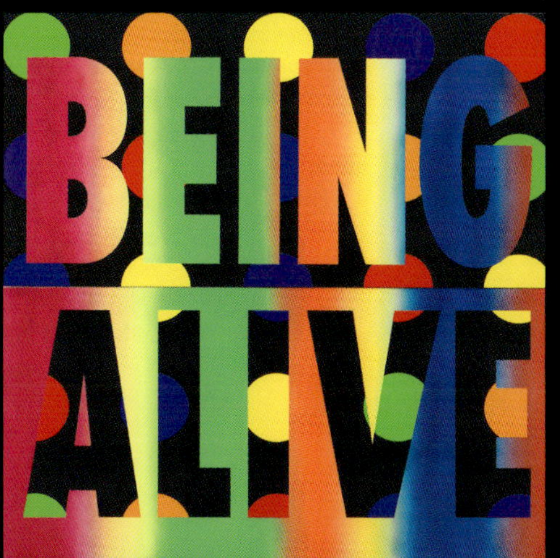

David Wojnarowicz's acclaimed artwork *Untitled (One Day This Kid)* pictures the artist as a happy child posing for a school photo, full of hope for the future. Made with an early projection photocopier known as a photostat, the image of the unsuspecting child is surrounded by text outlining the destructive consequences of homophobia that will impact his life as he grows up to discover 'he desires to place his naked body on the naked body of another boy'. The artist's black-and-white juxtaposition of childhood innocence and the harm caused by prejudice calls for real change, which starts with the personal.

One day this kid will get larger. One day this kid will come to know something that causes a sensation equivalent to the separation of the earth from its axis. One day this kid will reach a point where he senses a division that isn't mathematical. One day this kid will feel something stir in his heart and throat and mouth. One day this kid will find something in his mind and body and soul that makes him hungry. One day this kid will do something that causes men who wear the uniforms of priests and rabbis, men who inhabit certain stone buildings, to call for his death. One day politicians will enact legislation against this kid. One day families will give false information to their children and each child will pass that information down generationally to their families and that information will be designed to make existence intolerable for this kid. One day this kid will begin to experience all this activity in his environment and that activity and information will compell him to commit suicide or submit to danger in hopes of being murdered or submit to silence and invisibility. Or one day this kid will talk. When he begins to talk, men who develop a fear of this kid will attempt to silence him with strangling, fists, prison, suffocation, rape, intimidation, drugging, ropes, guns, laws, menace, roving gangs, bottles, knives, religion, decapitation, and immolation by fire. Doctors will pronounce this kid curable as if his brain were a virus. This kid will lose his constitutional rights against the government's invasion of his privacy. This kid will be faced with electro-shock, drugs, and conditioning therapies in laboratories tended by psychologists and research scientists. He will be subject to loss of home, civil rights, jobs, and all conceivable freedoms. All this will begin to happen in one or two years when he discovers he desires to place his naked body on the naked body of another boy.

Untitled (One Day This Kid),
David Wojnarowicz, 1990–1991,
photostat and silkscreened text,
78.1 x 104.1 cm (30¾ x 41 in)

Death Drop, 1973, **Mark Bradford**,
1973, single-channel video, no audio,
20-second loop

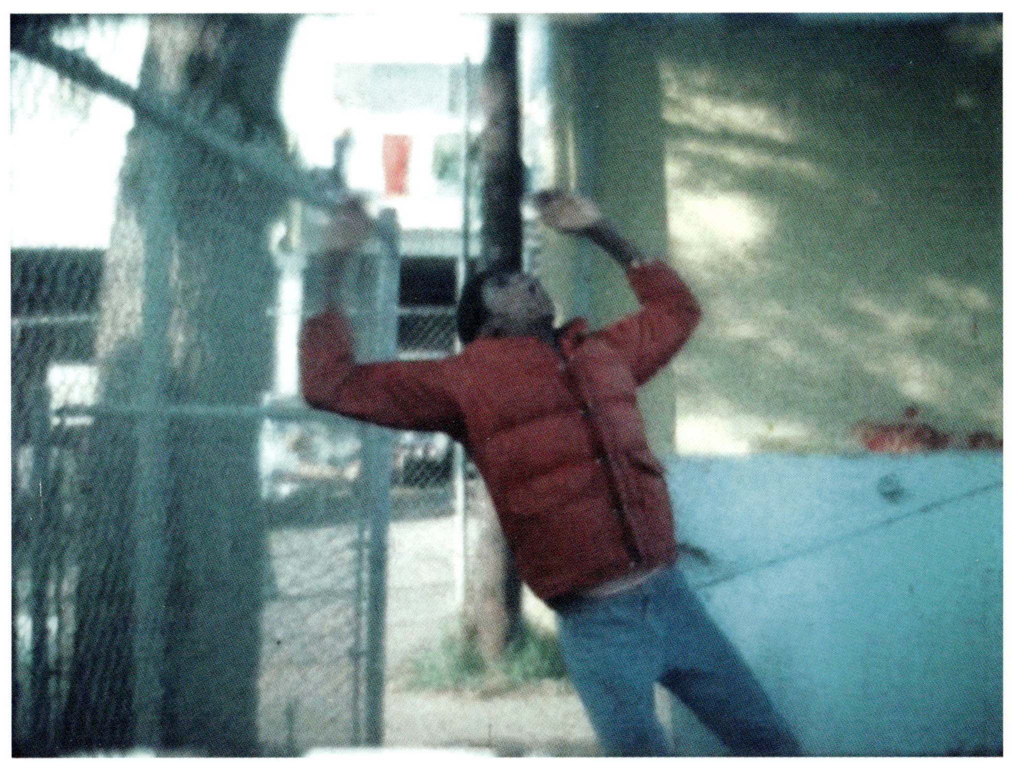

Mark Bradford's video *Death Drop, 1973* is
a 20-second loop of footage taken from a
Super 8 home movie that he directed and
starred in at the age of 12. The slow-motion
clip, which plays in silence, features the young
artist falling to the ground, arms flung high,
as if struck by a bullet. Each time the loop
begins again the figure appears upright,
only to be knocked down by some invisible
force that repeatedly and relentlessly throws
him to his feet. The motion resembles the
'dip' dance move that originated in ballroom
spaces and has come to be known as a 'death
drop' in popular queer culture. The piece
demonstrates the artist's awareness, even
from a very young age, of the vulnerability
of Black queer bodies. Here we see the
ongoing threat of violence turned on its
head in a poignant declaration of resistance
and resilience.

"Untitled" (Portrait of Ross in L.A.) is one of 20 'Candy Works' made by Felix Gonzalez-Torres in the 1990s, most of which are on display in major museums around the world. A sprawling pile of candies in brightly coloured wrappers sits in the corner of the gallery; as visitors take them away to eat, the candies are replenished. The work's title refers to the artist's partner Ross Laycock who had died in 1991 from AIDS-related complications; five years later Gonzalez-Torres succumbed to the same illness. The installation instructions state that the dimensions of the artwork may vary but the ideal weight of the candy should be 79.4 kg (175 lbs), the average weight of a healthy American adult male in the 1990s. By offering us the chance to interact with this deeply personal artwork, Gonzalez-Torres asks us to consider loss and our own sense of collective responsibility, and the endless supply of candy speaks to an everlasting love and queer resilience.

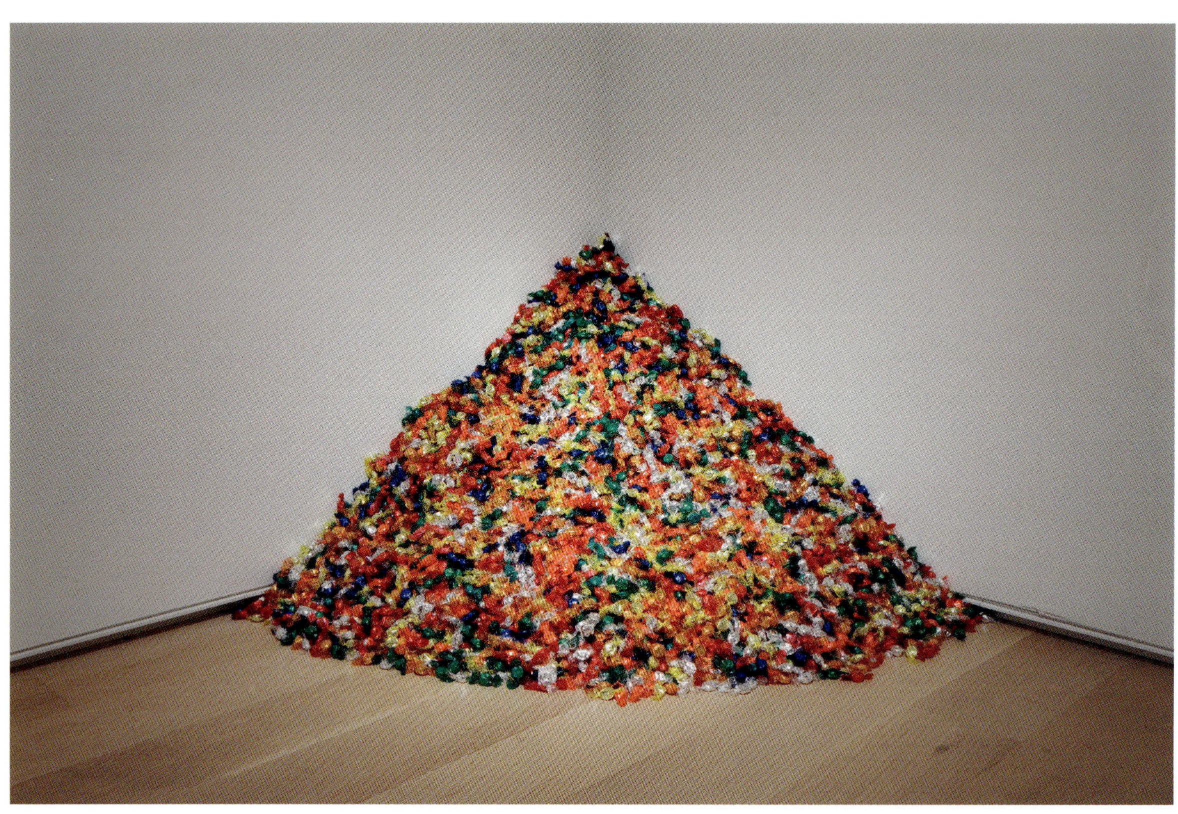

"Untitled" (Portrait of Ross in L.A.), **Felix Gonzalez-Torres**, 1991, candies in variously coloured wrappers, endless supply, overall dimensions vary with installation (ideal weight 79.4 kg /175 lbs), installation view, Art Institute of Chicago, 2010

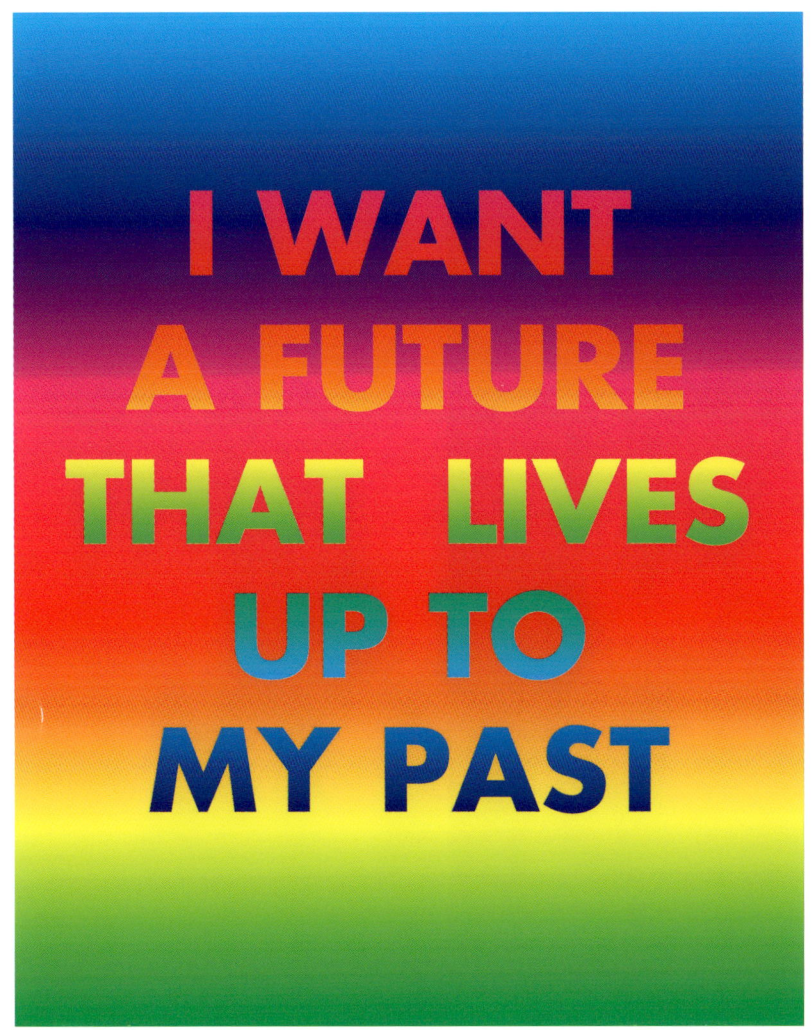

I want a future that lives up to my past
from the series 'Rainbow Aphorisms',
David McDiarmid, 1994

I want a future that lives up to my past is part of a 31-piece laser print series titled 'Rainbow Aphorisms' made by David McDiarmid between 1993 and his death from AIDS-related illnesses in 1995. The Australian artist and designer, who had his beginnings in activism with the Melbourne Gay Liberation Group, applied his political outlook to his creative work, which tackled queer identity and history. Inspired by Gilbert Baker's 1978 Rainbow Flag, which had become a symbol for gay people around the world, the computer-generated images superimpose bold sans-serif statements over vibrant colours. Ranging from a witty take on the tabloid media's vitriolic AIDS-related headlines to melancholy reflections, the aphorisms speak directly to the complex emotions of being fatally ill and the wider realities of the gay male experience in the 1990s.

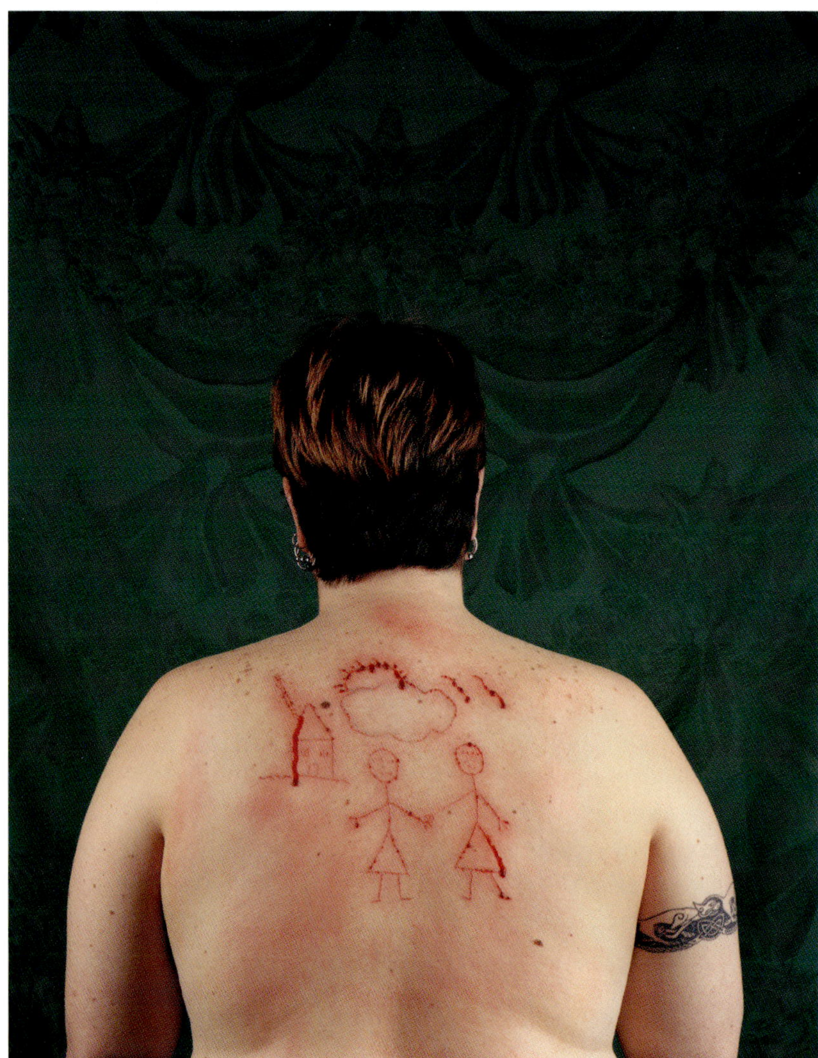

Catherine Opie

Catherine Opie made *Self-Portrait/Cutting* in 1993, the year she began her photographic series 'Portraits', which features members of her community, particularly lesbians, dykes, non-binary and transmasc figures. In the 1990s, Opie's approach to queer visibility – treating each of her subjects with a sensitivity, respect and sense of empowerment – was at odds with mainstream portrayals of LGBTQIA+ people in the United States. In this self-portrait Opie boldly places herself at the centre of the image: her own vulnerability and longing are revealed as both painful and hopeful.

Referencing her involvement in BDSM, she challenges the demonization of the leather community and confronts the notion that her sexuality is at odds with her desire to live and thrive routinely. Opie revisited *Self-Portrait/Cutting* in two later self-portraits that use the same formal qualities of sixteenth-century European portrait painting: *Self-Portrait/Pervert* (1994) and *Self-Portrait/Nursing* (2004). The suite of photographs played a critical role in bringing a dialogue around the queer experience to mainstream culture and continues to influence and inspire many contemporary artists.

With poignant realism and perfected composition, Jess T. Dugan's 'To Survive on This Shore' takes us into the lives of transgender and gender non-conforming American older adults. Bringing together photography and interviews, in collaboration with social worker and academic Vanessa Fabbre, Dugan tackles the lack of representation and advocacy for the trans community. *SueZie, 51, and Cheryl, 55, Valrico, FL* depicts the unbreakable bond shared by a couple of 20 years whose interview reflects on the improvement to their lives following SueZie's transition from male to female. Over a five-year period, Dugan and Fabbre sought out subjects whose lived experiences exist within the complex intersections of gender identity, age, race, ethnicity, sexuality, socioeconomic class and geographic location. By travelling from coast to coast, the pair created a much-needed historical record of survival outside the confines of binary gender in America.

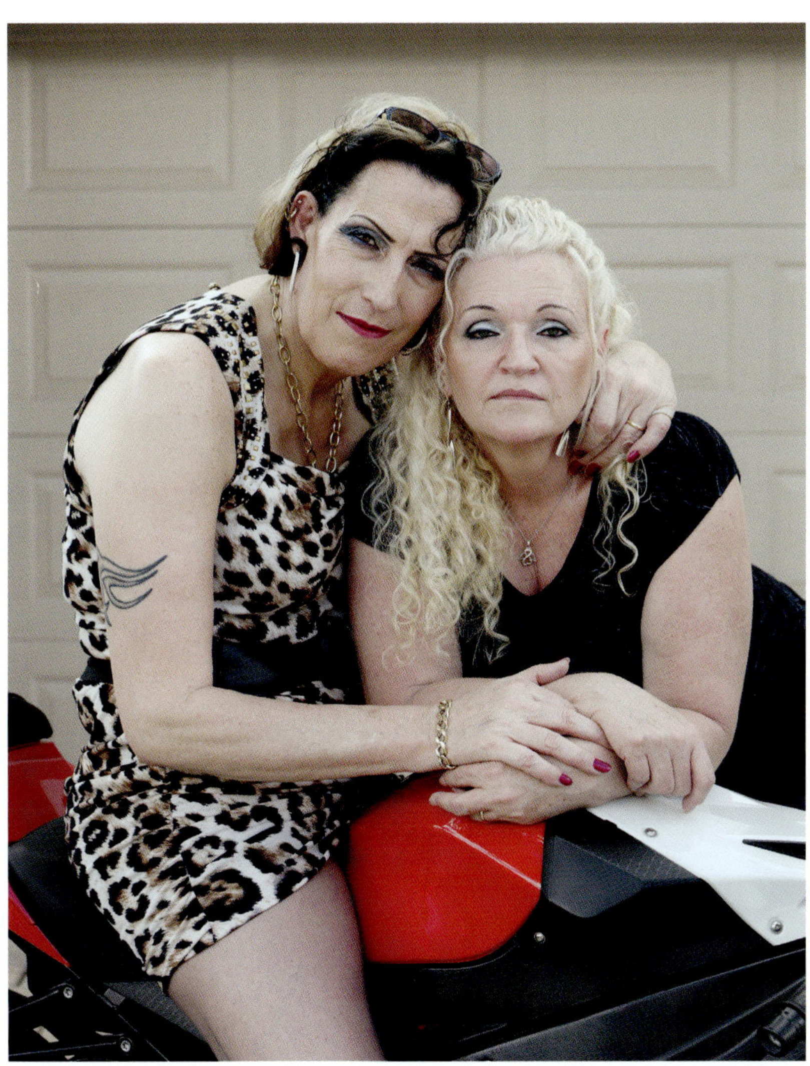

SueZie, 51, and Cheryl, 55, Valrico, FL from 'To Survive on This Shore: Photographs and Interviews with Transgender and Gender Nonconforming Older Adults', **Jess T. Dugan**, 2015, archival pigment print, 101.6 x 76.2 cm (40 x 30 in)

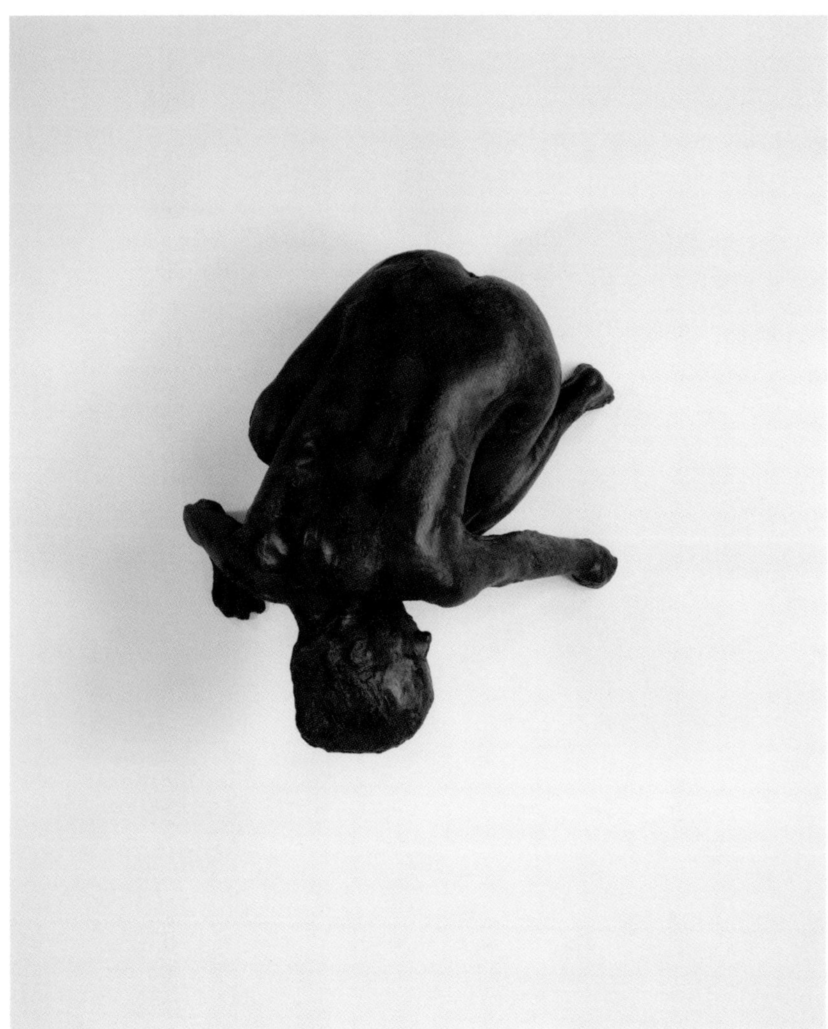

Lilith, **Kiki Smith**, 1994, silicone bronze and glass, 83.8 x 69.6 x 48.3 cm (33 x 27½ x 19 in)

Kiki Smith

Kiki Smith has been a prominent artist since the 1980s exploring embodiment and the natural world through her multidisciplinary practice. Her bronze sculpture *Lilith* hangs upside down, staring at viewers with piercing blue glass eyes. Lilith is a figure from Jewish folklore, a demonic female made from the same soil as Adam – unlike Eve who was made from his rib – who refused to be subservient to him and chose to leave the Garden of Eden. Smith harnesses the powerful and dangerous female sexuality from this ancient projection of woman, presenting her in animalistic form, crouched on all fours, empowered by her primal instincts. The figure presents a new way of looking at the female body that transcends socially prescriptive notions of gender and sexuality.

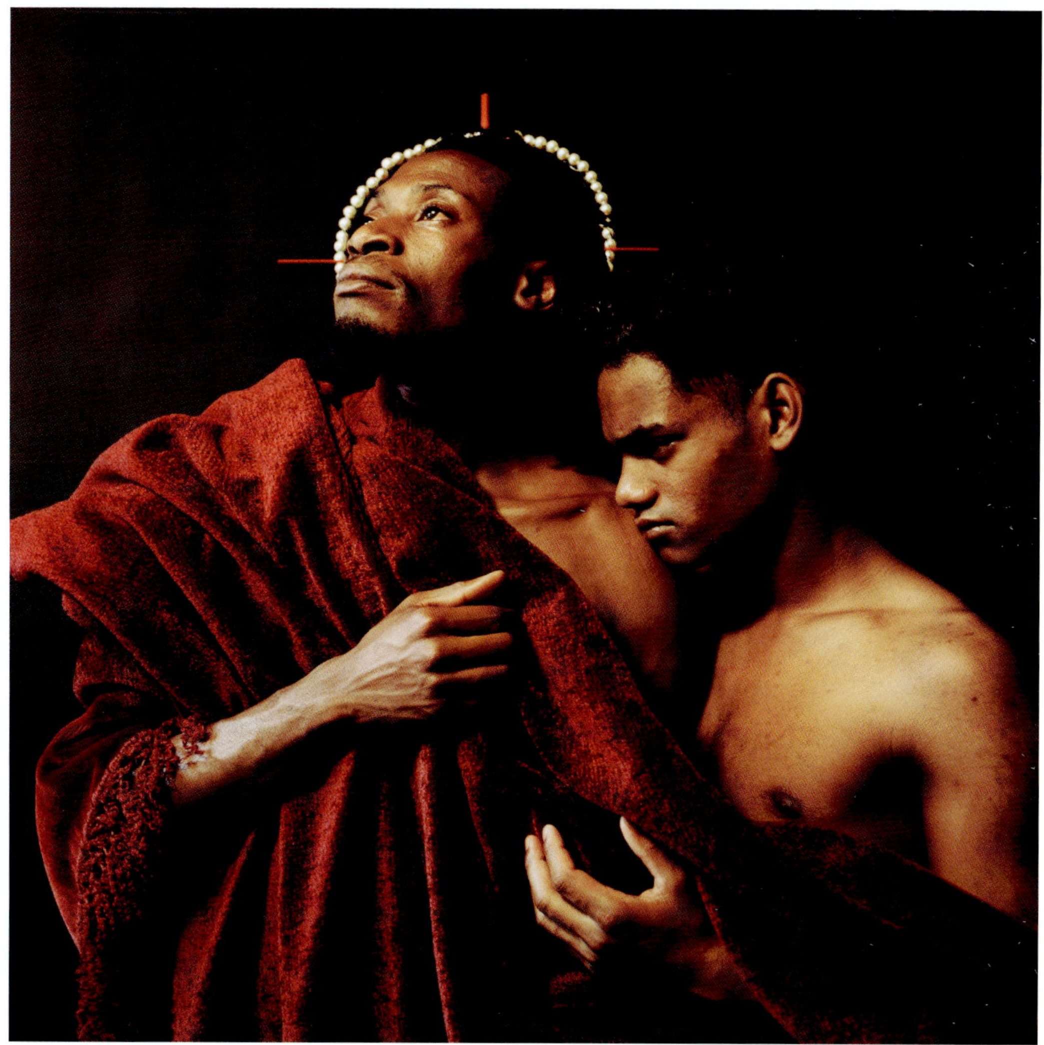

Made during the global AIDS epidemic and in the last year of his life, Rotimi Fani-Kayode's *Every Moment Counts* brought Black gay men to the forefront at a time of increased homophobia and racism in Margaret Thatcher's Britain, where the work was made. Part of the 1989 series of coloured prints 'Ecstatic Antibodies', the image introduces us to the 'technique of ecstasy' as two figures share a tender embrace adorned with references to Christian and Yoruba iconography. After fleeing a military coup in Nigeria, Fani-Kayode moved to Brighton, UK and later studied in the United States, before returning to the UK and becoming a member of the Brixton Artists Collective and cofounder of the Association of Black Photographers (now known as Autograph) in London. With his captivating and radical imagery, Fani-Kayode was able to make his mark on history before his death at only 34 years old.

Every Moment Counts from the series 'Ecstatic Antibodies', **Rotimi Fani-Kayode**, 1989, archival C-type print, 50.8 x 61 cm (20 x 24 in)

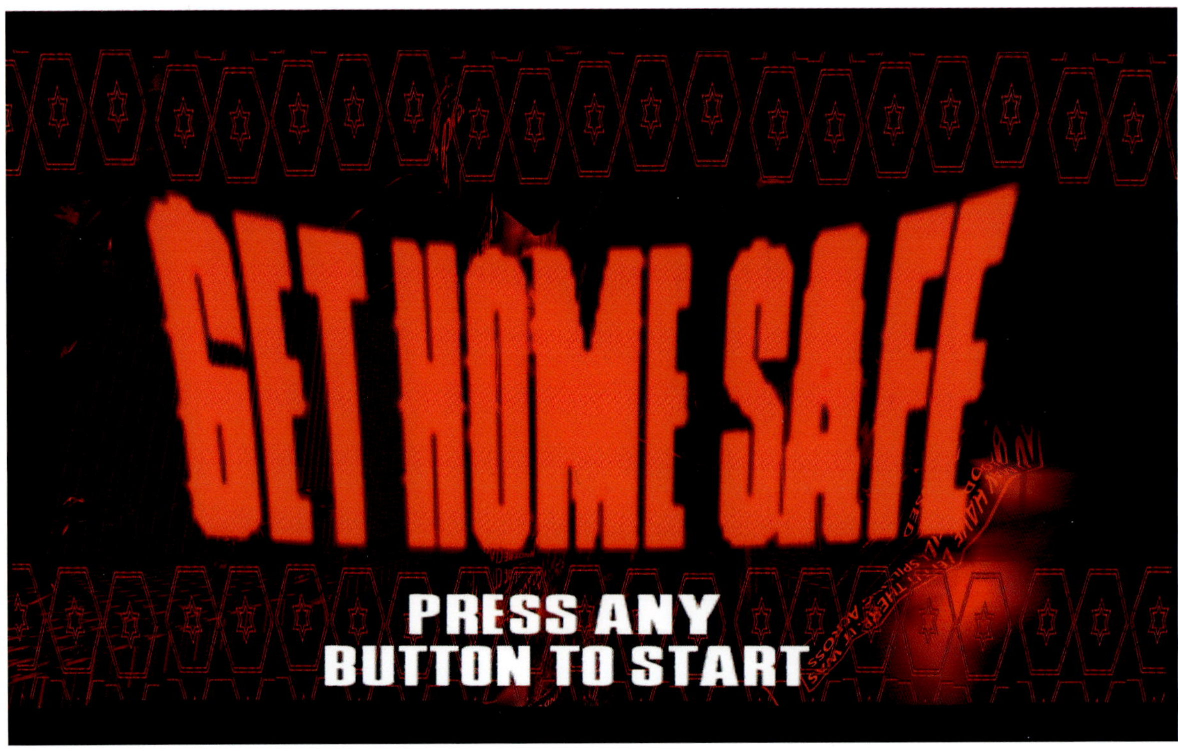

Describing herself as a 'virtua trans myst artist', Danielle Brathwaite-Shirley's work usually takes the form of video games. Taking the word 'myst' from a gaming franchise that inspires her aesthetic, Brathwaite-Shirley has adopted the term to describe a mist that appears in her own games as a protective force for Black trans life. Channelling her passion and activism into the art of archiving Black trans lives, she creates worlds that promote the health, safety and wellbeing of her community. *Get Home Safe* is an interactive work that asks what it means to get home safe when your safety is not guaranteed. Navigating the streets alone at night, as you quicken your pace, look over your shoulder and grip your keys in your pocket, you consider what needs to change for the outside world to become a safe space for Black trans people.

     Survival

Rindon Johnson is an artist and poet whose work, which moves between physical object-based works and immersive virtual space, is rooted in language. Questioning assumed realities, he explores the impact of capitalism, climate and technology on how we see and construct ourselves and navigate the world around us. *I First You (11/11)* is a digitally rendered film in which the viewer spins across a hilly glass island situated within a placid sea. The landscape is haunted by disembodied anonymous heads, bouncing eyeballs, indecipherable floating animals and architectural remnants – monuments to another time or fragments with which to rebuild. Accompanied by an ominous soundscape, Johnson sentimentally recounts tender stories of queer resilience. As his soft voice describes the sanctuary of a lover's bed, a stark contrast to the sparse and unpredictable terrain, he proclaims 'Let them come for us, we will step out of the way'.

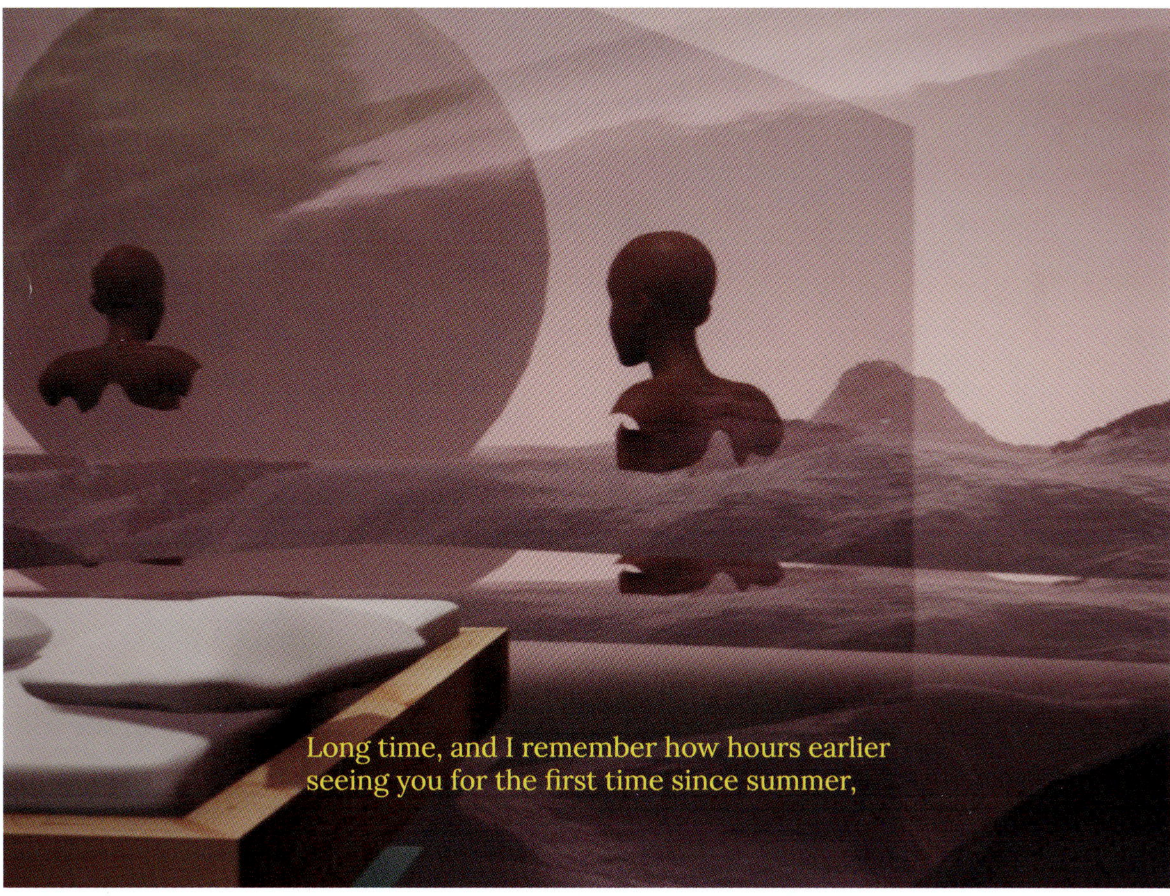

I First You (11/11), **Rindon Johnson**, 2018,
digitally rendered film, 5 mins 28 secs

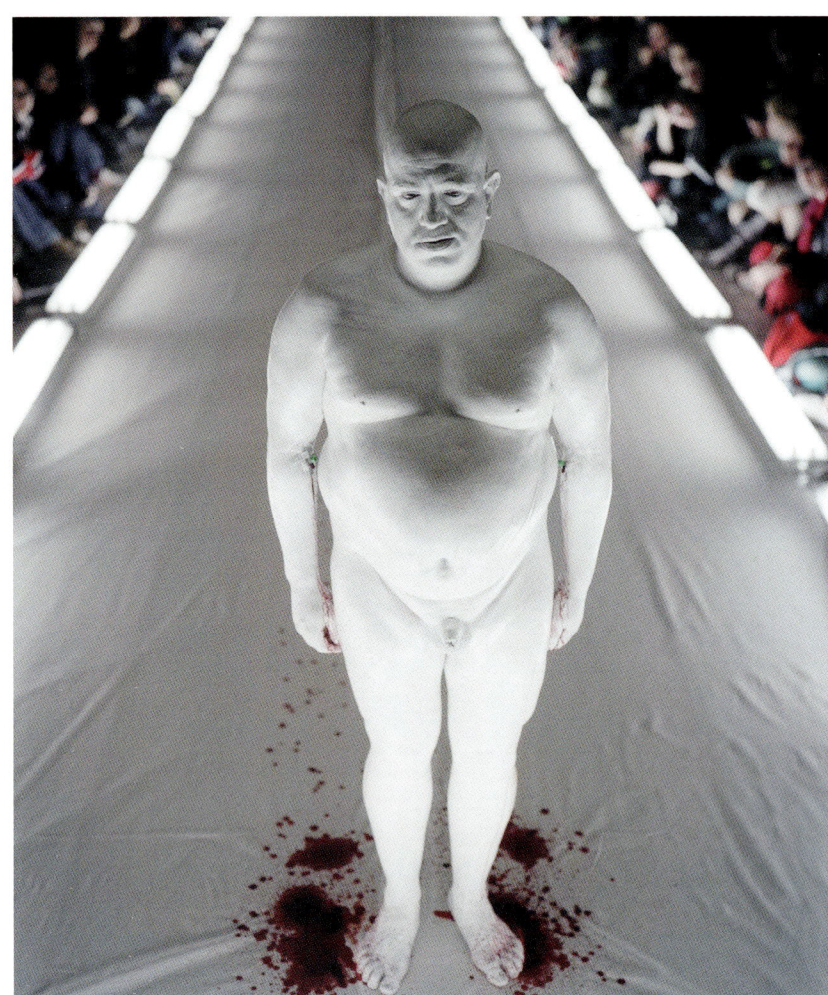

I Miss You, **Franko B**, 1999–2005, performance at Palais des Beaux Arts, Brussels, Belgium, 2005

Franko B rose to prominence in the 1990s with his performance and body-based work that often involved the process of bloodletting. First performed in 1999 in Antwerp, *I Miss You* sees his completely naked heavily tattooed and pierced body painted white walking the length of a white canvas catwalk, bleeding from his cannulated arms until he is too weak to continue. He subtly pumps his fists to increase the flow of blood, which pours down his body staining the canvas below. Through the visceral performance, the audience is confronted with the pain and fragility of the human body. Tapping into the childhood trauma of his Italian Catholic roots, which he excavates, shares and releases through his work, and addressing the fear and stigma attached to blood and the queer body following the AIDS epidemic, the artist uses the ritualized violation of his own body to take back control and assert his own lived experience.

Franko B

Although she only produced a small amount of work before her untimely death at the age of 32, Tessa Boffin's photography had an important role to play in queer art of the late 1980s and early 1990s. A leading lesbian artist of the period, her work addresses queer desire and LGBTQIA+ representation, centralizing women and gender non-conformity. Under the care of friend and fellow photographer Sunil Gupta, Boffin's photographic archive was posthumously reprinted in 2023, 30 years after her death, receiving long overdue public attention. *Untitled #5* is part of the five-part series 'Angelic Rebels: Lesbians and Safer Sex', which celebrates female sexuality and promotes safe sex. Bringing together religious iconography and bondage, the harnessed angels challenge the notion of lesbian 'purity' during the AIDS epidemic, presenting a powerful reminder that queer women are also at risk of the disease.

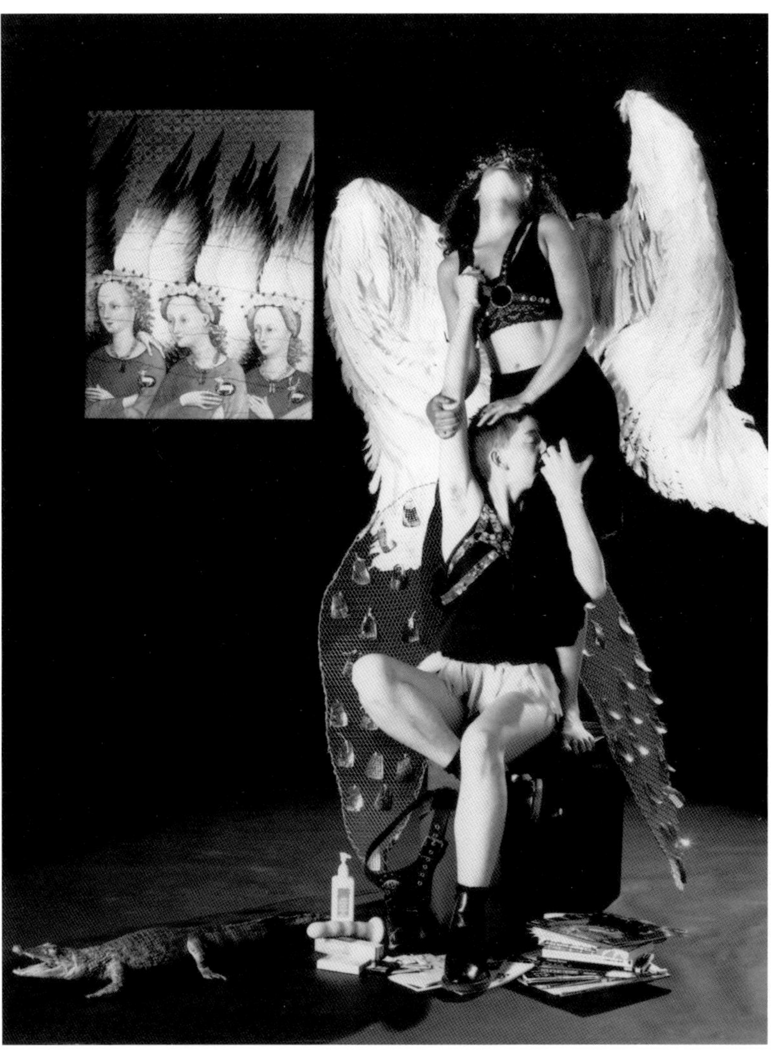

Untitled #5 from the series
'Angelic Rebels: Lesbians and Safer Sex',
Tessa Boffin, 1989, archival inkjet print:
89.3 x 70.6 cm (35⅛ x 27¾ in),
paper: 111.5 x 76.2 cm (43⅞ x 30 in)

Maggi Hambling's *Wilde and the Wallpaper* is a portrait of Oscar Wilde, who has appeared in her paintings throughout her long career. His expressionistically rendered head floats amid a dark and murky abstract plane as a pattern of sycamore seeds dances above. First hearing Wilde's stories as a school child, Hambling describes feeling like a voice from a different world was talking to her, a world in which she felt a sense of belonging. The title refers to the mythologized moment when, on his deathbed in a run-down Parisian hotel, the flamboyant writer said something along the lines of 'My wallpaper and I are fighting a duel to the death. One or the other of us has to go.' Wilde's death aged 46 followed a life of persecution due to his homosexuality, including public scandal, imprisonment and exile, and yet his writing continues to be viewed as some of the most important of the nineteenth century.

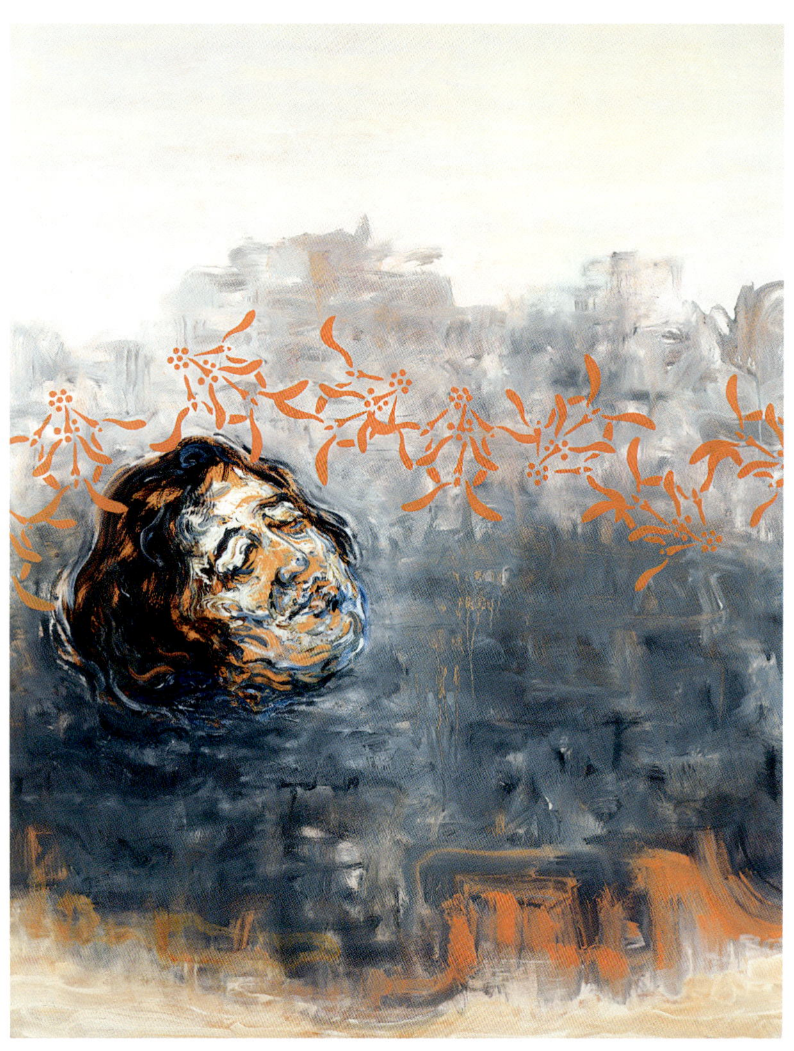

Wilde and the Wallpaper, **Maggi Hambling**, 1996–1997, oil on canvas, 122 x 91.5 cm (48 x 36 in)

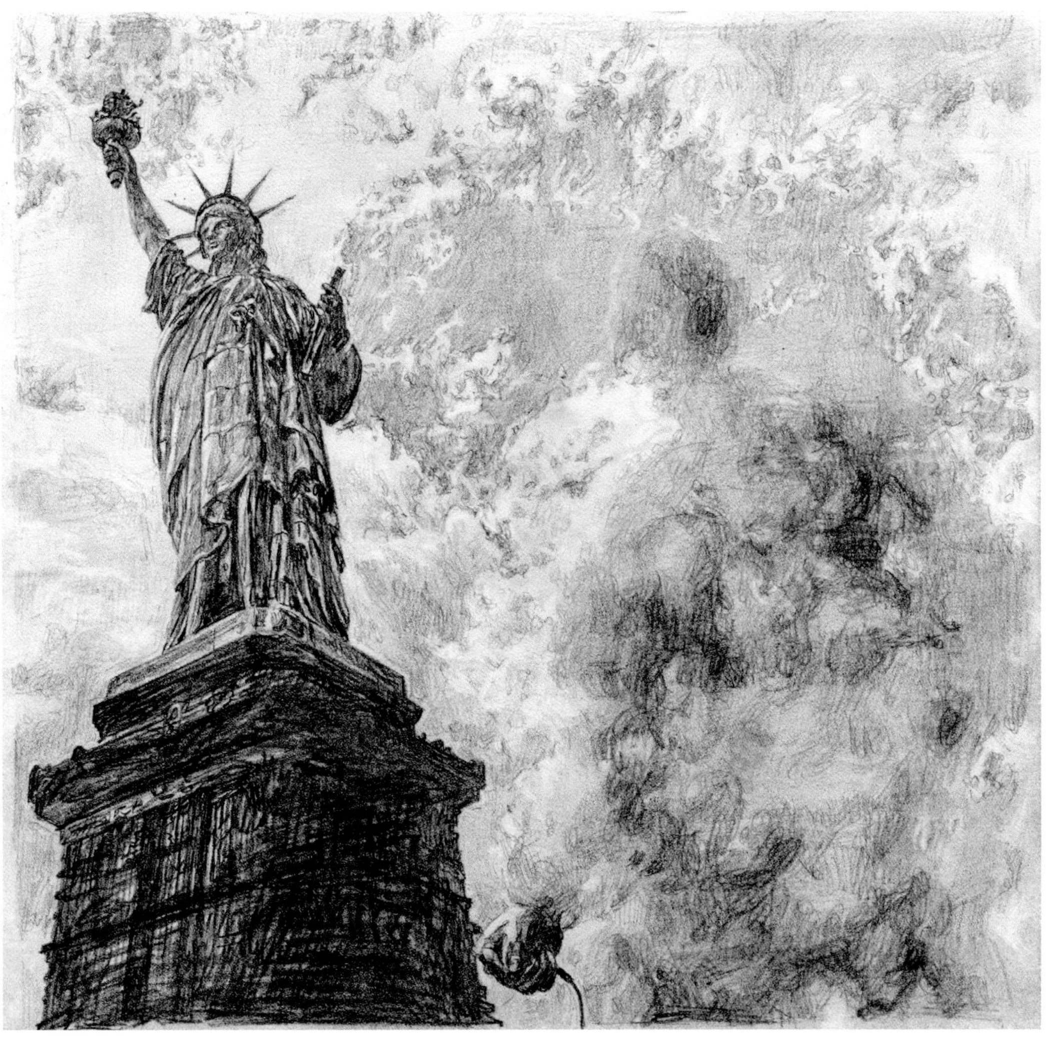

Erasure is central to the work of Kang Seung Lee. *Untitled (Tseng Kwong Chi, New York 2, New York, 1979)* is part of a series of pencil drawings in which the artist recreates well-known photographs of, usually gay and often BIPOC (Black, Indigenous and people of colour), male bodies. He removes the central figure from the image, instead drawing a ghostly shadow or cloud of smoke in their place. This image is based on the photographic series 'East Meets West' (1979) by Asian-American artist Tseng Kwong Chi, who photographed himself at well-known tourist destinations in the United States.

Dressed in a Zhongshan, or Mao suit, Tseng questioned issues of identity, belonging and cultural difference during the height of the AIDS epidemic. Kang, ruminating on the loss of key cultural figures (many of whom died of AIDS-related complications) by leaving them absent from his drawings, encourages us to consider the reduced odds of LGBTQIA+ survival, the resulting generational trauma and the legacies of queer creatives.

Untitled (Tseng Kwong Chi, New York 2, New York, 1979), **Kang Seung Lee**, 2019, graphite on paper, 20 x 20 cm (8 x 8 in)

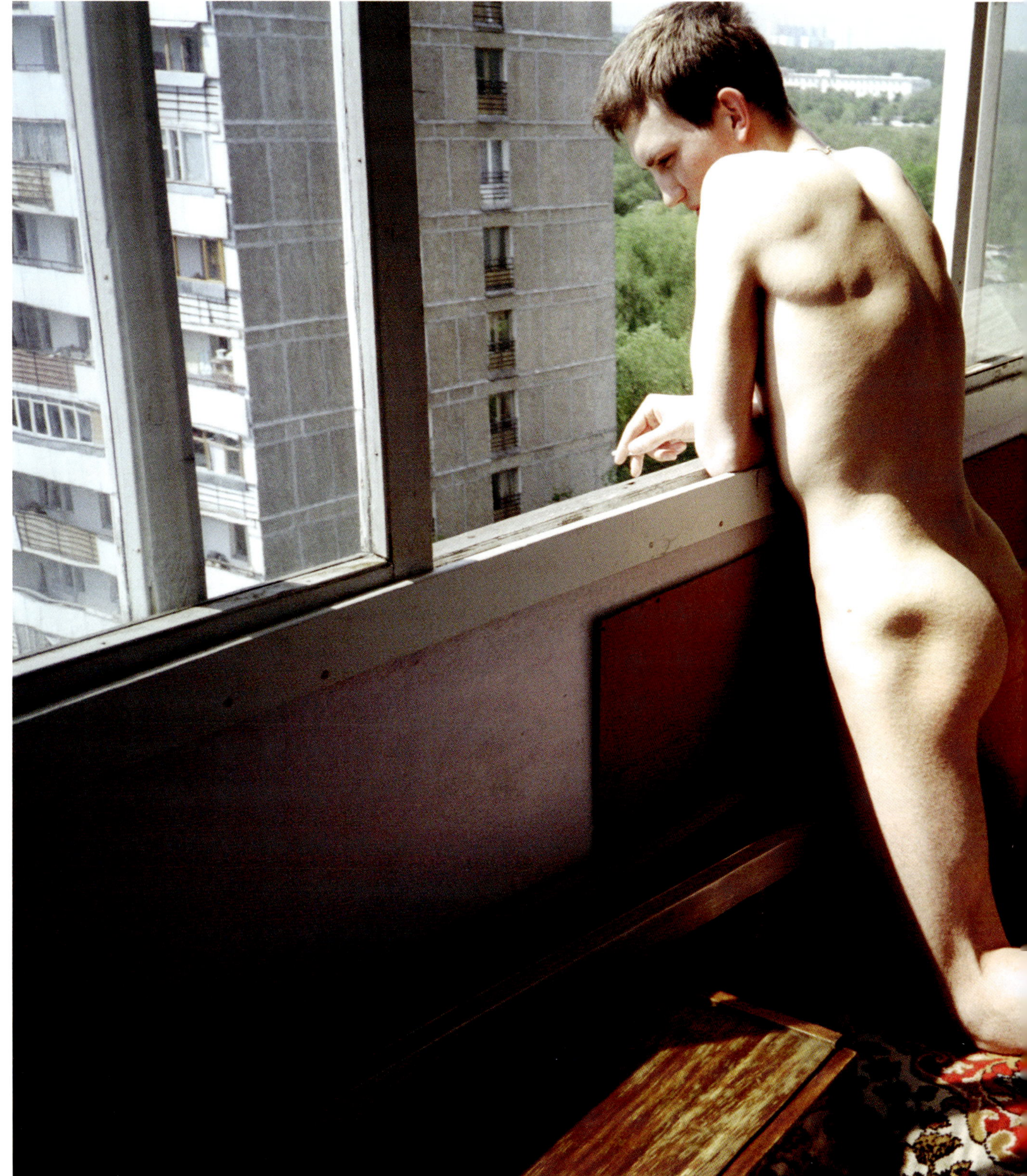

146   **Survival**

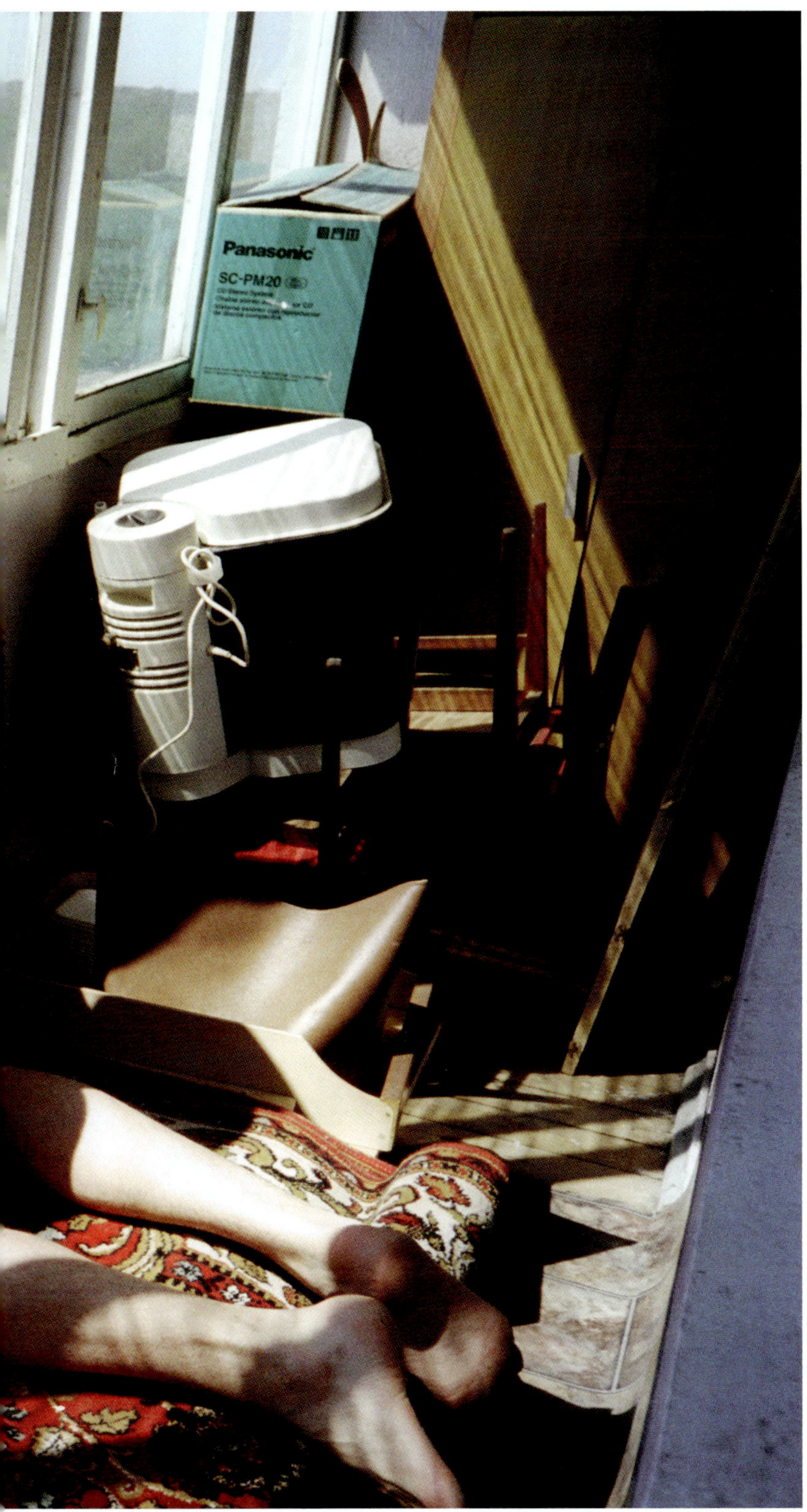

Slava Mogutin

Forced to flee his country in 1995, Slava Mogutin became the first Russian to be granted political asylum in the United States on the grounds of homophobic persecution. *Anton Smoking* is a portrait of his ex-lover taken during his first trip back home after several years in exile in the United States. He wanted to capture 'the rebellious spirit and optimism of the Russian youth' at a time of dramatic economic and political changes in his native country. It was a fleeting moment of freedom during the painful transition from the post-Soviet quasi-democratic society to the nationalist authoritarian regime of Vladimir Putin's newly elected government. The picture belongs to Mogutin's 'Lost Boys' series, which became his first solo exhibition in New York City (2001) and a monograph (2006). Through his own tumultuous relationship with Russia, Mogutin's photography reflects the enduring resilience and defiance of the country's queer community in the face of ongoing oppression.

Anton Smoking from the series 'Lost Boys', **Slava Mogutin**, 2000, analogue print

power

queer

Act III

Queer people, like other marginalized and oppressed people, have found innovative ways to reclaim power. There is a resilience unique to queerness formed in response to long-standing constraints on how LGBTQIA+ people love and live, and the silencing and erasure of queer experiences. Living freely and finding ways to thrive is in itself an act of resistance. Art is a powerful tool of that resistance, used to document and make visible, love and honour, dream and hope. As queer people have found their power, artists have been central in the self-organization, collective action and amplification that has led to change. The collaborative installation *Gay Power* (see pages 152–153) by Sharon Hayes, Kate Millett and the Women's Liberation Cinema, incorporating footage shot by the collective of the 1971 Christopher Street Liberation Day Parade and Gay-In in New York City, connected artists across decades to reflect on the radical bravery involved in those early protests.

Art is a place to take risks and many queer artists are bold in their risk taking, daring to directly challenge the status quo. In 2006, the curatorial initiative Ridykeulous led by Nicole Eisenman and A.L. Steiner published a zine featuring queer and feminist art by many leading artists that hilariously critiqued the art world and culture at large. Many artists have taken power into their own hands by launching queer-led platforms and spaces in which to bring artists and audiences together, to find solidarity and devise creative solutions for change. In the hands of queer people, art has the power to shape narratives, relationships, spaces and destinies. Much of the progress for LGBTQIA+ people that we experience today is the result of the power of queer love – self-love and love within the community.

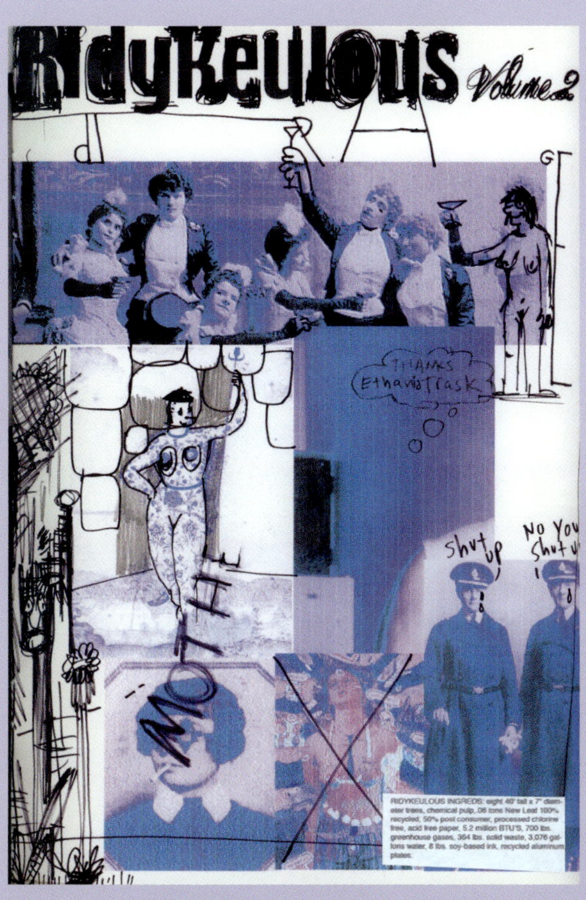

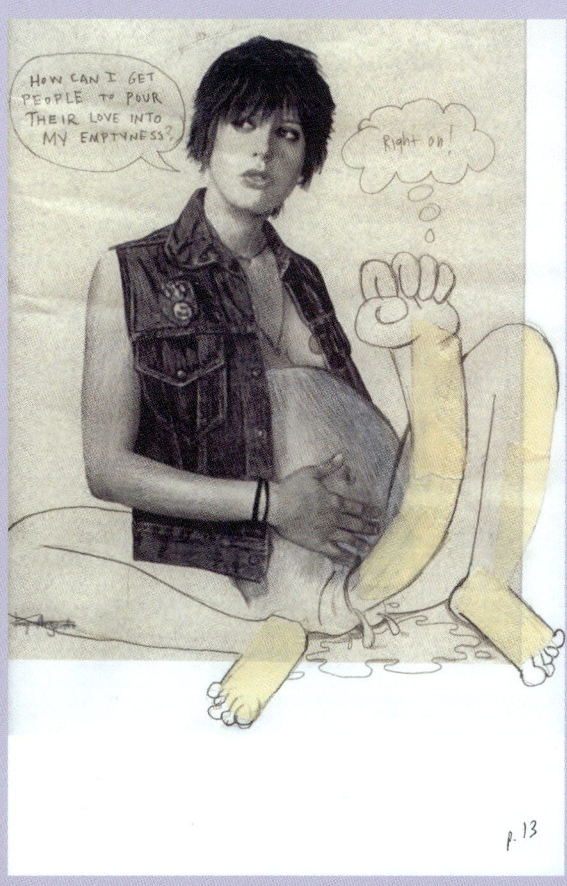

Pages from *Ridykeulous* zine, Nicole
Eisenman and A.L. Steiner, 2006

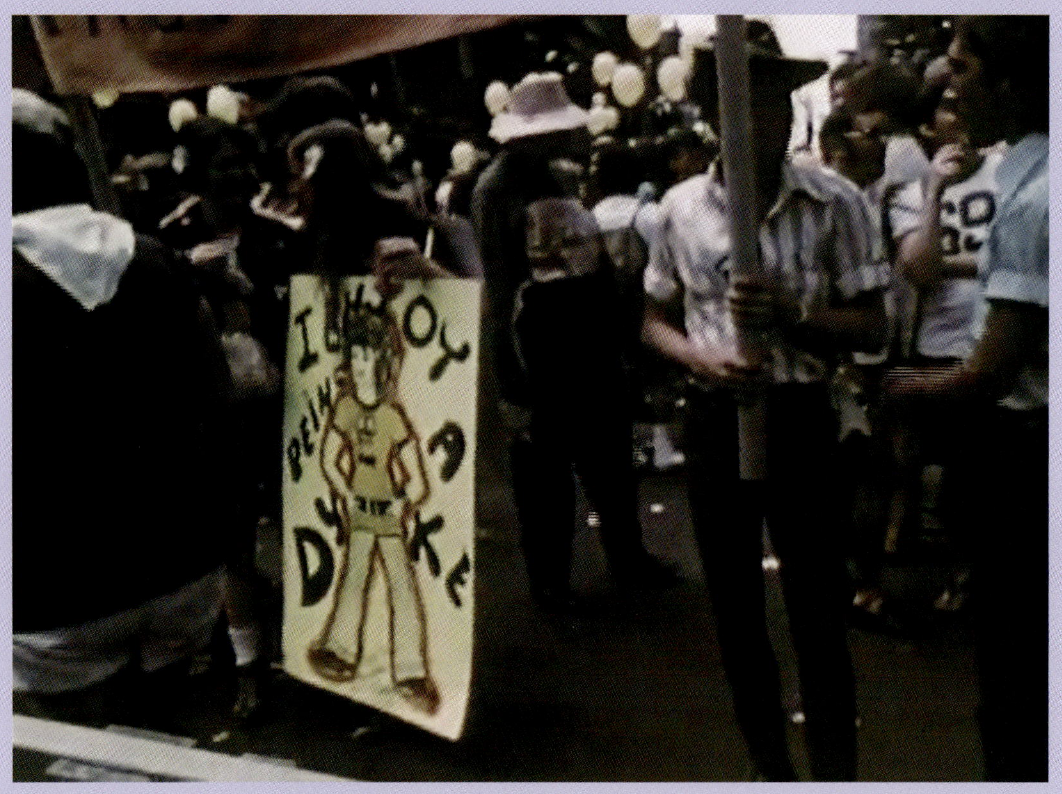
I'M OY A
DY KE
BEIN

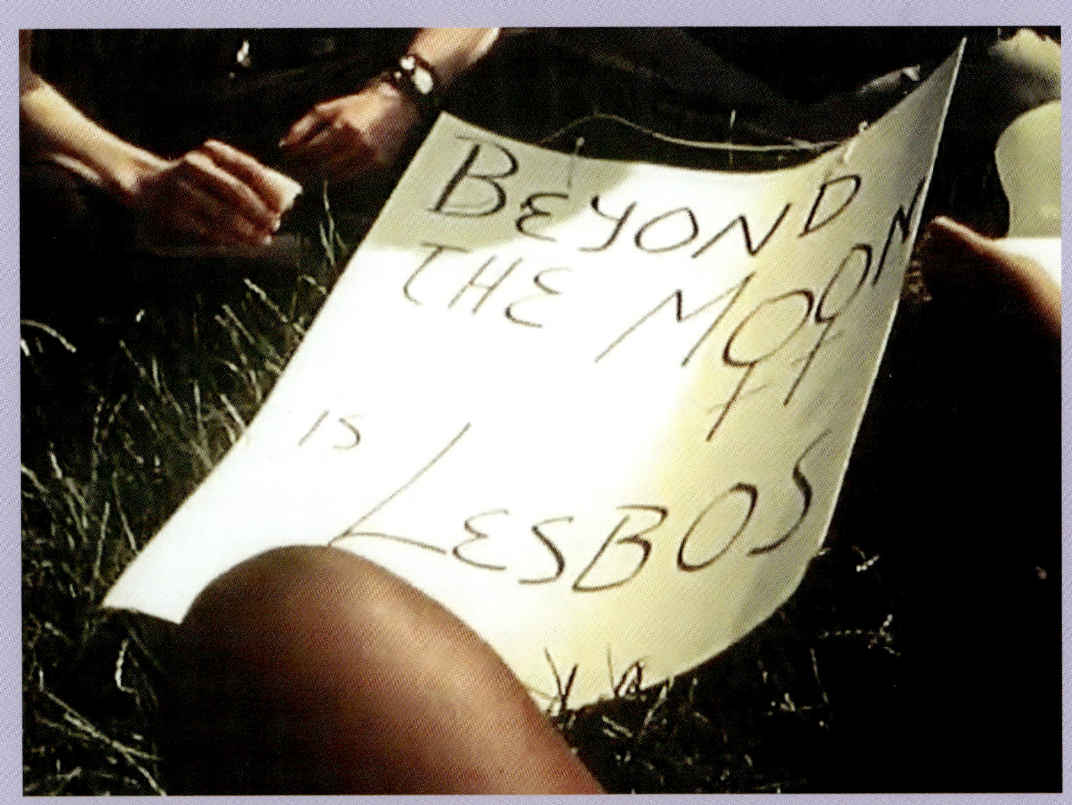

BEYOND
THE MOON
IS
LESBOS

Visibility

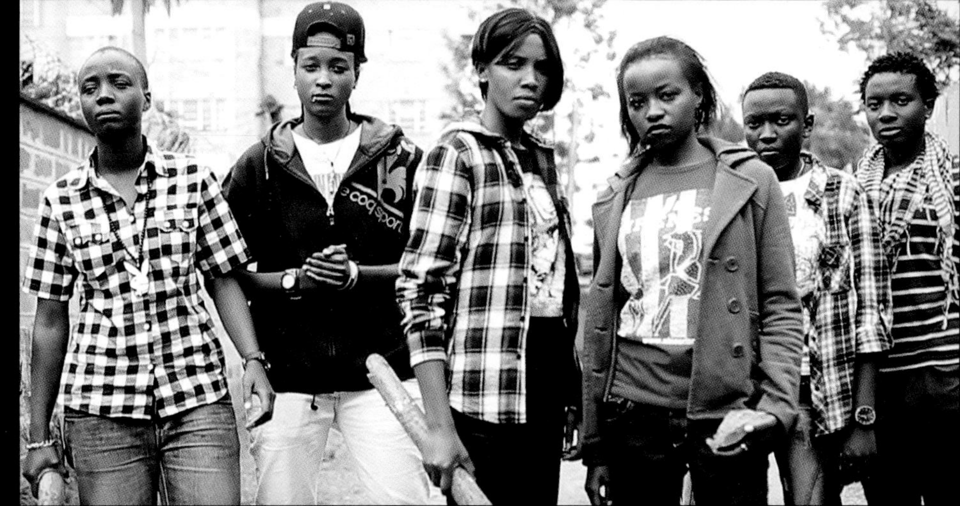

Whoever we are, hearing stories that we can relate to and seeing ourselves reflected in art and culture is vital. It's how we begin to understand and form our own identities, to develop a sense of belonging and validation. In much of the world, historical accounts of LGBTQIA+ life have been suppressed or erased, while the stories that do survive represent a particular perspective brought to light through the privileges of gender, race or class. In contexts where there are risks associated with being visible, traces of queerness are only identifiable through coded visual languages, objects and relics imbued with meaning, or images disseminated via underground publications. By portraying their own lives and those of their communities, often long before queer people appear in mainstream culture, artists become pioneers of queer visibility. The lens of queer artists brings meaningful and authentic visibility to the queer experience, articulating nuanced realities with sensitivity and respect, claiming space and countering homophobic and transphobic narratives.

Artists have embarked on ambitious journeys and undertaken large-scale projects in the name of visibility. For their anthology of short films about LGBTQIA+ life in Kenya, *Stories of Our Lives* (2013, see above), the Nest Collective, a group of multidisciplinary artists based in Nairobi interviewed more than 250 people from around the country. In times and regions

    Visibility

where queer life has been forced underground the work of
creating much-needed visibility is most challenging. Working
to diversify queer cultural narratives, contemporary artists
uncover and share the stories of those facing the most barriers
to existence, centralizing the experiences of non-white and
non-Western queers, trans and gender non-conforming people,
and bodies of different shapes and abilities. Many female artists
use their work to tackle the historical exclusion of women
and lesbian erasure, such as G.B. Jones, who published a
series of drawings in the 1990s called *Tom Girls*, based on the
highly popular work of Tom of Finland (see page 161), which
inserted women into the format of gay male homoerotic art
dominating queer culture at the time. Appropriating familiar
contexts from art history or using the visual language of the
media and mainstream culture are techniques used by many
artists to highlight a lack of visibility. Across an extensive range
of mediums artists find canny ways to express the beauty of
LGBTQIA+ life, taking control of the narrative and making the
multifaceted queer experience visible.

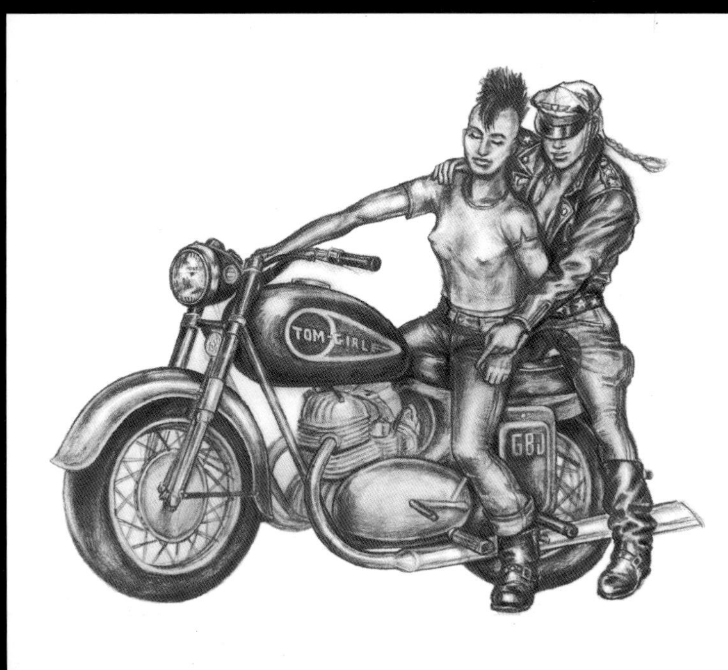

orcycle Girls,
Jones, 1987

Months after the New York Stonewall Uprising in 1969, Harmony Hammond moved to Manhattan. A pioneer of the emerging feminist art movement, she co-founded A.I.R., the first women's co-op art gallery, and the journal *Heresies: A Feminist Publication on Art and Politics*. Like many feminists, she rejected painting as a 'masculine' art form and embraced women's traditional textile arts and the art of non-Western cultures. *Presences* are among Hammond's best-known works. Constructed of fabric from women artist friends, they literally put Hammond's life in her work. Fabric strips were dipped in acrylic paint, then tied and stitched together into forms suggesting larger-than-life sized figures or ritual garments, suspended from the ceiling. The *Presences*, like all Hammond's work of this period, are intended to claim and occupy female space through materials (fabric) and process (accumulation), asserting the power of collective creativity.

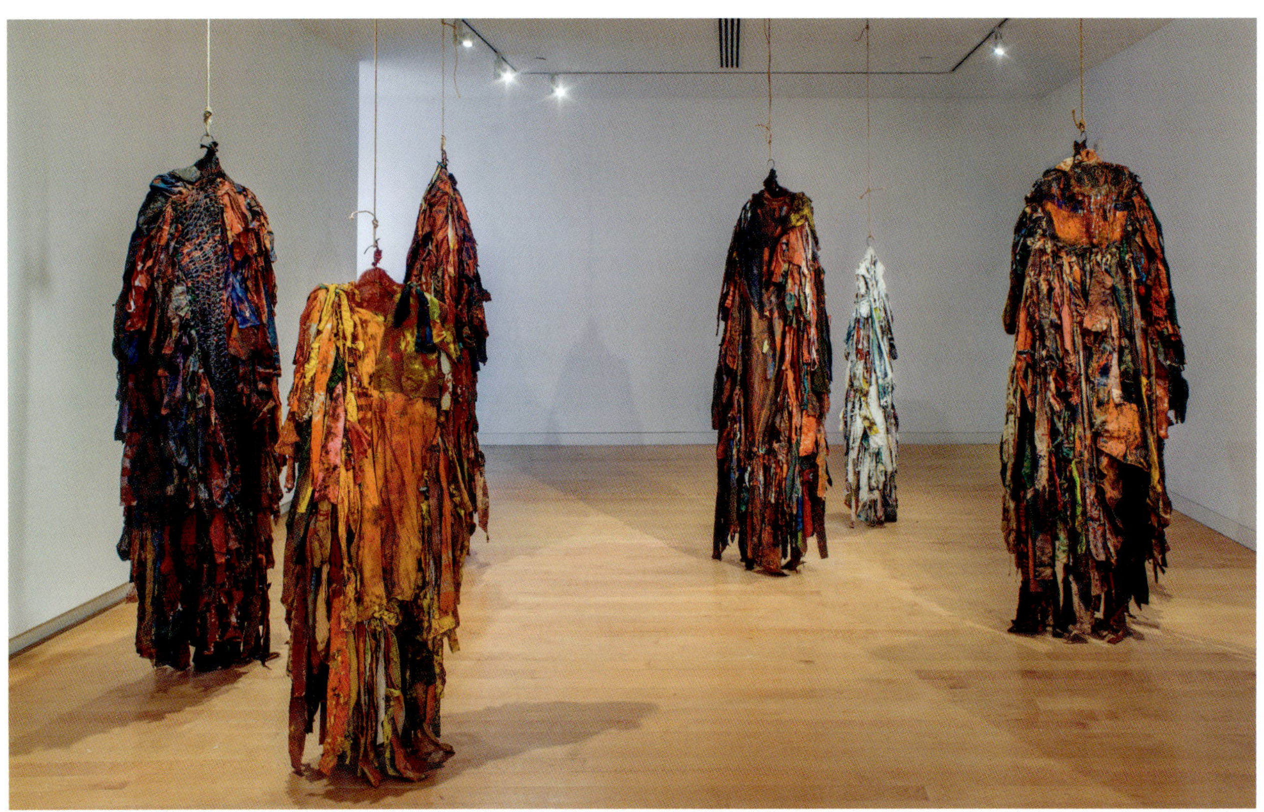

Presences, **Harmony Hammond**,
1971–1972, installation view,
'Harmony Hammond: Material Witness,
Five Decades of Art', The Aldrich
Contemporary Art Museum, 2019

My Courbet… or, a Beaver's Tale,
Mary Patten, 1991–1992, installation
view at the Art Institute of Chicago, 1992

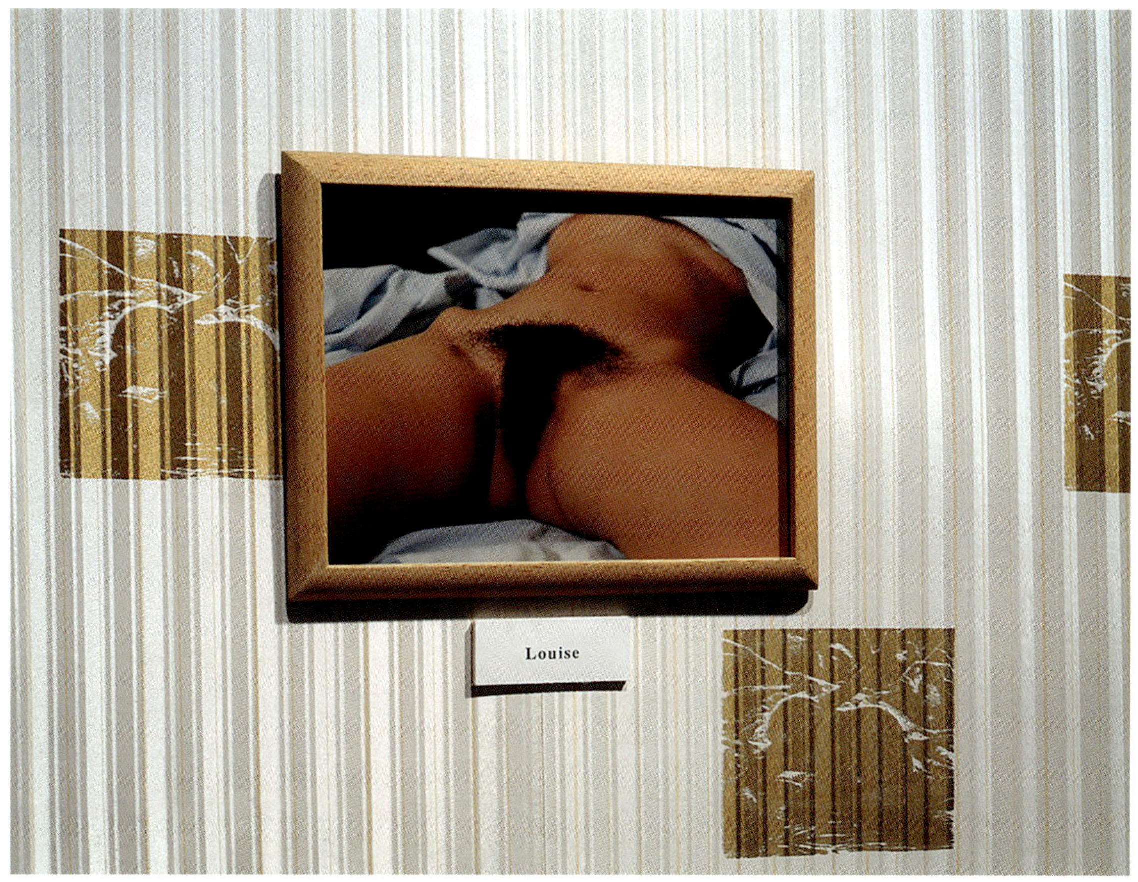

Mary Patten is an artist who has been engaged in political activism since the 1960s. She was involved with early feminist groups, the Gay Liberation Front and AIDS activist movements, and in the 1980s spent 10 months in Rikers Island prison for protesting against apartheid in South Africa. Her artwork deals with the socio-political issues for which she passionately campaigns, and her multimedia installation *My Courbet… or, a Beaver's Tale* is a key piece of American lesbian art history.

Nine framed portraits of women recreating the pose of Gustave Courbet's famous painting *L'Origine du monde* (*The Origin of the World*) hang on beaver-patterned wallpaper accompanied by a tongue-in-cheek documentary about lesbian representation through history. Patten is one of many artists of the period who used representational 'cunt imagery' to reclaim female sexuality through empowered depictions of women's bodies and the lesbian gaze.

'Gay Semiotics' is Hal Fischer's 1977 photo-text project that examines male cruising culture of the late 1970s in San Francisco. Annotations on black-and-white photographs decipher indicators of sexual preference, including the specific placement of earrings, keys or handkerchiefs. Images dissect archetypal gay looks seen on the streets or in the media, from leather to jock to hippie, and interpret queer paraphernalia such as amyl nitrate and bondage devices. The 'hanky code', also known as flagging, became popular in the United States and wider cruising culture during the 1970s to indicate sexual interests and fetishes through the positioning of colour-coded handkerchiefs in back pockets. By revealing these intricate signifiers, the seminal series gave visibility to gay life in the Castro, San Francisco's gay neighbourhood. Fischer's formal approach to deciphering queer visual coding, emphasized by his choice of title, uses the language of academics to give legitimacy to a largely undocumented culture.

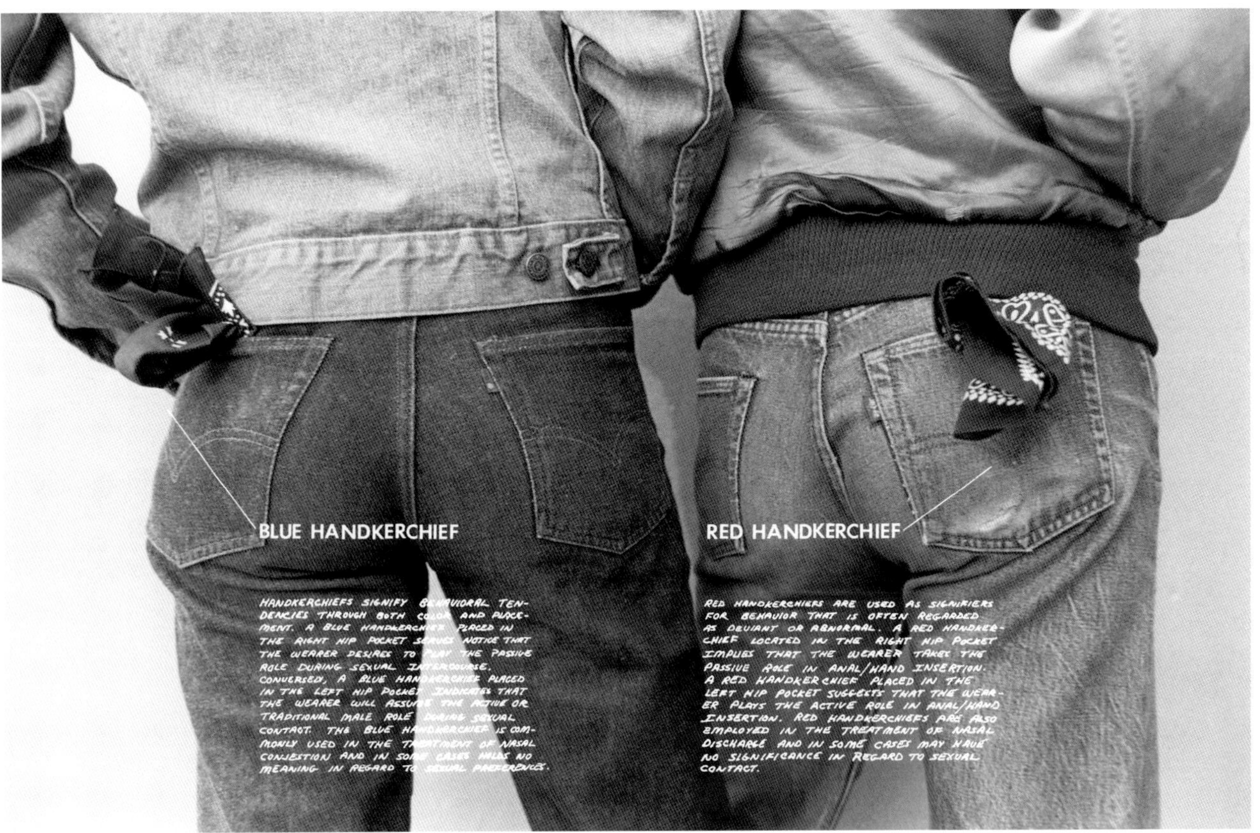

Handkerchiefs from the series
'Gay Semiotics', **Hal Fischer**, 1977/2017,
carbon pigment print, 61 x 76.2 cm
(24 x 30 in)

Tom of Finland

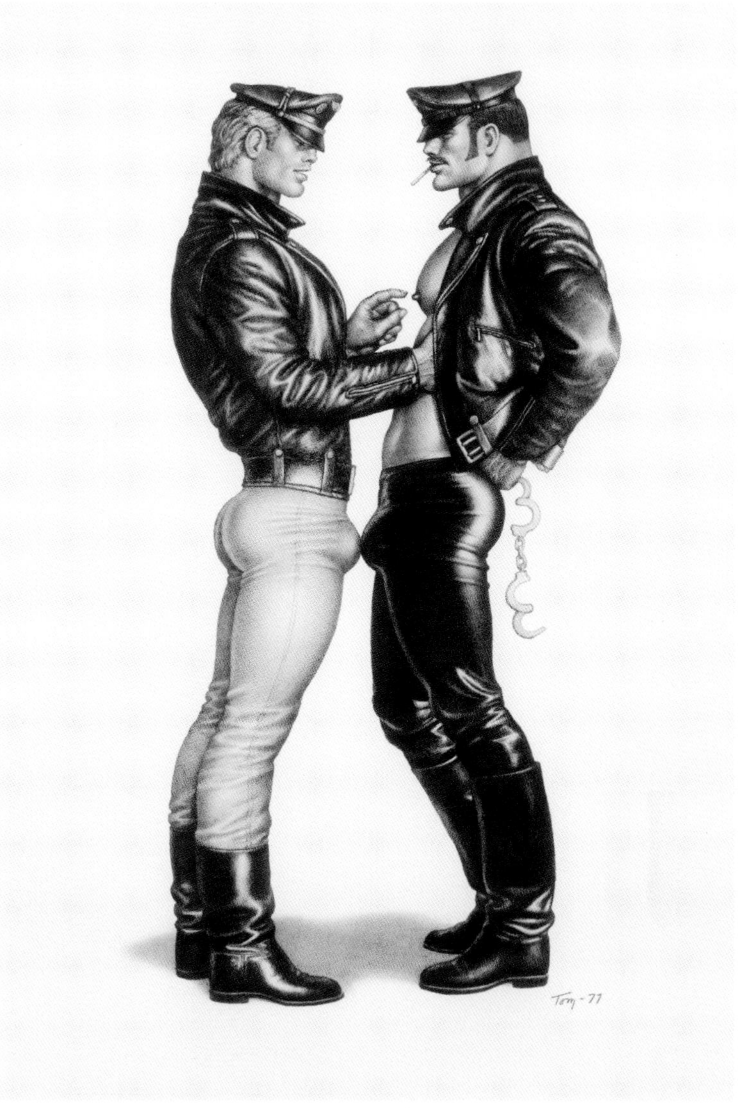

Tom of Finland (Touko Laaksonen) is perhaps the most successful queer artist to have penetrated mainstream culture. His detailed pencil drawings of explicit homoeroticism have provided identification and hope to queer people since the 1950s. A self-taught artist with a professional background in marketing, he astutely studied the drawings of Michelangelo and Leonardo da Vinci as he developed his own highly skilled penmanship. His figures represent the height of masculinity – police officers, bikers and soldiers with rippling muscles and huge glistening cocks bulging in pristine uniforms and leathers. His images were initially disseminated via the notorious publication *Physique Pictorial* and other 'beefcake' magazines that navigated the censorship of homoerotic imagery by posing as part of the fitness genre, and later via mail order commissions for fans around the world. Following the decriminalization of homosexuality in Finland in 1971, Tom began publishing his own erotic comic books and showing his work in exhibitions. Amassing a huge international following, his art had a significant influence on the development of queer culture.

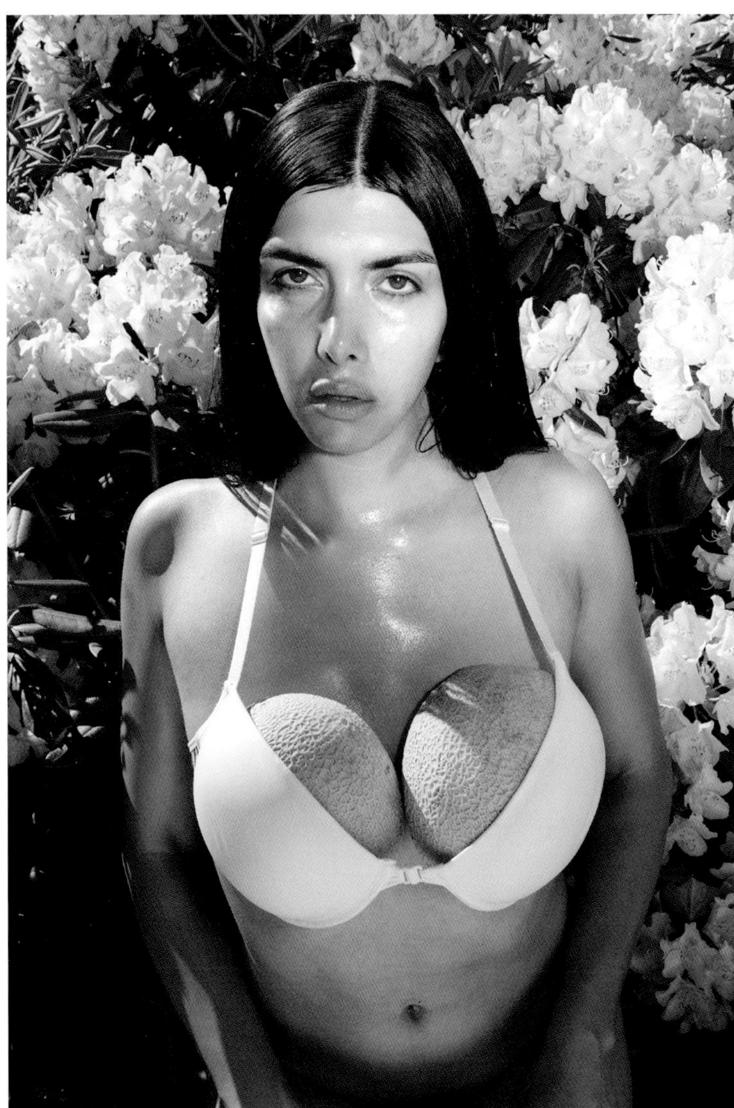

Body En Thrall, p.112 from *Indigenous Woman*, **Martine Gutierrez**, 2018, offset-printed artist magazine, 41.9 x 27.9cm (16½ x 11 in)

Martine Gutierrez

The editorial photographic series 'Body En Thrall' (2018) was produced by Martine Gutierrez for her magazine *Indigenous Woman*, which she began producing in 2014. Taking on the role of model, stylist and photographer, the artist centralized her own identity as an Indigenous, Latinx, trans woman in an exploration of gender and beauty norms within high fashion and wider culture. The intention of her gaze is 'set upon the reorientation of the body, the nuances of intimacy that continue to unearth the contemporary repressions of our historical conquests'. Describing the series, Gutierrez says, 'The title itself is a play on words, a shifting between in thrall, which means being under someone else's power, morally or mentally enslaved, and enthral, to capture the attention of another, to bewitch, ensnare or fascinate. There is a subtle yet extremely significant shift in control between the two.'

Throughout her career, Lula Mae Blocton has been fighting for visibility and acceptance of LGBTQIA+, feminist and Black communities. Her work is concerned with two key factors: a love of formal and precise abstract art and a passion for human dignity and civil rights. Part of the Black abstractionist movement, her work incorporates triangles, diamond shapes and repeated patterns found in African art. Design elements refer to Kente cloth, a Ghanaian textile recognized globally, particularly by African Americans, to represent African identity. Comprising the colours of the rainbow and those representing the Black and Brown communities, *Rainbowmalicongo 1* and its companion piece *Rainbowmalicongo 2* symbolize progress, harmony and the possibility of social justice for queer people. Speaking to the different aspects of Blocton's identity across gender, sexuality and ethnicity, the paintings reflect on the complex layering and sometimes dark nature of human experience, through a vibrant lens of hope.

Rainbowmalicongo 1 (top) and
Rainbowmalicongo 2 (bottom),
Lula Mae Blocton; both images 1999,
coloured pencil on rag paper,
76.2 x 76.2 cm (30 x 30 in)

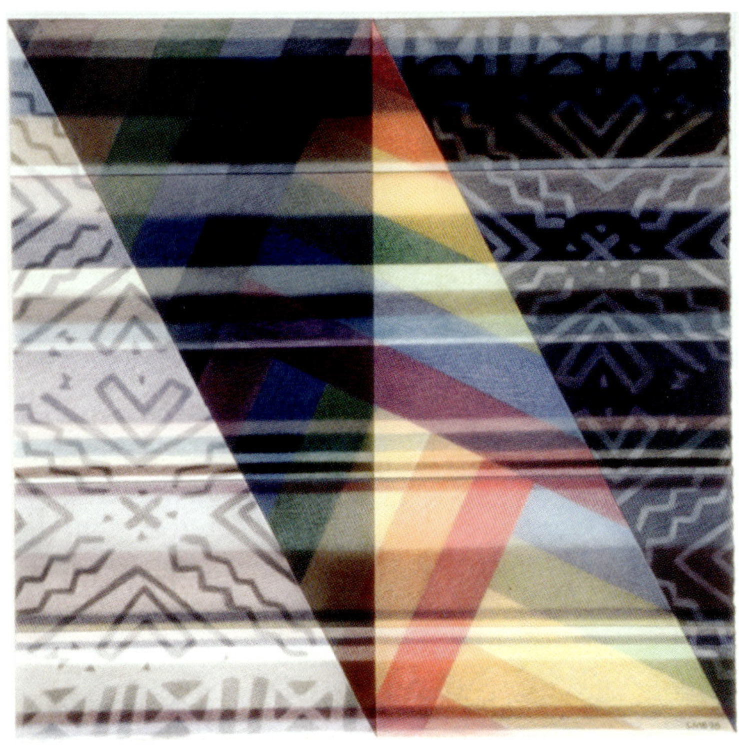

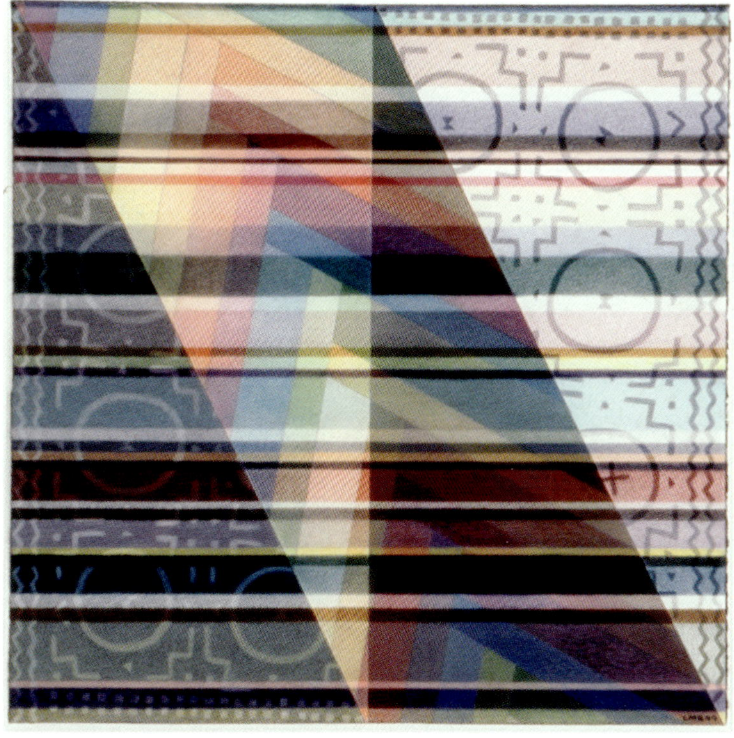

JEB (Joan E. Biren) began taking photographs of lesbians in the 1970s because she had never seen a picture of two women kissing so she created her own. This formative moment sparked one of the most significant contributions to lesbian visibility in America. JEB embarked on a road trip across the country to photograph lesbians, which she presented in her 1979 book *Eye to Eye: Portraits of Lesbians*. Originally self-published, as no publisher was interested in such a project, the book was rereleased in 2021 by Anthology Editions. *Kady and Pagan in Their Cabin, Monticello, NY* is the book's cover image, a bold photograph of two older lesbians gazing lovingly into each other's eyes. Posing for JEB's book was an act of resistance and bravery since every woman who agreed to be featured risked having their children removed, losing their jobs, their families or facing deportation for being out.

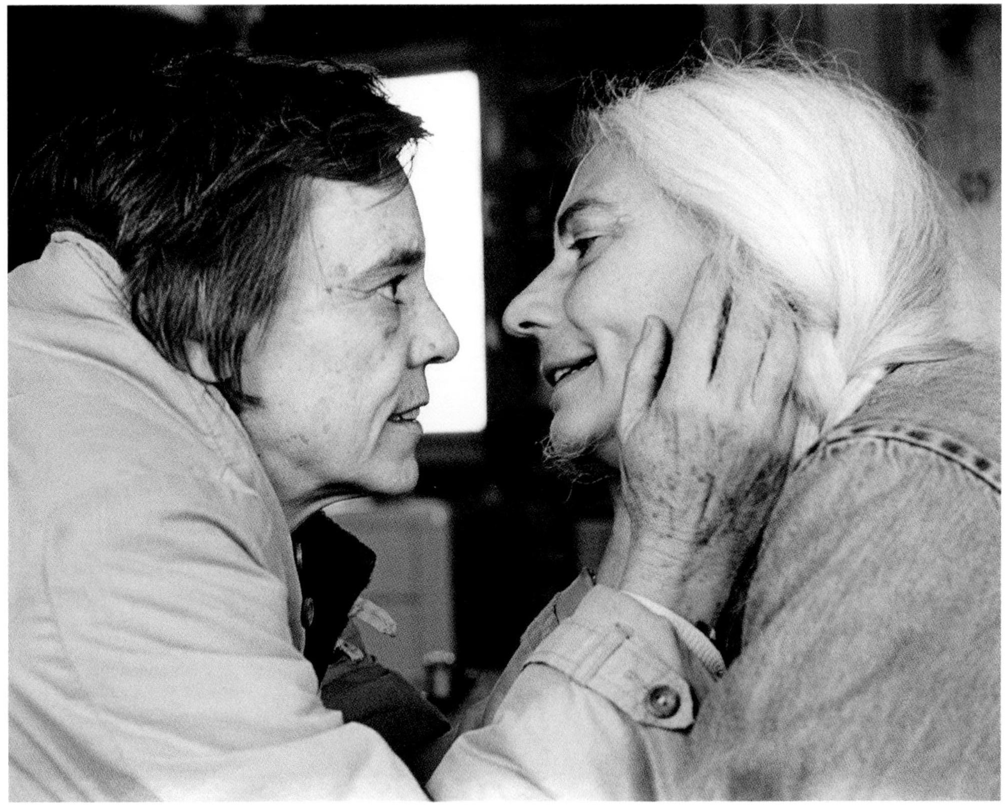

Kady and Pagan in Their Cabin, Monticello, NY, **JEB (Joan E. Biren)**, 1978

Superdyke, **Barbara Hammer**, 1975,
16mm film on video (colour, sound),
17 mins 34 secs

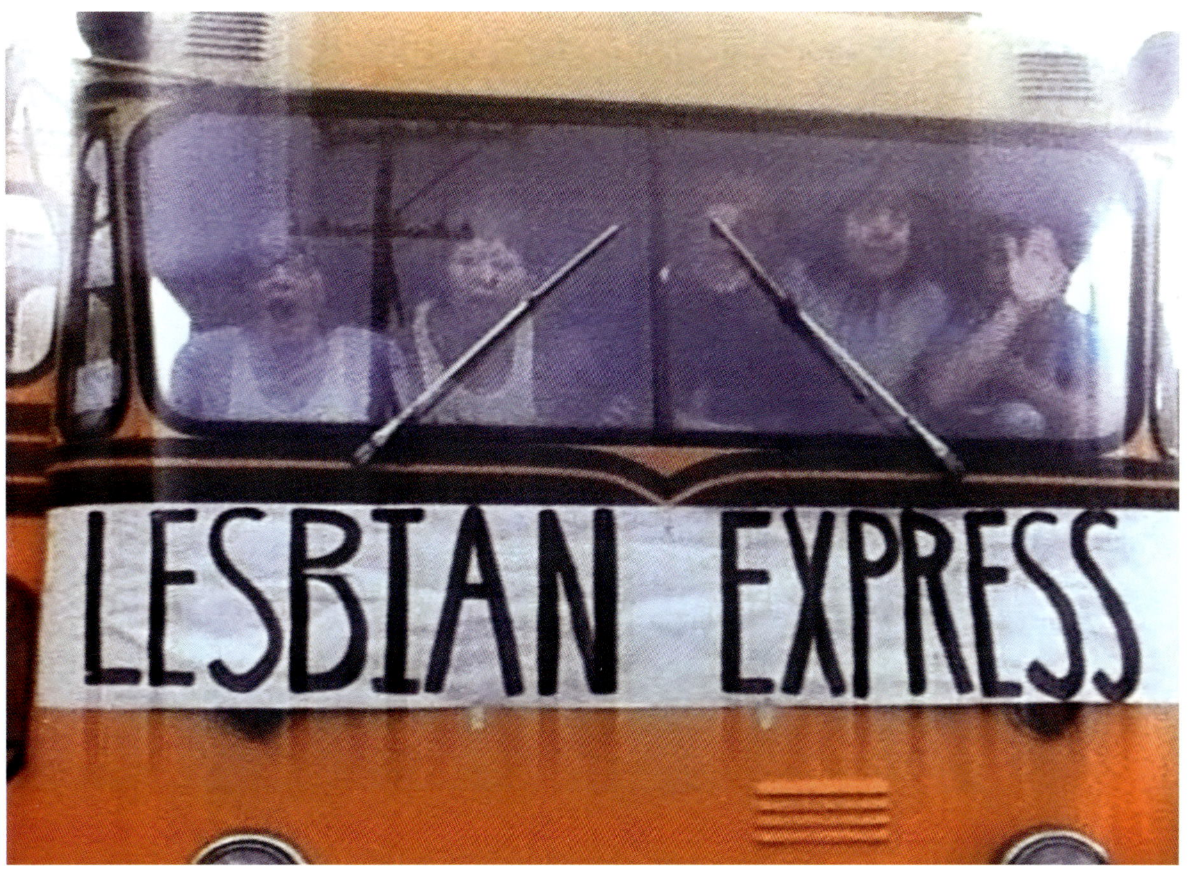

Celebrated as a pioneer of queer cinema, Barbara Hammer used film to challenge societal norms with political precision and a sense of humour. Her early film *Superdyke* was made during a time of new-found liberation for gays and women. Drawing attention to the exclusion of lesbians from both movements, her 'superdykes' are a troupe of powerful women bearing Amazonian shields as they take to the streets and overturn the city's institutions. Shot on 16mm with a handheld camera, the comedic film offers an insider's perspective of the lesbian revolution. Hammer's lesbians inhabit a multitude of roles, from leading the charge and flexing muscles, to relaxing in the country and sharing intimate moments, as she gives visibility to lesbians and centralizes the multifaceted experience of being a queer woman.

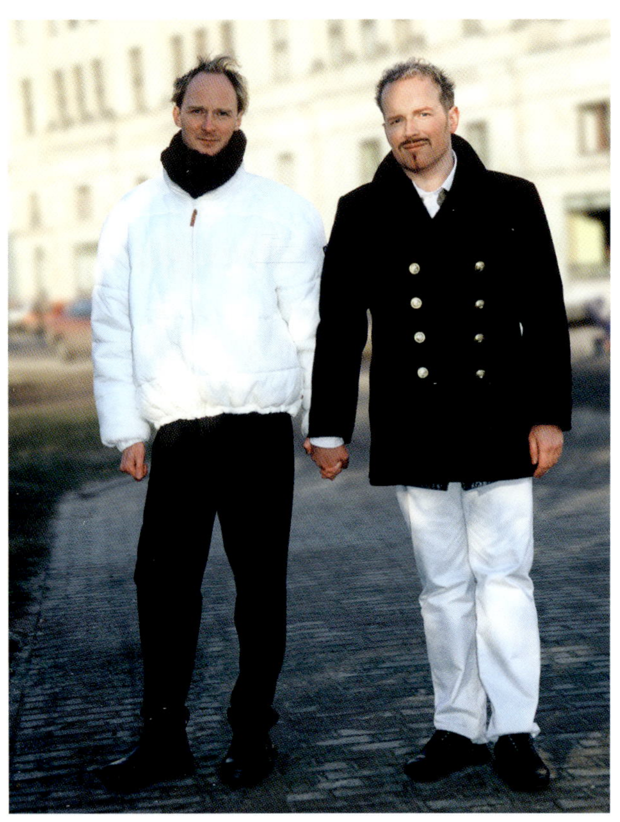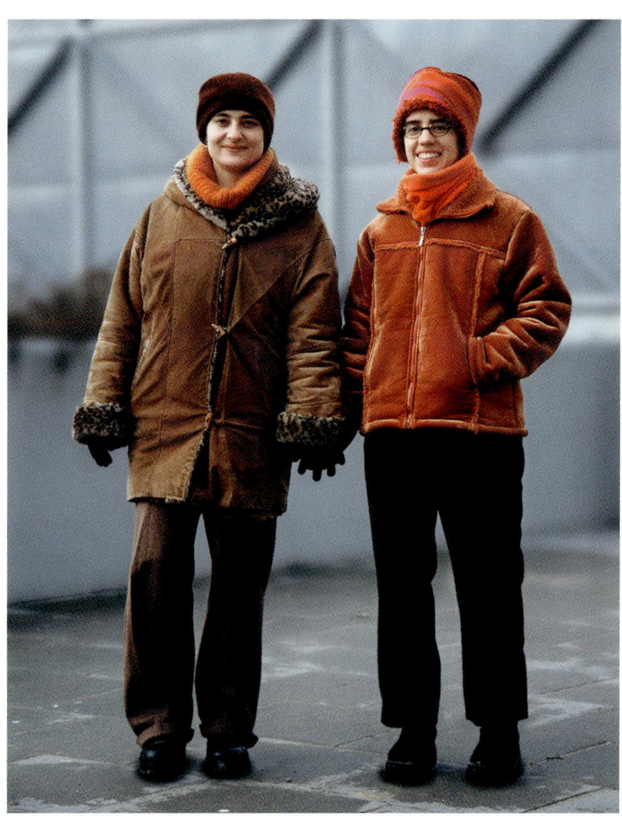

Karolina Bregula

Karolina Bregula's 'Let Them See Us' is a series of 30 photographic portraits of gay and lesbian couples holding hands. The project was made in response to homophobia in Poland, fuelled by growing support for the League of Polish Families, a recently formed political party with far right views. The photographs gave visibility to queer people during a time when it did not feel safe to be out in the country and the very act of holding hands in public could put a couple at risk of discrimination or violence. Bregula's series appeared in exhibitions and on billboards as part of the organization Campaign Against Homophobia's first gay rights social campaign. The billboards were met with much opposition and were often vandalized, demonstrating the strength of the anti-LGBTQIA+ sentiment in the country and the need for such a public gay rights campaign.

Gilbert Prousch and George Passmore view themselves as a singular artist – Gilbert & George. Meeting at art school in 1967 they fell in love at first sight and have collaborated ever since. Taking inspiration from their local east London neighbourhood and incorporating self-portraiture, their distinctive graphic photo-based work portrays the world as they see it; as they state: 'nothing happens in the world that doesn't happen in the East End'. *Existers* is a collage-like composition including portraits of the artists among a large group of young men consisting of 28 individually framed photographic prints. Applying their characteristic bold block colours to their subjects' clothing, hair, ears and lips as they strike a variety of elegant poses, the artists highlight the beauty of young men and reinforce their right to exist.

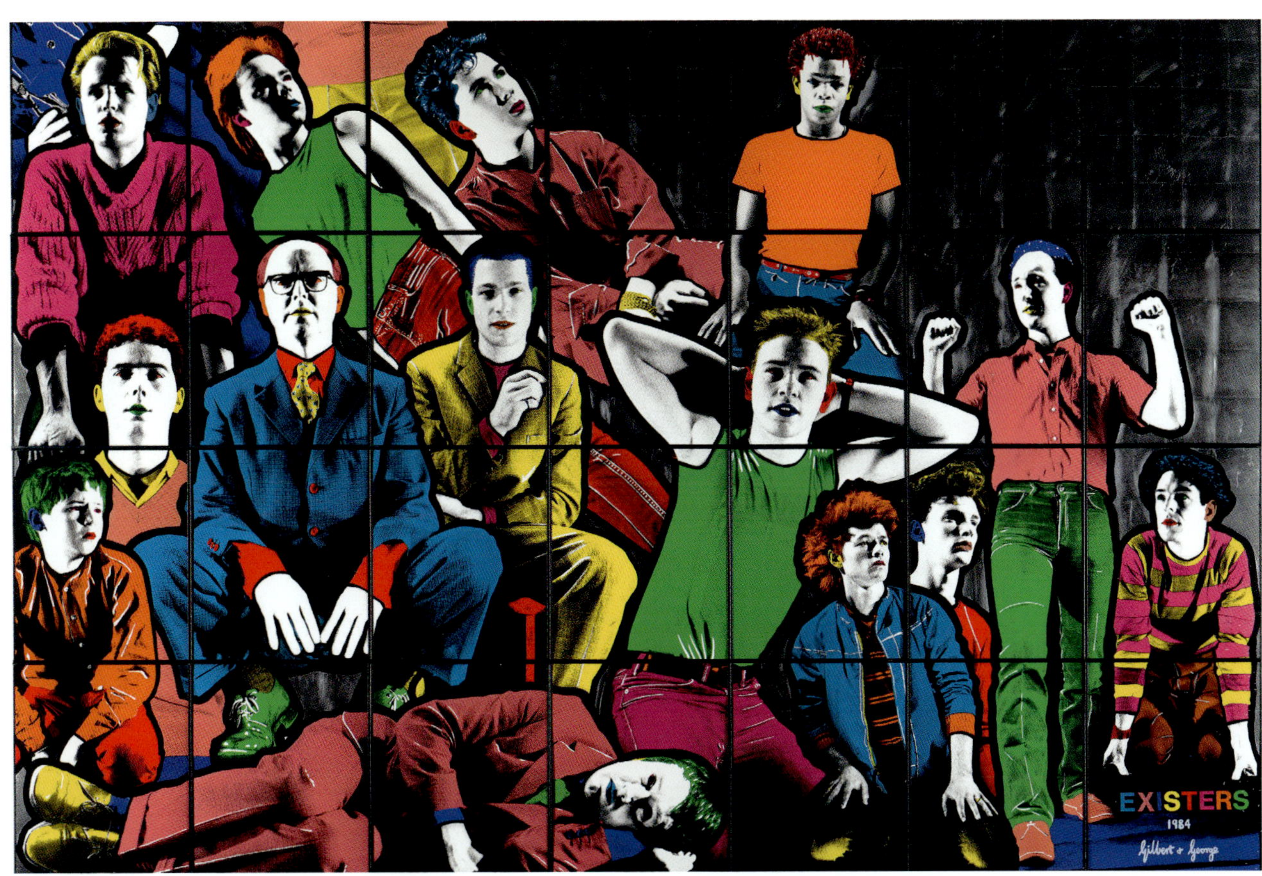

Existers, **Gilbert & George**, 1984, photographic prints, 242 x 353 cm (95¼ x 139 in)

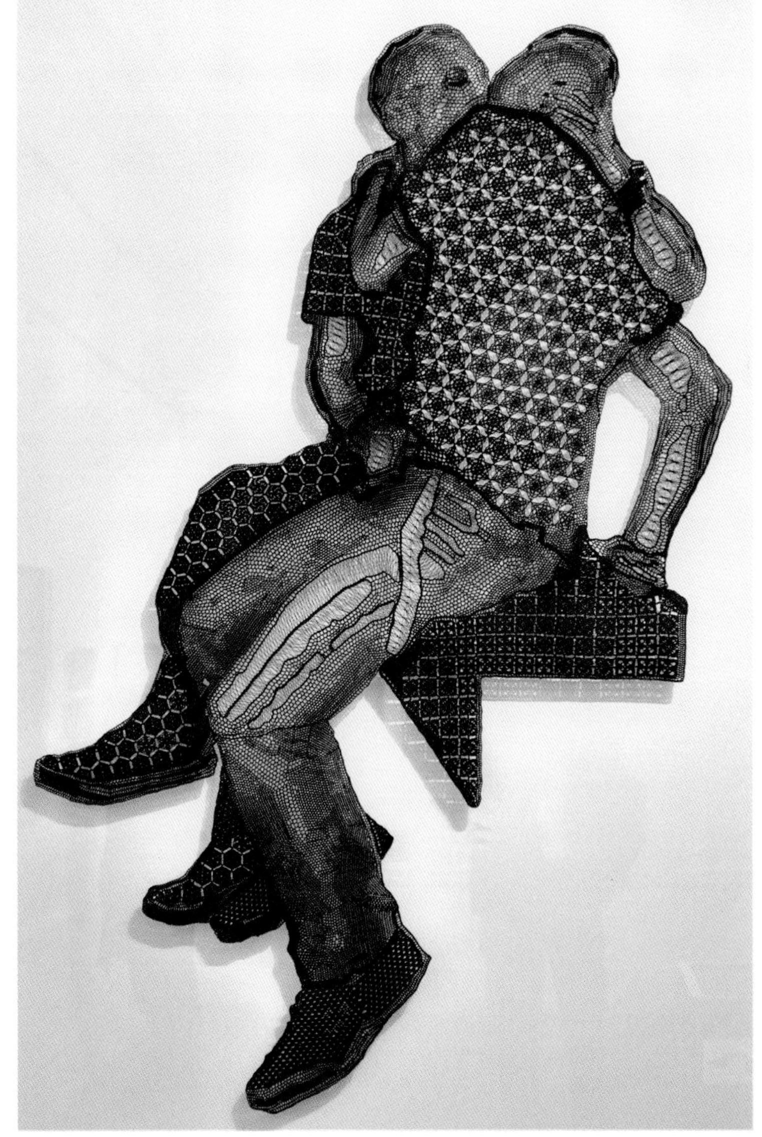

The Kiss, **Pierre Fouché**, 2007, crocheted mercerized cotton, 200 x 120 cm (78¾ x 47¼ in)

Lace-maker and teacher of contemporary bobbin lace Pierre Fouché is celebrated in the international world of craft for combining technique, tradition and innovation. He employs traditional craft techniques to represent queer bodies, celebrating the beauty of gay men in tender moments of solitary reflection or intimate connection. With an air of romanticism, his source imagery is drawn from domestic photography found online or captured by himself or friends, as he gives visibility and openness to scenes that would otherwise be private. At two metres (around six-and-a-half foot) tall, his crochet cotton portrait *The Kiss* hangs in the national art gallery of his native South Africa, where it proudly promotes equal love and takes space for queer people.

The erotically charged female figures in Ghada Amer's *you my love* are embroidered in a painterly fashion, the tangle of hair-like threads suggesting the artist's hand never left the canvas. Having left her native Cairo as a child and resettled in France where she studied art, Amer navigates the different ways in which women are perceived according to the global context. Her work responds to the underlying misogyny, restrictions of female power and erasure of individual identity that are consistently experienced by women regardless of location. Her choice of embroidery is a nod to traditional women's roles. Throughout her practice the artist addresses the absence of women from art history, centralizing them in her work to create female-led narratives. By lifting her figures from pornographic magazines and positioning them in poses suggestive of lesbian acts, she gives visibility to queer female love and power to female anatomy.

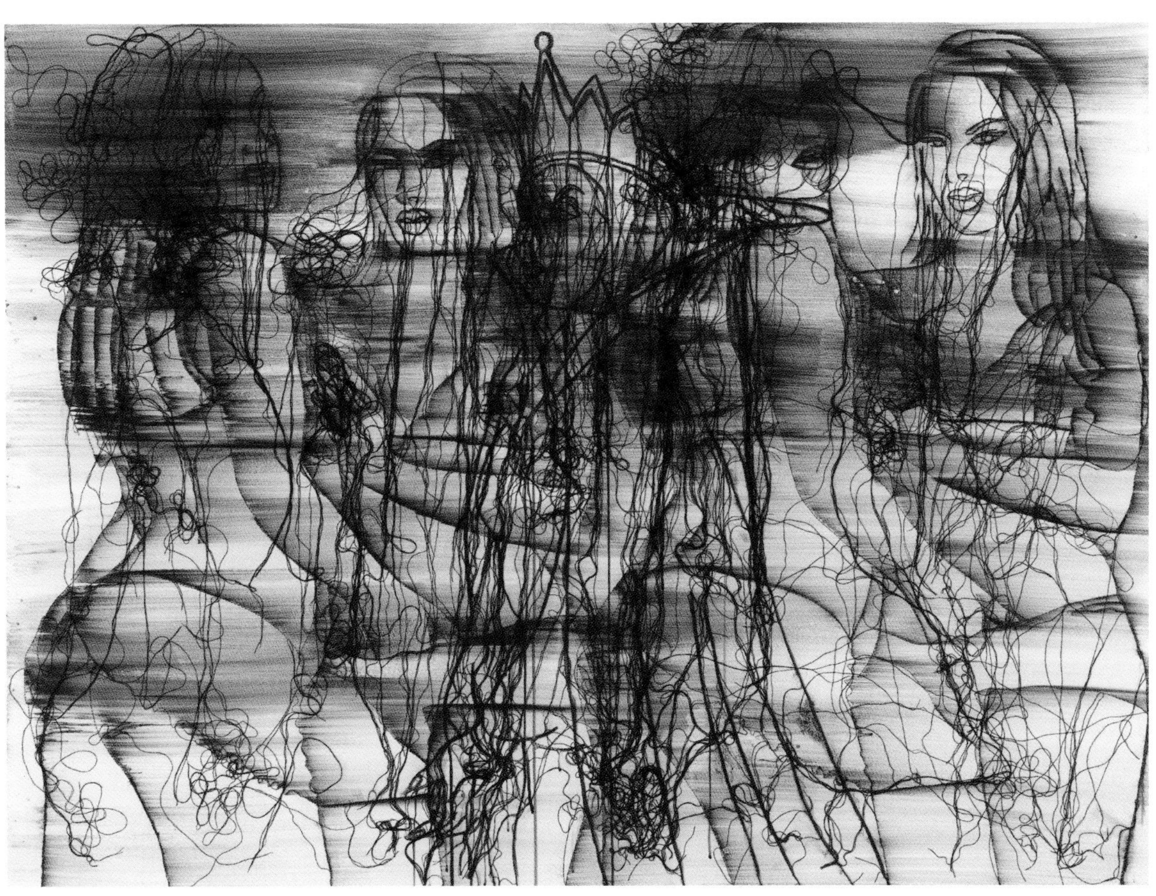

you my love, **Ghada Amer**, 2011, acrylic, embroidery and gel on canvas, 127 x 165.1 cm (50 x 65 in)

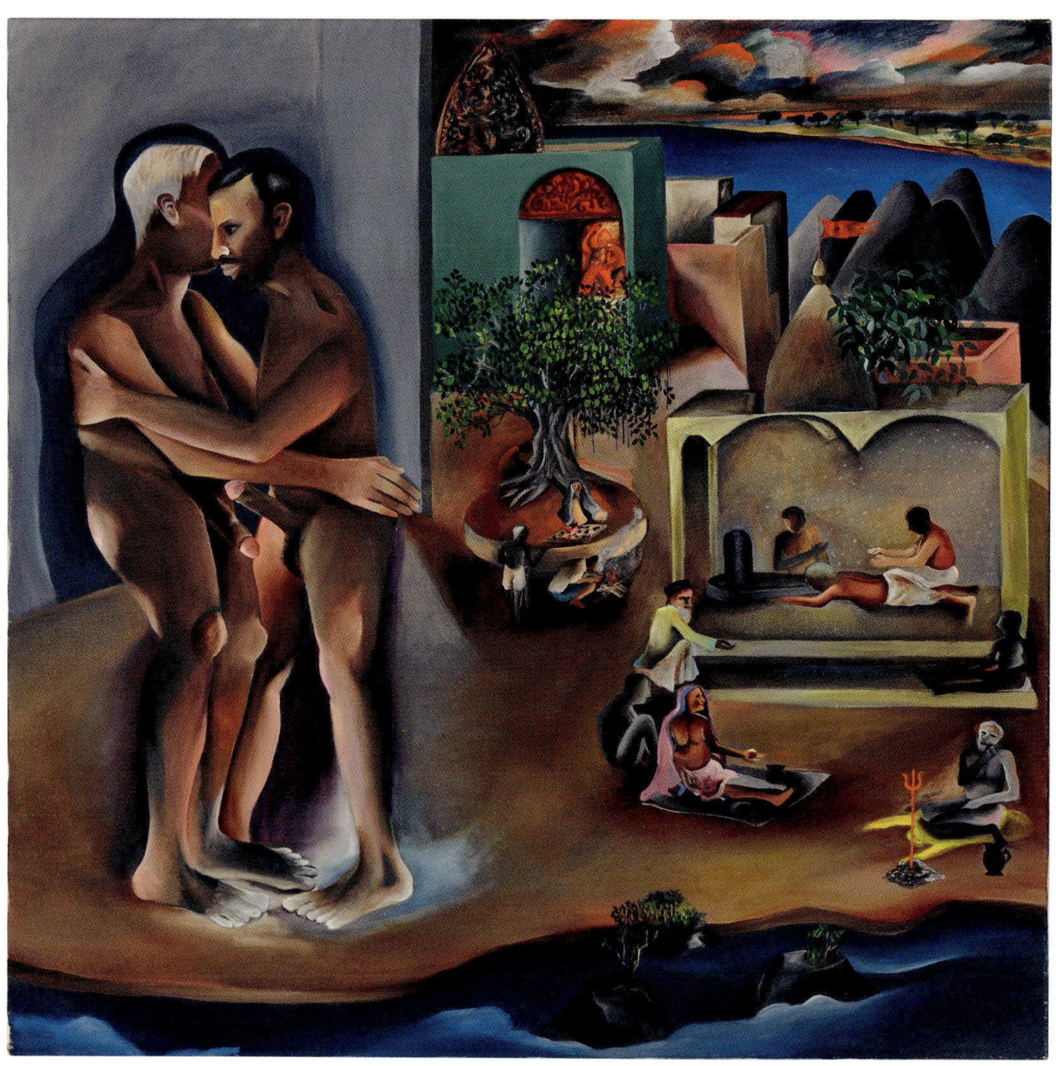

Bhupen Khakhar is celebrated as a central figure in modern Indian art. Blending everyday life with personal reflections, his work plays an important role in LGBTQIA+ visibility in India, and queer culture more broadly. Having spent time in England in the late 1970s, where he experienced the gay rights movement and connected with British pop artists, he began coming out in his painting. *Two Men in Benares* is the most explicit example of his newfound boldness and open sexuality. Two male nudes embrace against the dusty map-like backdrop of Varanasi, also known as Benares, one of the oldest living cities in the world and the pilgrimage capital of India. Among the *sadhus* (holy men), the smoky shrines and the aged trees of this ancient landscape, the pair's homosexual love appears gloriously spiritual.

Two Men in Benares, **Bhupen Khakhar**, 1982, oil on canvas, 160 x 160 cm (63 x 63 in)

  Visibility

Glenn Ligon's iconic text-based work *Untitled (I Am a Man)* remembers the signs carried by striking sanitation workers in Memphis, Tennessee in 1968 that became a symbol of the American civil rights movement. The protests against racial discrimination, unsafe working conditions and low wages, which often met with police violence, were joined by Dr Martin Luther King the day before his assassination. Ligon's image uses the same capitalized black font against a white background as the appropriated placards but deliberately formats the line breaks differently, distinguishing his declaration from the source. The statement against oppression reappears at times when human rights are being challenged in America. As a Black gay man, Ligon harnesses the power of protest found in these resounding words to assert his presence and demand unequivocal acceptance and dignity for all parts of his identity.

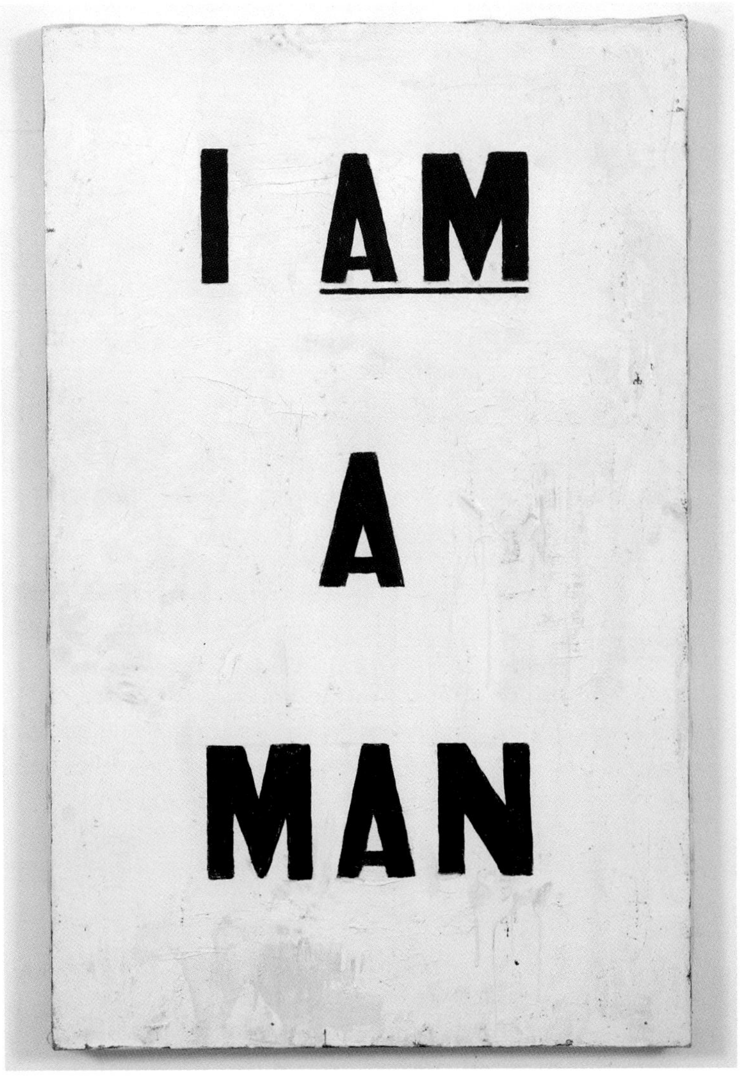

Activism

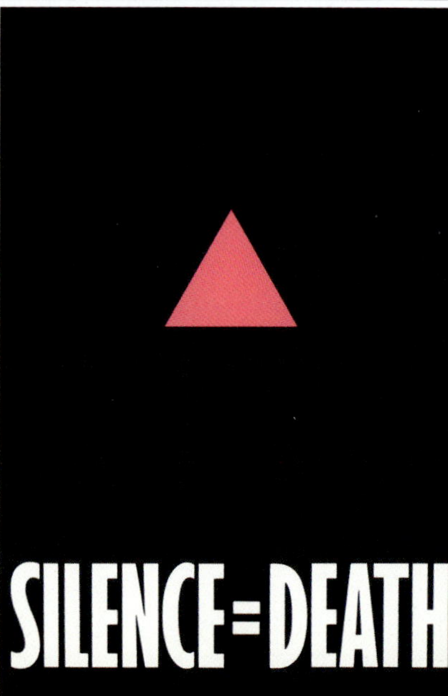

Silence = Death poster,
ACT UP, 1987

Throughout history the queer community has been marginalized. With a longstanding and ongoing lack of representation in positions of influence and decision making, LGBTQIA+ people have been excluded from societal systems and their needs have gone unmet. Within these circumstances queer people have turned to activism to make themselves visible and heard, to make demands for basic human rights and equality. Drawing attention to the reality of lived LGBTQIA+ experiences, queer activism responds to systemic failings, cultural biases and gaps between public opinion and government policy. All around the world queer people have had to, and continue to have to, fight for the reversal of anti LGBTQIA+ laws, healthcare reforms, state recognition, safety from violence (inflicted by the police and others), equal marriage, parenting rights and more. In the ongoing fight for social justice, queer activists also have a history of using their voices to support those dealing with wider global issues, such as climate change and conflict, and the causes of other marginalized groups and oppressed people, from miners to migrants.

Artists have played a key role in queer activism, from the use of artistic platforms to engage with activist messaging, to creative contributions to campaigns and involvement in collective action. Many artists featured in this chapter would describe themselves as artists *and* activists, frequently bringing the two threads together in traditional art world contexts and activist settings. The art of activism is often quickly created in response to urgent situations. Historically this has taken the form of work that can be easily reproduced using photocopiers and printers, often in black and white, appropriating the easily digestible visual language of media and marketing that combines text and graphic imagery. With the birth of social media, queer activist art takes a digital form that can be disseminated faster and further. The creativity of queer artists has been harnessed to enhance the traditional format of protest, through banners, placards, public installations and performance.

In the West, there have been some pivotal moments in the fight for LGBTQIA+ rights led by grassroots activist groups including and working in close collaboration with

Activism

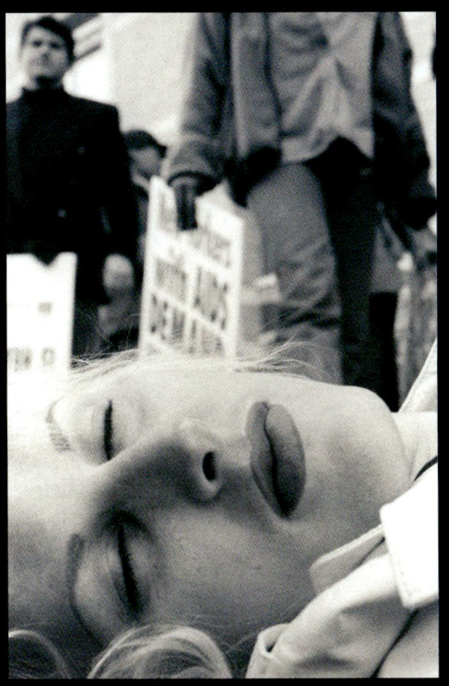

Chloe Dzubilo, ACT UP die-in, New York City, photo by Alice O'Malley, c. 1994

artists: from the Stonewall Riots and the gay liberation and lesbian activist movements that followed, to ACT UP (AIDS Coalition to Unleash Power) whose 'silence = death' slogan appeared in many artworks and who staged legendary 'die-ins' involving thousands of people simulating death, to the rapidly growing movement in support of trans rights. As the situation for queer people continues to be unsafe in many areas of the world and new anti LGBTQIA+ legislations are passed, artists are using their platforms to contest the discrimination of their communities and to engage with global dialogues. There is a rich history of queer activist art that continues to grow as artists make critical and creative contributions to changing the conditions that marginalize their communities.

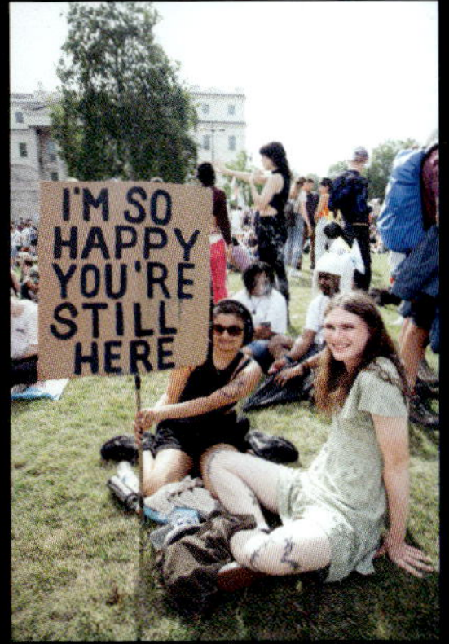

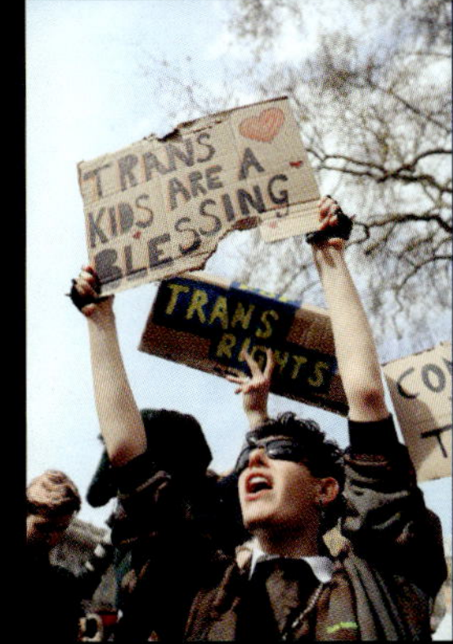

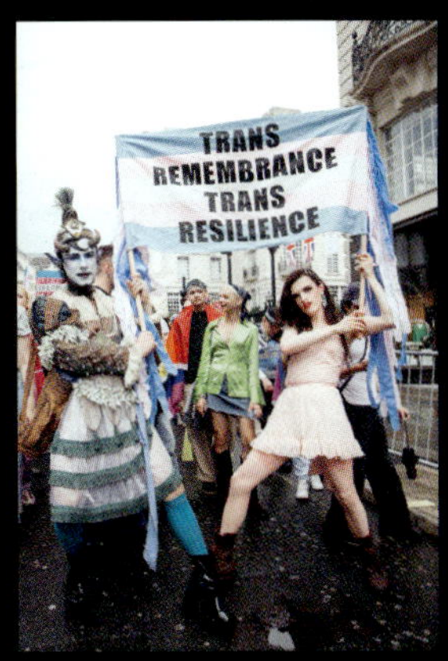

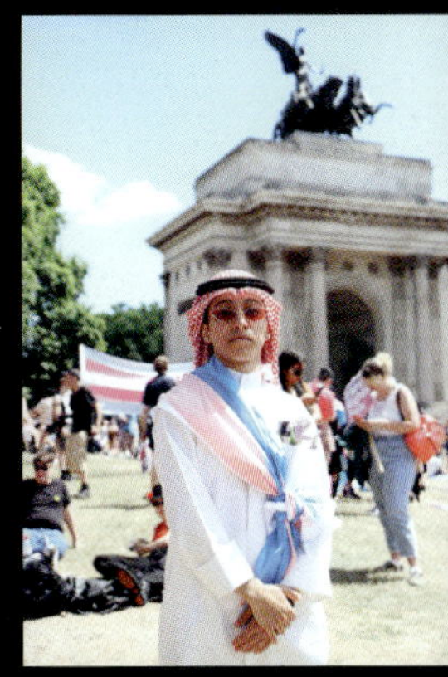

Clockwise from top left: *I'm So Happy You're Still Here* (London Trans+ Pride 2023), *Trans Kids Are a Blessing* (Ban Conversion Therapy protest, 2022), *Yousef* (London Trans+ Pride 2022), *Trans Remembrance Trans Resilience* (London Trans+ Pride 2023); all photos by Bex Wade

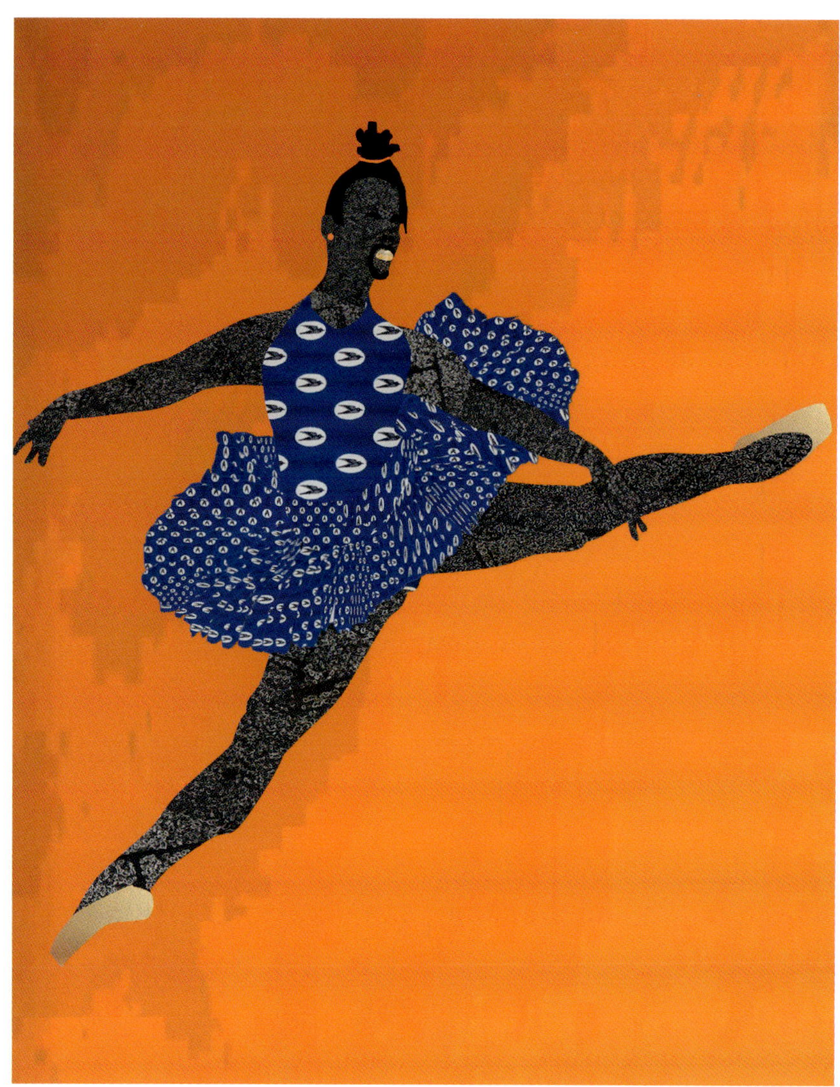

Becoming Sochukwuma, **Osinachi**, 2019, digital, 4400 x 3400 pixels

Nigeria's leading crypto artist, Osinachi's NFT and digital print *Becoming Sochukwuma* was inspired by an essay written by Chimamanda Adichie in response to Nigeria's 2014 Anti-Gay Law. The legislation imposed jail terms for homosexual marriage, public displays of same-sex relationships and belonging to LGBTQIA+ rights groups in addition to the existing sodomy laws, which had already largely forced queer life underground in the country. The award-winning writer's text titled 'Why Can't He Just Be Like Everyone Else?' uses the example of Sochukwuma, a young boy who knows he's different before he even has the language to describe his sexuality, to challenge the new law. Osinachi imagines Sochukwuma as an adult, wearing a beautiful blue dress, golden lips and ballet shoes, grown to love himself to the point of dancing across the image.

Russian-born Brazilian performance artist Fyodor Pavlov-Andreevich uses his own body to stage site-specific installations and guerrilla-style interventions that challenge the way we interact with the world, often drawing attention to global issues relating to the human experience. *Temporary Monument 0* was a durational live piece created in response to Chechnya's anti-LGBTQIA+ campaign that began in 2017 and in which people targeted for their sexual orientation, mostly gay men, were systematically detained, tortured and even executed. The artist's body, wrapped in a rug that references both Muslim prayer rituals and Chechen funeral ceremonies, was suspended from the second-floor window of Gazelli Art House, London, for five hours. The artist's head sticking out of the rug with no physical support caused him excruciating pain throughout the performance, which he says is of 'little significance' compared to the suffering of Chechnya's queer victims.

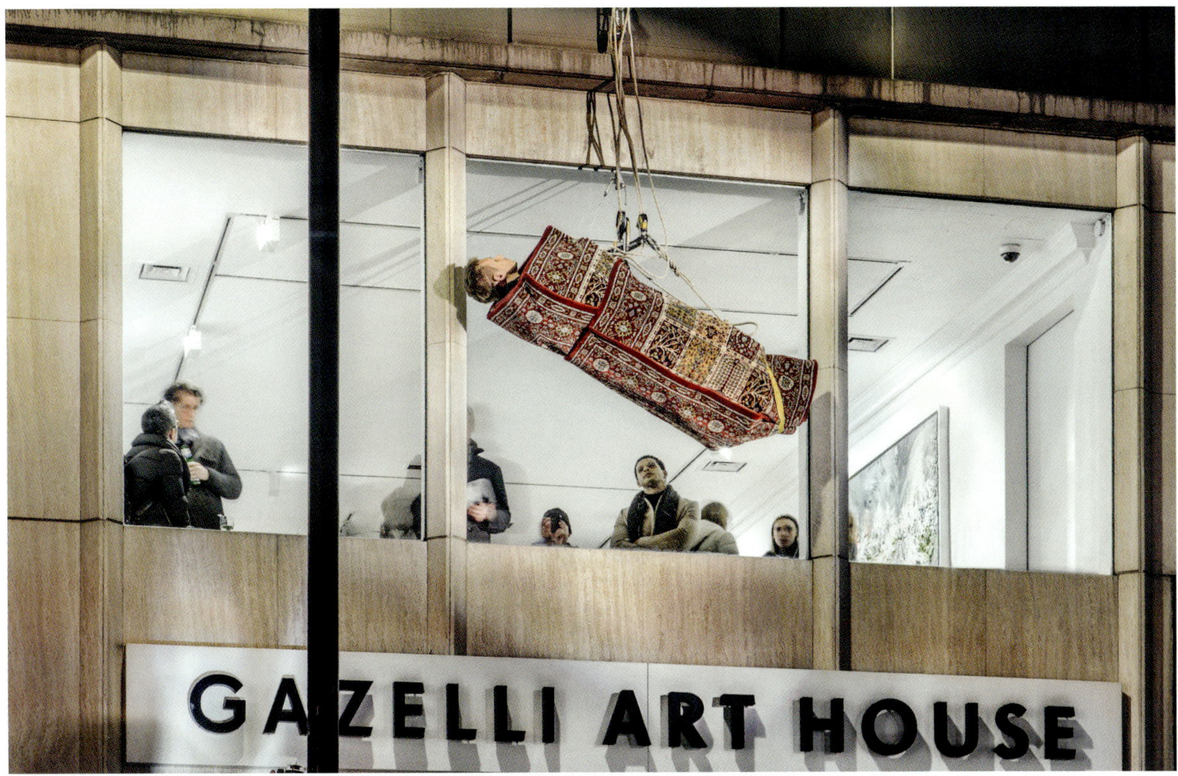

Temporary Monument 0,
Fyodor Pavlov-Andreevich, 2018,
five-hour live endurance performance,
Gazelli Art House, London

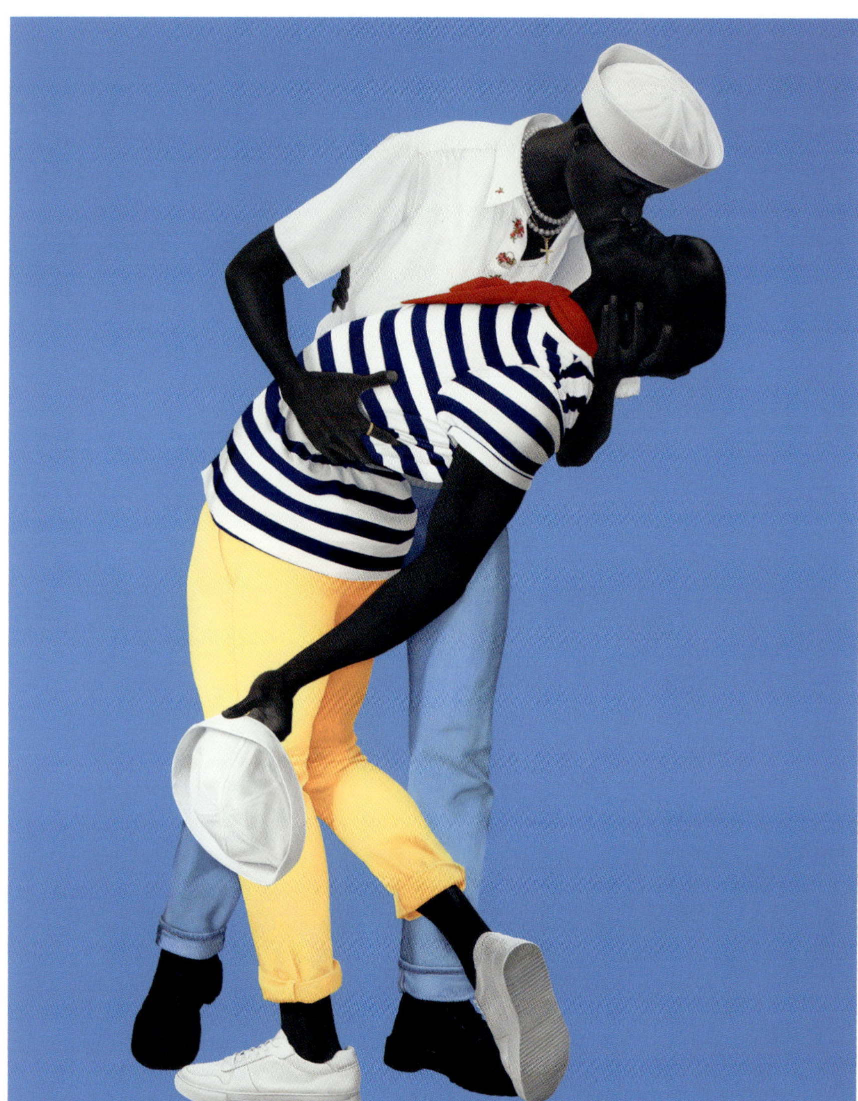

Amy Sherald's *For Love, and For Country* depicts a passionate kiss between two Black men wearing sailing garb. One figure swoons into the kiss while the other grabs his waist and tenderly cups his head in his hand. The painting is a recreation of a famous photograph by Alfred Eisenstaedt called *V-J Day in Times Square*, in which a US Navy sailor kisses a woman on Victory over Japan Day in New York City's Times Square in 1945. A painter of the Black experience, Sherald calls to mind the Black soldiers whose contributions to the war effort often go unrecognized. As an ally, she queers the pose in response to the unfair treatment of LGBTQIA+ people in the United States. At more than three metres (ten feet) tall, the painting is one of the artist's largest, and a monumental statement of love.

Activism

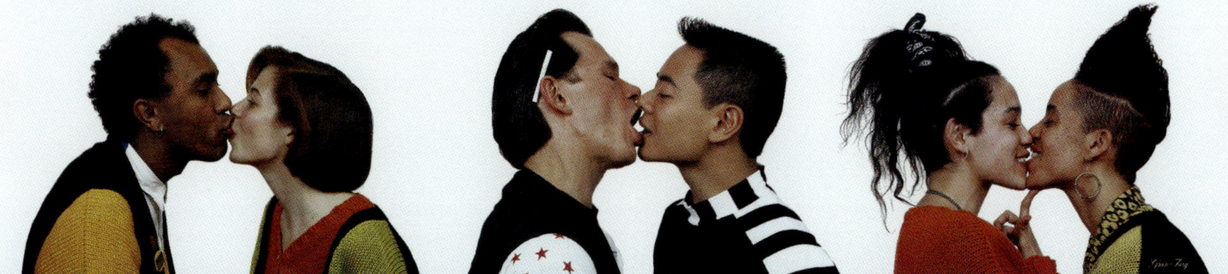

Gran Fury was a collective of artists and designers that emerged from ACT UP (AIDS Coalition to Unleash Power). Spurred on by a lack of official action in response to AIDS, leading to confusion and fear, the group's public art served a legitimate need to share factual information about the disease, how it spreads or doesn't spread and who it affects (everyone). The *Kissing Doesn't Kill, Greed and Indifference Do* poster campaign draws attention to the lack of medical support and the stigmatization and complacency impacting those living with and dying from the disease. The poster is inspired by the 'kiss-ins' orchestrated by ACT UP during the late 1980s, large groups of activists would publicly kiss to undermine homophobia and the incorrect belief that kissing could spread the disease. In demonstrating the joy and normalization of queer affection, the three diverse kissing couples serve as a rallying cry for acceptance and action.

General Idea was a multimedia conceptual art collective founded in Toronto, Canada in 1969 by three artists, AA Bronson, Felix Partz and Jorge Zontal. Their collaborative work dismantled the media, popular culture and the art market through satire and queer punk aesthetics. From 1987 their subversive projects prioritized the AIDS epidemic, which was ripping through their community and would eventually bring an end to the collective when the disease claimed the lives of Partz and Zontal in 1994. *AIDS (Wallpaper)*, one of the first works expressing the new focus of the collective's practice, was inspired by Robert Indiana's pop art love motif made in the mid-1960s. The wallpaper became an advertisement campaign of sorts to help the public engage with and normalize the word AIDS, which simply wasn't being talked about enough, despite the disease having become a national crisis by this point.

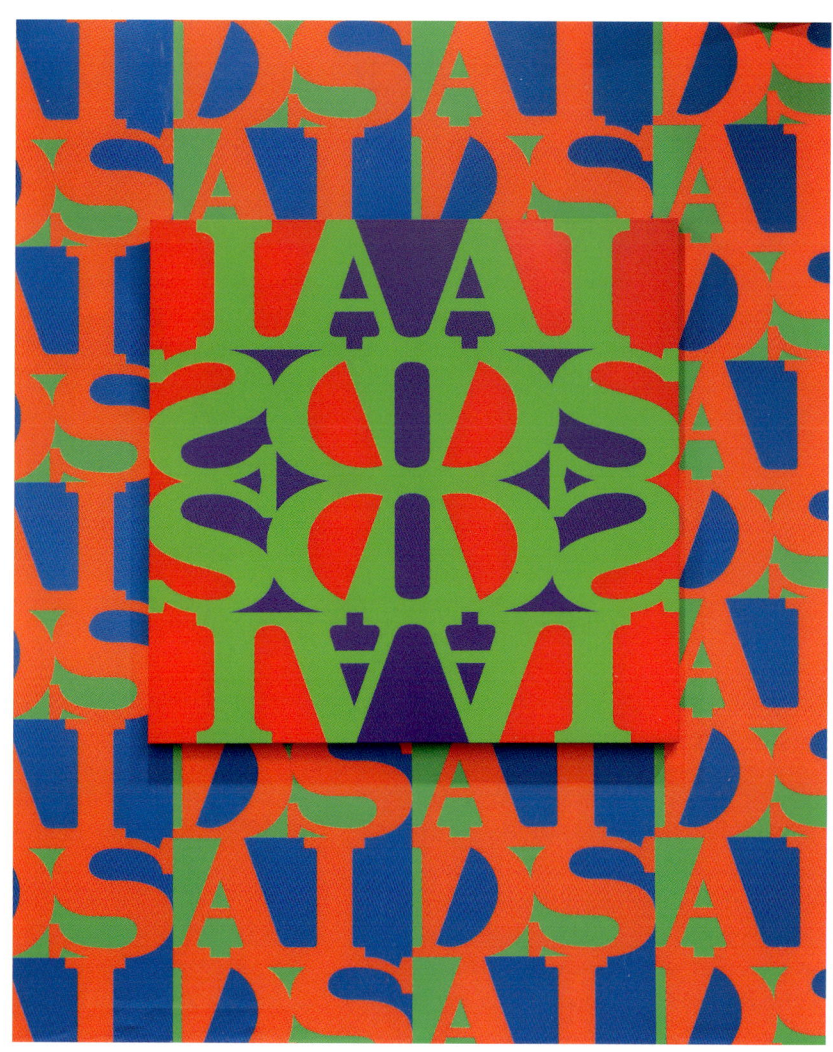

Great AIDS (Cadmium Green Yellow) and *AIDS (Wallpaper)*, **AA Bronson + General Idea**, 1990/2018, installation view at Maureen Paley, London, 2018

I want a dyke for president. I want a person
with aids for president and I want a fag for
vice president and I want someone with no
health insurance and I want someone who grew
up in a place where the earth is so saturated
with toxic waste that they didn't have a
choice about getting leukemia. I want a
president that had an abortion at sixteen and
I want a candidate who isn't the lesser of two
evils and I want a president who lost their
last lover to aids, who still sees that in
their eyes every time they lay down torest,
who held their lover in their arms and knew
they were dying. I want a president with no
airconditioning, a president who has stood on
line at the clinic, at the dmv, at the welfare
office and has been unemployed and layed off and
sexually harrassed and gaybashed and deported.
I want someone who has spent the night in the
tombs and had a cross burned on their lawn and
survived rape. I want someone who has been in
love and been hurt, who respects sex, who has
made mistakes and learned from them. I want a
Black woman for president. I want someone with
bad teeth ~~and an attitude~~, someone who has
eaten ~~that nasty~~ hospital food, someone who
crossdresses and has done drugs and been in
therapy. I want someone who has committed
civil disobedience. And I want to know why this
isn't possible. I want to know why we started
learning somewhere down the line that a president
is always a clown: always a john and never
a hooker. Always a boss and never a worker,
always a liar, always a thief and never caught.

I Want a President, **Zoe Leonard**, 1992,
typewritten text on paper, 27.9 x 21.6 cm
(11 x 8½ in)

Zoe Leonard's *I Want a President* was written in the run-up to the 1992 US presidential election, which took place at the height of the AIDS epidemic. The piece, which was inspired by poet Eileen Myles's bid for presidency, was initially written for an underground LGBTQ magazine that ceased publication and was instead photocopied and circulated among friends. The typeface and poster format of the image was consistent with the visual language of contemporaneous activist groups calling out the establishment's negligence regarding the impact of AIDS, such as ACT UP (AIDS Coalition to Unleash Power) and Gran Fury. The artwork has since reappeared in popular culture, going viral on social media in response to Donald Trump's presidential win in 2016 as women, people of colour and queer people anticipated further marginalization under his presidency. Whenever progressive leadership has appeared unattainable, Leonard's poem has become a symbol of solidarity, collective action and hope.

The late 1970s were a tumultuous time in Britain, marked by civil unrest and economic gloom, and culminating in Margaret Thatcher's Conservative government coming to power in 1979. Jill Posener documented graffiti on the streets of London that gave a voice to the disillusioned and frustrated people of the city, publishing the images in the 1982 photobook *Spray it Loud* as a reminder that there is 'resistance and rebellion'. Slogans in the book respond to a range of political issues, including a national housing crisis, nuclear war and gender-based violence. *Dalston* is one of many billboards featured in the book whose sexist advertising has been subverted by feminist activists. The hilarious improvements to the text offer a tongue-in-cheek call to action in response to a climate of lesbian erasure, lack of female agency and women regularly being made to feel unsafe.

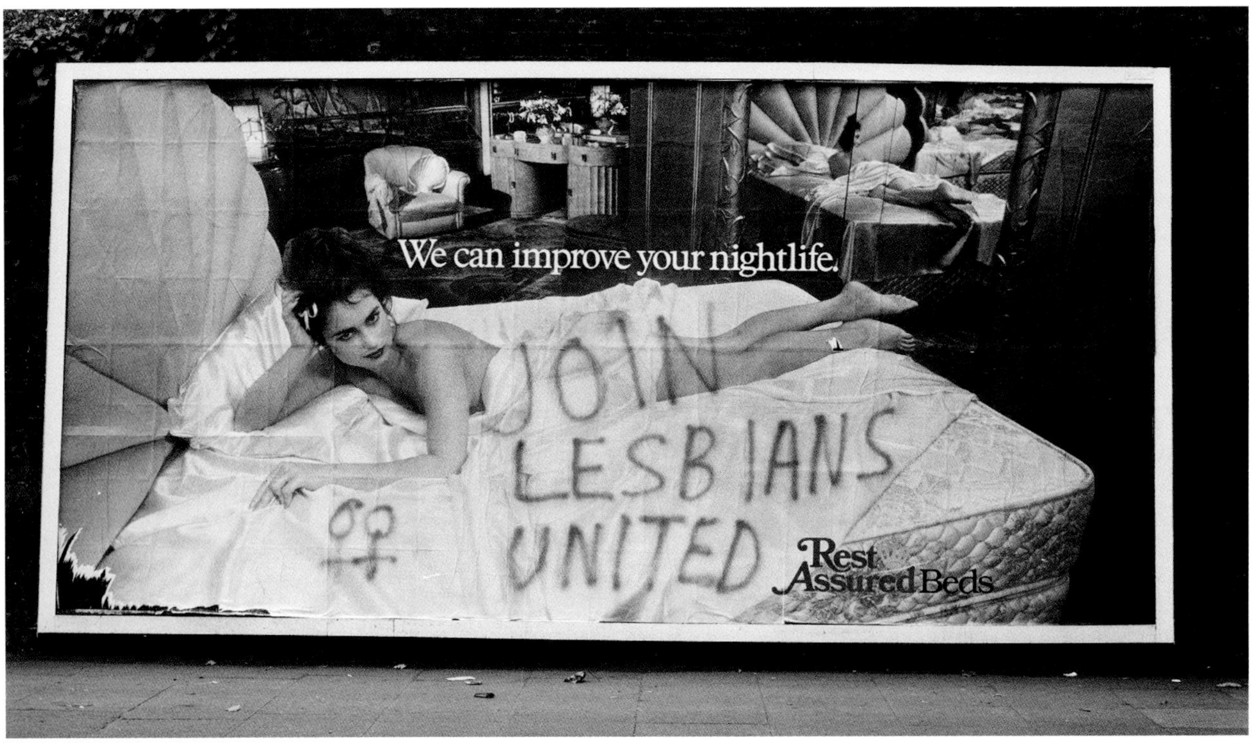

Dalston, **Jill Posener**, 1981, gelatin silver
print from a 35mm negative,
dimensions variable

Dyke Action Machine! (DAM!)

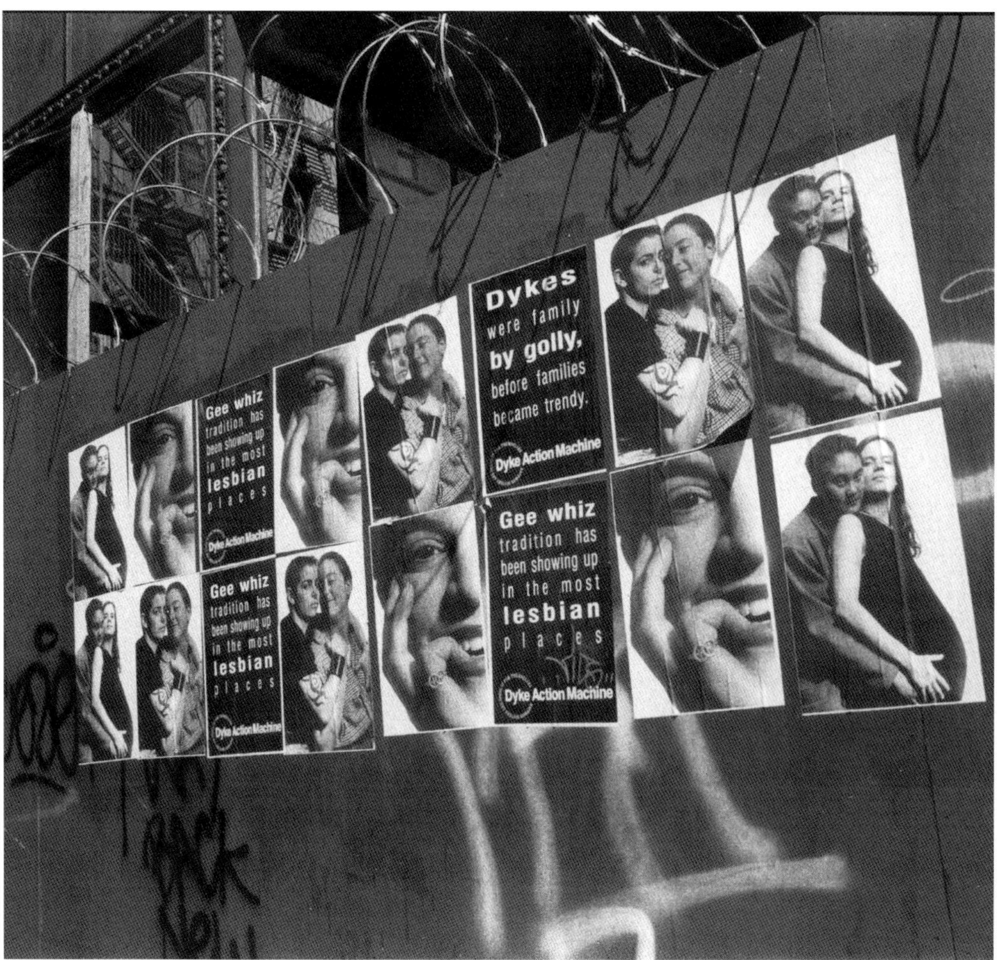

Dyke Action Machine! (DAM!) is a two-person public art project founded in 1991 by artist Carrie Moyer and photographer Sue Schaffner. Between 1991 and 2004, the pair, who remained anonymous for many years, wheat-pasted Xeroxed posters across New York City, inserting lesbians into recognizably commercial contexts. Delivered with wry wit, their mission was to offer the lesbian viewer 'all the things she'd been denied by the mainstream: power, inclusion and the public recognition of identity'. The 1992 campaign *Family Values* riffed off a campaign of the same year by *Family Circle* magazine that positioned the nuclear family as a trendy marketing tool. DAM!'s images of fluid queer families challenged the heteronormative framework dominating mainstream media and questioned the influence of the Christian right's aggressive family values rhetoric.

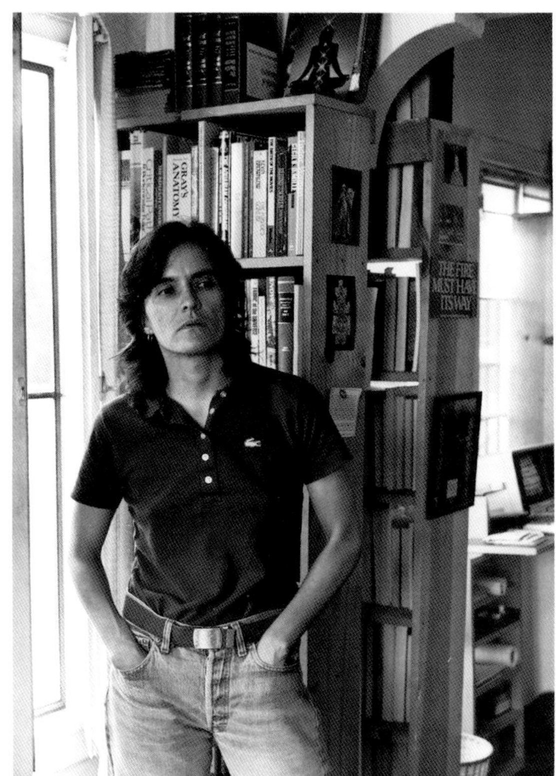

Yolanda from the series 'Latina Lesbians',
Laura Aguilar, 1987, gelatin silver print,
35.6 x 27.9 cm (14 x 11 in)

My latina side infuses my lesbian side with chispa
& pasión. I am a lifelong lesbian and I think that
women hold powerful promise for changing conditions
on the planet. You think I look hostile? Maybe
it has to do with a passion for and an impatience
with a vision. Maybe it comes from comparing
what could be with what is. ¿! Y qué?!

Laura Aguilar's 'Latina Lesbians' is a landmark series of black-and-white photographs of people who self-identify as lesbian and Latina, taken between 1986 and 1990. Each one is accompanied by a handwritten note in which the subject speaks to their relationship with their identity. Yolanda Retter is one of many well-known Chicanx creatives included in the series. She was a librarian, archivist and author respected for her lifelong commitment to activism, as illustrated by the background carefully selected in collaboration with Aguilar. Retter's confrontational manner, which earned her the nickname 'Yolanda the Terrible', was demonstrated when she appeared on *The Oprah Winfrey Show* alongside other separatists and challenged the host's view of man-hating lesbians. By celebrating the personalities and multifaceted experiences of the individuals in the photographic series, Aguilar recognizes the collective contributions of her community.

Sunil Gupta created his series '"Pretended" Family Relationships' in response to Margaret Thatcher's British government introducing a series of laws, known as Section 28, that prohibited the 'promotion of homosexuality' by local authorities and the teaching in schools of 'the acceptability of homosexuality as a pretended family relationship'. The 1988 laws had severe consequences for the LGBTQIA+ community in the UK and were widely protested against until their repeal 25 years later. There are three parts to each of Gupta's images: a colour photograph of an unnamed couple, a poem by his then partner Stephen Dodd and a black-and-white image from one of the many demonstrations against Section 28. In *Untitled #4*, a gay male couple reclining on a bed is juxtaposed with a protester holding a triangular placard that reads 'FIGHT'. As all three figures lock eyes with the viewer we are reminded that the relatively mundane scene of queer domesticity is in fact hard-won.

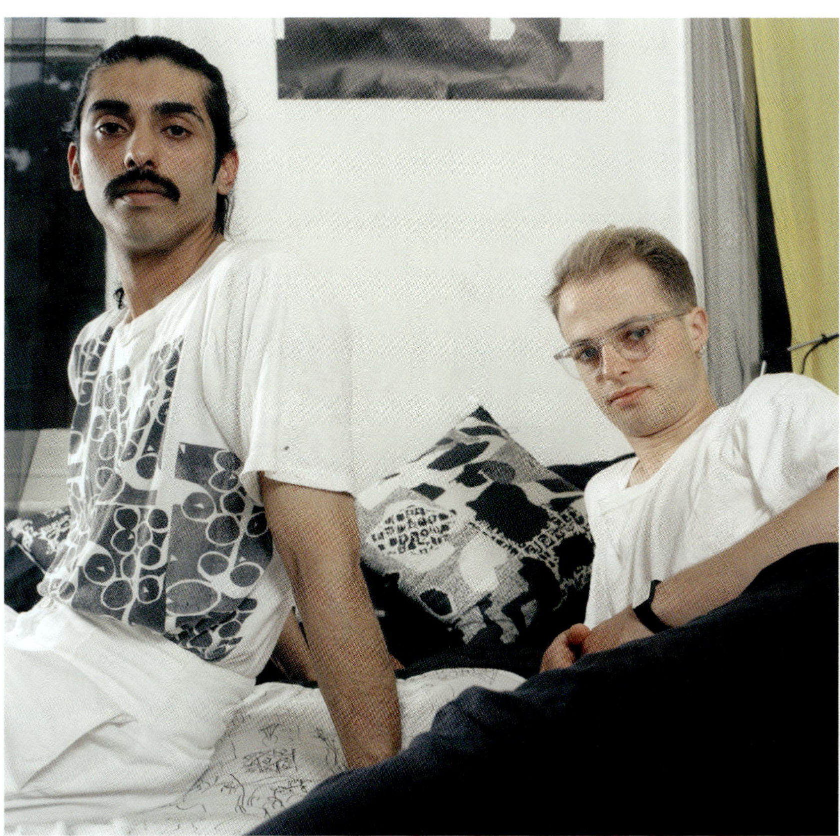

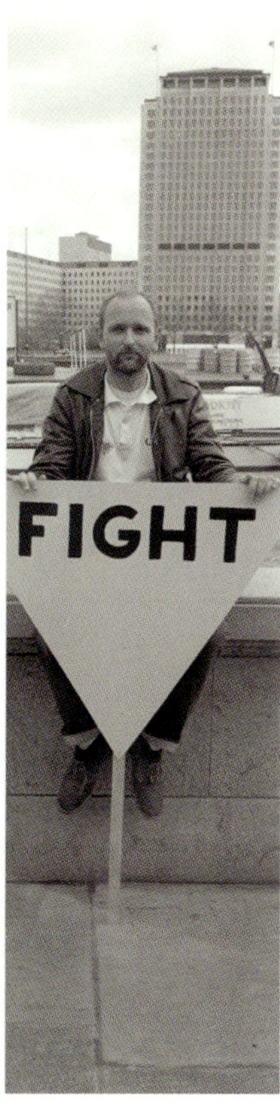

Untitled #4 from the series '"Pretended" Family Relationships', **Sunil Gupt**a, 1988, archival inkjet print, 70 x 91 cm (24 x 36 in)

Keith Haring is one of the best-known artists of the twentieth century. He was prolific during his short lifetime and his distinctive pop art now appears throughout mainstream culture, from high to low. Engaged in social issues from the start of his career, he made posters against nuclear war and apartheid. Once the AIDS epidemic began, deeply impacting his community in New York City and eventually taking Haring's own life, the disease became the central focus of his work. The iconic 1989 poster *Ignorance = Fear* features slogans used by activist groups and a pink triangle that is a symbol of the LGBTQIA+ community. His yellow figures see no evil, hear no evil and speak no evil, like the American public and authorities whose inaction exacerbated the crisis. The artist made this work the year before he died, the same year he founded the Keith Haring Foundation, which perpetuates his artistic legacy and the AIDS-related fundraising and research he was so passionate about.

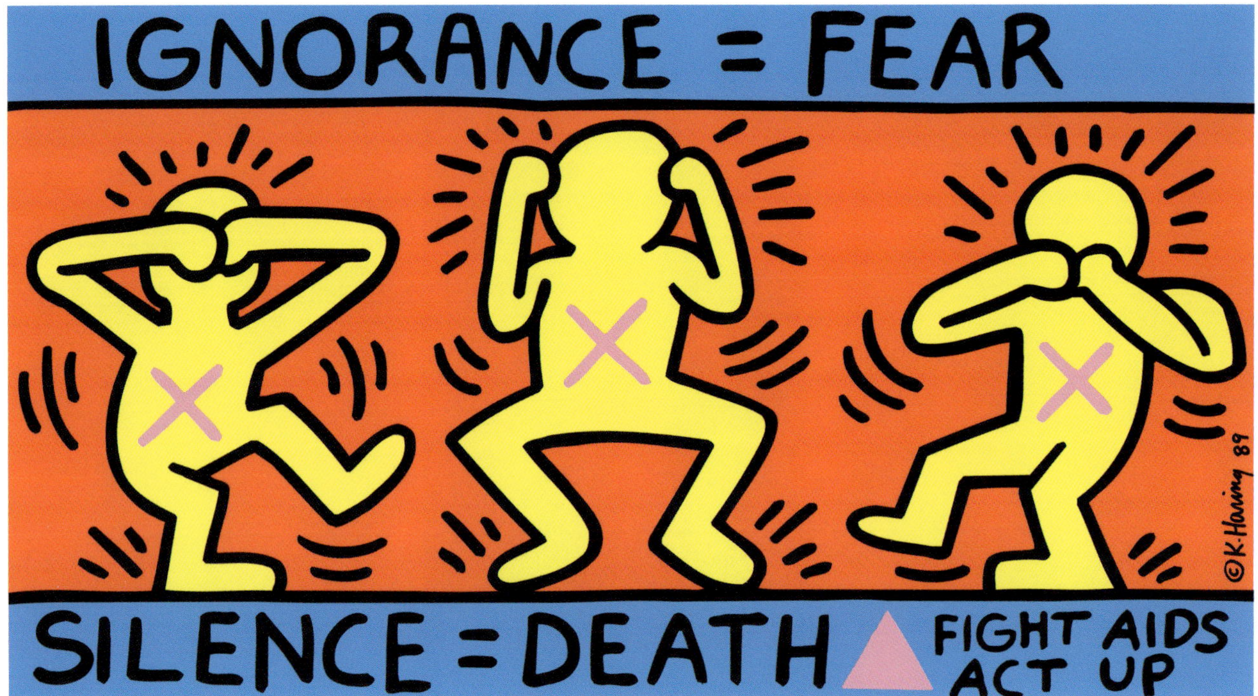

Ignorance = Fear, **Keith Haring**, 1989, poster, 61 x 110 cm (24 x 43¼ in)

He Kills Me, **Donald Moffett**, 1987,
offset lithograph, 59.7 x 95.3 cm
(23½ x 37½ in)

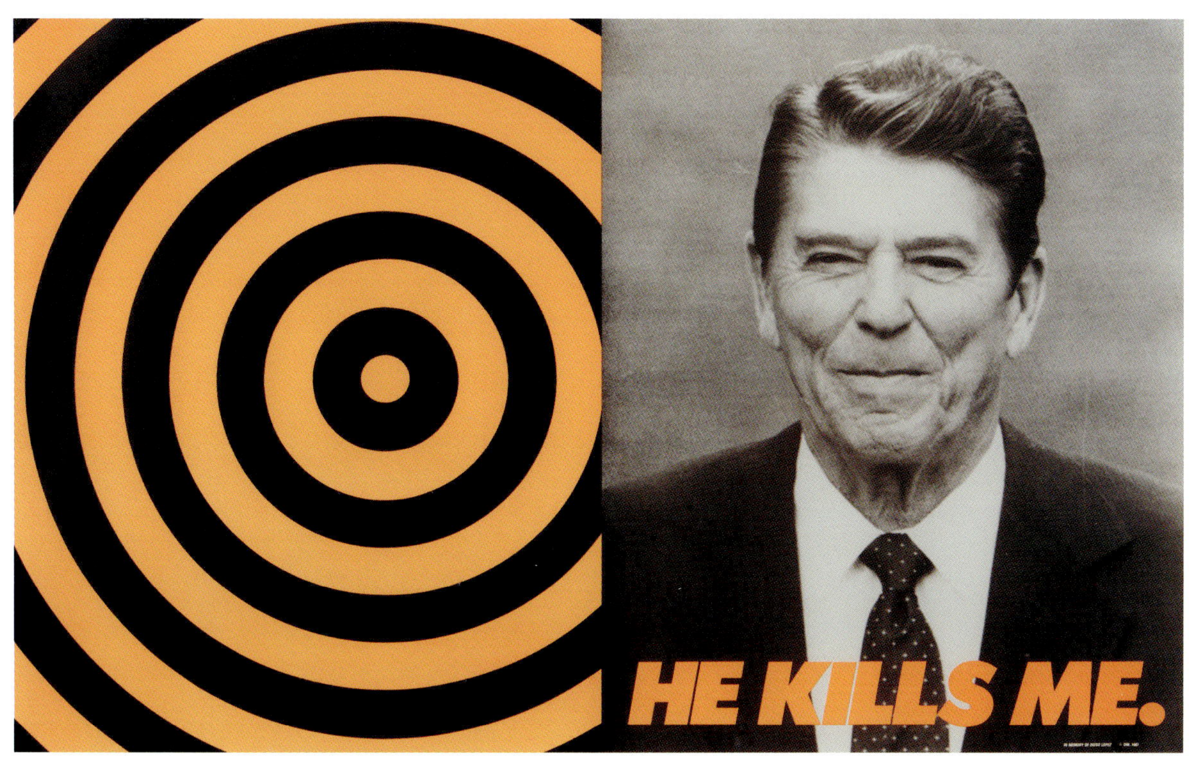

Donald Moffett emerged as an artist and activist in late 1980s America. He was a founding member of the collective Gran Fury and formed the transdisciplinary studio Bureau in partnership with fellow activist artist Marlene McCarty. Moffett's poster *He Kills Me* was made for a demonstration organized by ACT UP (AIDS Coalition to Unleash Power) in response to Ronald Reagan's Presidential Commission on the HIV Epidemic. Six years after health officials first became aware of AIDS, the 1987 commission was formed to investigate the deadly effects of the disease. However, activists were frustrated by the lack of gay representation among the appointed team and were sceptical about their expertise. Appropriating the visual language of mass media through the combination of image and text, the poster directly calls out the president's silence, holding him responsible for the thousands of deaths that occurred during this long period of inaction.

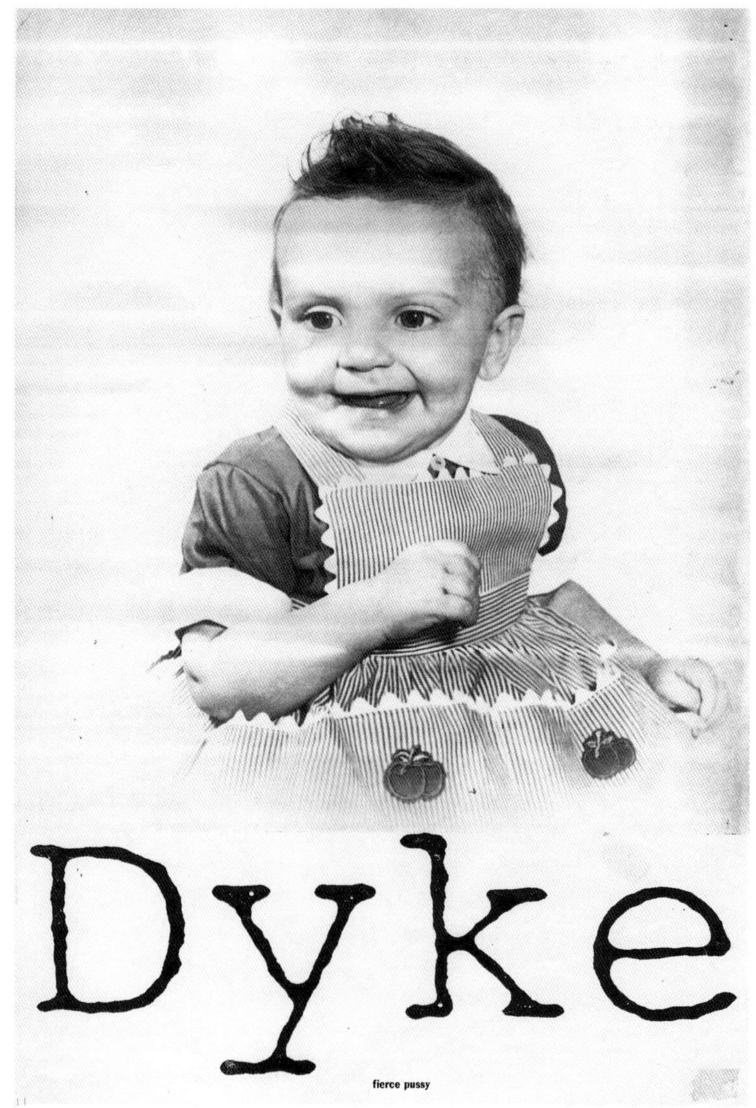

DYKE poster from the series 'Family and Found Photographs', **fierce pussy**, 1991

fierce pussy was founded by Joy Episalla, Carrie Yamaoka, Nancy Brooks Brody and Zoe Leonard who, originally members of ACT UP (AIDS Coalition to Unleash Power), formed a women-only collective. They were active between 1991 and 1996 and again from 2008. The core of their early collaborative work was public art that addressed the homophobic rhetoric of American conservative propaganda. Their posters parodying right-wing campaigns appeared around the streets of New York City, where they were wheat-pasted to trucks, walls and billboards. The group encouraged their audience to make and disseminate copies of their posters, which were originally printed on the photocopy machines in the magazine offices where they worked (they often credit Condé Nast for its unwitting support). This image from 'Family and Found Photographs' challenges the Christian right's claim that gay people are against family values by pairing a photo of a beaming baby with the word 'dyke', a proud reclaiming of a stigmatized term that uses humour to tackle a painful issue.

'Faces and Phases', **Zanele Muholi**,
2006–present, installation view at
GL Strand, Copenhagen

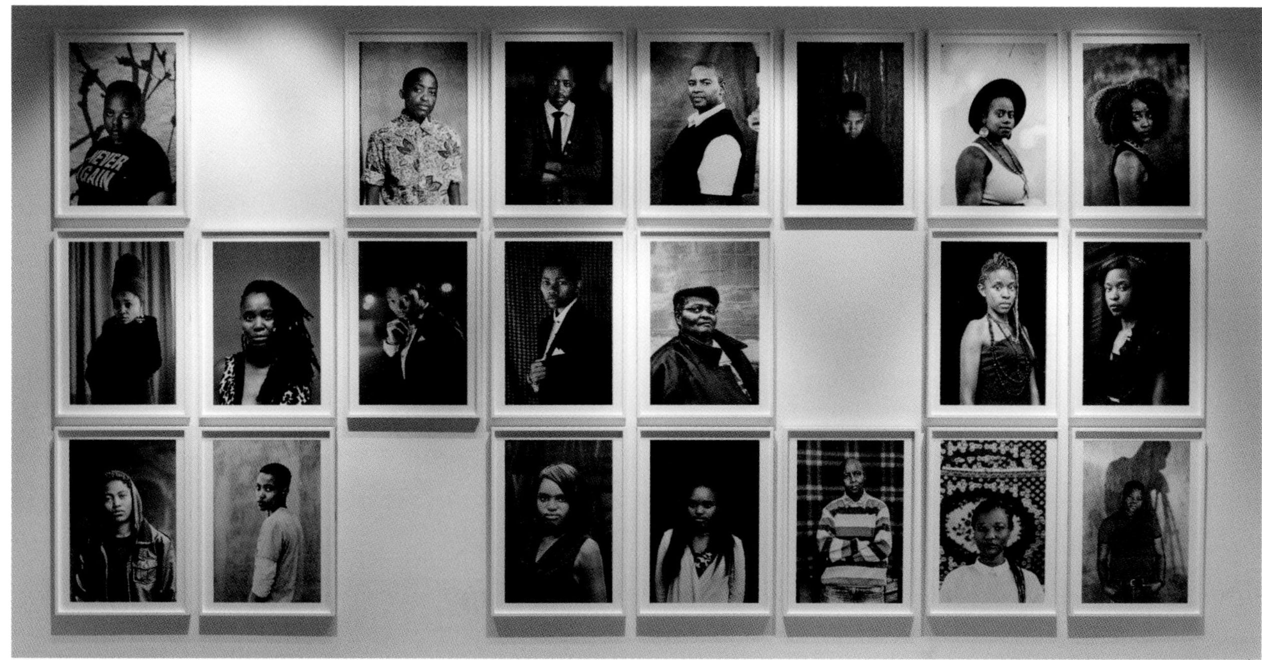

Working across photography and film, Zanele Muholi describes themself as a visual activist. Begun in 2006, 'Faces and Phases' is a landmark photographic series archiving the queer faces of post-apartheid South Africa. Inspired by the portraits of lesbians done by JEB (Joan E. Biren), Muholi's project is an ambitious undertaking in the representation of Black lesbians and genderqueer individuals. Each sitter locks eyes with the viewer as we are asked to consider the multifaceted experience of being an African lesbian. Compiled as a book in 2010 and exhibited all around the world in extensive grids, the portraits celebrate the richness and diversity of the community, presenting a nuanced exploration into the construction of identity. By building relationships with sitters and photographing many individuals multiple times over the years, Muholi gives each person the opportunity to write their own history as they collectively call for recognition, respect and validation for their community.

Love

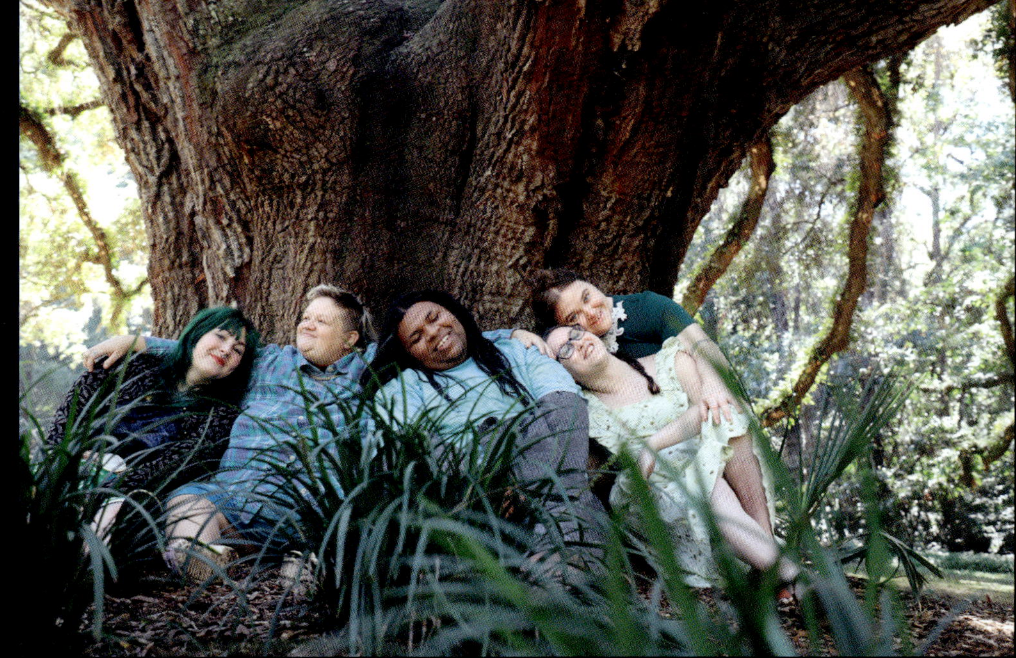

Everyone deserves unconditional love. For LGBTQIA+ people access to love has not always been a universal right. In the face of rejection or a lack of understanding, from family, community or self, queer people have been forced to seek out those who accept them for who they are and share their values. The relationships that make us feel safe, loved, help us grow and bring us joy take all sorts of configurations: from caregiving and mentoring, to romance, friendship and creative collaborations. 'Chosen family' – as depicted in the work of photographer Shoog MacDaniel, for example – is an important concept for the queer community. A lot of love is found in queer spaces, particularly the bars, clubs and parties where many LGBTQIA+ people find acceptance and the safety to be their true selves for the first time.

Loving connections with other queer people and allies, whether transient or enduring, are vital stepping stones in the journey towards self-love. Artists candidly capture these meaningful relationships and tender connections in their work, showing love for their subjects by immortalizing them through

Live Oak Love, **Shoog McDaniel and**

art. For others, artistic practice is a way to excavate the past, reclaiming the elements of lost familial and cultural histories that have meaning, and which become an integral part of their future selves.

The way queer people love has been restricted by society, from the risk of violence when displaying affection in public, to laws prohibiting LGBTQIA+ people from having sexual relationships, cohabiting or getting married. As rights to equal marriage are granted at different rates around the world, artists use their practice to reflect on the nuances of queer relationships and appeal for equality. While many LGBTQIA+ people reject marriage as a heteronormative institution with a long history of rejecting queer people, others claim their right to marriage in the name of equal rights, to pay respects to those who fought for it and to formally recognize relationships. Made in 2002, when same-sex marriage was still illegal in America, Patricia Cronin's *Memorial to a Marriage* (see left) depicts herself and her partner, artist Deborah Kass. Designed for a burial plot and installed in a cemetery, the sculpture highlights the fact that their relationship would only be officially documented upon their deaths through wills or healthcare paperwork. Similar restrictions apply to parenting, with LGBTQIA+ people historically perceived as a threat to children, when in reality those lucky enough to be raised by queer people are deeply wanted and loved. Throughout history, scenes of domestic and other loving partnerships and family structures – real or imagined – have been the only traces of queer relationships. Art reflects the magic of queer bonds, the freedom that comes from existing outside of restrictive heteronormative traditions, and the excess of love found within the queer community.

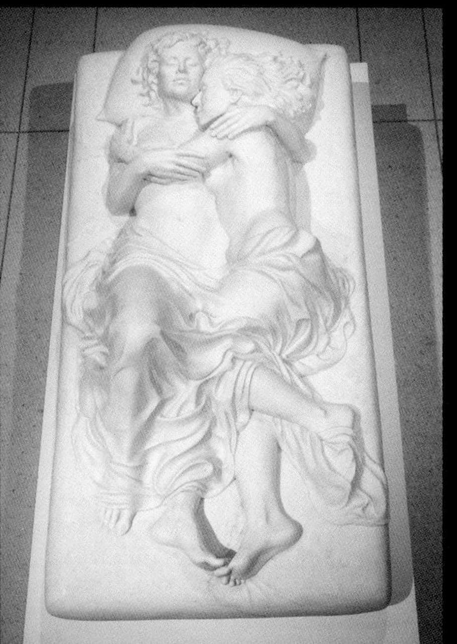

Memorial to a Marriage,
Patricia Cronin, 2002

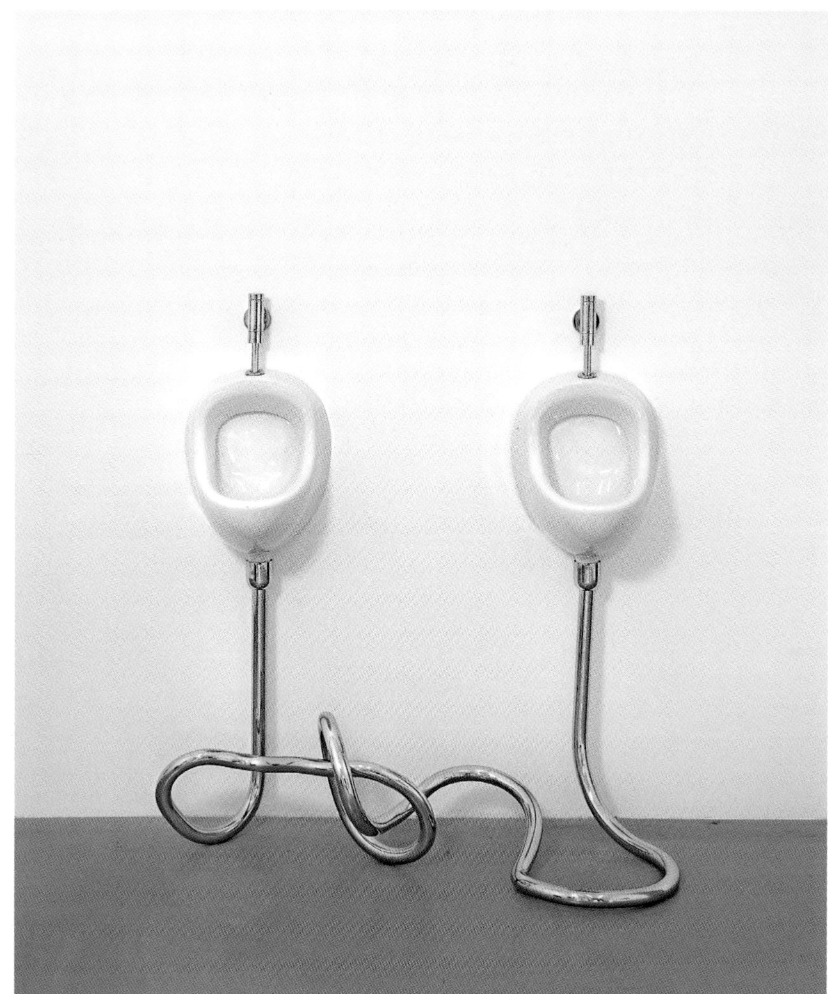

Elmgreen & Dragset

Elmgreen & Dragset's sculpture *Gay Marriage* consists of a pair of wall-mounted porcelain urinals linked together by an intertwining stainless-steel pipe that rests on the floor below in a knot. In the precursors to this work, *Marriage* (2004) and *Second Marriage* (2008), both pairs of sinks, difference is denoted in subtle details such as a bar of soap or opposing tap positions. The urinals are identical, their sameness brings harmony. The queer balance is offset as the pipe buckles where they meet, a moment of tension reflecting the restrictions imposed by the institution of marriage not built for same-sex couples. Although Elmgreen & Dragset ended their romantic relationship in 2004, they continue to collaborate artistically. They have likened their ongoing partnership to this sculpture, to the complex nature of entanglement with another, the joys and challenges it brings and the deep love and connection underpinning it all.

Born in 1960s northern England to Jamaican parents, Ajamu X grew up with a lack of images of Black men, who appeared in the media only as sports stars or the subjects of police clashes. His own photography addresses this lack of representation, and he creates images that resonate with his own experience and challenge dominant narratives around masculinity and Blackness. His work, which was inspired by events such as the National Black Gay Men's Conference, which began in London in 1987, and the gay male sex parties that he began hosting in the 1990s, serves as an important contribution to Black queer art and photography. *Long Time Companion* is one of many tender photographs that celebrate sexuality, desire and what he refers to as 'pleasure activism'. The love shared by the companions appears deeply sensual, spiritual and unbreakable.

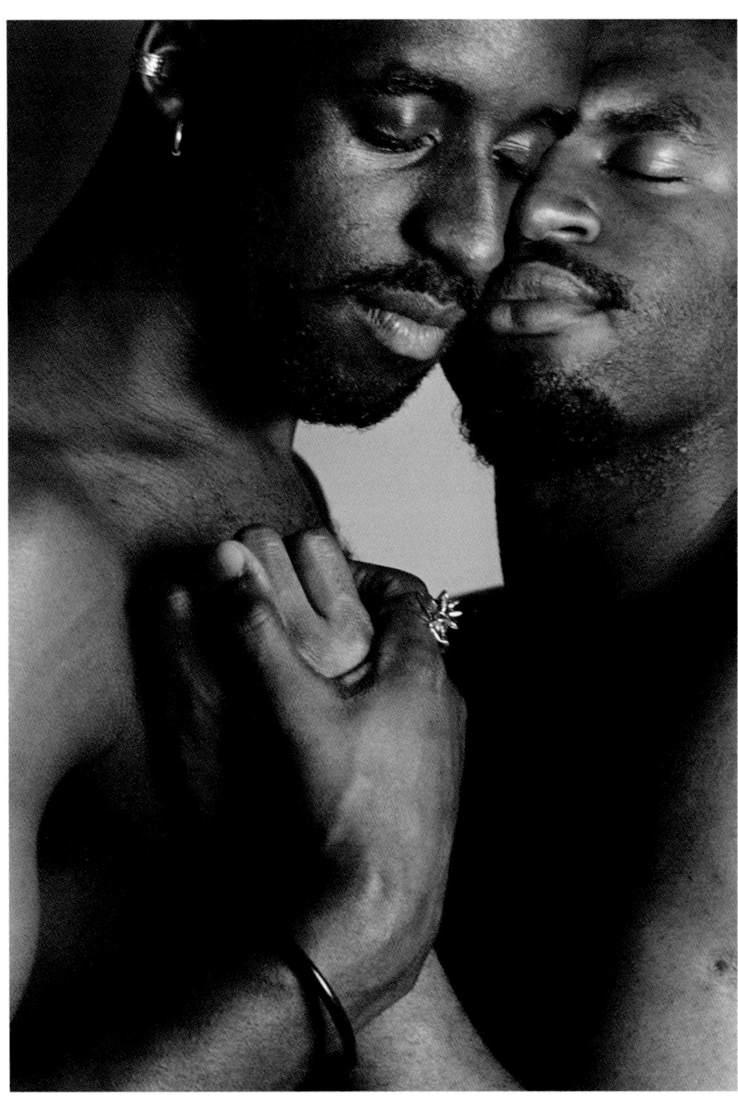

Long Time Companion, **Ajamu X**, 1992

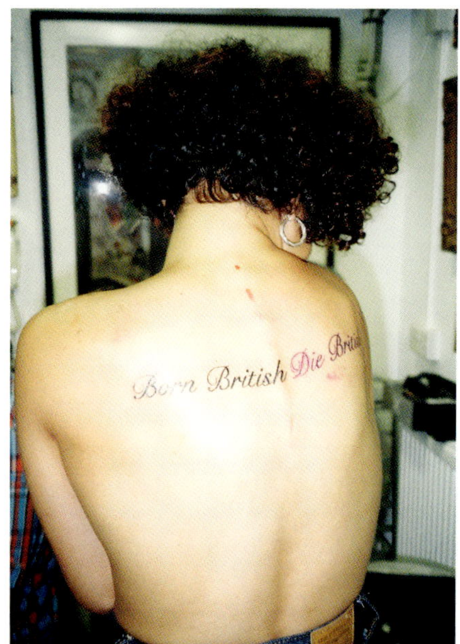

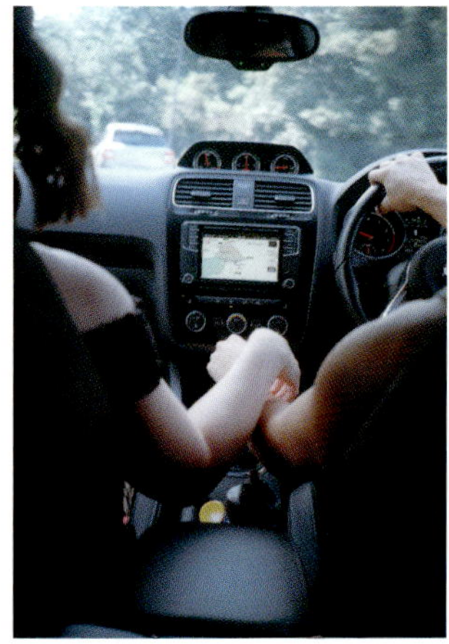

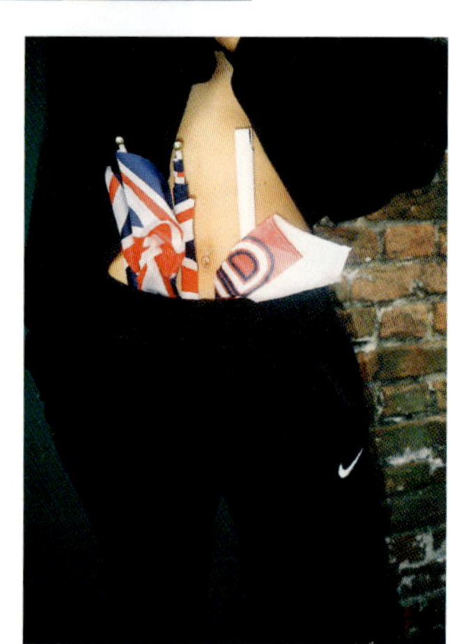

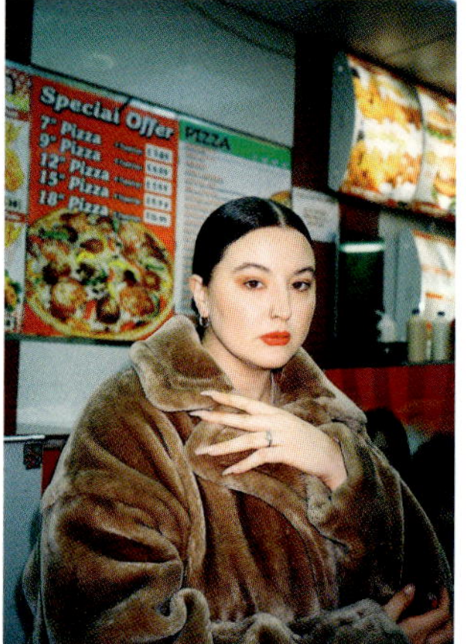

'flags for countries that don't exist but bodies that do', **Rene Matić**, 2018–2021, inkjet prints; from left to right: Jenny and *Zac Holding Hands* (2019), *Rene at New Wave Tattoo* (2020), *VE Day, Skegness III* (2020), *Maggie in Morleys* (2020), *Mia and Cait Snogging I* (2020)

Rene Matić's practice occupies a space they call 'rude(ness)', an 'evidencing and honouring of the in-between'. They take inspiration from dance and music movements such as Northern Soul, Ska and 2-Tone as a tool to delve into the complex relationship between West Indian and white working-class culture in Britain. This photographic series explores the intimacies, familial bonds and shared joys experienced by LGBTQIA+ people in resistance to an oppressive world.

Immortalizing moments of celebration within the queer art world, the images feature key figures from a young generation driving change, such as singer Campbell King and writer Travis Alabanza. Matić's subjects beat the odds against layered marginal identities, finding belonging in London's subcultural creative scene. Through their lens we bear witness to the love and solidarity found in the friendships – both fleeting and deep rooted – that constitute queer community.

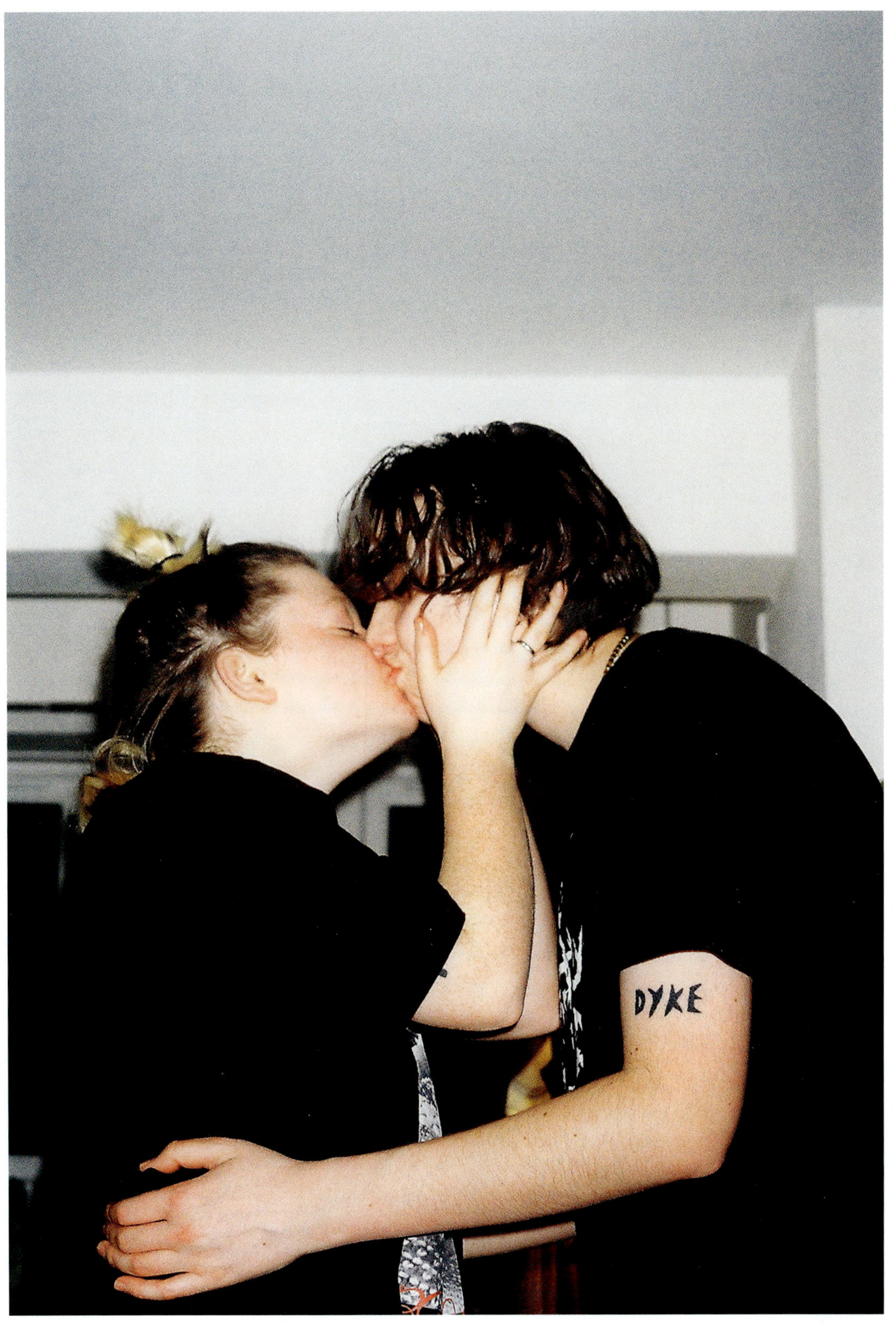
DYKE

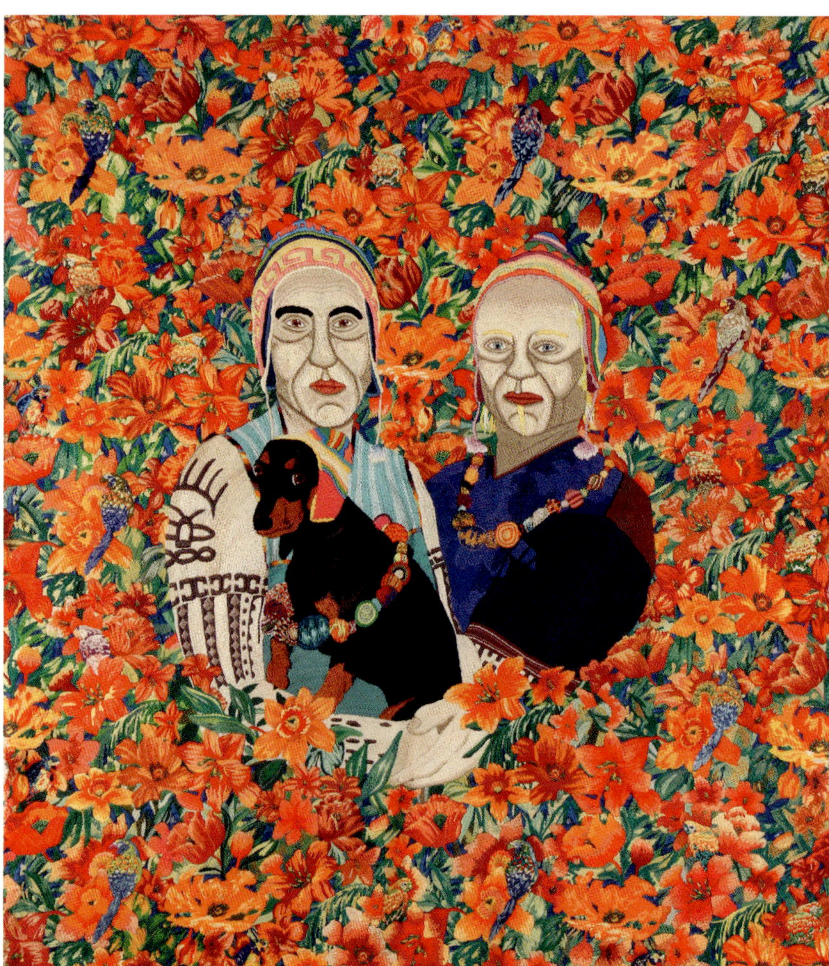

Family Coyita, **Chiachio & Giannone**, 2011–2012, cotton thread on fabric, 160 x 130 cm (63 x 51 in)

Chiachio & Giannone

Artist couple Leo Chiachio and Daniel Giannone have collaborated on art since meeting in 2003. Their vibrantly coloured maximalist textile work redefines the traditional family portrait. In *Family Coyita* their dazzling hand embroidery depicts two men and a dog, a family unit representative of contemporary queer society. 'Coyita' is the diminutive of 'Coya' or 'Kolla', a group of Indigenous people from the northern provinces of Argentina. Incorporating motifs and patterns referencing their Latin American culture, Chiachio & Giannone's work reflects the home they share in Argentina and their wider community. Beginning with sketches that are transferred to canvas and stitched with cotton yarns, wool, rayon or jewel-effect threads, the pair work on each of their pieces for more than seven months. Fabric is often sourced from friends, adding layers of meaning to the work, which represents their joyful dreams of a loving home.

Brenda Goodman's *Double Portrait* depicts herself and her partner Linda, who she'd been with for 20 years at the time of painting. Despite Goodman identifying as a lesbian for most of her life, *Double Portrait* is her only painting that's so explicit in its queerness. Kept private, perhaps to protect the sacred bond shared by the couple, the painting wasn't exhibited until recently. This is the first time it's been published in a book, other than appearing in the background of a later self-portrait – Goodman was waiting for the right context within which to present it. Painting since the 1960s, Goodman is now recognized as a leading figure in American art, applauded for her technical experimentations that push the limits of abstraction and figuration. Typical of her earthy palette, *Double Portrait* is a textured study of the aging female body that emanates peace, contentment and strength.

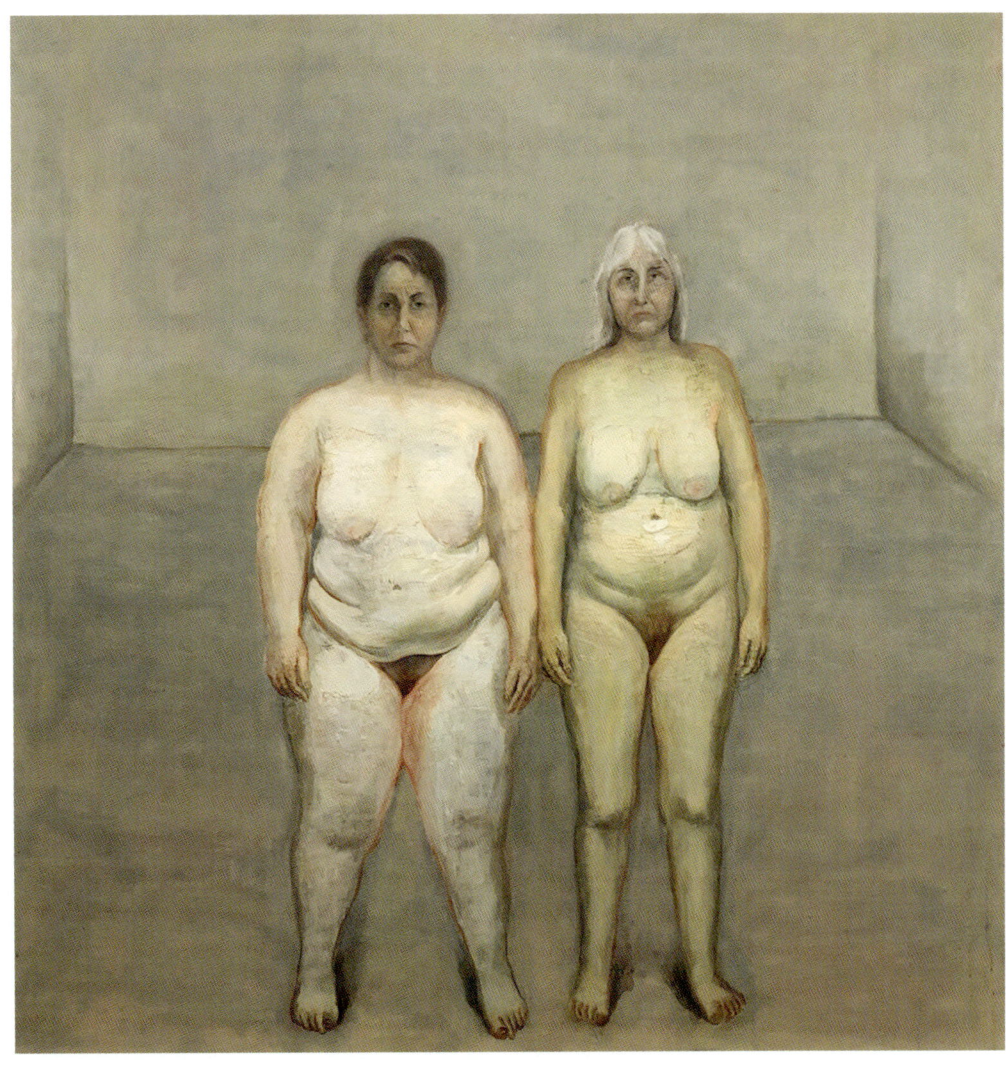

Double Portrait,
Brenda Goodman, 2006, oil on wood,
162.6 x 152.4 cm (64 x 60 in)

Yuki Kihara's 'Paradise Camp' reflects on pertinent local and global issues from the unique perspective of Fa'afafine – Sāmoa's third gender community to which she belongs. Comprising black-and-white portraits, large-scale colour photographs and films of a witty talk show and beauty pageant, the work was presented at the 59th Venice Biennale where Kihara was the first Pacific artist to be presented in the New Zealand Pavilion. Central to the body of work is

Fonofono o le nuanua: Patches of the rainbow (after Gauguin), a highly saturated tableau photograph featuring a local ensemble photographed on Upolo Island, Sāmoa. Referencing the colonial gaze underpinning Gauguin's celebrated position in art history, Kihara highlights the dark realities under the surface of the colourful depiction of the Pacific paradise – a lack of recognition and legal rights for her community and the compounding effects of climate change.

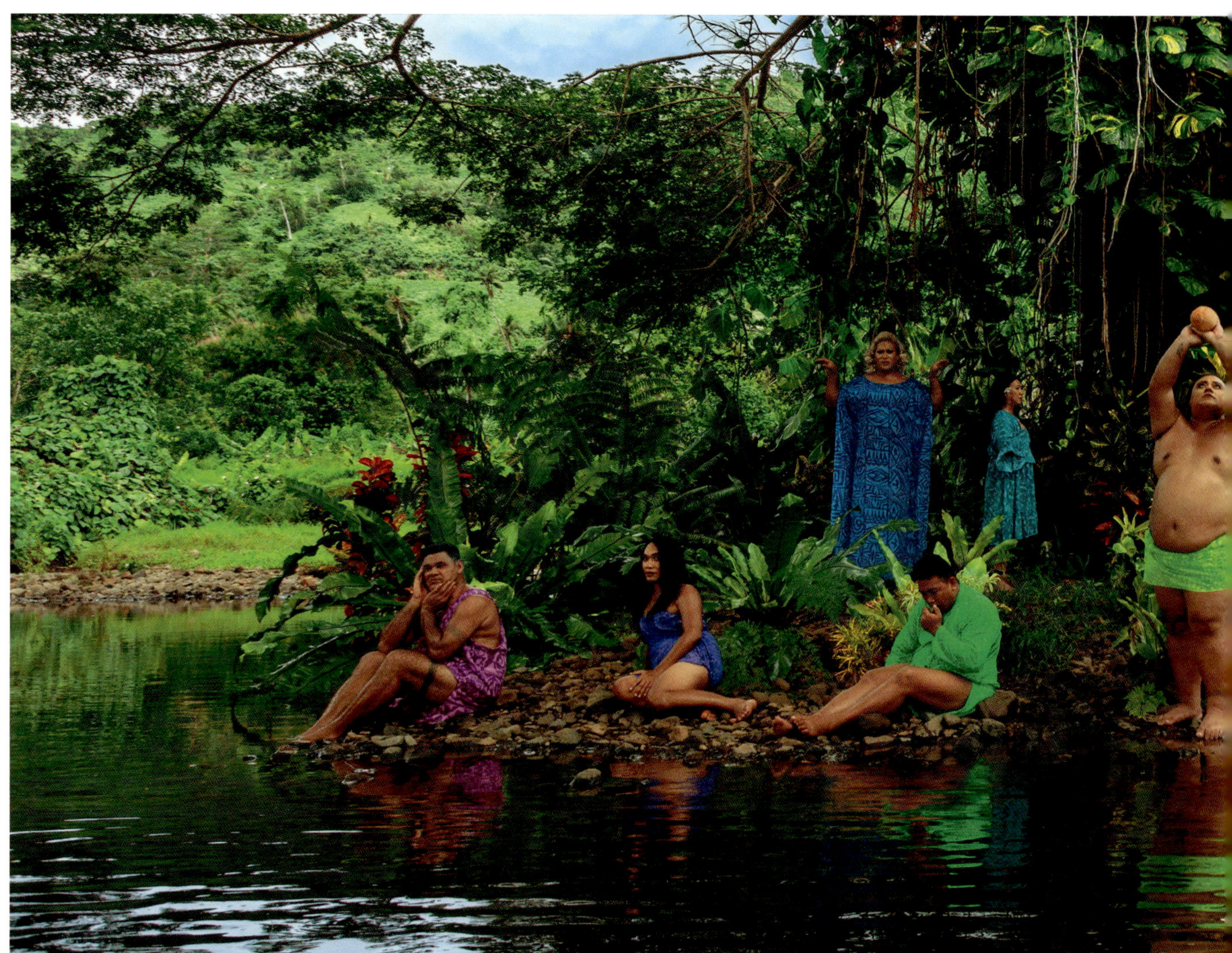

Fonofono o le nuanua: Patches of the rainbow (after Gauguin) from the series 'Paradise Camp', **Yuki Kihara**, 2020, quadriptych, C-print mounted behind acrylic glass, 139 x 375 cm (54¾ x 147⅝ in)

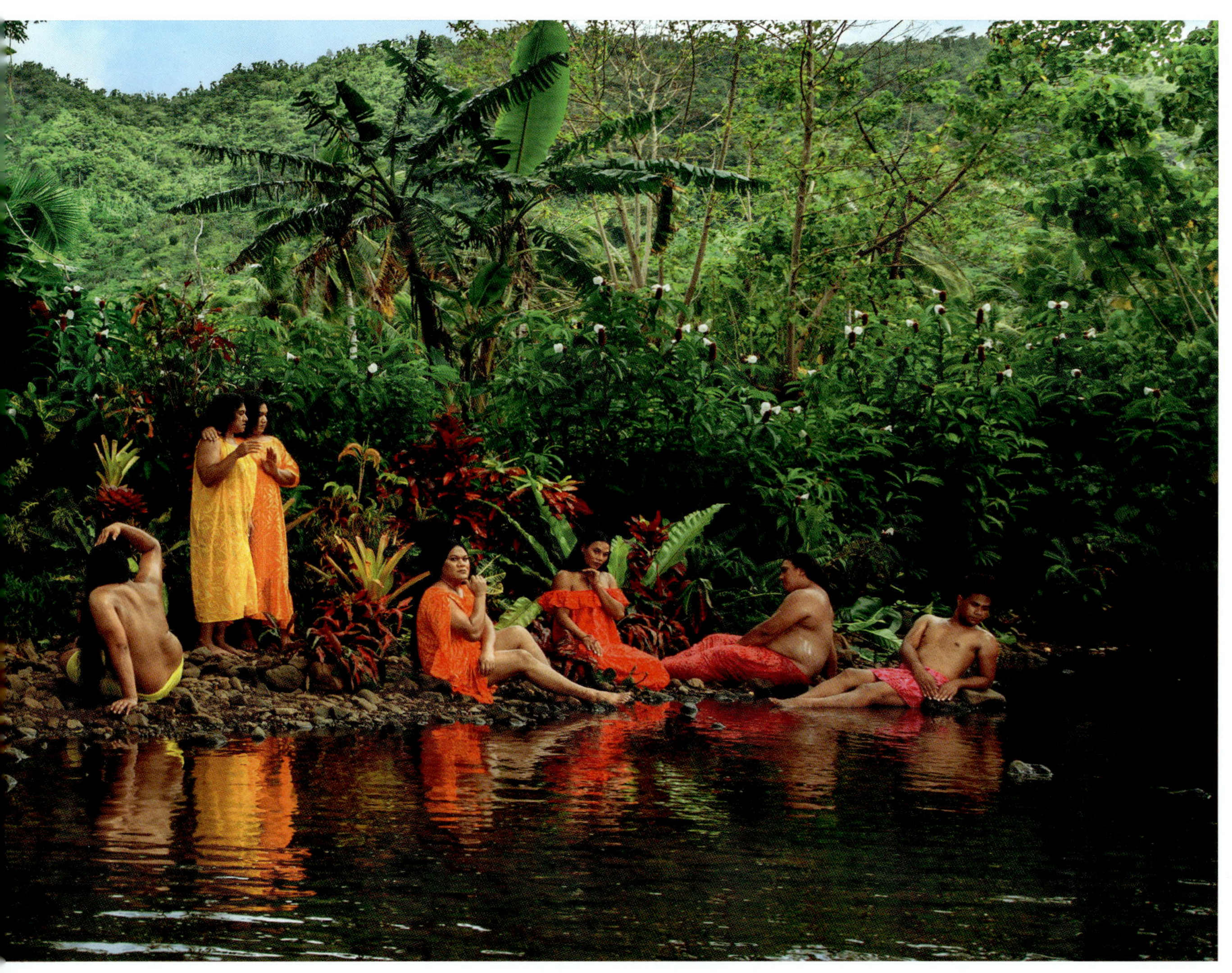

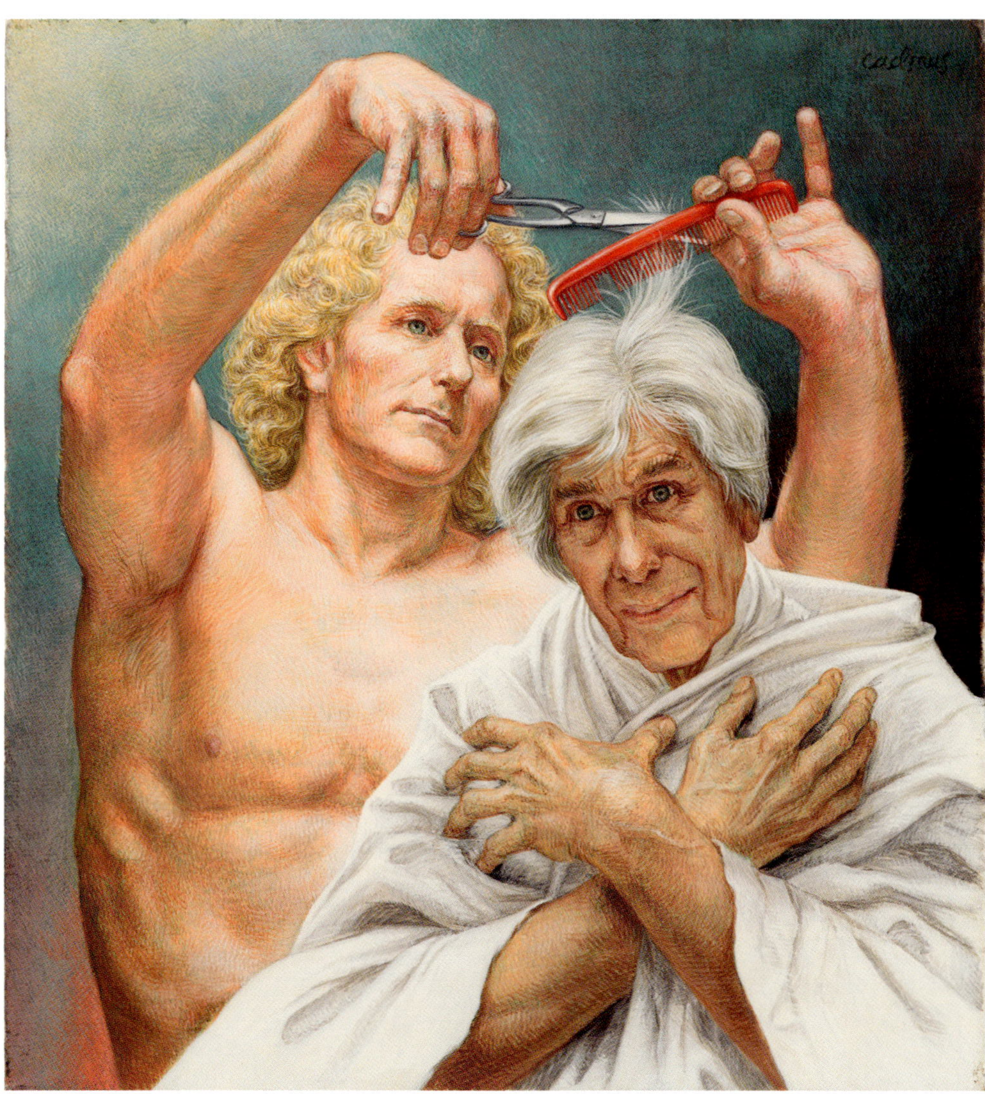

Since Paul Cadmus began painting in the 1930s his work has drawn huge controversy, largely due to its homoerotic undertones. His 1934 painting *The Fleet's In!*, a wild scene of drunken women and sailors in buttock-hugging outfits, caused a national scandal and was censored by the US Navy. The queer signifiers in his work that attracted so much negative attention were also the source of inspiration for generations of gay artists for whom depictions of their existence were scant. *The Haircut* (1986) is a portrait of the artist with his partner Jon Anderson, who

he met on a pier on Nantucket in 1965 and stayed with until his death 35 years later. Jon was the subject of much of Paul's work, from intimate nude sketches to large paintings of the couple. This late work captures a moment of love and care shared during their decades together.

The Haircut, **Paul Cadmus**, 1986, egg tempera on fibreboard, 53.3 x 48.2 cm (21 x 19 in)

     Love

Robert Indiana was a leading figure in American art from the 1960s until his death in 2018. Describing himself as an 'American painter of signs', his distinctive style of pop art explores national identity and personal history through abstraction and language. Indiana became famous for his recognizable image *LOVE*, which was first created in 1964 as a card that he sent to friends and later turned into paintings, prints and sculptures.

His compact arrangement of the word, which reveals his passion for symmetry, now appears throughout mainstream pop culture from clothing to homeware. The piece, which originally read FUCK, was created as Indiana's relationship with the abstract painter Ellsworth Kelly was coming to a rocky end. Interpreted by many as a desperate gesture of love, the image has been adopted as a global symbol of optimism and hope.

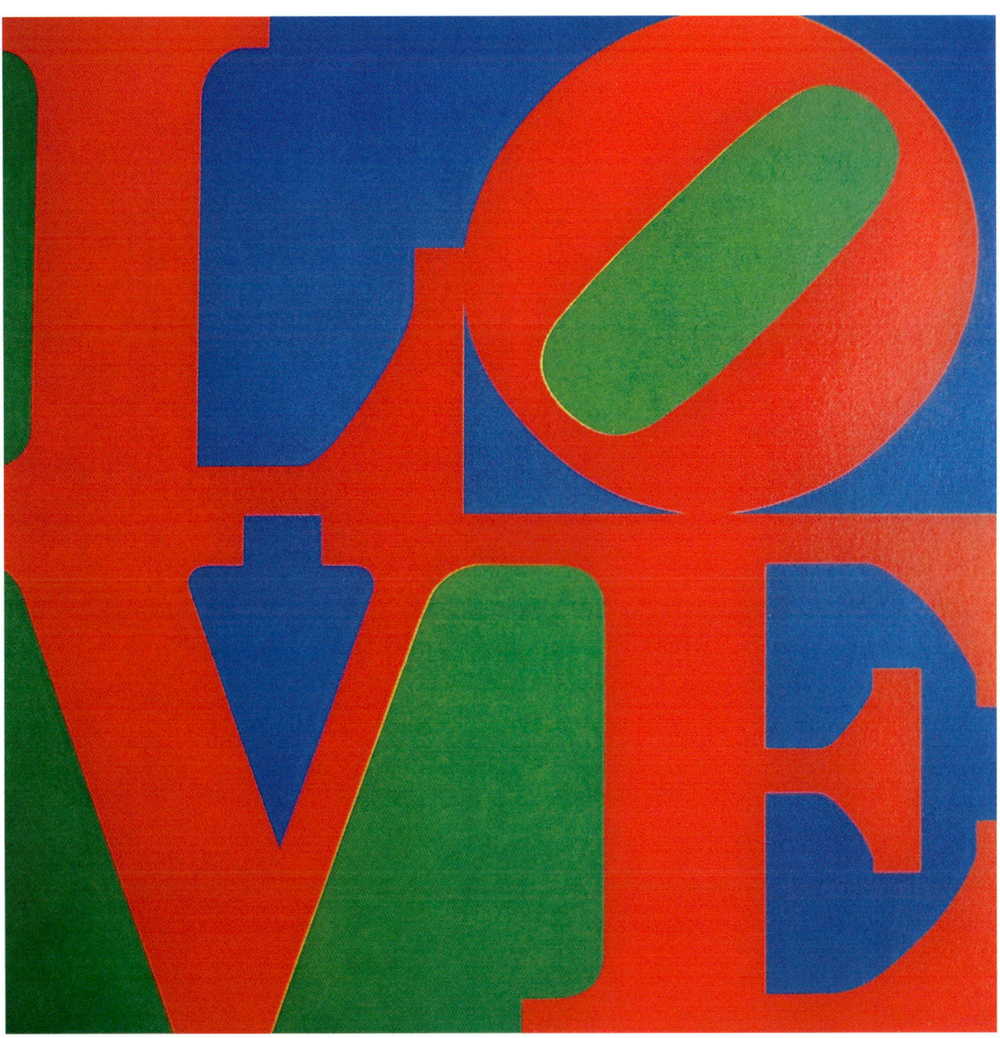

LOVE, **Robert Indiana**, 1968

Inspired by Janet Jackson's 1993 hit single of the same name, *That's the Way Love Goes* is part of a larger group of hanging textile pieces whose visual language collectively envisions a future of love. These works blur the line between image and text, painting and craft, past and present struggles and future hopes. By referencing pop music, Jeffrey Gibson creates a sense of familiarity for those that share the contemporary queer experience. His Choctaw and Cherokee heritage and appreciation for global cultures inspire his vibrant colours and shapes and the use of hide and beads. The work acts as a vivid celebration of queer and Indigenous communities and a powerful rallying call for their empowerment.

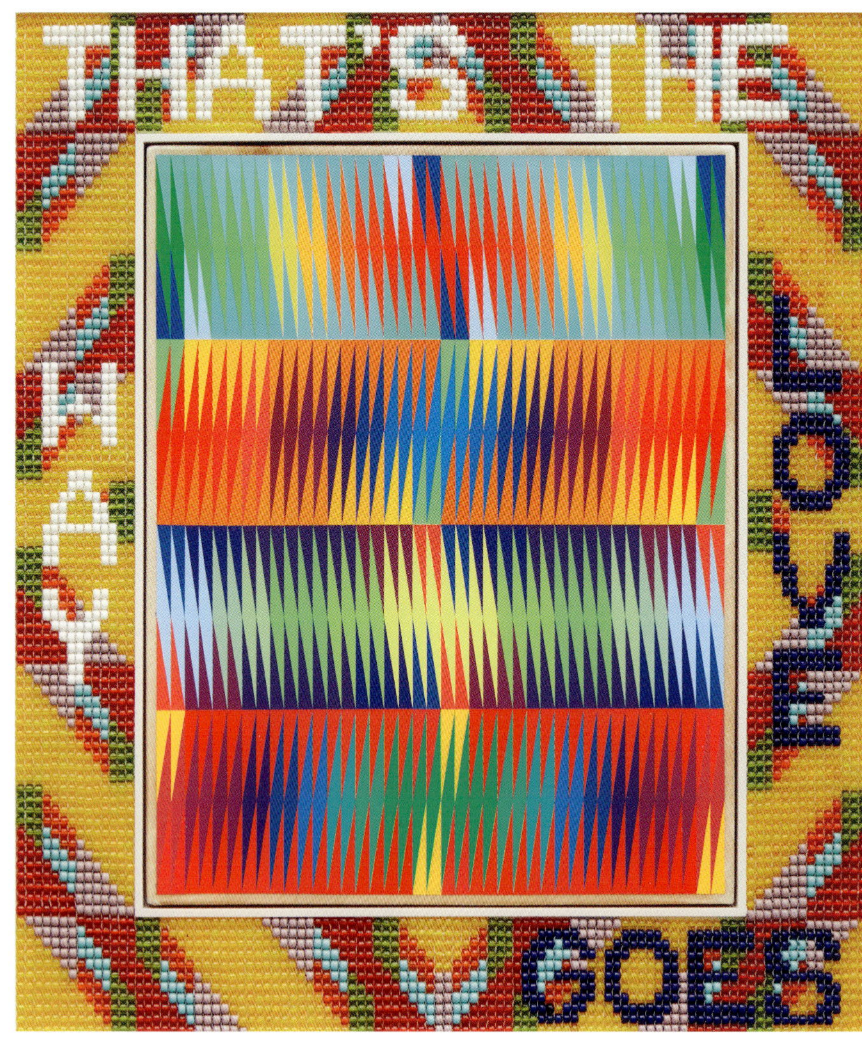

That's the Way Love Goes, **Jeffrey Gibson**, 2021, acrylic paint on hide, glass beads, artificial sinew, inset in custom wood, 87.6 x 73.3 cm (34½ x 28⅞ in)

    Love

'Ebika Bya ba Kuchu mu Buganda
(Kuchu Clans of Buganda) II',
Leilah Babirye, installation view,
Stephen Friedman Gallery,
London, 2021

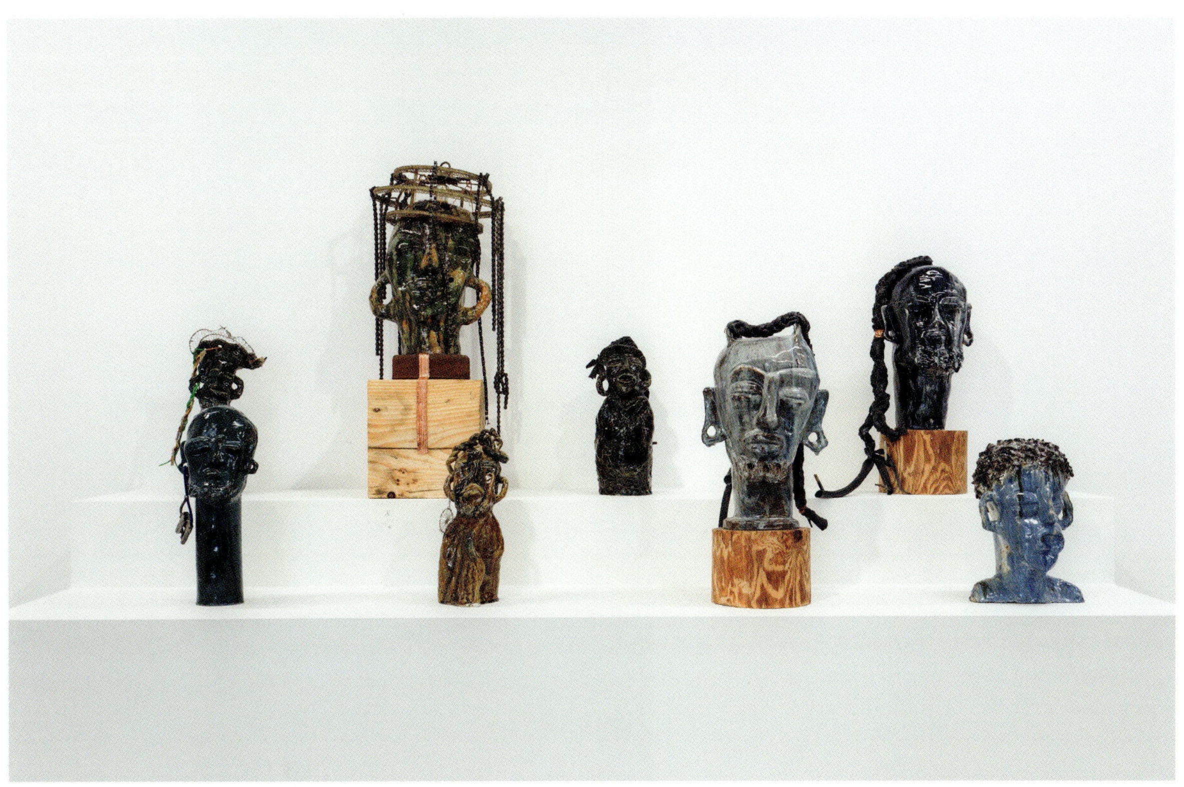

Leilah Babirye's sculpture represents queer bodies coming together as chosen families in the format of the traditional clan structures of the Kingdom of Buganda. 'Ebika Bya ba Kuchu mu Buganda (Kuchu Clans of Buganda)' was made in New York City, where the artist took refuge after being outed by a local newspaper in her native Uganda. The work celebrates the familial and humanizing aspects of all figures of Ugandan lineage, regardless of their gender identities and sexualities. Combined with carved wood and glazed ceramic, found materials such as nuts, bolts, copper wire and tyres are transformed from discarded everyday materials into treasure. Since these works were made, the Anti-Homosexuality Act 2023 was signed into law by Ugandan President Yoweri Museveni, endangering the lives of LGBTQIA+ Ugandans. Connected through the power of love and kinship, Babirye's figures are a call to action to overturn this life-threatening law that renders her community in Uganda unsafe and resourceless.

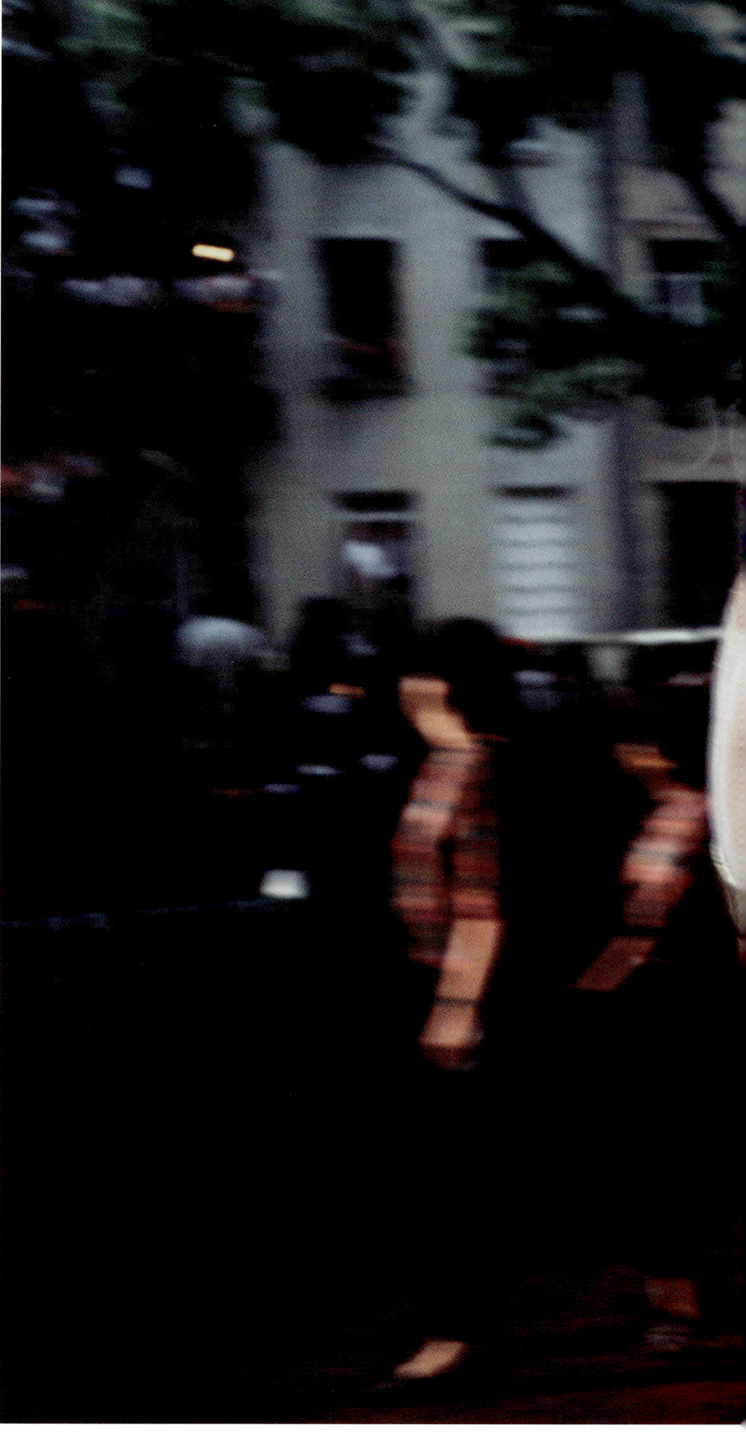

Jimmy Paulette on David's Bike, NYC is part of Nan Goldin's series 'The Other Side', which marks her first forays into photography and the beginning of a long career as a leading voice in contemporary art. Begun in the 1970s when she first visited Boston's drag queen bar The Other Side, the portraits document the daily lives of the friends who became her whole world, taking an intimate and loving viewpoint of their vibrant creativity and rich connections. Goldin photographed Jimmy Paulette many times, along with several other drag queens with whom she was particularly enamoured, saying 'I wanted to pay homage, to show them how beautiful they were'. The movement in this photograph, conveyed through a blurred background, is a beautiful example of the cinematic effect of Goldin's very distinctive and influential photography.

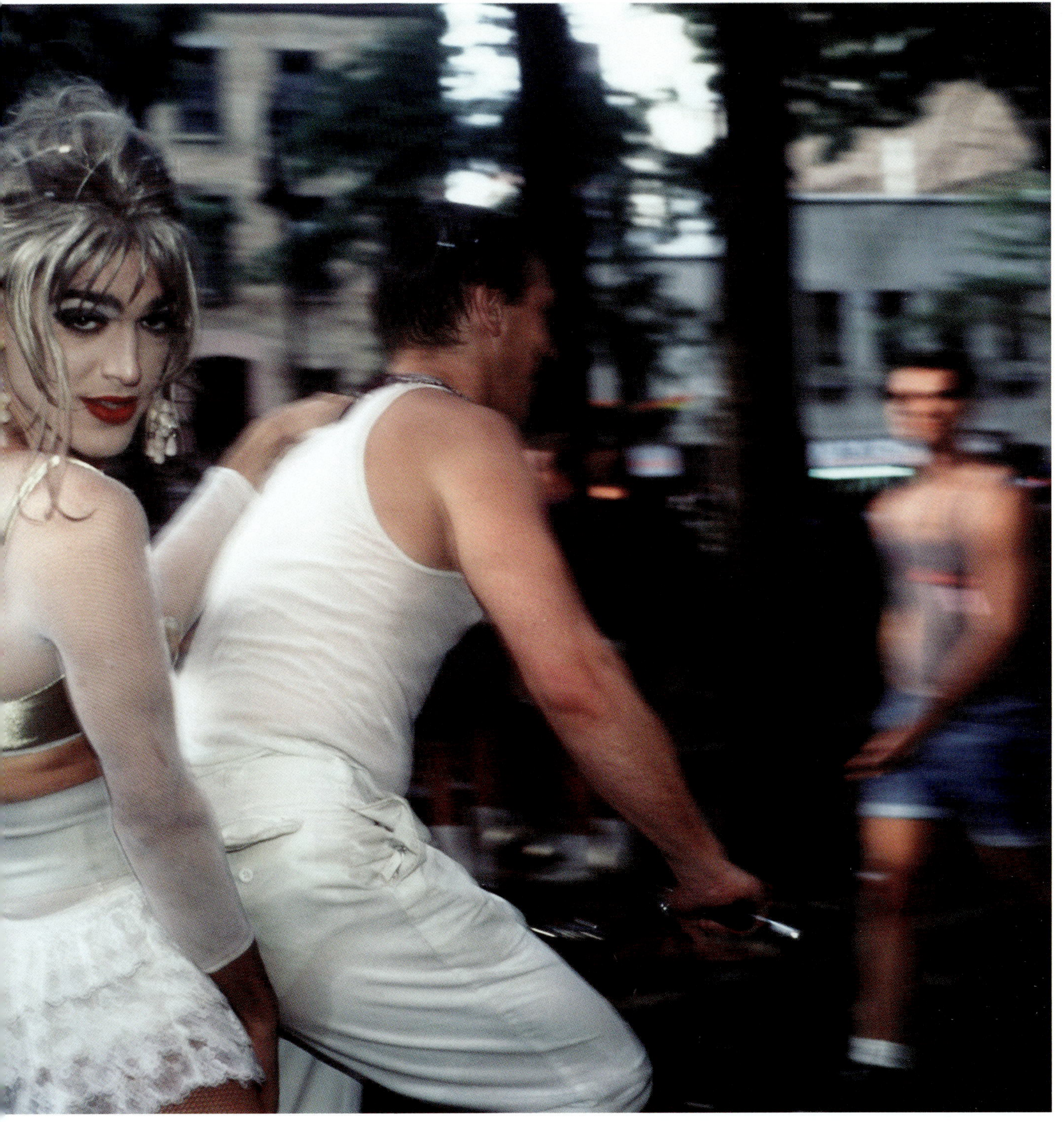

Jimmy Paulette on David's Bike, NYC from the series
'The Other Side', **Nan Goldin**, 1991, dye destruction
print, 38.7 x 59.1 cm (15 ¼ x 23 ¼ in)

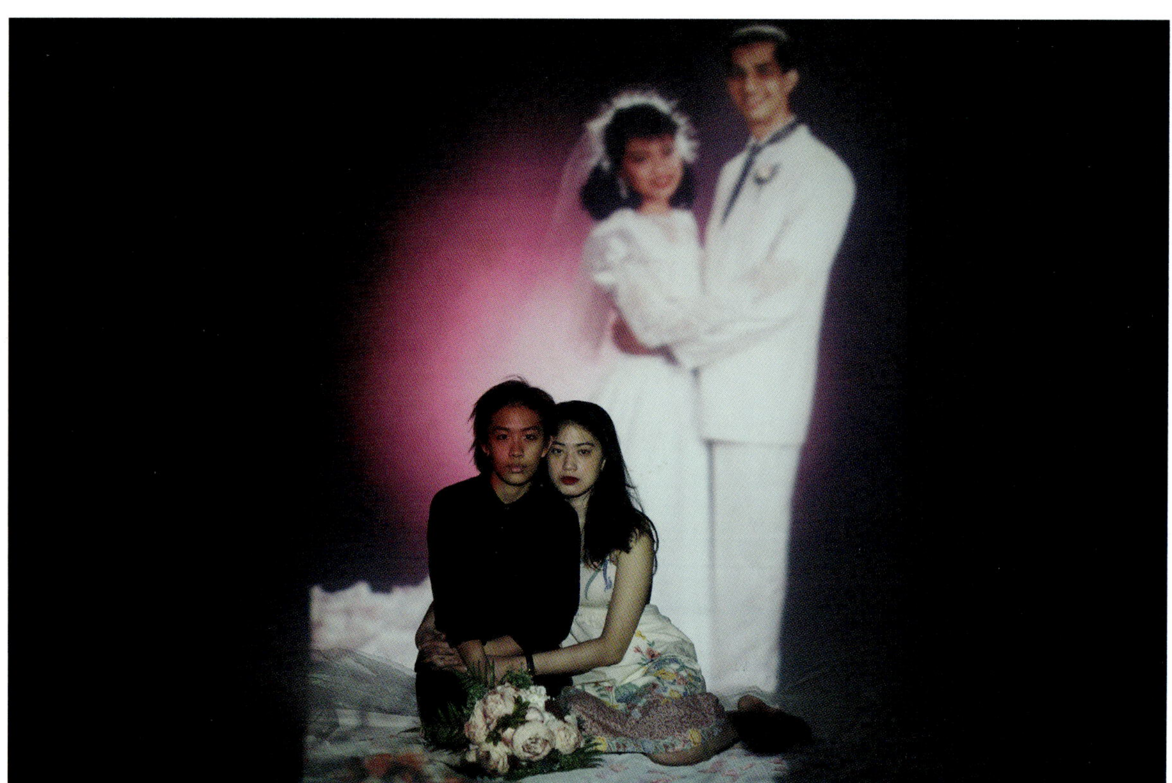

Charmaine Poh's photographic series 'How They Love' stages queer Singaporean couples and individuals in scenes of romantic bliss. In these images, sexuality, gender expression and gender identity have room to breathe. The young sitters assert their presence and the validity of their love – wearing wedding garb, holding flowers and nestling their heads together. The sitters are covered by a softly projected image of one of their parents' wedding photographs, their figures disrupting the dated image. Poh's work responds to social and legal restrictions affecting the rights of LGBTQIA+ people in Singapore; through photography she looks to the future of queer life and love in Singapore, reckoning with archaic notions of gender and sexuality while creating necessary and life-saving visibility.

Francis Bacon is widely acknowledged to be one of the most important artists of the twentieth century. His compelling work painted in entirely his own style features nightmarish figures that respond to his own existential turmoil and the horrors of war. He painted his lover George Dyer obsessively throughout their eight-year relationship and continued to do so after Dyer's untimely death. The triptych *In Memory of George Dyer* was painted the year Dyer died from a drug and alcohol overdose in the bathroom of the Hotel des Saint-Pères in Paris two days before the opening of Bacon's retrospective at the Grand Palais. The centre panel shows a ghostly figure in front of a stairway based on one in the Paris hotel. The painting made using oils and dry transfer lettering marks the start of Bacon's 'black triptych' phase, which is characterized by a deep grief at his lover's passing.

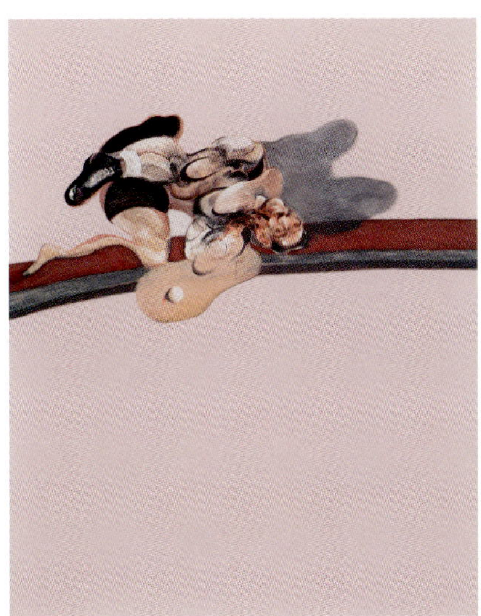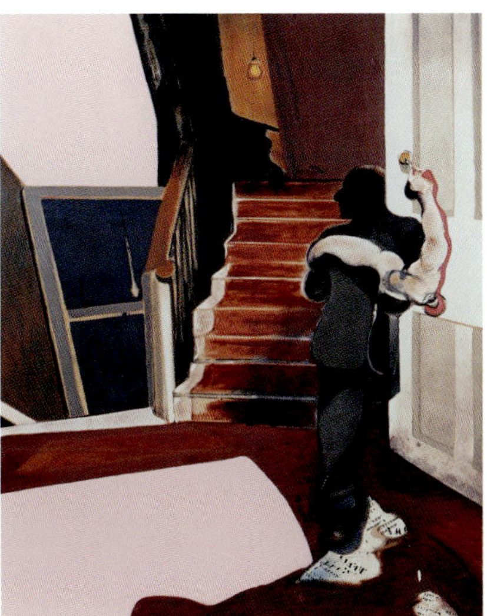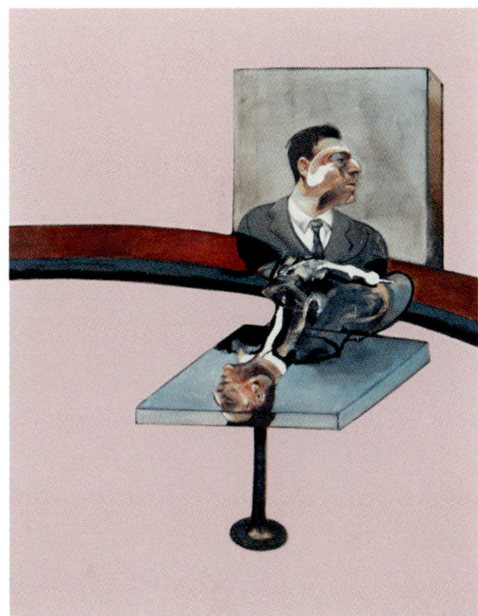

In Memory of George Dyer, **Francis Bacon**, 1971, oil and dry transfer lettering on canvas, triptych, each panel 198 x 147.5 cm (78 x 58 in)

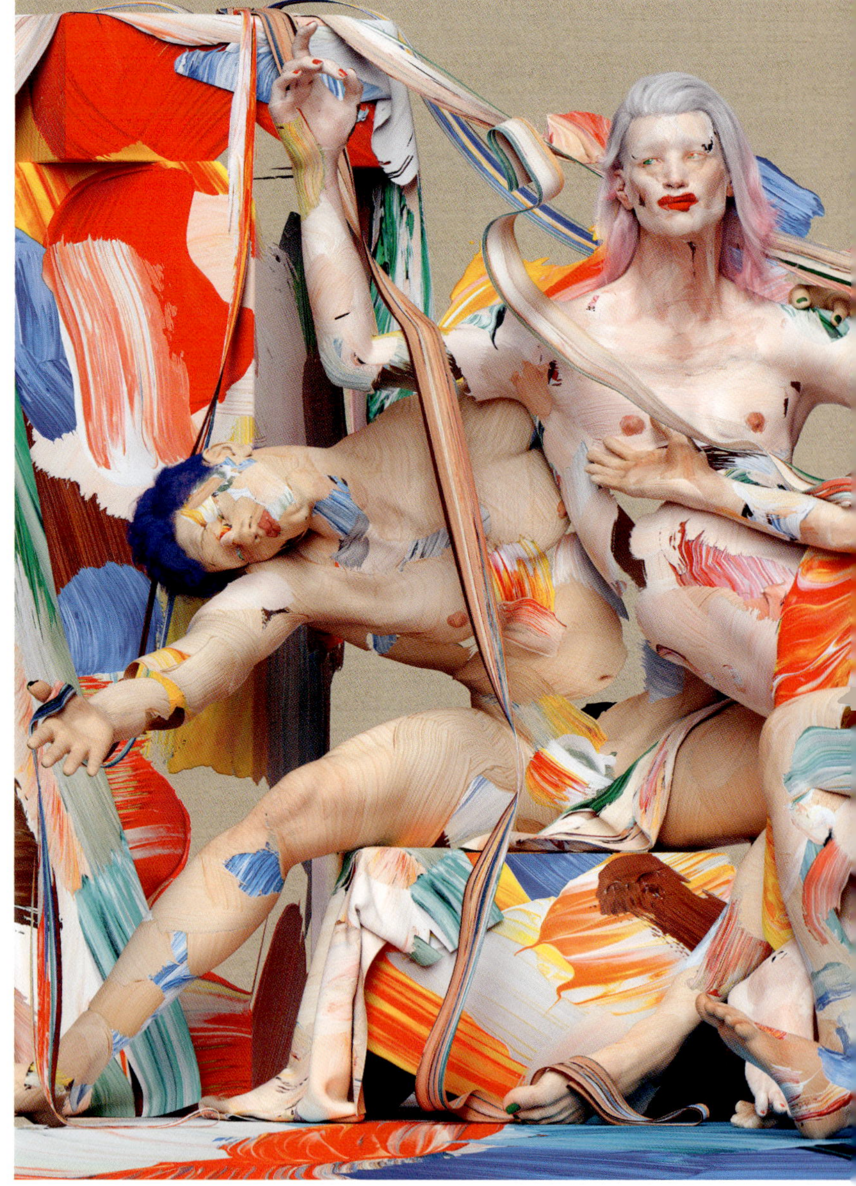

Matthew Stone's *Together* is a digital painting printed onto linen. The sprawling composition is made from brushstrokes painted directly onto glass, which are then scanned and transformed into three-dimensional paint gestures. Five figures occupy the digital space, their gestural bodies entwined, connected by swathes of fabric and ribbon, and unified by flashes of rainbow hues. The image captures the strength, energy and tenderness of queer bodies as they come together in love and solidarity. In the words of the artist, 'It is … my intention to create images that show people together and at ease with each other. That togetherness is a part of the reality I see around me, but also a part of a vision I hold for a future that is defined by collective healing, which includes my own transformation.'

Together, **Matthew Stone**, 2019, digital
print on linen, 160 x 300 cm (63 x 118 in)

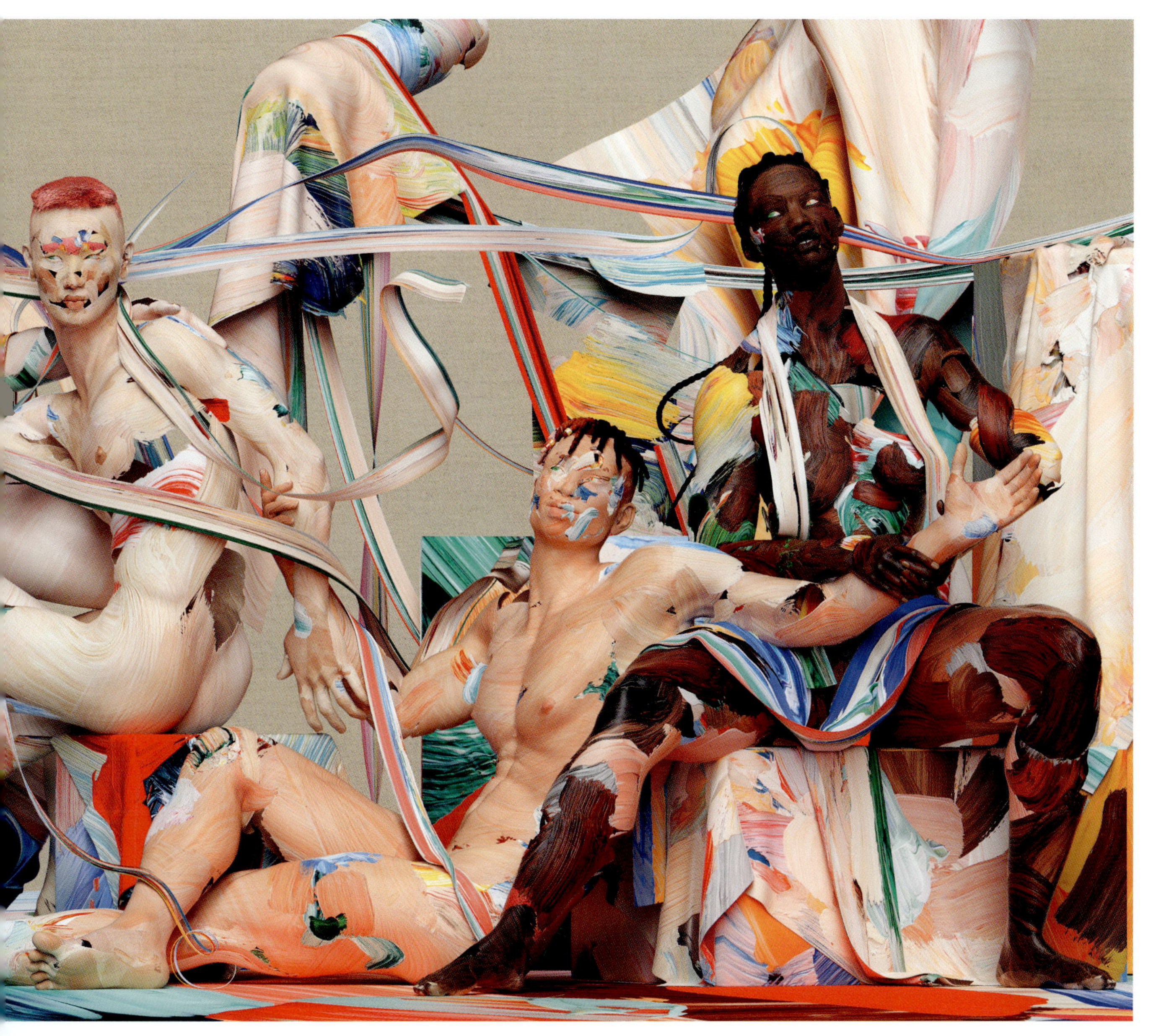

Queertopia

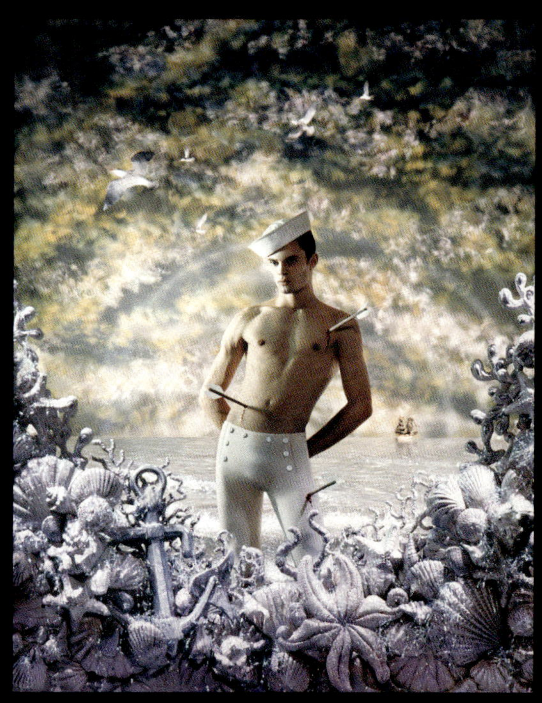

Queerness engenders resilience. Queer people channel the power of creativity to redress realities: excavating queer histories and distilling the lessons of the past to create a foundation upon which to project, manifest and build better futures, new ways of being and new worlds. Queer happiness and belonging has always been the stuff of fantasies, a revolution of the imagination where everyone is always free, a freedom found in queer-designed utopias: queertopia. There are examples of LGBTQIA+ people coming close to successfully creating and living their dreams of queertopia. Some take the form of communities established beyond the restrictions of mainstream society, offering escape from discrimination, momentary freedoms or entirely new realities. One such place that attracts and inspires many artists is Fire Island in the state of New York, specifically the island's neighbouring hamlets Cherry Grove and the Pines, which have a long history of welcoming LGBTQIA+ tourists. Artists, writers and creatives have played a key role in enriching the vibrant queer life found on the beaches of Fire Island and have documented the magic-filled summers shared by those seeking queer liberation. Elsewhere, within towns and cities, LGBTQIA+ people have carved out space for their communities in geographic areas indicated by a critical mass of queer-owned and queer-inhabited venues or residential buildings. These become known as gay villages and gayborhoods and offer sanctuary to their communities. But true queertopia goes far beyond the here and now, as envisioned by artists whose longing for more takes them into new realms. Taking elements from mythology, folk stories, religious iconography and science fiction, we see new lands imbued with queer spirituality, magic and radical futuristic possibilities, like the work of Pierre et Gilles, whose art transports us to dreamlike landscapes that are rich with exquisite beauty and queer mysticism. The nourishing powers of abundant natural landscapes or the supernatural qualities of imagined worlds offer hypothetical environments in which to thrive. Harnessing the possibilities of new technologies, artists explore queertopia in new digital frontiers. Rashaad Newsome's video work, for example, presents a path out of the very real dangers of contemporary society for LGBTQIA+ people (particularly Black trans people, proportionately at higher risk of hate crime) that rests on the destruction and rebuilding of worlds. Artists present alternative worlds bursting with the potentiality, thereby undermining the systems and ideologies that hinder constructive growth and happiness for everyone, not just those affected by marginalization.

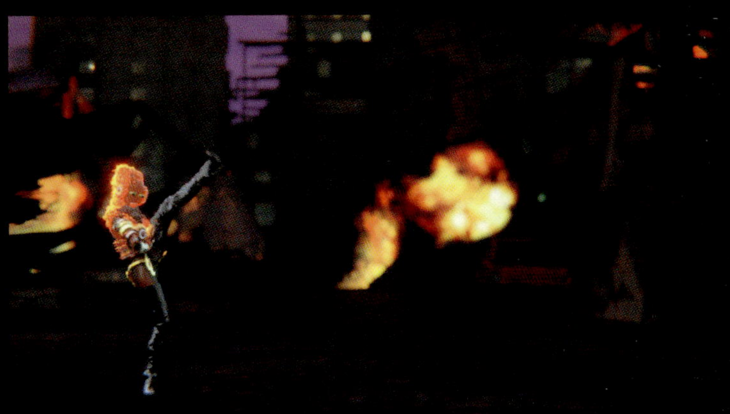

Build or Destroy, **Rashaad Newsome,** 2021

Tom Bianchi shot his Polaroid series between 1975 and 1983, when Fire Island Pines, New York, was one of the few safe spaces for gay men to interact openly and freely in the United States. During the 1970s, when Bianchi began visiting Fire Island, homosexuality was still illegal across the majority of states and it was not until the end of the decade that civil rights and protections began being introduced. Bianchi's images capture the men he spent summer vacations with in the Pines as they live their best lives away from the reality of the city. Faces often turned away or slightly out of shot, the focus is on the sun-drenched muscles and oiled bodies of figures lounging around the pool or partying on the beach. The Polaroids offer a glimpse into a magical world of gay abandon at a particular moment in the history of the utopian gay destination, before the community was deeply impacted by the AIDS epidemic.

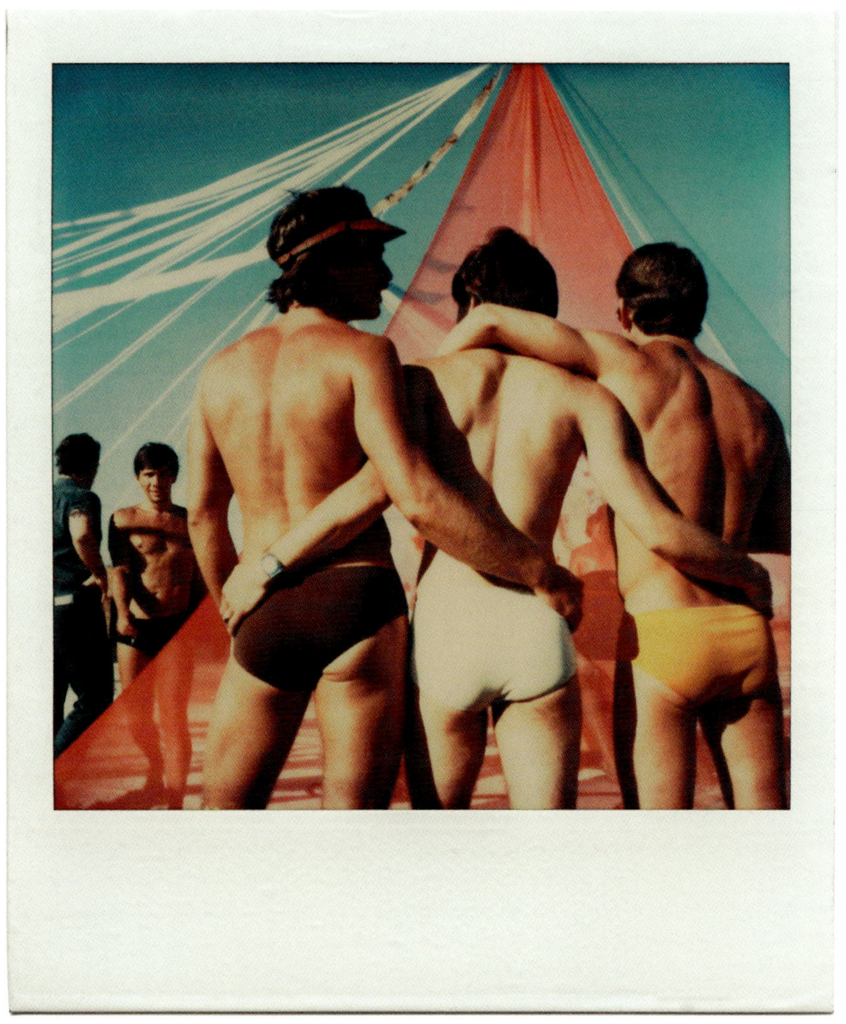

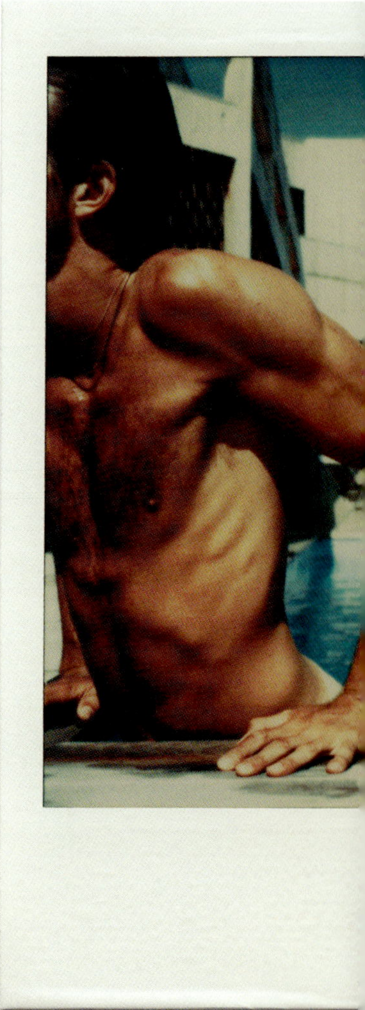

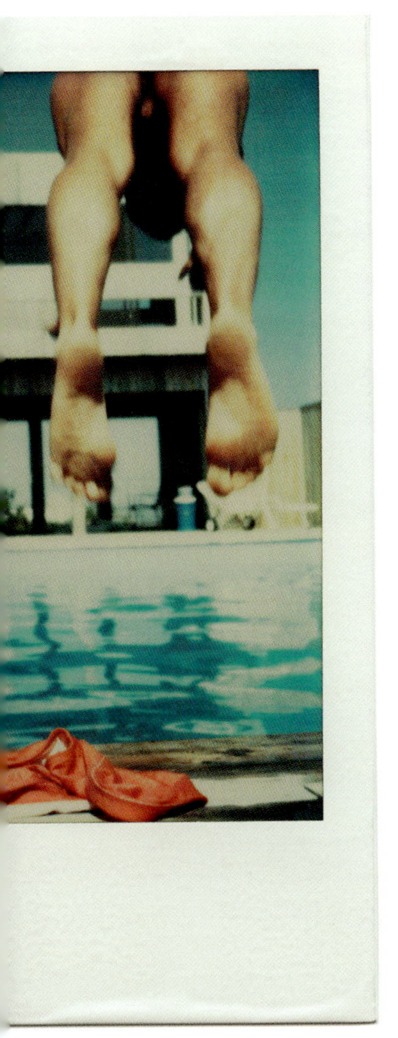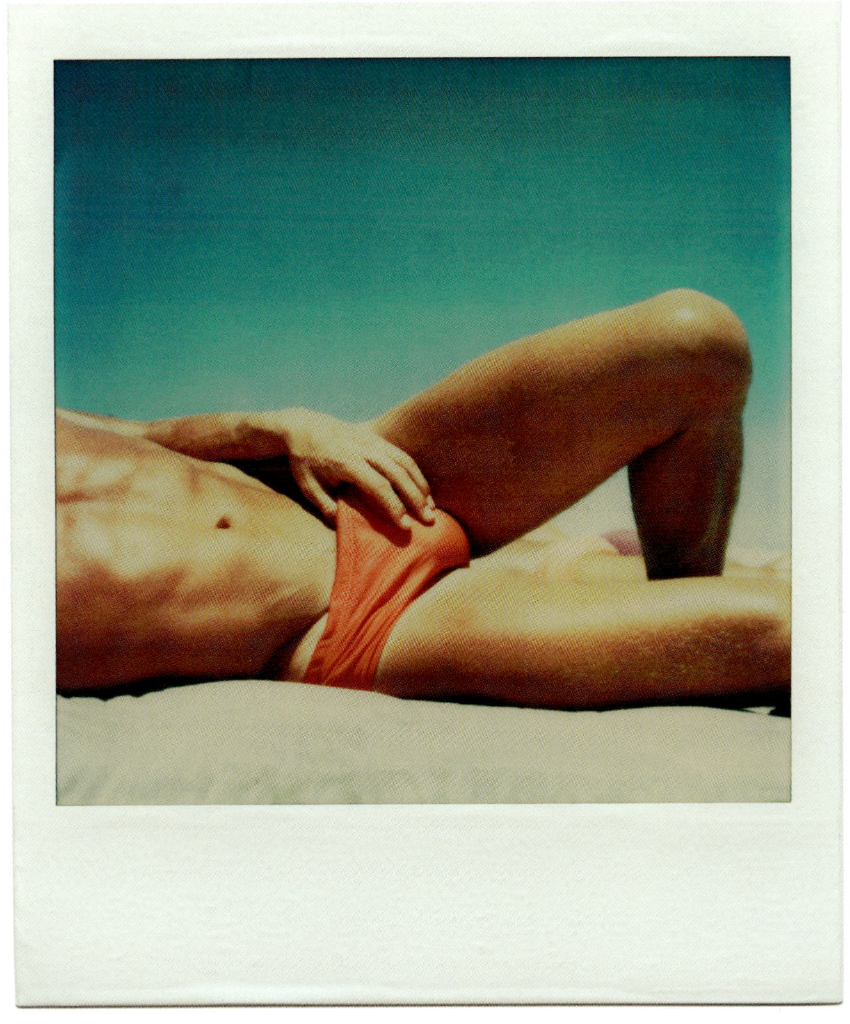

Flags, Fire Island 2022, **Joe McShea and Edgar Mosa**, 2022, ribbon and bamboo, each flag 200 x 300 cm (78¾ x 118 in) on variable height poles

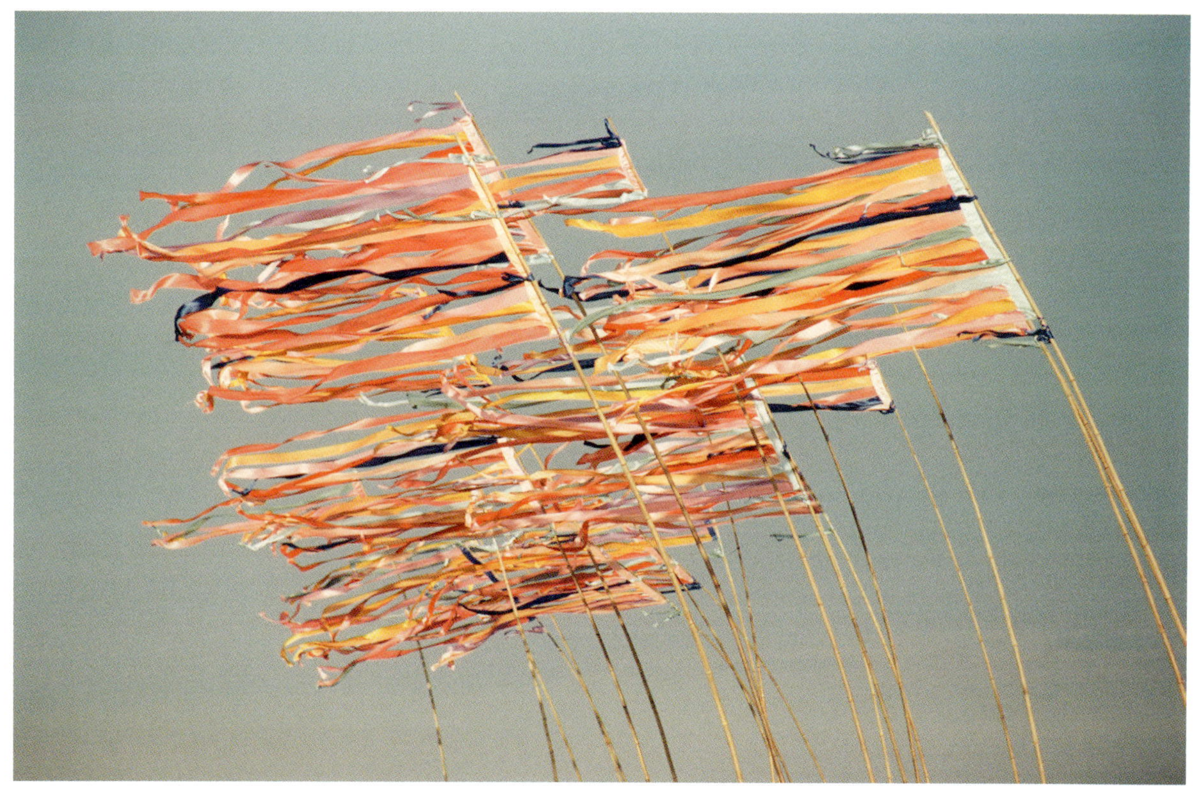

Partners in work and life, Joe McShea and Edgar Mosa made their first flag together during an artist residency in Italy in 2018. They became fascinated by the process of recontextualizing an object so typically entrenched in meaning, stripping it of the heavy layers of power, politics and identity. The pair began installing their flags on the beaches of New York's Fire Island, to which they'd moved from New York City after the first Covid-19 lockdown and quickly built a community of like-minded queer artists and creatives who would congregate on the beach for dance parties. The flags, which towered high above the sand catching the island wind, would draw people to them and create a safe enclave. Playing with the format of a traditional flag and calling to mind the long history of the rainbow pride flag, hundreds of candy-coloured silk ribbons flutter a message of optimism and love.

TM Davy's paintings from Fire Island, New York, depict the close-knit community of queer creatives that he is deeply embedded in. Once known as a destination for body beautiful muscle gays, the queer beach town's visitors are becoming increasingly diverse. With a rich cultural history featuring numerous well-known queer creatives, including an infamous visit from Oscar Wilde, and now home to multiple artist residencies and arts initiatives, the island attracts artists, writers, actors and musicians during the summer season. *Hari Sea* depicts Hari Nef, the American actress, model and trans icon. Davy's exquisite and distinctive use of pastels gives a luminous quality to his figures, imbuing them with a mythical aura. As Hari frolics in the sea, the waves breaking against her body and the light catching her skin, we get a sense of the freedom, joy and queer magic that people seek at Fire Island.

TM Davy

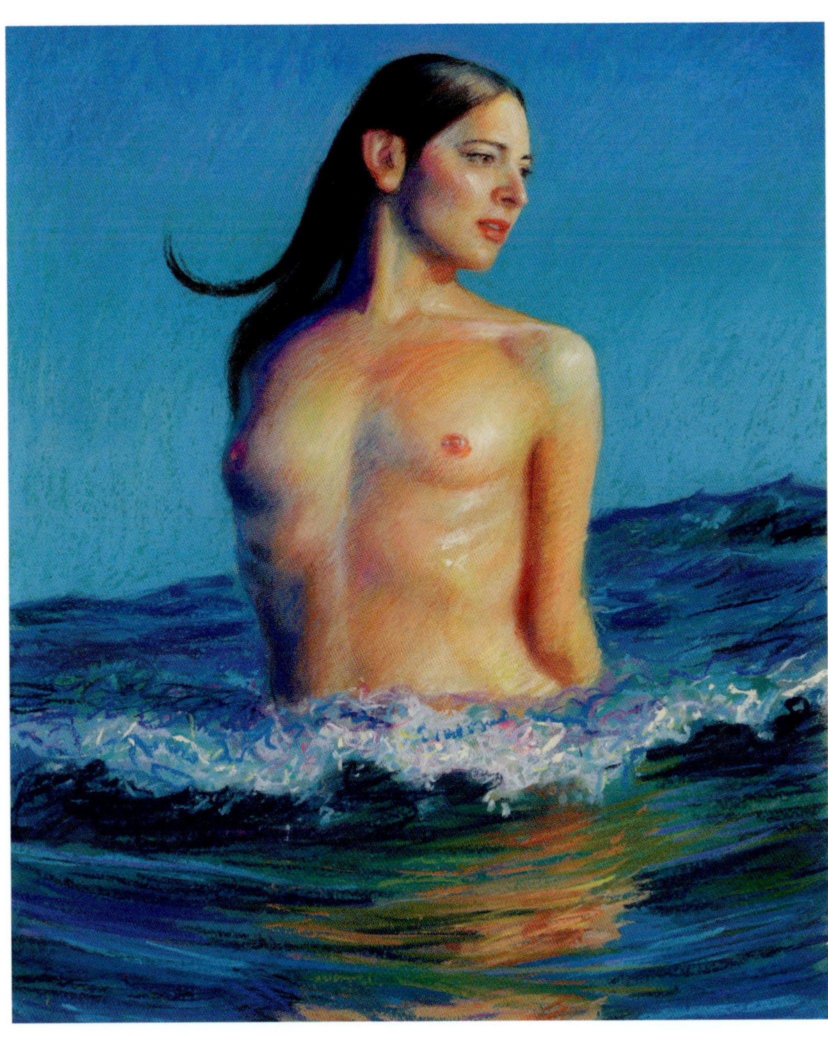

Hari Sea, **TM Davy**, 2021, pastel and gouache on toned paper, 60.9 x 45.7 cm (24 x 18 in)

Garden of Earthly Delights X, **Raqib Shaw**, 2004, acrylic liner, acrylic paint, glitter, enamel, rhinestones and mixed media on board, 243.8 x 457.2 cm (96 x 180 in)

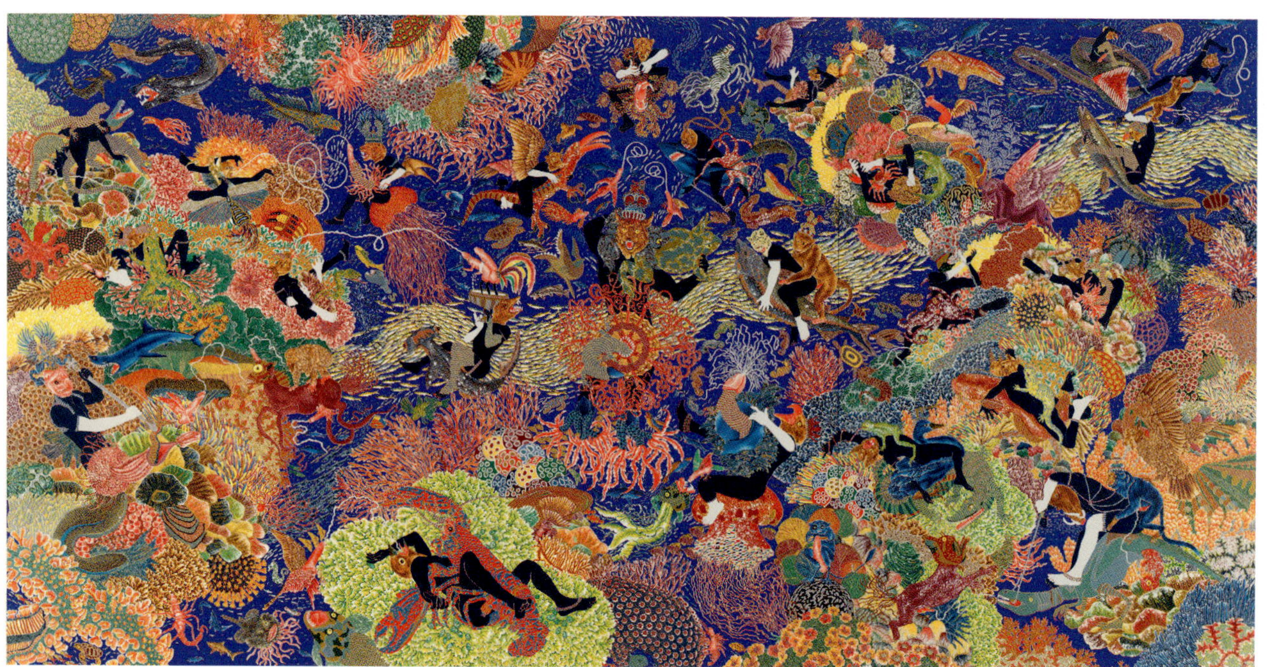

Raqib Shaw's art is distinctively opulent, ornate and rich in texture. He meticulously creates highly imaginative worlds from painted enamel, inlaid coloured jewels and embossed gold. Inspired by his upbringing in Kashmir, India, where he was surrounded by the luxurious products of his family's carpet-making and shawl-trading business, his work combines influences from both East and West. Working with a scale and level of detail reminiscent of the old masters, his painting series 'Garden of Earthly Delights' reimagines Hieronymus Bosch's large triptych of the same title. Shaw's sexually charged scene is an underwater world filled with vibrant plant life and fantastical figures that are part animal, part human, part mythical creature. As the bodies are liberated from their inhibitions, a captivating hedonistic spirit runs through the image, promising the possibility of transcendence.

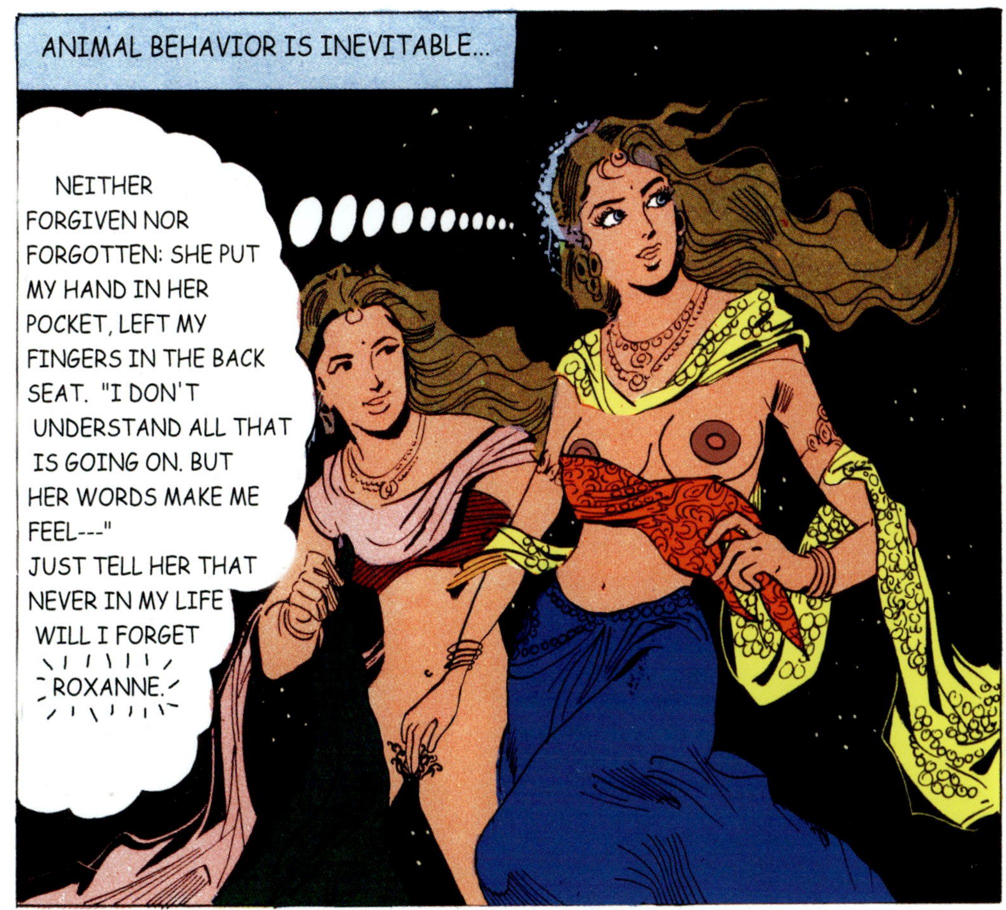

Chitra Ganesh

Born and raised in Brooklyn, New York, Chitra Ganesh unites her South Asian cultural heritage with feminist queer social theory in her work. Employing a comic book format, her 21-part series 'Tales of Amnesia' centres on a female protagonist with mystic powers similar to those of Hindu goddesses. The artist takes inspiration from popular comics that she read as a child – *Amar Chitra Kartha* teaches children Indian history and Hindu myths, reinforcing their social codes. She queers this framework by empowering the main character, Amnesia, to elude social stereotypes and defy cultural expectations of compliance, obedience and subversiveness. Playing with a recognizable and accessible format, the artist rewrites popular history in order to challenge social structures and present an alternative world powered by female autonomy and sexual freedom.

In 'A Countervailing Theory' Toyin Ojih Odutola constructs an ancient mythology where women rule. Forty monumental monochromatic drawings made with pastel, charcoal and chalk are accompanied by an immersive soundscape to communicate the artist's elaborate fictional narrative. Born in Ilé-Ifẹ, Nigeria, Ojih Odutola contends with her own displacement by using her work to deconstruct harmful Western narratives and ideologies about Blackness, Africa, queerness and power. Taking inspiration from Nigerian Ifẹ heads and Nok culture, the narrative takes place in a surreal landscape informed by the rock formations of Nigeria's Plateau State. In Ojih Odutola's world, women are superior, men serve and homosexuality is compulsory. The story's turning point is a forbidden love between a woman and a humanoid man, whose perspective is heard by his lover as the act of listening becomes the stepping stone to political change.

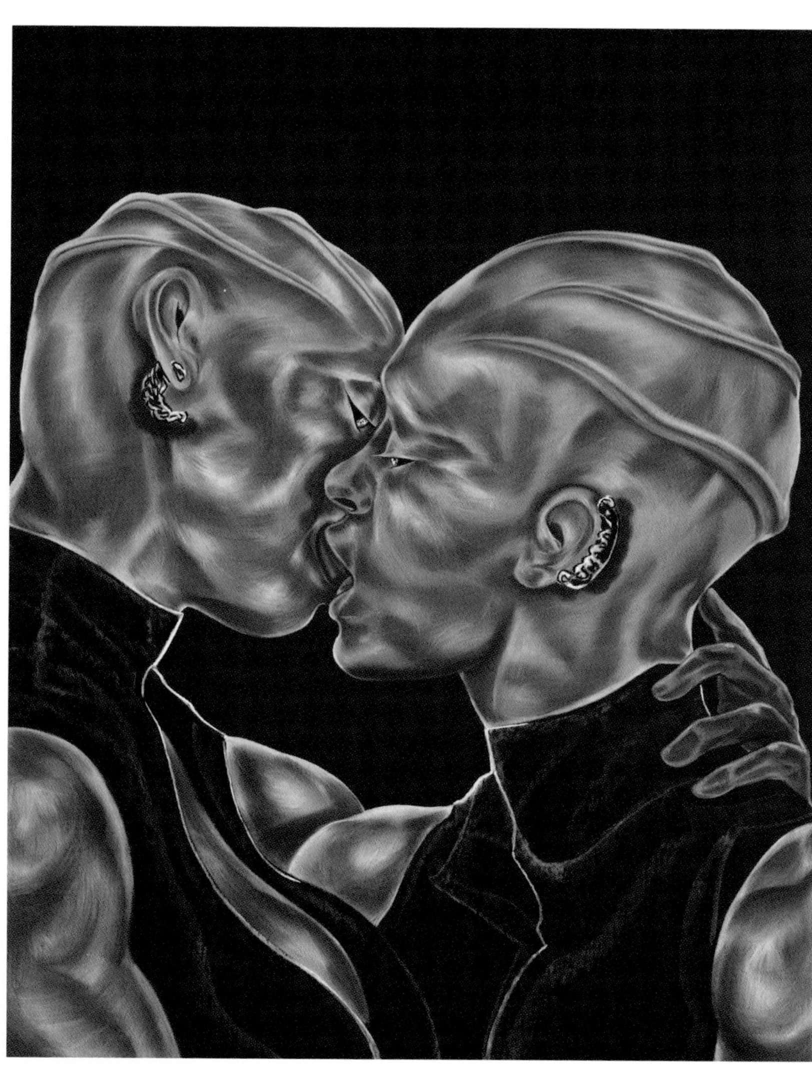

A Parting Gift: Hers and Hers Only from the series 'A Countervailing Theory', **Toyin Ojih Odutola**, 2019

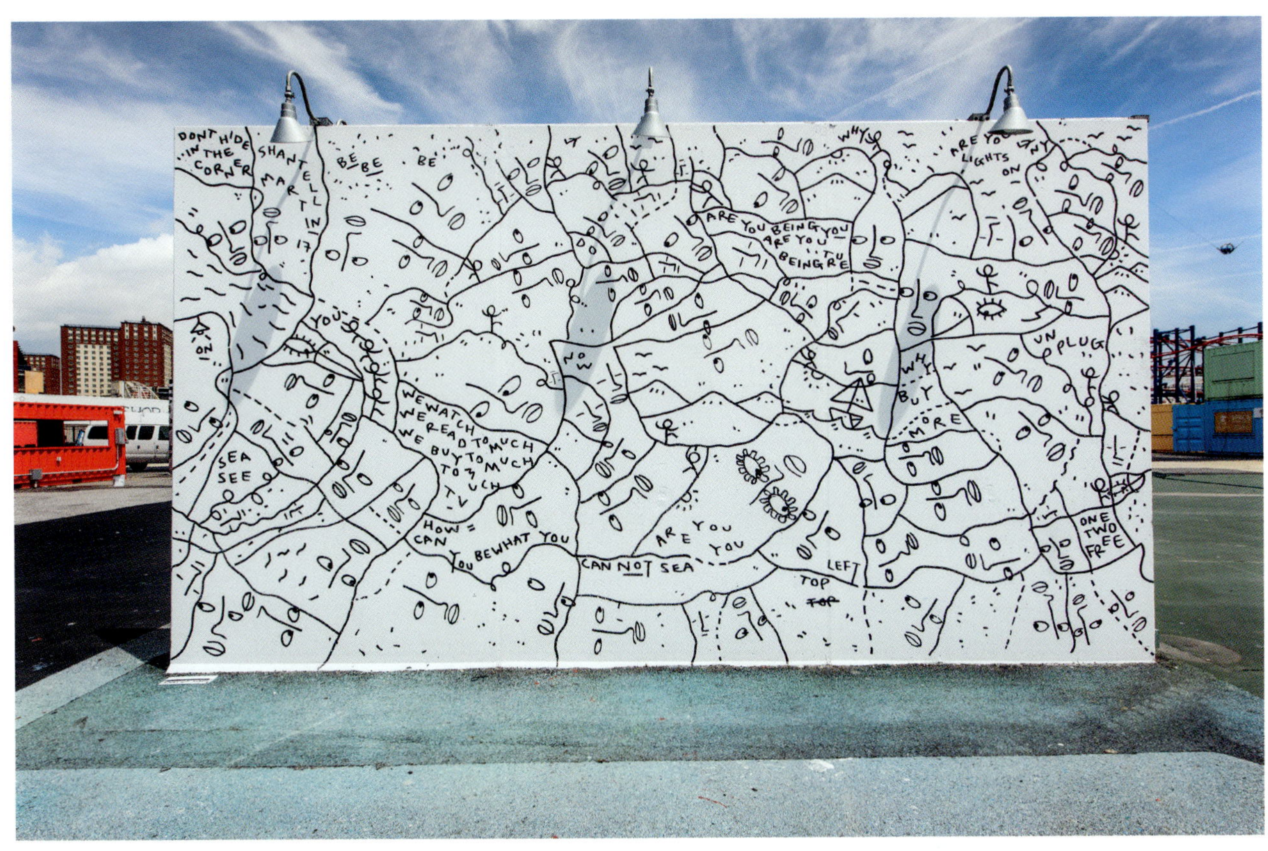

Shantell Martin engages a vast audience through her uplifting and thoughtful drawings. The recognizable monochrome visuals appear across culture from social media and clothing to performance collaborations and public installations. Both autobiographical and dreamlike, the work reflects on her own experiences of marginalization as a Black queer woman and offers strong messages of empowerment and hope. Her sprawling cartographic drawings combine text with line work akin to surrealist automatism, using word and image, play and *double entendres* to pose provocative and contemplative questions. Her installation for Coney Art Walls, an outdoor art museum curated by Joseph Sitt and Jeffrey Deitch, takes the social history of the seaside resort as a starting point to ask 'are you being you, are you being true?'.

Shantell Martin

The practice of multidisciplinary artist Than Hussein Clark is a convergence of art, design, film and theatre. His highly conceptual, research-based work is both historical and futuristic in its exploration of desire, beauty, theatricality and excess. In his first feature-length film, *Love at the Frankfurt Autoshow*, the aesthetic and treatment of character so recognizable in his exhibitions, installations and performances is translated into film format. Drawing on the languages of melodrama, police thriller and film noir, the film follows a famous industrial family whose launch of a self-driving car has been sabotaged by a mysterious professor and his accomplice. Clark presents a high camp world of colour-blocked costumes and exaggerated speech through which to consider the complexity of relationships, family dynamics and economies of desire.

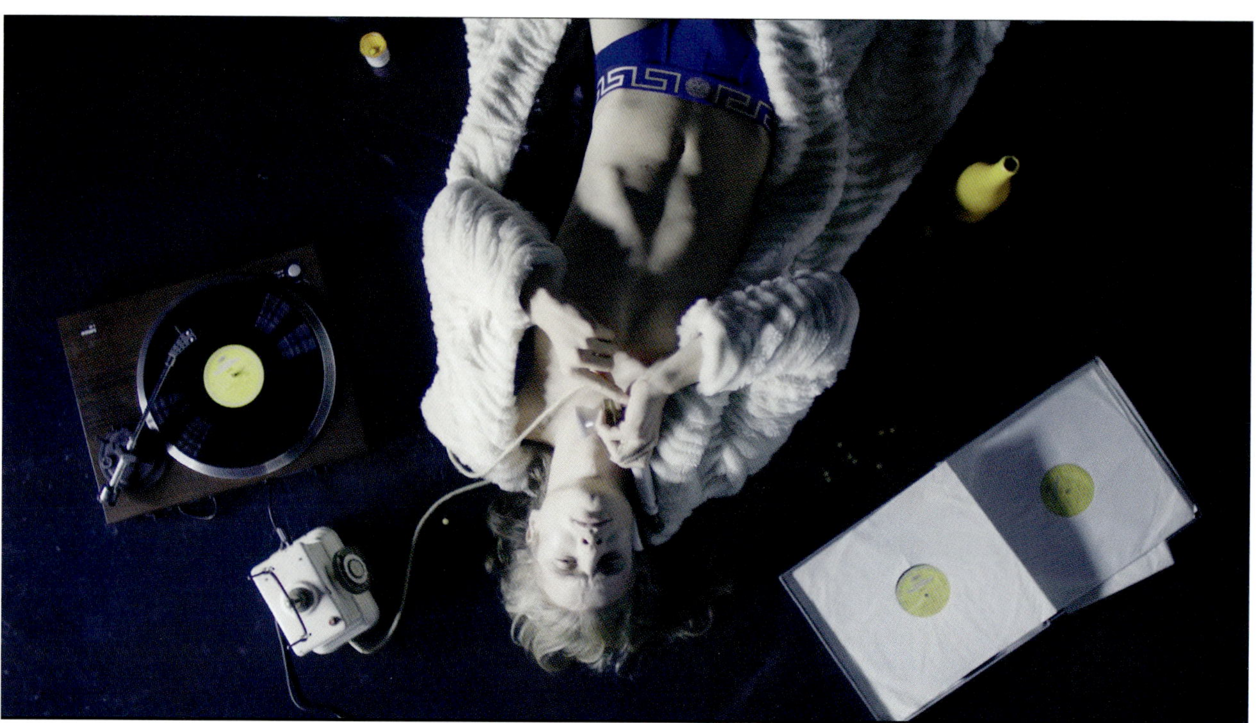

Love at the Frankfurt Autoshow,
Than Hussein Clark, 2017,
video, 2 hrs 26 mins

BEAST TYPE SONG, **Sophia Al-Maria**,
2019, single-channel HD video,
38 mins 3 secs

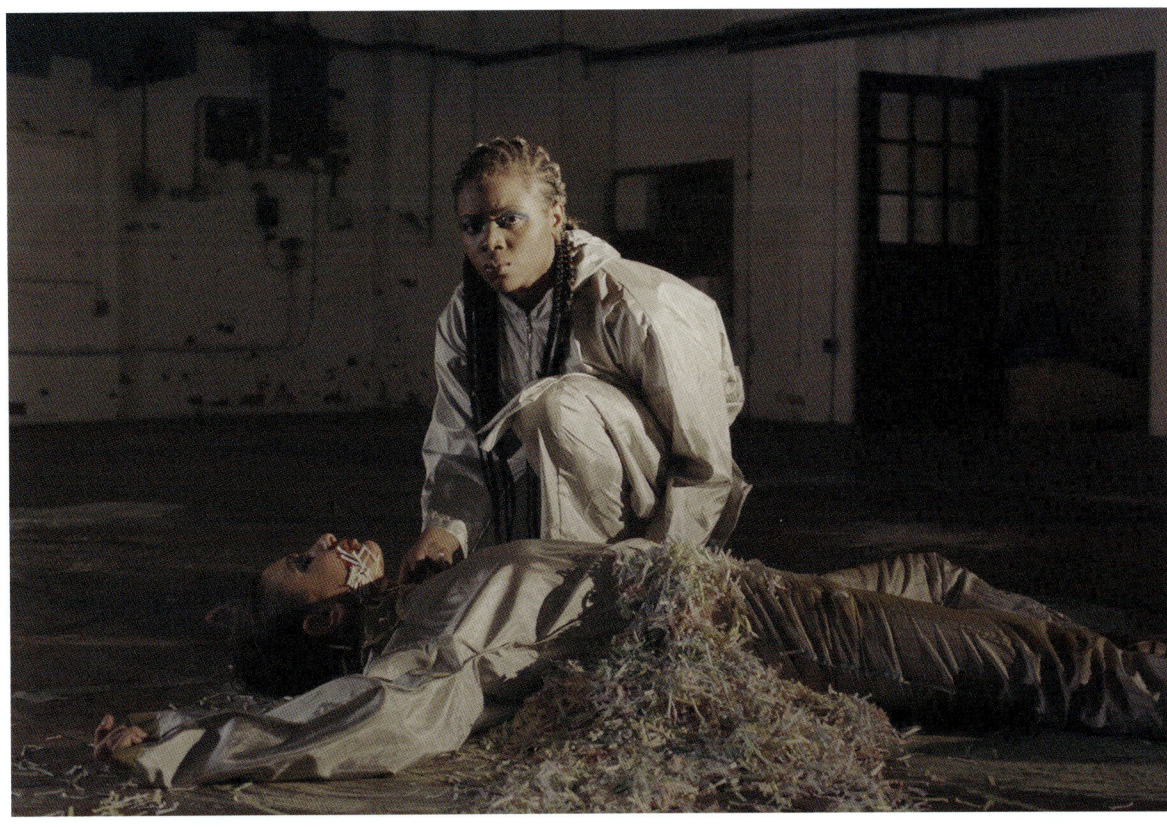

Sophia Al-Maria

Qatari-American artist Sophia Al-Maria is known for coining the term Gulf Futurism, a futuristic aesthetic reinterpreted from Islamic Arabism that appears in the hyper modernized urban planning, architecture and art of the Gulf States. She builds her own worlds through drawing, storytelling, music and film, combining myth with fantasy. *BEAST TYPE SONG* is a single-channel video that examines the erasure and revision of identities and histories in order to present alternative futures. Al-Maria queers the traditional format of filmmaking, presenting a series of different sections that could be viewed in any order, from drawings accompanied by voiceover, to written scenes and those improvised by performance artist Tosh Basco. Shot in the derelict former campus of Central Saint Martins in London, the film, which centres on a science fiction solar battle, is rewritten and revised as it unfolds on screen offering an escape from fixed and imposed narratives.

Ad Minoliti's practice combines Latin American geometric abstraction with speculative futurism to create a new visual language that explores the future possibilities of queer and feminist theory. *Abstracción geométrico-galáctica* is a large-scale inkjet print across three canvas panels set within a spaceship inhabited by three figures formed of abstract geometric shapes that the artist describes as 'non-binary geometries'. The pink interior is inspired by the animated television show *Steven Universe*, Cartoon Network's first series created solely by a non-binary person and celebrated for featuring LGBTQIA+ themes. Through the spaceship window we can see a distant futuristic landscape lifted from artist-designed space colonies commissioned by NASA in the 1970s. The cosmic scene imagines an alternative universe that goes beyond the binary and beyond the human to offer, in Minoliti's words, a 'democratic, open and safe space'.

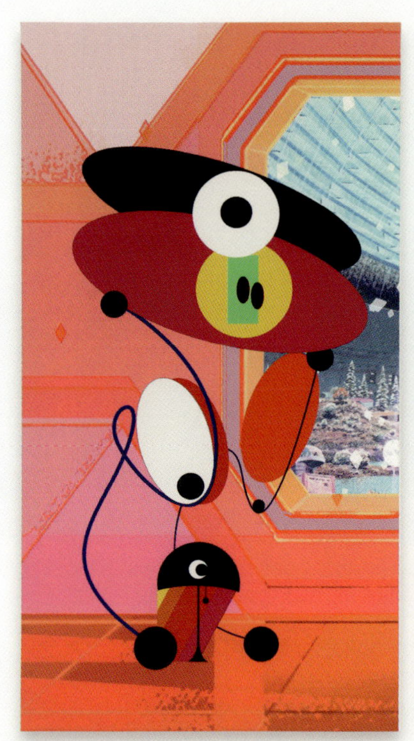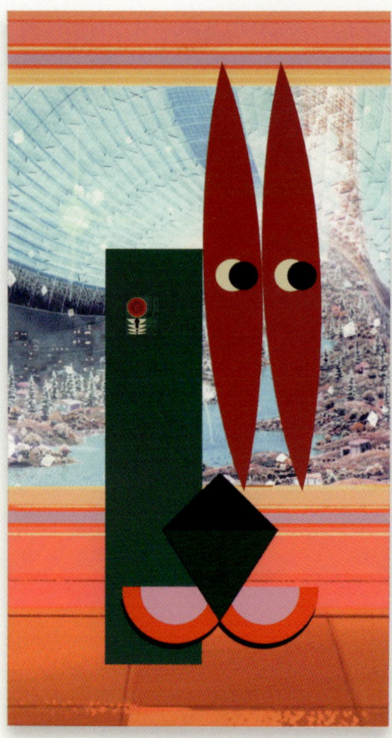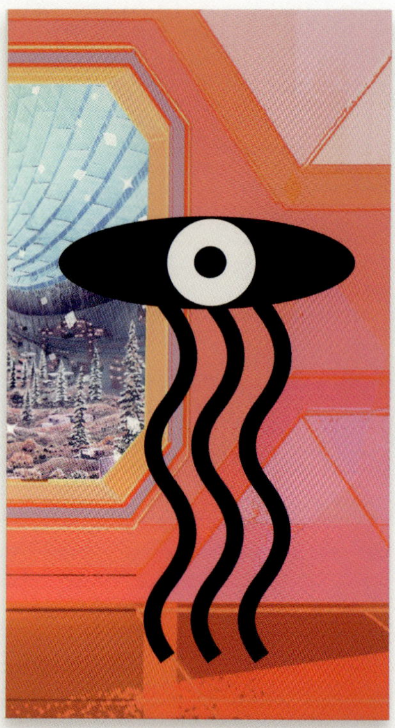

Abstracción geométrico-galáctica,
Ad Minoliti, 2019, unique eco-solvent
inkjet print on canvas, three panels:
150 x 250 cm (59 x 98½ in),
each panel: 150 x 80 cm (59 x 32 in)

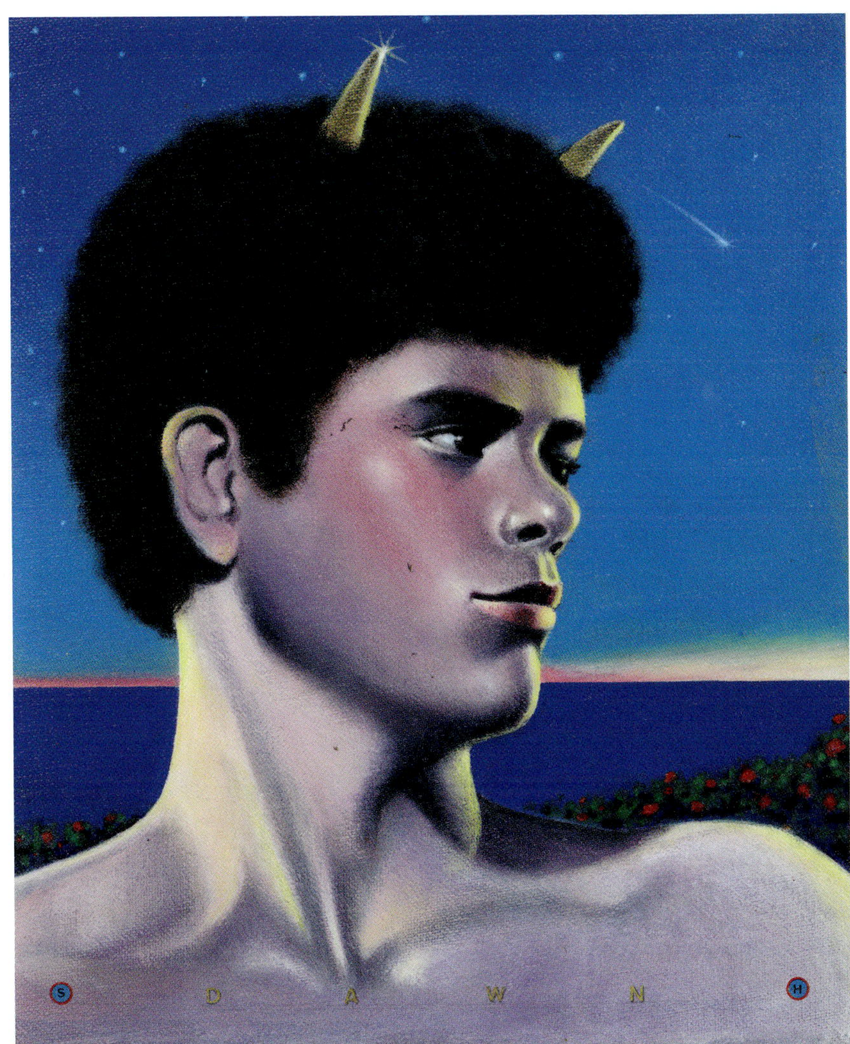

Dawn, **Sadao Hasegawa**, 1980, acrylic on board, 27 x 22 cm (10½ x 8½ in)

Sadao Hasegawa creates a world that merges eroticism, mythology and fantasy. His illustrated and painted figures represent Japanese homoeroticism and queer desire mixed with elements from Indian, South East Asian and African religious and mythological art, BDSM culture and popular Anglo-American cartoons. His detailed depictions of the male physique, inspired by Western beefcake magazines and the machismo of gay imagery that flourished in Japan in the post-war period, cause him to be commonly referred to as 'Japan's Tom of Finland'. After the artist's death from suicide at the age of 54, Hasegawa's family planned to destroy his archive until a note was discovered bequeathing his art to Tokyo-based Gallery Naruyama, which continues to preserve his legacy. In the work illustrated here, an ethereal faun-like figure with luminous skin and glistening horns, backlit by shooting stars and a glowing horizon, invites us into a technicolour realm that offers queer power and agency.

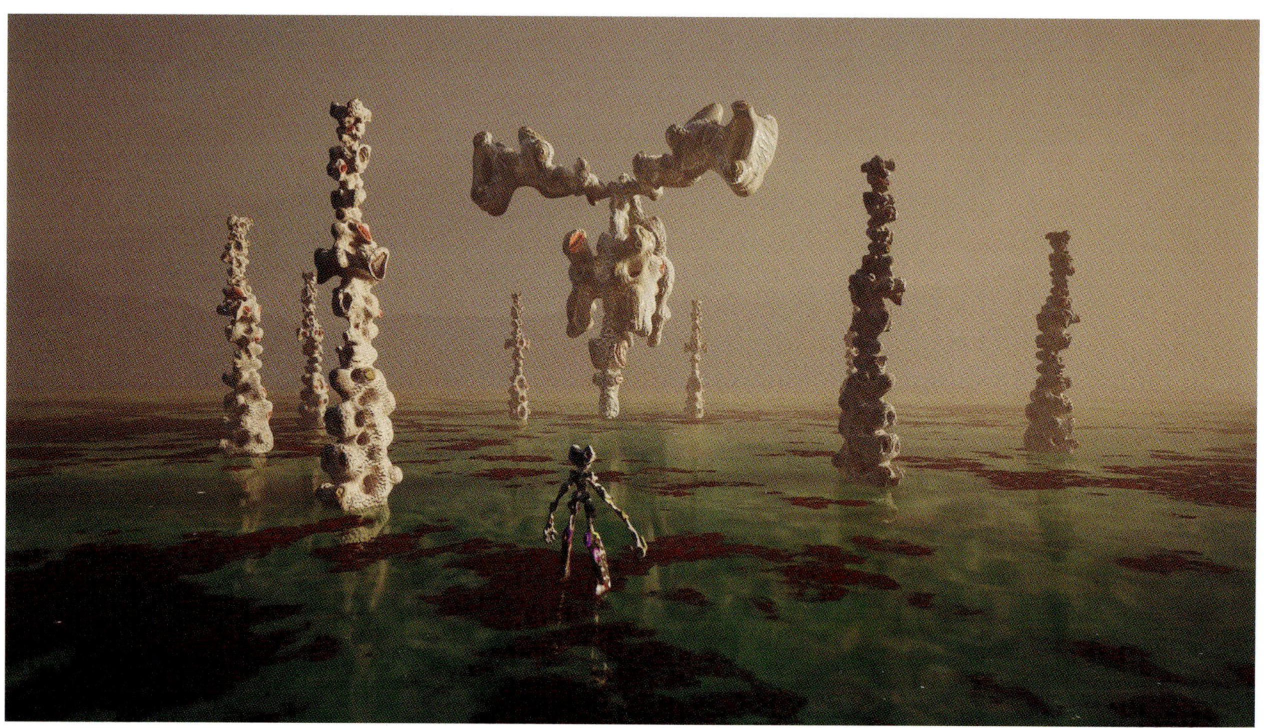

Gabriel Massan

Third World: The Bottom Dimension is a free-to-download, multi-level, single-player PC game built by Gabriel Massan in collaboration with Castiel Vitorino Brasileiro, Novíssimo Edgar and vocalist and music producer LYZZA, commissioned and produced by Serpentine Arts Technologies. Massan works across 3D animation, digital sculpture, games, sound and interactive installations to build worlds and create experiences rooted in a conceptual practice they call 'fictional archaeology'. Designed as a consciousness-raising tool, the game takes us on a journey through the Black Brazilian experience, offering players the perspective of those trapped by a system of inequality. Through the lenses of decoloniality, queerness and decentralization (technological, social, economic and ideological), the game 'challenges us to rethink the ways in which we understand and orient ourselves in the world'.

Jacolby Satterwhite builds digital worlds using a very personal visual language drawn from his own life experience and popular queer culture. Referencing dance, BDSM and mainstream television shows that represent LGBTQIA+ visibility, he creates safe spaces in which Black queer bodies thrive. His deep love of folklore and immersive languages are inspired by the books of Tolkien, the role-playing game *Dungeons & Dragons* and the video game *Final Fantasy* that he got lost in as a child. *Reifying Desire* is a six-part video series in which Satterwhite's 3D modelled body inhabits worlds based on the annotated drawings of his late mother who suffered from schizophrenia. Structured around a queer gestation cycle, the films see the artist voguing through utopian realms in a surrealist exploration of memory, family and fantasy that is full of promise for the future.

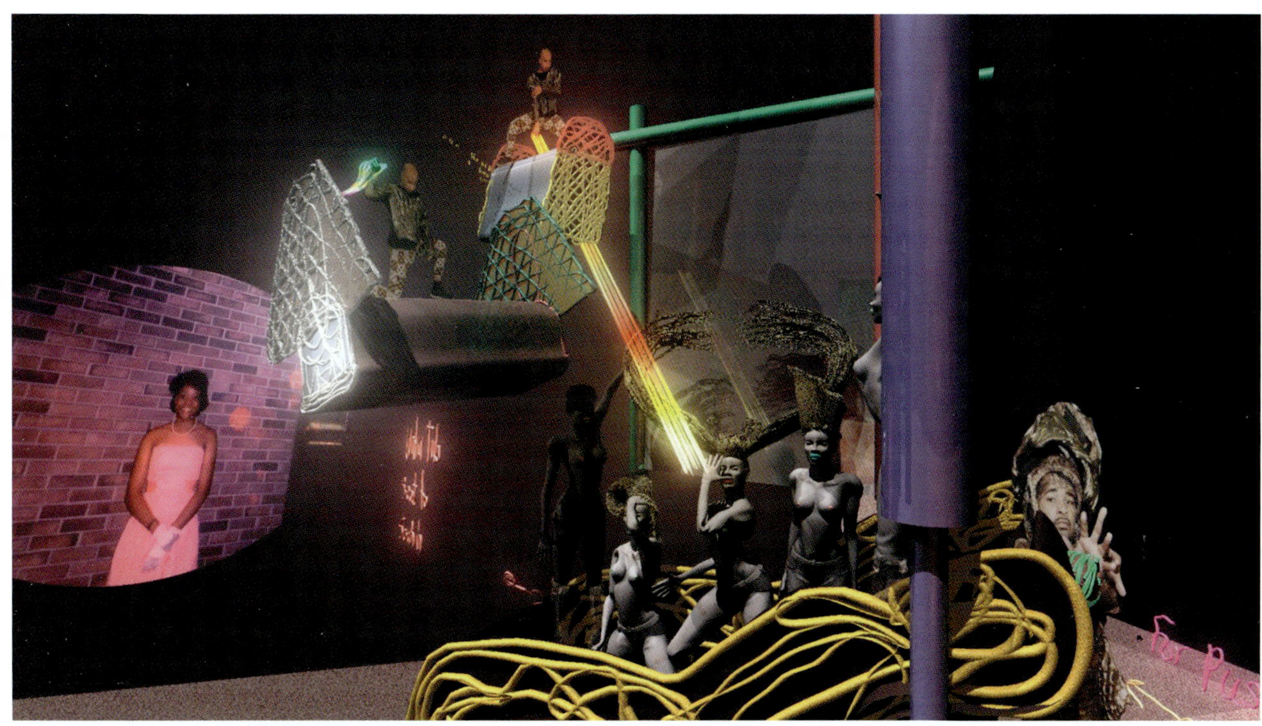

Reifying Desire 5, **Jacolby Satterwhite**,
2013, HD digital video with sound,
RT: 8 mins 51 secs

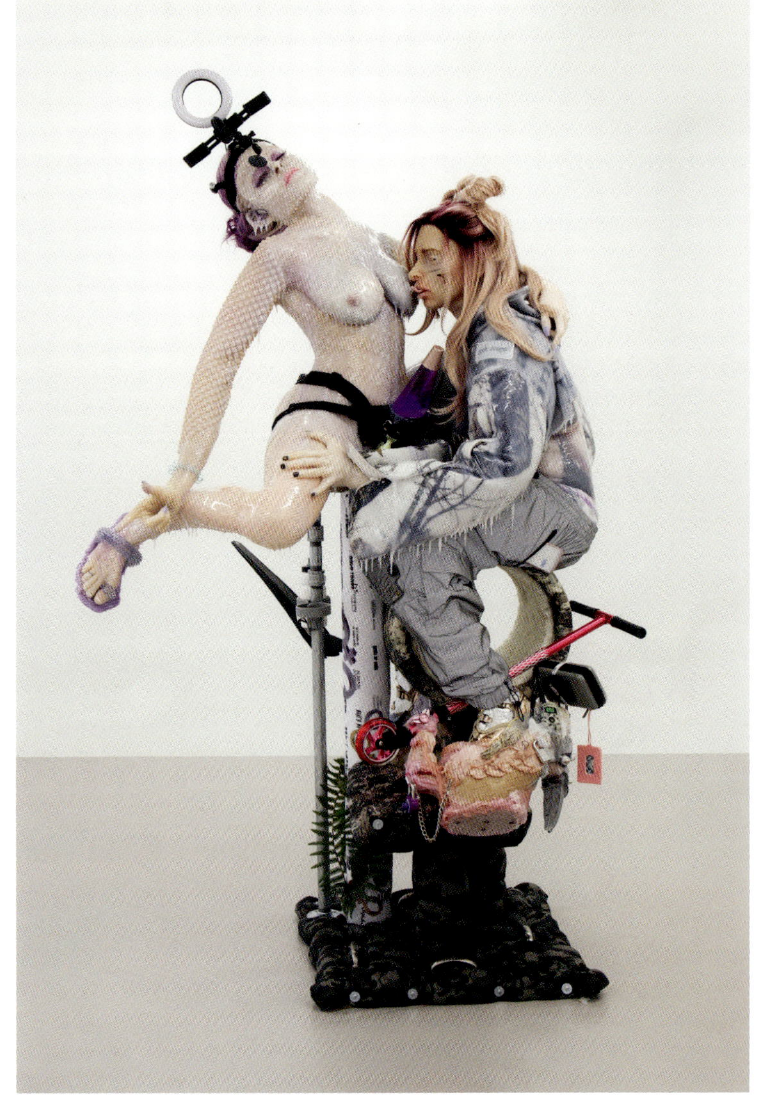

Aqua Aura, **Cajsa von Zeipel**, 2020, silicone and mixed media, 233.7 x 104.1 x 127 cm (92 x 41 x 50 in)

Cajsa von Zeipel disrupts the sculptural canon with her larger than life-size depictions of femmes and queer women and their cats and babies. Skilfully working with silicone, she quite literally stretches the possibility of sculpture with the construction of fantastical yet life-like bodies that she refers to as 'futuristic lesbians'. In *Aqua Aura* a pair of female lovers, each somewhere between cyborg, sex doll, mannequin and statue, are adorned with hi-tech gadgets and shiny objects – a ring-lit magnifying headband, a strap-on lava lamp, keychains, padlocks and a toothbrush. Each detail of the assemblage reveals more of the girlfriends' story. Dripping with a layer of ectoplasm, the erotically charged monumental figures represent a future dominated by lesbians, where women take charge of their own narratives and femmes reign.

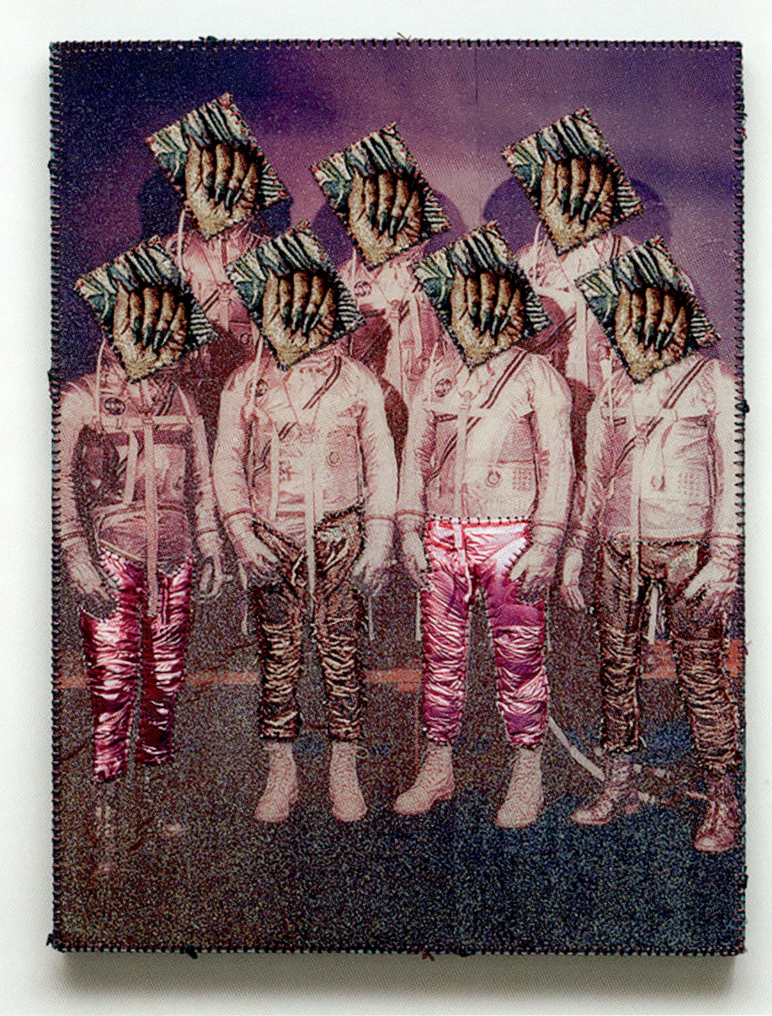

The First Atlanticans, **April Bey**, 2021, digitally woven tapestry, metallic cord, glitter, hand-sewing and epoxy resin on wood panel, 121.9 x 90 cm (48 x 36 in)

April Bey's work is about a fictional planet created by her father to explain why their family 'looked differently from white people and why that was a problem here on earth'. Fuelled by childhood imagination and a sense of possibility, and later inspired by Afrofuturism, Bey named the planet Atlantica – a world that's free from prejudice and celebrates difference, which offers solace from the harmful rules on earth. Often based on real people, Bey's figures are selected as model Atlantican citizens for their ability to boldly go where no earthling has gone before by defying societal norms and pressures. In her pivotal work we see the first Atlanticans, ready for space travel in shiny pink suits and helmets made of Black female hands with long beautiful acrylic nails, one of the many motifs in the artist's work celebrating African diasporic culture. Usually presented as large-scale installations comprising paintings, tapestries and wall hangings, Atlantica continues to grow in detail, from fashion lines, plant life and agricultural systems, all of which lead back to the planet's currencies – love and glitter.

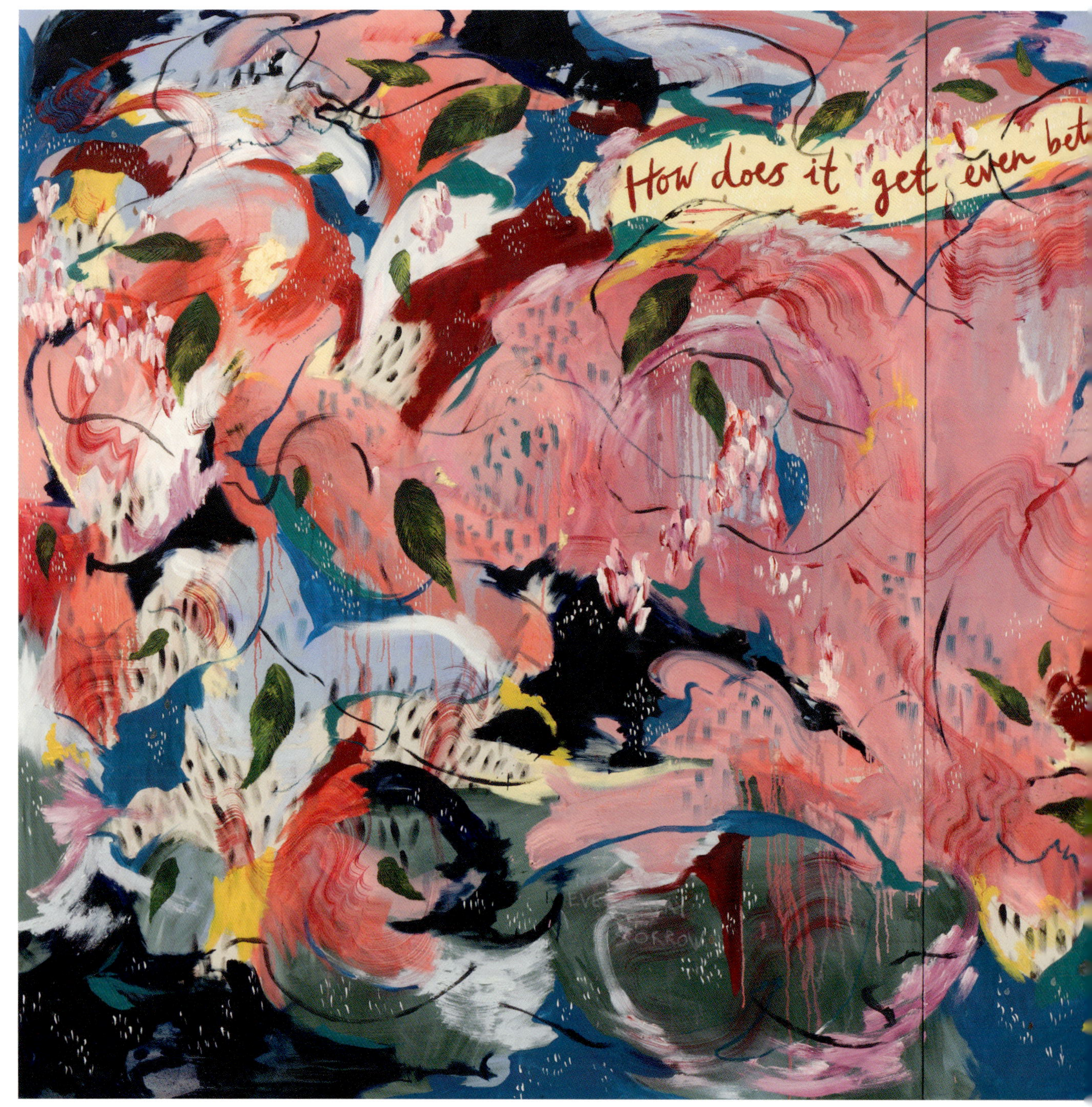

A Conduit for Joy, **Michaela Yearwood-Dan**,
2021, oil, acrylic, ink, gold leaf and Swarovski
crystals on canvas, two panels: 221 x 360 cm
(87 x 141¾ in), each panel: 221 x 180 cm
(87 x 70⅞ in)

232   **Queertopia**

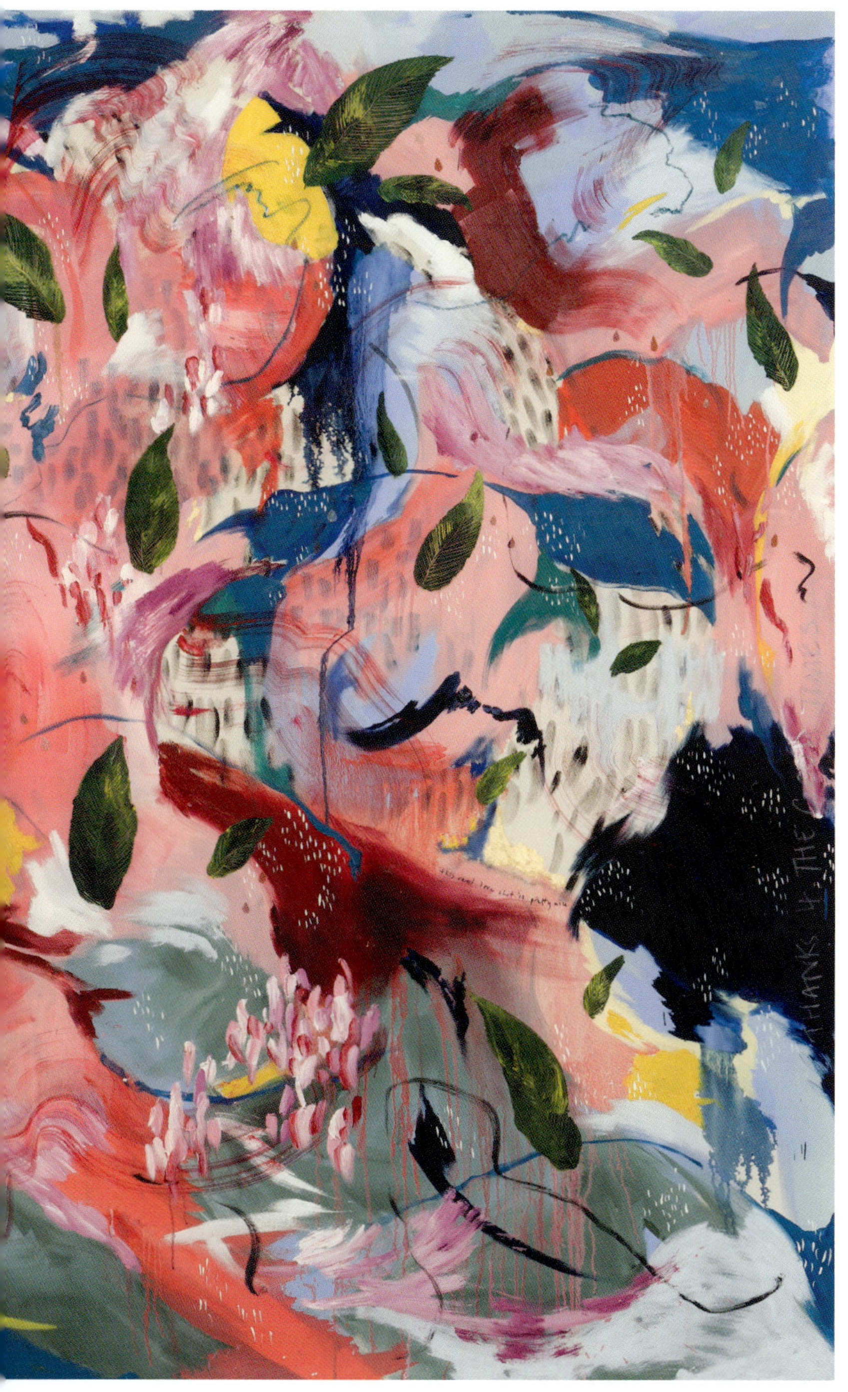

Through painting, Michaela Yearwood-Dan creates vibrant dynamic worlds bursting with joy, liberation and possibility. Swirling abstract forms coalesce with flora and fauna overlaid with words lifted from popular culture and those of the people who inspire her. Often built on a rich pink base mixed with shades of orange and blue, in reference to the lesbian and bisexual flags, her work draws visual references from Blackness, queerness, femininity, healing rituals and carnival culture. *A Conduit for Joy* is made of two vast canvas panels painted with oil, acrylic and ink, embellished with gold leaf and Swarovski crystals, and has the words 'how does it get even better?' scrawled across the top of the painting in the artist's flowing red handwriting. By incorporating the question she grew up hearing her father rhetorically ask anytime something good happened, the artist encourages us to take a pause and consider the countless ways we can go from here.

Index

Picture Credits

Front cover:
Seyon Amosu, Muse, Ajamu X, 2020.
© Ajamu Ikwe-Tyehimba. All rights reserved, DACS 2024.

Interior images:
9 © Estate of Derek Jarman. Image courtesy Keith Collins Will Trust. Photo © Manchester Art Gallery / Bridgeman Images; 10 Photo by Janice Wilde; 11 Fred W. McDarrah/MUUS Collection via Getty Images; 15 © Ingrid Pollard. All rights reserved, DACS/Artimage 2024; 16–17 Courtesy of the artists and Studio Voltaire. Photo Credit Francis Ware; 20 © Estate of Duncan Grant. All rights reserved, DACS 2024. Image courtesy The Charleston Trust; 21 © Coyote Park; 22 © Zackary Drucker and Rhys Ernst. Courtesy of the artists and Luis De Jesus Los Angeles; 23 © Jarvis Boyland; 24 Liam Warren, Arthur Eskenazi and members of RML. Photo Credit Robin Plus; 25 Whiskey Chow. Photo by Ge Cheng; 26 Courtesy of Hilary Harkness and P·P·O·W, New York. Photo: Genevieve Hanson; 27 Courtesy Skuja Braden and the Latvian Centre for Contemporary Art, Riga. Photo: Aleksejs Beļeckis; 28 © David Hockney. Photo Credit: Art Gallery of New South Wales/Jenni Carter; 29 © Kudzanai-Violet Hwami. Courtesy the artist and Victoria Miro; 30–31 Courtesy of the artist and Jessica Silverman, San Francisco; 32 © Amy Sillman. Courtesy the artist, Gladstone Gallery, New York and Thomas Dane Gallery; 33 © ARS, NY and DACS, London 2024. Photo Courtesy Alexander Gray Associates, New York. © 2023 Estate of Hugh Steers/ Artists Rights Society (ARS), New York; 34 © Sarp Kerem Yavuz;
35 Courtesy of Stars Gallery. Copyright © Clifford Prince King; 36–37 © Laurence Philomène; 40 Photo © Dave Swindells; 41 Courtesy of Reynaldo Rivera and Reena Spaulings Fine Art NY/LA; 42 Courtesy of the Artists and Arcadia Missa, London; 43 © James Bartolacci/Private Collection; 44–45 © Salman Toor; Courtesy of the artist and Luhring Augustine, New York.

Collection of the Whitney Museum of American Art. Photo: Farzad Owrang; 46 © Assume Vivid Astro Focus; 47 © The estate of Patrick Angus; 48 Courtesy the artist and Phillida Reid, London; 49 Courtesy the artist, Galerie Isabella Bortolozzi, Berlin; 50 Alternative Miss World, established by Andrew Logan. Photo © Lurie Lewis; 51 Courtesy Electronic Arts Intermix (EAI), New York; 52 © Sadie Barnette/Photo: Adam Reich; 53 © Chantal Regnault, *Voguing and the House Ballroom Scene of New York 1989–1992*; 54–55 © Nina Chanel Abney. Courtesy of the artist and Jack Shainman Gallery, New York; 56–57 Courtesy of the artist, Victoria Miro, London, and Jessica Silverman, San Francisco; 60 © ARS, NY and DACS, London 2024. Photograph used courtesy The Alvin Baltrop Trust and Galerie Buchholz.; 61 © ADAGP, Paris and DACS, London 2024. Photo Courtesy of Sotheby's; 62 Courtesy the artists and NOME, Berlin; 63 © Nash Glynn/Tate Modern; 64–65 *Caretakers*; *Constant Gardener*: Mervyn Metcalf Collection; *Migration*: Robert Shiell Collection; *The Herd*: Hort Family Collection. All images: Copyright the artist. Courtesy of Edel Assanti; 66 Courtesy of the artist and Temnikova & Kasela Gallery; 67 © Eve Fowler; 68 © Sola Olulode; 69 © Hernan Bas. Courtesy the artist and Lehmann Maupin, New York, Hong Kong, Seoul, and London and Victoria Miro; 70 Copyright Martin Wong Foundation. Courtesy of the Martin Wong Foundation and P·P·O·W, New York; 71 Courtesy of the artist and blank projects, Cape Town. © Sabelo Mlangeni; 72–73 © Leasho Johnson; 74 Courtesy the artist and Stephen Friedman Gallery. Photo by Todd-White Art Photography; 75 © Ro Robertson. Image courtesy of the artist, Yorkshire Sculpture Park, Wakefield and Maximillian William, London. Photography: Nick Singleton; 76 © The Estate of Bernice Bing, Executor Frieda Weinstein; 77 © Leah DeVun, courtesy of the artist; 78–79 © Adham Faramawy;
83 © Robert Mapplethorpe Foundation.

Used by pemrission; 84–85 © ADAGP, Paris and DACS, London 2024. Photo Credit Riccardo Banfi. Courtesy Delfina Foundation and Arts Council England. ADAGP; 88 © 2024 The Andy Warhol Foundation for the Visual Arts, Inc./ Licensed by DACS, London. Photo: Museum of Fine Arts, Houston/Photo: Bridgeman; 89 Courtesy of Chiffon Thomas; 90 Courtesy of Christina Quarles, Pilar Corrias, London, and Hauser & Wirth; 91 Carlos Motta and Christina Motta, editors. Front cover of *We Who Feel Differently*, CTRL+Z Publishing, 2011. Courtesy of Carlos Motta and P·P·O·W, New York; 92 © Yasumasa Morimura; Courtesy of the artist and Luhring Augustine, New York; 93 © Del LaGrace Volcano; 94 Rennie Collection, Vancouver. © Lubaina Himid. Image courtesy the artist and Hollybush Gardens, London. Photography Gavin Renshaw; 95 Courtesy of the artist and Company Gallery, New York; 96 Courtesy the artist and Galerie Isabella Bortolozzi, Berlin; 97 Courtesy the artist and Soft Opening, London. Photography Theo Christelis; 98 Knoxville Museum of Art, 2018 purchase; © The Estate of Beauford Delaney, by permission of Derek L. Spratley, Esquire, Court Appointed Administrator; Courtesy of Michael Rosenfeld Gallery LLC, New York, NY; 99 © Estate of Greer Lankton. Photo: Paul Monroe; 100 © Collier Schorr. Courtesy 303 Gallery, New York; 101 © Ghada Khunji; 102 © Estate of Lorenza Böttner. Image courtesy Leslie Lohman Gallery; 103 © Juliana Huxtable; 104 Courtesy of the artist and New Discretions; 105 Image courtesy the Artist and Hales Gallery. Copyright the artist. Photo by Damian Griffiths; 106 © 2024 The Peter Hujar Archive/Artists Rights Society (ARS), New York, DACS London; 107 © Shikeith, Courtesy Yossi Milo, New York; 108–09 © Lyle Ashton Harris; 112t © The Tee Corinne Papers, Coll. 263, Special Collections & University Archives, University of Oregon Libraries; 112b © ADAGP, Paris and DACS, London 2024. Image courtesy Weinstein

Gallery; **113** © Lin Zhipeng (aka No.223); **114** Courtesy of the artist; **115** © Wolfgang Tillmans; **116** Courtesy of the artist and Vielmetter Los Angeles; **117** © ARS, NY and DACS, London 2024. Photo by Todd-White Art Photography, Courtesy The Artist, David Kordansky Gallery, and MASSIMODECARLO; **118** © Roni Horn. Photo: Roni Horn Studio; **119** © Doron Langberg. Courtesy the artist and Victoria Miro; **120** Courtesy of Jessie Darling and Sultana, Paris © Aurélien Mole; **121** Image copyright of the artist, courtesy of Video Data Bank, School of the Art Institute of Chicago; **122** Courtesy of the Artist and Company Gallery,New York; **123** Photo: Trevor Good. Courtesy the artist and Plan B Cluj, Berlin; **124–25** © Nicole Eisenman. Courtesy the artist and Hauser & Wirth; **126–27** © Kehinde Wiley. Courtesy of the Rubell Museum, Miami; **130** © 2024 The Peter Hujar Archive/Artists Rights Society (ARS), New York, DACS London. Digital image, The Museum of Modern Art, New York/Scala, Florence; **131** © Deborah Kass. ARS, NY and DACS, London 2024; **132** Copyright Estate of David Wojnarowicz. Courtesy of the Estate of David Wojnarowicz and P·P·O·W, New York; **133** © Mark Bradford, Courtesy the artist and Hauser & Wirth; **134** © Estate of Felix Gonzalez-Torres. Courtesy Felix Gonzalez-Torres Foundation; **135** Reproduced with the permission of the copyright holder Dr Sally Gray and the David McDiarmid estate; **136** © Catherine Opie, Courtesy Regen Projects, Los Angeles, and Thomas Dane Gallery, London and Naples; **137** © Jess T. Dugan; **138** © Kiki Smith, courtesy Pace Gallery; **139** © Rotimi Fani-Kayode. Courtesy of Autograph, London; **140** Courtesy of the artist and David Kordansky Gallery; **141** Courtesy the artist; **142** © Franko B. All rights reserved, DACS 2024. Photo: Hugo Glendinning; **143** Courtesy of the Estate of Tessa Boffin, the Gupta+Singh Archive and Hales London and New York; **144** © Maggi Hambling; **145** © Kang Seung Lee; **146–47** © Slava Mogutin; **151** *Ridykeulous* zine, Nicole Eisenman and A.L. Steiner. Courtesy of the artists; **152-53** Sharon Hayes, Kate Millett and the Women's Liberation Cinema; **156** *Stories of Our Lives*, The Nest Collective, 2014; **157** Courtesy of

the artist and Cooper Cole, Toronto; **158** Courtesy the artist and Alexander Gray Associates, New York. © Harmony Hammond/VAGA at ARS, NY and DACS, London 2024. Photo: Jason Mandella; **159** © Mary Patten; **160** Image courtesy of the artist and Project Native Informant, London © Hal Fischer; **161** © 1977 Tom of Finland Foundation/Artists Rights Society (ARS), New York/DACS, London 2024; **162** © Martine Gutierrez; Courtesy of the artist and RYAN LEE Gallery, New York; **163** © Lula Mae Blocton; **164** © JEB (Joan E. Biren); **165** Courtesy of the Estate of Barbara Hammer, New York; Electronic Arts Intermix (EAI), New York; and Company Gallery, New York; **166** © Karolina Bregula. Courtesy of lokal_30 gallery; **167** © Gilbert & George; **168** © Pierre Fouche. Collection: Iziko South African National Gallery; **169** © Ghada Amer. Courtesy of the artist and Marianne Boesky Gallery, New York and Aspen; **170** © Estate of Bhupen Khakhar. Courtesy of Sotheby's; **171** © Glenn Ligon. Courtesy the artist, Hauser & Wirth, New York, Regen Projects, Los Angeles, Thomas Dane Gallery, London, and Galerie Chantal Crousel, Paris; **174** ACT-UP/public domain. Photo: Brooklyn Museum; **175t** © Alice O›Malley; **175b** All 4 photos © Bex Wade; **176** © Osinachi; **177** © Fyodor Pavlov-Andreevich. Photographer: Thierry Bal; **178** © Amy Sherald. Courtesy the artist and Hauser & Wirth; **179** Gran Fury/public domain; **180** © AA Bronson + General Idea, courtesy Maureen Paley, London; **181** © Zoe Leonard. Courtesy the artist; **182** Courtesy of the artist; **183** Courtesy the artists and Alexander Gray Associates, New York. © 2024 Carrie Moyer and Sue Schaffner; **184** © Laura Aguilar Trust of 2016; **185** © Sunil Gupta. All rights reserved, DACS/Artimage 2024; **186** Keith Haring artwork © Keith Haring Foundation; **187** Copyright: © Donald Moffett. Courtesy of the artist and Marianne Boesky Gallery, New York and Aspen; **188** © fierce pussy; **189** © Zanele Muholi. Courtesy Stevenson, Cape Town/ Johannesburg and Yancey Richardson, New York. Photo: David Stjernholm; **192** © Shoog McDaniel and Erin McDaniel; **193** © 2023 Patricia Cronin/Artists Rights Society (ARS) New York; **194** © Elmgreen & Dragset.

Courtesy the artist and Victoria Miro; **195** © Ajamu Ikwe-Tyehimba. All rights reserved, DACS 2024; **196-97** Courtesy of the Artist and Arcadia Missa, London; **198** © Chiachio & Giannone; **199** © Brenda Goodman; **200-01** Courtesy of Yuki Kihara and Milford Galleries, Aotearoa New Zealand; **202** © Lucas Museum of Narrative Art, Los Angeles. Image Courtesy of DC Moore Gallery, New York; **203** © Morgan Art Foundation Ltd./ Artists Rights Society (ARS), New York, DACS, London 2024. Photo: flab/Alamy; **204** Images courtesy Jeffrey Gibson, Stephen Friedman Gallery, London; Sikkema Jenkins & Co, New York; and Roberts Projects, Los Angeles. Photography by Jason Wyche; **205** Copyright Leilah Babirye. Courtesy the artist, Stephen Friedman Gallery and Gordon Robichaux, New York. Photo by Mark Blower; **206-07** © Nan Goldin. Courtesy Gagosian Gallery. Image: San Francisco Museum of Modern Art, Accessions Committee Fund purchase.; **208** © Charmaine Poh; **209** © The Estate of Francis Bacon. All rights reserved. DACS 2024. Photo: Bridgeman Images; **210-11** Courtesy the artist & The Hole; **214** © Pierre et Gilles; **215** Courtesy Rashaad Newsome; **216-17** © Tom Bianchi; **218** © Joe McShea & Edgar Mosa; **219** © TM Davy; **220** © Raqib Shaw. All Rights Reserved, DACS 2024. Digital image, The Museum of Modern Art, New York/Scala, Florence; **221** © Chitra Ganesh; **222** © Toyin Ojih Odutola. Courtesy of the artist, Corvi-Mora, London and Jack Shainman Gallery, New York. Photo: Charlie J Ercilla/ Alamy; **223** © Shantell Martin. Photograph by Roy Rochlin; **224** Courtesy the artist and VI, VII; **225** Courtesy the artist, Anna Lena Films, Paris and Project Native Informant, London; **226** KADIST collection, courtesy the artist and Crèvecoeur, Paris. Photo: Aurélien Mole; **227** © Sadao Hasegawa/ Gallery Naruyama; **228** © Gabriel Massan and Serpentine; **229** © Jacolby Satterwhite/Courtesy of the artist and Mitchell-Innes & Nash, New York; **230** © DACS 2024. Image courtesy of the artist and Company Gallery, New York; **231** © April Bey; **232-33** Courtesy of the artist and Marianne Boesky Gallery, New York and Aspen.

Acknowledgements

Many wonderful people have been involved in producing this book. Thank you to everyone at Quarto, who believed in my vision, worked tirelessly to make this book the best it could possibly be and helped get it out into the world: Stephen Behan, Laura Bulbeck, Clare Churly, Alice Graham, Lewis Laney, John Parton, Leonardo Collina. To the dear friends and collaborators who helped with research and editing: Amelia Abraham, Mollie Barnes, Cas Bradbeer, Ariel Collier, Fiontan Moran. To all of the galleries, institutions and individuals who helped with sourcing images and securing image rights. To my friend Kate Bryan who suggested I write a book in the first place. To my wonderful wife, Danielle, who read every single caption as I was writing and supported me throughout the process. To my children and chosen family for inspiring me to make a book that hopefully makes the world a bit better. And to the artists in this book and beyond, thank you for helping us make sense of ourselves and for creating space for our community in the worlds you create.

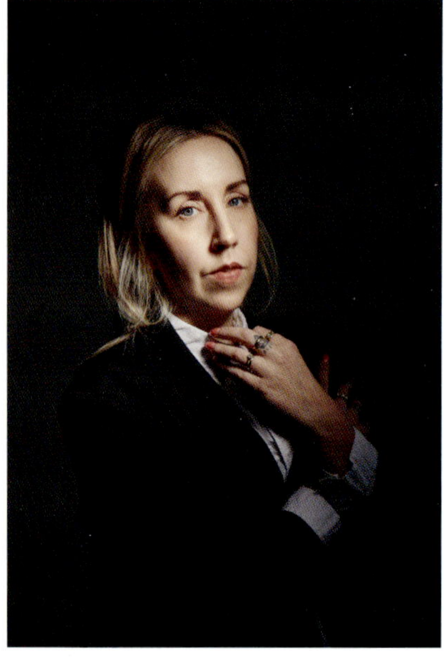

Author Bio

Gemma Rolls-Bentley has been at the forefront of contemporary art for almost two decades, working passionately to amplify the work of queer artists and provide a platform for art that explores LGBTQIA+ identity. She curates exhibitions, builds art collections and leads projects internationally. Most recently she curated the group exhibition 'Dreaming of Home' at the Leslie Lohman Museum of Art in New York and the Tom of Finland Art & Culture Festival in London. She curated the 'Brighton Beacon Collection', the largest permanent display of queer art in the UK. Gemma is a visiting lecturer at the Royal College of Art and she has sat on the boards of numerous organizations and charities that support diversity in the arts.

Acknowledgements / Author Bio